**A Gift to
the Vista Library
from
Joan Brandt Hawkins
in Honor of her mother
Irene Brandt**

George Gershwin

Early formal portrait of George Gershwin, circa 1923. (© Library of Congress, Music Division)

George Gershwin

A New Biography

WILLIAM G. HYLAND

PRAEGER

Westport, Connecticut
London

Library of Congress Cataloging-in-Publication Data

Hyland, William, 1929–
    George Gershwin : a new biography / by William G. Hyland.
      p. cm.
    Includes bibliographical references (p.) and index.
    ISBN 0–275–98111–8 (alk. paper)
    1. Gershwin, George, 1898–1937. 2. Composers—United States—Biography. I. Title.
ML410.G288H95   2003
780'.92—dc21
   [B]   2003046303

British Library Cataloguing in Publication Data is available.

Library of Congress Catalog Card Number: 2003046303
ISBN: 0–275–98111–8

First published in 2003

Praeger Publishers, 88 Post Road West, Westport, CT 06881
An imprint of Greenwood Publishing Group, Inc.
www.praeger.com

Printed in the United States of America

The paper used in this book complies with the
Permanent Paper Standard issued by the National
Information Standards Organization (Z39.48–1984).

10 9 8 7 6 5 4 3 2

To James, John, Victoria, and William

Contents

Note: Photo essay follows Chapter 7.

Preface and Acknowledgments

This book grew out of my experiences of fifty years ago. In 1951–52 I was a private in the United States Army stationed in Germany. A call went out in the Seventh Army for volunteers to play in a GI symphony orchestra to be formed to perform for German audiences. Before being drafted I had been an aspiring jazz trumpet player, but nevertheless I decided to audition. To my surprise I was chosen by the conductor, a young corporal named Sam Adler, a Harvard graduate and student of Paul Hindemith and Walter Piston. He went on to become a renowned American composer and a professor of composition at the Eastman School of Music.

Adler wisely chose to present programs that featured American music, ranging from Roy Harris and Walter Piston to Richard Rodgers and George Gershwin. We played the *Rhapsody in Blue* many times. I enjoyed the jazzy trumpet parts, played with wah-wah mutes and appropriate growls and flutter tongues. The Germans were delighted; musicians would even come backstage to examine my "jazz" trumpet. The *Rhapsody* was my introduction to the "other" Gershwin. I knew his music from his many standard songs, played by the dance bands of that era, but I was largely ignorant of his concert music.

More than three decades later, my wife and I were living in New York and savoring the variety of music that is so easily accessible. One of our favorite Broadway shows, *My One and Only*, was loaded with Gershwin's music. It piqued my interest in Gershwin's life.

The Performing Arts Library at Lincoln Center offered a treasure not only of Gershwin but of his contemporaries, Irving Berlin, Jerome Kern, Richard Rodgers, and Cole Porter. This led me to write a book, a collection of mini-biographies of that group. That led, in turn, to a biography I wrote about the life of Richard Rodgers.

I could not help but think of Rodgers as I began to write about Gershwin. It turned out that they were friends and respected each other's work, but they were quite different. Rodgers was a man of the theater; he wrote music only when he had a show to complete. Gershwin, on the other hand, would noodle endlessly at the piano, often producing memorable music. Ironically, Rodgers studied music formally at what was the predecessor to Juilliard, but he confined his music to Broadway. Although Gershwin's formal studies were sketchy, he boldly "crossed over" to the concert hall.

For twenty years, both Rodgers and Gershwin were each linked almost exclusively to one lyricist: Rodgers to Larry Hart and George Gershwin to his brother Ira. Both suffered the indignities of the early days of Hollywood musicals. Rodgers and Hart finally fled back to New York, as George and Ira returned to Hollywood for the last year of George's life. Rodgers was temporarily in Hollywood when Gershwin died and wrote his wife that "the town is in a daze."

Rodgers was difficult to know; even his partner, Oscar Hammerstein, admitted that. Rodgers wrote an autobiography, but for some years there was no major biography, possibly because Rodgers lived until 1979. On the other hand, George Gershwin's death in 1937 was followed by an avalanche of books, articles, TV shows, and even one movie biography. Nevertheless, in the end the biographers had to discover the "real" Gershwin. That is one of the themes of this book. My other objective is to express an appreciation of all his glorious music.

I am indebted to many: to Ray White of the Library of Congress, who guided me through the labyrinth of the Gershwin collection; to Eric Levy, my editor at Greenwood Press, who was receptive to an early draft; to Katharine Weber, the granddaughter of Kay Swift and a fine novelist, who offered valuable insights and read some of the early drafts; to Professor David Schiff, who read some early drafts and passed on his valuable comments; to Kitty Carlisle Hart, who knew the Gershwins and reminisced for me from time to time; to Sam Adler, who answered my occasional musical questions and urged me to continue writing; to Harry Haskell, of Yale University Press and a fellow Kansas Citian, who also encouraged me to continue when things were not going so well; finally, to my family, especially my wife, Evelyn, who tolerated my frustrations and irritations in trying to complete this book.

Introduction

On New Year's Day 1898, amid snow and rain, Greater New York City was born: Brooklyn as well as Queens, Staten Island, and the Bronx were consolidated with Manhattan into one metropolitan area. The new city encompassed over three hundred acres and was second only to London in population. It was already the financial hub of the nation; the largest, busiest port; and the center of popular culture. This was George Gershwin's town. He was born in Brooklyn in September 1898 and would live all but the last year of his life in Greater New York, spending most of his youth in the crowded Lower East Side, where the massive influx of Jewish immigrants from Eastern Europe and Russia settled.

The European immigration created a new city and a new nation. The first wave came from Ireland and Germany; then came Italians and, finally, the most powerful surge—Jews, mainly from Poland, Russia, and Galicia. The new Jewish immigrants were not all peasants, as so appealingly romanticized by the show *Fiddler on the Roof*. Many were tradesmen, artisans, and workers from the clothing and textiles industries of Russia. George Gershwin's father was one of them.

In New York and other northern cities, there was also an internal migration. Rural America was moving to the urban areas, and black Americans from the deep South were moving to the northern cities. Harlem would become the informal capital for African Americans, but before the Great War it had been an area for middle- and upper-class Jews, including the Gershwins, for a brief time. In the early part of the century young George Gershwin would roam around 125th Street. Within a decade this became home to black jazz musicians, many of them Gershwin's friends. "Uptown" was where he could hear Bessie Smith or Louis Armstrong at Connie's Inn, or Duke Ellington at the Cotton Club.

In short, the great melting pot was emerging. It was represented in a stage play that could have foreshadowed Gershwin's career. The central character in Israel Zangwill's play *The Melting-Pot* was a Russian Jewish immigrant, a musician who composed an "American Symphony." His music reflected a vision of America as a "waiting, beckoning, shining" land. George Gershwin too would envision his music as representative of the great melting pot. The tentative title of his *Rhapsody in Blue* was "American Rhapsody."

To be sure, the anti-Semitism that had plagued European Jews for centuries followed them to the New World, manifested in the resurrection of the Ku Klux Klan. Nevertheless, as Gershwin was growing up before the Great War, the mood of the country was generally optimistic. The economy was growing, jobs were more plentiful, farm prices were rising, and technology offered new horizons. A British visitor, Frederic Harrison, wrote in 1901: "Life in the States is one perpetual whirl of telephones, telegrams, phonographs, electric bells, motors, lifts, and automatic instruments." Within a few years he would have been able to add automobiles to the list. In 1903, Henry Ford started his own company, and in December of that year the Wright brothers flew their aeroplane at Kitty Hawk.

New York had already entered a period of remarkable growth and change. The first license to the American Bell Telephone company was issued in 1877. Edison's lights illuminated Wall Street in 1882. St. Patrick's Cathedral opened in 1879. The Waldorf Hotel and the Astoria were open for business in the 1890s, and the magnificent Flatiron Building was completed in 1902. Leopold Damrosch formed a symphony orchestra in 1878, and the Metropolitan Opera House opened in 1883. It was still a city of contrasts and contradictions, however. Not far from the turmoil and squalor of the Henry Street markets were the stately mansions of the Vanderbilts, the Whitneys, and the Morgans along Fifth Avenue (some are still standing).

Nevertheless, the era of Edith Wharton's "old New York" was ending. By 1914, when war broke out in Europe, New York City had changed almost beyond recognition. A visitor from 1870 would not have recognized the city of 1914; it had already assumed the contours of the current modern city. New roads and bridges had been built, along with an elevated railway, a subway, and some so-called skyscrapers. Grand Central Terminal opened in 1913. The flood of immigration had increased the population to over 4.8 million.

The new city could not be easily governed by the old political machines, which were increasingly unable to stem the tide of reform. The spirit of reform would flourish during the Progressive Era championed by Theodore Roosevelt and continued for a time by Woodrow Wilson. The reformers wanted government to protect the poor, minorities, women, and children. In New York, Lillian Wald founded the Henry Street Settlement; it was at the Christadora House where "George Gershvin" [*sic*] first played in public in 1914. In Chicago, Jane Addams created Hull-House, where Benny Goodman learned to play the clarinet. In New York, City College was opened to Jews; Ira Gershwin and "Yip"

Harburg were students there, as were Bernard Baruch and Felix Frankfurter. The slums did not disappear, but conditions were better.

By the end of the war, reform was all but dead and a new period—the Jazz Age—was beginning. This was to be Gershwin's era.

Indeed, the Jewish ghettos of New York and elsewhere yielded a whole new generation of entertainers, performers, songwriters, and composers who would revolutionize popular American culture. The Gershwin brothers would be among the leaders; so too were Irving Berlin, Richard Rodgers, Larry Hart, Harry Ruby, Harold Arlen, Yip Harburg, Fanny Brice, Eddie Cantor, Ed Wynn, and of course Al Jolson.

This, then, was the city that was home to George Gershwin for almost his entire life. It was the city where he would join the world of popular music—a field in which talent counted.

In New York there was almost every kind of music, from orchestral concerts and piano recitals—often attended by the Gershwin brothers—to raw burlesque, struggling vaudeville, saccharine operettas, and bright and sassy musical comedies. George Gershwin would be drawn into almost all of it, as a journeyman "song plugger," in Tin Pan Alley playing and selling his publisher's songs, a budding songwriter, a skillful ragtime pianist, and a successful composer. He worked with Victor Herbert, the father of the American operetta, and with his early idol Jerome Kern, who would revolutionize musical comedy. He even volunteered as an apprentice to Irving Berlin, who advised him to follow his own talents. He did a stint in vaudeville as the piano accompanist to the famous Nora Bayes, who wrote "Shine on, Harvest Moon."

Not surprisingly, in New York the most popular song was "Sidewalks of New York." Irving Berlin wrote amusing ethnic songs like "Sadie Salome Go Home" for Fanny Brice. But it was a graduate from vaudeville, George M. Cohan, whose songs dominated the prewar era—"Give My Regards to Broadway" and "The Yankee Doodle Boy," as well as "You're a Grand Old Flag." And then after the United States entered the war in April 1917, he wrote "Over There." Cohan became the title character in one of his plays, *The Man Who Owned Broadway*.

When George Gershwin was young, ragtime was the rage. Irving Berlin's great breakthrough was "Alexander's Ragtime Band." The purer forms of ragtime, written by Scott Joplin, were bowdlerized by musicians and songwriters who could not play the more complex patterns. Most of this music was not ragtime at all, but it was syncopated and carried the word "rag" somewhere in the title. The young George Gershwin wrote a song entitled "Rialto Ripples (A Rag)." It was a far cry from "Alexander's Ragtime Band," but he was only nineteen; then he wrote "Swanee," which Al Jolson turned into a mega-hit.

New York became the hub not only for entertainers but for the business of printing and publishing popular music. At first the heart of the new music business was located downtown around Union Square. There were also important centers in Chicago, Detroit, and Kansas City. The publishing firm of Jerome H.

Remick's, where Gershwin first broke in, originated in Detroit. Even in Sedalia, Missouri, a small firm published the songs of an obscure pianist named Scott Joplin.

As the city expanded northward so too did the music business, to an area called Tin Pan Alley on 28th Street between Fifth and Sixth Avenues. Music publishing became rewarding. By 1910, sheet music sales were over $5.7 million. There were about 25,000 songs entered for copyright in 1909, and over 27 million phonograph records and cylinders were manufactured. George Gershwin began recording piano rolls in late 1915.

The Broadway theater district began on 13th Street but gradually moved north. Perhaps the most famous theater for musicals was the New Amsterdam on West 42nd Street, often called the most gorgeous playhouse in New York, which opened in 1903. It was here that the Viennese import, Franz Lehar's *The Merry Widow*, took New York by storm in 1907. The operetta had already captured the heart and imagination of New York theater audiences, because they were accustomed to the fine operettas of Victor Herbert. He wrote some of the most wistful, romantic love songs of the prewar era, such as his famous "Kiss Me Again." George Gershwin worked for him as the rehearsal pianist for a show written by Herbert and Jerome Kern. Herbert's "Suite of Serenades" was performed on the same program as *Rhapsody in Blue*.

It was Herbert who performed two services for his fellow songwriters. In court he won the right to be compensated for any production of his songs—an invaluable legacy to his fellow composers that would make many of them very wealthy. He also gave shape to songwriting as a profession. Along with eight other composers (including soon thereafter both Jerome Kern and Irving Berlin), in late 1913 he helped to establish the American Society of Composers, Authors and Publishers (ASCAP). ASCAP imposed a small fee for a license to perform a member's music. A common treasury was established and the songwriters were paid a percentage of the overall revenue, which flourished into a multimillion-dollar operation. In the lean years of the Great Depression, the Gershwin brothers would live off their earnings from ASCAP.

Gershwin and other Broadway songwriters would also owe a debt to Jerome Kern. His seminal achievements were the scores for the Princess Theater musicals beginning in 1915 that would change the history of the American musical stage. Along with Guy Bolton and P.G. Wodehouse, Kern's shows integrated the music, the lyrics, the plot, and the characters. The Gershwin brothers saw most of these shows and greatly admired them. Later, Bolton and Wodehouse would write librettos for Gershwin's shows.

This was the musical world that drew in George Gershwin. He admired the elegance of Herbert and Kern on the one hand and the popularity of Cohan and Berlin on the other. To some degree he embraced all of their achievements, but he also traveled his own road; he sought out serious teachers who introduced him to the study of Chopin and Liszt, which led him into the concert hall and finally into the opera house.

His story is a variation on the great American success saga. His parents were Jewish immigrants from the Russian Empire. Just before the turn of the century they settled in New York. They were not a musical family, but when a piano arrived, George devoured it. One of his piano teachers declared him to be a genius. Soon he plunged into the professional world, song plugging at age fifteen and songwriting at seventeen. The sights and sounds of New York, its blues, jazz, Tin Pan Alley, and the Great White Way were his sources and inspiration.

In 1936, he put aside New York, Broadway, and the concert halls. He and his brother—his collaborator and confidant—flew to Hollywood to write the score for *Shall We Dance*, starring the popular team of Ginger Rogers and Fred Astaire. Within a year he would die there of a fatal brain tumor. He was only thirty-eight.

His music would not die. More than sixty years after his death, his music is still heard everywhere, from the White House to Broadway to the Metropolitan Opera. When the president of China visited the United States, he was treated to the traditional lavish White House dinner in the East Room. Afterward, the National Symphony Orchestra led by Leonard Slatkin performed a thirty-minute program of music by American composers. The centerpiece was George Gershwin's *An American in Paris*. When the New York Philharmonic, under Kurt Masur, ended its 2001 season, the conductor chose *Rhapsody in Blue*. When the Academy Awards ceremony in Hollywood presented a special film tribute to New York, after the tragedy of September 11, 2001, the background music for the film opened with the sweeping clarinet sounds of *Rhapsody in Blue*. On Broadway, every few years award-winning shows have been built around Gershwin's music—*My One and Only* and *Crazy for You*.

It is not surprising that Gershwin's music is still so appealing. But so is the story of his life: Because of his early and tragic death in 1937 and the greatness of the works he composed during his short life, he became an almost legendary figure in the music world. No one doubts that had he lived longer he would have scored new triumphs. The Gershwin story is still fascinating.

Chapter 1

Youth

The Gershwin story began in St. Petersburg, the capital of the Russian Empire. George and Ira Gershwin's parents emigrated from there to the New World in the 1890s. Their mother, Rosa Bruskin (or Brushkin), and her family arrived about 1891-92, when Rosa was fourteen or fifteen. A young man from St. Petersburg, Moishe Gershowitz, was also part of the flood of emigration. Moishe apparently knew Rosa in Russia; this is quite possible since the Jewish community in St. Petersburg must have been rather small. The romanticized story is that he followed her to America; the fact is that he arrived in New York on August 14, 1890, according to his application for citizenship—that is, before Rosa arrived. Still, it is a nice story.

As Jewish residents of St. Petersburg, both families must have earned unique advantages. In Imperial Russia the vast majority of Jews were confined to the Pale of Settlement, an area specifically designated for Jews that covered parts of Poland, Byelorussia, and the Ukraine. In fact, it was illegal to live "beyond the Pale" without special permission.

Moishe's grandfather apparently was a rabbi and his father was a "mechanic," who invented some kind of firearm used by the Czarist armies. It was for this achievement that the family was given the privilege of residing outside the Pale. Nevertheless, Moishe became eligible for military duty (a mandatory service of twenty-five years) and decided to leave the country to join his uncle in Brooklyn. For some reason this uncle, referred to only as Greenstein, seems to have disappeared from the Gershwin history.

Rosa Bruskin's family also must have been privileged to reside in St. Petersburg. However, Kate Bruskin Wolpin, Rosa's sister, claimed that they were from Vilna (in Lithuania, which was then part of the Russian Empire). They may have moved to St. Petersburg. Frances Gershwin speculated that her mother claimed to be from St. Petersburg because it was more elegant than the backwater Vilna. Rosa and Kate's father was a "furrier," probably a merchant, which could explain the family's privileges. The entire family—father, mother, and three children—emigrated. George eventually painted portraits of his maternal grandparents; sporting a bowler and a small goatee, grandfather Gerson (or Gerskin) Bruskin looks quite distinguished.[1]

Both families were caught up in the massive emigration that began in the 1880s. After the assassination of Czar Alexander II, the new Czar, Alexander III, resumed the lethal pogroms against the Jews, and the repressions grew increasingly severe. The prohibitions against Jews residing outside the Pale were radically tightened until a particularly gruesome purge was conducted in Moscow in 1891, when thousands of Jews were expelled from the city on the first day of Passover. Jews had no choice: They emigrated. Thousands fled in the 1880s and 1890s, until by 1906 nearly two million had left Russia and Eastern Europe. This wave of immigration overwhelmed New York's Lower East Side. The Jewish population of New York City grew to about one million, or almost one-quarter of the city's people.

Life was harsh in the New World on the Lower East Side of New York, where most Jewish immigrants settled. The grim conditions there, about the time Gershowitz and the Bruskin family arrived, were described rather pompously by the *New York Times* (July 1893): the area was the "eyesore of New York. . . . It is impossible for a Christian to live there because he will be driven out either by blows or the dirt and stench."

Many who came from the Lower East Side later recalled not only the difficult times and conditions, but happier memories. The lyricist E.Y. "Yip" Harburg, a good friend of the Gershwins, remembered: "We were poor, always out on the street with our furniture, and never knowing if the next rent would be paid." But he added, "I had an exciting time. More fun than I ever had in Hollywood. It was real."[2] Irving Berlin was only five when his family arrived in New York in 1893. He recalled eight or nine people living in four rooms, sleeping on the fire escape in the summer; poor parents, but never being hungry—there was always bread and butter and hot tea. Yet in retrospect, many from the area remembered their childhood as a happy time. As an adult Irving Berlin would return to the area to relive those early days.

The American world of entertainment, in particular, benefitted greatly from the exodus from Russia and Poland—it became a "creative crucible." A joyful spirit shines through in the comedy of Fanny Brice, Milton Berle, and George Burns; the songs and dances of Eddie Cantor; and the music of the area's most illustrious graduates, the Gershwins and Irving Berlin. In addition to the Gershwins and Irving Berlin there were Richard Rodgers' family and Harry Ruby ("Three Little Words"), who would become a song plugger with George Gershwin at Jerome H. Remick's; also among the immigrants on the Lower East Side were "Yip" Harburg, Ira Gershwin's classmate who wrote the words to "Over the Rainbow"; Irving Caesar, who would write the words to George Gershwin's

"Swanee"; and Al Jolson (not New York, but Washington, D.C., via Lithuania), who would turn "Swanee" into a great popular hit. When he died George Gershwin was working on the score for a movie produced by Samuel Goldwyn, a refugee from Poland.

It took courage to venture on a long hazardous journey, even if choosing to remain was dangerous. The journey from Russia to the port of embarkation, usually in Hamburg, Germany, was in itself hazardous. On arrival there was a bewildering confusion, to say nothing of the trauma of facing the dreaded health inspection in New York; and finally, adapting to a radically different environment. In the Gershwin family tradition there is a story that Moishe, while still on the boat from Russia, lost the name and address of his uncle in New York when the note in his hat blew off into the water. After his arrival, speaking a combination of Yiddish and Russian he eventually located his uncle in Brooklyn. If so, Moishe was not the first in the family to immigrate.

Rose and Morris, as they preferred to be known in their new country, were married on July 21, 1895. Rose was eighteen and Morris was twenty-five. Their wedding picture shows a very proper couple; Morris is wearing a watch chain and fob; Rose's hair is swept up in a fashionable mode. Eighteen months later, Ira (Israel) was born (December 6, 1896) on the Lower East Side at 69 Eldridge Street. About a year later the family moved to Brooklyn, and on September 27, 1898, George (Jacob) was born in the house at 242 Snediker Avenue. Ira recalled it as a spacious home for that time: a front room, a dining room, a kitchen, and a maid's room; upstairs there were three or four bedrooms; the rent was $14/month. One of the bedrooms was rented out for $3/month to Mr. Taffelstein, a collector for the Singer Sewing Machine Company. Ira remembered a vacant lot next door where he played and a grape arbor in the fenced backyard (until recently the house was still standing, rented by a Hispanic family, but is now a parking lot).

The family lived in Brooklyn for two or three years. Some time after George's birth, however, they moved back to Chrystie Street on the Lower East Side. Morris changed his profession from a designer of women's shoes ("leather worker" on George's birth certificate) to part owner of a Turkish bath on the Bowery. The family would move a total of twenty-five or twenty-eight times following Morris' peripatetic search for new jobs, according to Ira. Arthur was born in 1900, and Frances was born in 1906, exactly ten years to the day after Ira. Whether for business or some other reason, the family name was changed to Gershvin and then to Gershwin. George's birth certificate is written Jacob Gershwine, however, but supposedly that was a copying error by the physician.

Rose and Morris did not suffer the grinding poverty of tenement life. Morris was earning about $35 a week at the time George was born. He was obviously enterprising and started various businesses, often together with his brother-in-law, Harry Wolpin. Ira recalled Turkish and Russian baths in the Bowery and Harlem, two restaurants in Harlem and on the Lower East Side, a bakery, a cigar store, a pool parlor, and even a stint at bookmaking at the Brighton Beach race track. This lack of permanence in the family's life made Morris the subject of some light ridicule by Gershwin's biographers and the butt of various anecdotes by George. Morris' endeavors illustrate a more important point—he had to be industrious. To leave Russia by himself without the support of any family members was in itself a bold act. Moreover, whether as the owner of restaurants or Turkish and Russian baths, he saw to it that his family was supported. The Gershwins were relatively well off, no mean achievement for Jewish immigrants in that era.

After George died, some of the entries for him in various musical encyclopedias mentioned that he came from an "impoverished" family. Despite some efforts to romanticize George's youthful hardships, in fact his life was not the great American "rags to riches" story. On leaving the premiere of the movie of George's life, *Rhapsody in Blue*, Rose Gershwin objected to the portrayal of the family: "It's not the truth." They always had enough money for "Georgie's" piano lessons, because "Poppa" had twelve restaurants.[3] The lyricist "Yip" Harburg, who grew up in the same area, agreed that the Gershwins were not poor, that they owned restaurants. When he was a classmate of Ira's at City College, Harburg recalled going to the Gershwins' to hear their Victrola, in itself a mark of some affluence. Frances Gershwin remembers the family had a maid; and there is a photograph of Rose, her young children, and the maid.

As for family life, Gershwin's first biographer, Isaac Goldberg, claimed that there was the dignity inherent in the ancient matriarchal and patriarchal institutions.[4] After Gershwin died his friend Merle Armitage published a collection of observations; he wrote that he loved his family and they loved him. Armitage did not know George before 1936 and knew nothing of his family, but this is the standard version. And, indeed, on the surface Gershwin's family life seems to have been congenial. There was no sense of hostility or antagonism. George was over thirty when he finally moved out of his family's multilevel apartment. True, family life was unstructured and mildly chaotic, and occasionally George took a leave of absence for a few weeks to concentrate on writing a new musical score. But when a friend asked if the "busyness" did not distract him he demurred and said that it stimulated him.

Most accounts treat Morris sympathetically. He was described by George as a very easy going, humorous philosopher, which apparently meant passive, if not in business, then as a family member. The playwright S.N. Behrman, a longtime Gershwin friend, described him as "short, rotund, inclined to literalness," and a man who had that "singular and unerring faculty which certain originals have for saying, in any situation, that final thing beyond which there is nothing left to be said." In a letter to a friend in September 1931, the year before Morris died, Gershwin wrote: "Pop goes along uncomplainingly, taking things as they come—the happy philosopher."[5]

Frances said that Morris had a sort of Russian-Jewish accent. He was a "darling person," but she felt ashamed of his accent. On the other hand, George would go to parties and tell stories of his father, sometimes using a little accent as his father would use, Frances said. He had no sense of false pride about things like that. Their friend Sam Behrman wrote that a saga of anecdotes accumulated about Morris. When he would meet George or Ira, Behrman would simply ask, "What's the latest?"

Morris was not a strong father and was apparently cowed by his wife. Indeed, Rose was the dominant parent. George described her as nervous, ambitious, and purposeful; Behrman described her as level-headed and practical. According to Behrman, she steered the family through the early years and helped Morris to reach the eminence of a restaurant proprietor: It was not her fault that Morris was not always prosperous. Ira recalled being sent to the local pawn shop with Rose's diamonds to obtain enough to tide the family over during temporary hard times (where she got the diamonds in the first place is not explained).

She never pestered her children with excessive surveillance. After George died, Rose boasted in an interview that she was determined to see that her children were raised as "regular kids," conscious of both sides of "real life," knowing more than just how to walk gracefully out of a Fifth Avenue home. When the boys were young they adhered "rigidly to the Jewish faith," she claimed. Their home was strictly orthodox. They were taught by rabbis and were all bar mitzvah (this was certainly not true; this interview was tailored for a Jewish audience of the *Jewish Examiner*).[6] She was clearly ambitious for both sons, encouraging Ira in his education, and later sponsoring Frances in a brief career as a child performer in a traveling musical revue. George commented to Isaac Goldberg that his mother was the kind of woman that the songwriter wrote the mammy songs about; "only I mean them," he said. As an adult George was in fact solicitous of his mother after his father died, and wrote her letters frequently from Hollywood. He also supported her financially. According to Frances, Rose was very proud of George. She was Mrs. Gershwin. She took it upon herself to have all the "honors" such as special seats at restaurants. For his part, Frances said, "George was very sweet to my mother. He used to come up all the time after he had his own place and bring ice cream."[7]

In his biography of George, David Ewen wrote favorably of Rose: Gershwin held a touching adoration of his mother—a gentle little woman. This was published in 1958. Many years later, in a revised version, Ewen shifted his view: he portrayed Rose as a "proud and self-centered woman . . . frequently an unhappy woman." According to Ewen, "George shared Rose's strength of will and purpose, pride and even selfishness," but "he was often at odds with his mother." It was his father whom he adored.[8]

On the other hand, in his more critical biography (1973), Charles Schwartz treated Rose favorably. He claimed that George confided in his mother, sought her advice, and followed her counseling—things he could not have done with his father. And after his father's death George and his mother seemed to become closer than ever. George believed that he and his mother were much alike. Schwartz suggests that the critical views about Rose, as related by Ewen, stemmed from Rose's strained relations with Ira, who influenced biographers such as Ewen.[9] Ira was disdainful of Schwartz's book; he found it so painful that he stopped reading it.[10]

Edward Jablonski, in his major biography, tilts toward a more critical appraisal of Rose, but he too was influenced by Ira. According to Jablonski, "mother and son [George] were not truly close." Rose Gershwin and her son "often clashed" and even after he became a successful songwriter she "offered unsolicited advice and made demands." Moreover, the Gershwins' marriage was not a model one. Morris' failure at business led to clashes and family tensions.[11]

Frances Gershwin told Joan Peyser that Rose provided no role model for her. She was self-absorbed and narcissistic; there was no relationship between the parents and children in the family, not even with George. In her biography of George, Peyser concludes that the "real" Rose would periodically—according to her sister Kate Wolpin—ask George if he didn't think she deserved a new mink coat—then when he answered yes she would buy a sable; she took every opportunity to point out that other composers were getting more favorable reviews than he.[12]

She was a woman, according to Peyser, who moved her face away when her son tried to kiss her. A word is in order about pulling her face away when George tried to kiss her. This is an interpretation of a photograph in which Rose does look pained; but there is another photograph of this very same occasion in which Rose looks happy, and yet another in which she looks equally pained cheek-to-cheek with Ira. Nevertheless, most photographs of Rose usually seem to show her with a severe countenance, or at least not a very happy one. George's painting and drawings seem to bear out the preference for his father: his father's portrait, as painted by George, shows a kindly, affectionate warmth. But George's painting of his mother shows a stern, almost forbidding matron; it is a strange portrait; the background seems to be an odd rural setting, with a small farmhouse in the distance against stormy clouds.

George and Ira both spoke and wrote lovingly about their father. When their father died, however, George showed no great emotion, according to the later recollection of his valet Paul Mueller (perhaps a biased source since he was summarily dismissed by Leonore Gershwin after George died). A better illustration of George's true feeling for his father was an incident at a New Year's Eve Party at the White House on December 29, 1934, two years after Morris died. He attended as the guest of his friend, the journalist Kay Halle. She relates: "As we reached the entrance hall leading to the East Room, George's joy and excitement were so unbounded that he shot away from the receiving line to stand under the glittering chandelier, joyfully crying out, 'If only my *father* could see me now!' "[13]

Yet, it is also true that in his old age Ira kept a picture of his mother in his dressing room. He remarked to his assistant Michael Feinstein that he never really knew his father until near the end of Morris' life, when he finally perceived his father's character. Ira added that he resented the way his father was treated by his mother. Frances commented that it was a "family of individuals, each going separately." She well remembered how she almost had to raise herself. According to two Gershwin biographers: "the suggestion that here was family harmony that brought them together, each attentive to the others' need and wants, that is the myth," perpetuated by the film biography of George's life.[14]

In sum, Isaac Goldberg's original picture of a healthy, unspoiled, simple Jewish family is open to challenge. Edward Jablonski, explaining George's reluctance to marry, wrote that "he apparently did not want the kind of marriage that his parents endured." Moreover, Gershwin's ego-centrism may be explained by the feeling that his parents preferred Ira. After all, both parents assumed he would end up as a bum (vagrant). Yet after George died, Rose repeatedly said that he was her favorite.[15]

The life of the Jewish immigrant, impoverished or otherwise, was not especially conducive to music—although this same area (Brooklyn) produced both George Gershwin and Aaron Copland (born within a year of each other). For Copland, music was an art he discovered by himself: No one ever talked music to him or took him to a concert. But his sister played the piano and gave him lessons, and his brother was a skilled violinist. Jerome Kern's mother as well as Richard Rodgers' mother played the piano quite well. Rodgers attended the opera with his grandfather, and his parents played and sang excerpts from the latest operettas. Nothing like this was the case with Gershwin. As an adult Gershwin noted that, though of Russian parentage, he owed no sensitiveness to melodious sounds from that source. George rather weakly claimed that his father was musical—he played a comb wrapped in tissue paper!

While Copland, Rodgers, and Kern were drawn to a career in music, at first George was more attracted to the rough-and-tumble life of the streets—at least that is what he claimed. He earned the reputation of a "bad" boy. In later years he tended to exaggerate his image of the street urchin. He explained his fear of being known as a sissy ("maggie" was the term of those days). His biographers have all adopted these characterizations: He was a "rough-and-ready, muscular type" not "one of your sad and contemplative children."[16] Yip Harburg remembered that "George was a kid then, just a snip of a kid, and Ira sort of sloughed him off because George didn't care too much about education and had dropped out of school."[17] He was the athletic champion of his gang, playing street hockey, "cat," and roller-skating on the streets. According to his sister, George was a pretty wild boy. People used to tell her mother that she would have trouble with George. Frances said that George did not have much to do with Ira or Arthur. She "heard" he was an independent kid, on his own a lot. Of course, as she acknowledged, she could not remember George's youth since she was eight years younger.

Isaac Goldberg summed up: George was "frankly, a bad child," who might have become a "gangster." Writing sixty years later, Joan Peyser too is quite blunt: "He was a dirty, neglected child. His grades were bad. He seems never to have read. He fought, stole and played hookey."[18] This goes too far. Gershwin graduated from grammar school (P.S. 20), no mean achievement in 1910; many who became prominent in show business quit school at an early age. On the other hand, Harburg recalled that "The public schools were better then, too. I went to P.S. 64 on Avenue B and Ninth street. Great teachers—they were aware of the poverty conditions of the kids they were teaching."[19] Moreover, George moved on to the High School for Commerce for two years. It was intended that he study bookkeeping.

As for his rough play, this was more the norm in that era and in that locale. The future movie actor Edward G. Robinson, who attended the same grammar school as the Gershwins, said that the ambition of all his classmates was to win an athletic medal. "The street, not the home was your life," said Harburg. It was the studious Ira who was more of an exception.

It was on the streets that the children of Jewish immigrants were American-ized. Thus, George's fascination with writing "American music" may well have had its roots in this early environment. Indeed, his love of New York probably dates from these youthful days. After achieving fame on Broadway, Gershwin wrote:

> I was becoming acquainted with that which later I was to interpret—the soul of the American people. Having been born in New York and grown up among New Yorkers, I have heard the voice of that soul. It spoke to me on the streets, in school, at the theater. In the chorus of city sounds I heard it.[20]

Thus his environment was an important influence on his music. Irving Berlin wrote dozens of ethnic and novelty songs about Jews, Italians, Germans, and even Chinese. Although Gershwin lived in the same area of the Lower East Side, he did not write ethnic songs. In his concert compositions he was seeking a genuine American sound that evoked the melting-pot of New York. Thus, the original title for *Rhapsody in Blue* was *American Rhapsody*.

George's fondness for the "melting-pot" may well have been the result of the Gershwin children often being on their own, free to roam around their area that bordered the Italian and Irish districts and Chinatown. Ira Gershwin's recollec-tions, many years later, were mildly romantic: riding the horse-drawn street cars on Delancey Street, their stoves hot in the winter; trips with other kids to Chi-natown to buy sugar cane at about a cent a foot; learning to swim in the "mucky Harlem River"; picking up some Italian phrases to serve as passwords in case you were ganged up on around Mulberry Street; the laundry with a two-cent lending library side-line, and the Atlantic Gardens on the Bowery—"a nice great uncle took you—where you heard a sixteen piece lady orchestra, saw several acts, then a one reel movie, while you ate a sausage and drank a small beer."[21]

Family life was "indulgent," and as young boys George and Ira became quite self-reliant. Perhaps they had to, given the potentially hostile environment outside the Jewish quarter. Yip Harburg recalled fighting the Italians as well as the Irish, and both fought the Jews. For George this freedom in his early life was transformed into an unshakable self-confidence and an outsized ego; indeed, there was an early assertiveness in George Gershwin that bordered on aggressiveness. He alienated childhood friends with his rough game-playing. Some commentators noted that this aggressiveness was reflected in his music. Noting this independence in his youth, some of George Gershwin's biographers detect an inability to form a permanent attachment with women largely because of this early freedom from parental supervision.

George cooperated with Isaac Goldberg in the preparation of his biography, so he apparently not only did not object to descriptions of his rough childhood, he encouraged them. Probably he was laying the groundwork for claiming that it was music that rescued him. After he had achieved a certain degree of prominence he said that "studying the piano made a good boy out of a bad one. It took the piano to tone me down. It made me more serious. I was a changed person six months after I took it up."[22] If so, his "bad" boy period could not have lasted more than a year or two.

Even though music was considered an endeavor for "maggies," Gershwin claimed he was enchanted by music from an early age. He related several incidents in which he was inexorably drawn to music, even before the family acquired a piano. For example, his family briefly lived in Harlem; the area was then primarily Jewish; the black influx came later. When he was a young boy of about six, around 1904, George once stood outside a penny arcade in Harlem at 125th Street. He was mesmerized by the sounds tinkling from a battered player piano: he was barefoot, in overalls, drinking it all in, avidly. It was Anton Rubinstein's "Melody in F," and the particular jumps in the melody kept him rooted. George told this anecdote many, many times. It was used as the opening scene for his film biography (though he is barefoot in his own version, in the movie he is on roller-skates). In an early draft of the movie script, Ira appears and listens to the music and, perplexed, asks, "Where are the words?" Mercifully, this was never included in the film. Despite George's early infatuation with music there was no effort to follow up until several years later. Perhaps the incident was exaggerated.

George also related many times another, similar incident. When he was in grammar school (about ten) he was standing outside the school auditorium when he heard his classmate, the violinist Max Rosenzweig, playing "Humoresque." He was entranced and ran in the pouring rain to seek him out, but Max had left the school. They soon became friends and Rosen (formerly Rosenzweig) introduced him to the world of music. George gleefully added to this tale that Max's advice was for George to forget about music because he had no real talent. Fortunately, Max Rosen became a concert violinist, not a music critic.

NOTES

1. Immigration records show a family named Bruskin, including a daughter, Rosa, arrived on February 26, 1892 on the liner *Sorrento* from Hamburg, but Rosa's age is given as 19—too old unless a mistake was made by immigration officials, or unless she shaved a few years off her age later. The census of 1900 records the family of Gerskin Bruskin (age 48), his wife, Mary (age 42), their daughter, Katie [*sic*] (age 10), and their son, Barney (age 12), all born in Russia, living at 34 Orchard. By then Rosa was married. On George's birth certificate Rosa's name is spelled/or misspelled "Brushkin"; her age is twenty-two, but when she died in December 1948 she was listed as 71; accordingly, she was probably born in 1876 or 1877.

2. Max Wilk, *They're Playing Our Song* (New York: Zoetrope, 1986), p. 229.

3. *Time*, July 9, 1945.

4. Isaac Goldberg (supplemented by Edith Garson), *George Gershwin: A Study in American Music* (New York: Frederick Ungar Publishing, 1958; originally published New York: Simon and Schuster, 1931), p. 30.

5. Library of Congress, Gershwin Collection; Correspondence Folders: letter to Rosamund Walling.

6. *Jewish Examiner*, September 2, 1938.

7. Robert Kimball and Alfred Simon, *The Gershwins* (New York: Bonanza Books, 1963), pp. 47–48.

8. David Ewen, *George Gershwin: His Journey to Greatness*, 2nd enlarged ed. (New York: The Ungar Publishing Company, 1970), p. 5. The first edition was published in 1958; subsequent editions have been revised, but not extensively. The author claimed that Ira and Leonore Gershwin were helpful sources.

9. Charles Schwartz, *Gershwin: His Life and Music* (New York: Bobbs-Merrill, 1973; reprint, New York: Da Capo, 1979), p. 8.

10. Benny Green, *Let's Face the Music* (London: Pavillion Books, 1989), p. 209.

11. Edward Jablonski, *Gershwin: A Biography* (New York: Doubleday, 1987), p. 4.

12. Joan Peyser, *The Memory of All That* (New York: Simon and Schuster, 1993), pp. 18, 21.

13. *Washington Post*, February 5, 1978.

14. Edward Jablonski and Lawrence D. Stewart, *The Gershwin Years* (New York: Doubleday & Company, 1958; third ed., New York: Da Capo, 1996), p. 332. There have been several editions. Each new edition has incorporated significant changes, especially in the final chapters and the bibliography. Stewart was an assistant to Ira Gershwin, so his evaluation carries weight.

15. Jablonski, *Gershwin*, p. 298. Considered by many to be the definitive text. A subsequent edition contains an updated discography.

16. Goldberg, *George Gershwin*, p. 53.

17. Wilk, *They're Playing Our Song*, p. 230.

18. Goldberg, *George Gershwin*, p. 57; Peyser, *The Memory of All That*, p. 23.

19. Wilk, *They're Playing Our Song*, p. 229.

20. George Gershwin, "Jazz is the Voice of the American Soul," *Theatre Magazine*, March 1927; reprinted in *Gershwin in His Time: A Biographical Scrapbook, 1919–1937*, ed. Gregory R. Suriano (New York: Gramercy Books, 1998).

21. Ira Gershwin, "But I Wouldn't Want to Live There," *Saturday Review of Literature*, October 1958.

22. Interview with Katharan McCommon, probably 1924; Library of Congress, Gershwin Collection.

Chapter 2

Song Plugging

A piano was a status symbol for a Jewish family. The Jewish daily newspaper *Forward* wrote: "There is no question that a piano in the front room is preferable to a boarder. It gives spiritual pleasure to exhausted workers." The songwriter Harry Ruby asserted (only half-jokingly) that the great songwriters from the Lower East Side were produced by the omnipresence of the piano. Contemporary accounts in the *Forward* graphically explained the prevalence of both the Victrola and the piano in Jewish families:

> God sent us the Victrola, and you can't get away from it unless you run to the park. As if we didn't have enough problems with cockroaches and children practicing the piano next door. . . . There are pianos in thousands of homes . . . but it is hard to get a teacher. They hire a woman for Moshele or Fennele and after two years decide they need a "bigger" teacher. But the bigger teacher listening to the child finds it knows nothing. All the money—down the drain. Why this waste? Because Jews like to think they are experts on everything.[1]

One afternoon in 1910 a secondhand upright piano was hoisted through the second floor window in the Gershwins' apartment. Since it was a sign of affluence and culture, plus the fact that Rose Gershwin's sister Kate had a piano, Rose decided to follow. The piano was intended for Ira. When it was delivered to the Gershwins, George immediately sat down and played a popular song of the day, according to the version related by Ira, who was impressed by George's dexterous use of his left hand. The family's surprise was explained by the fact that George had been playing and practicing at a friend's house by imitating the movement of the keys on a player piano. When he was an old man Ira offered a startlingly different version. Before the Gershwins owned a piano, one day George returned from school and announced that he had played at the school assembly. Ira was surprised; he said he didn't know George could play, and George replied, "I didn't know I could either."[2] Apparently, he had actually been playing for some time!

Young George's attraction to music and the piano is a minor mystery. As noted, he was mesmerized by the sound of a player piano in a penny arcade when he was about six, but nothing came of it. Indeed, it was about six or seven years before he learned to play by imitating the depression of the keys on a friend's player piano. Why, then, did he not ask for his own music lessons? Was it, as Goldberg claims, that he was afraid of being thought a "sissy"? If so, what changed him? Was it, perhaps, rivalry with Ira?

In any case, Ira began to take lessons, and George had to be "shooed" away from the piano. But Ira soon gave up and George began to take lessons, probably sometime in 1911 when he was twelve or thirteen. His first teacher may have been the same Miss Green who was Ira's first teacher (Ira also took a few lessons from his Aunt Kate). George later said that he had three women teachers. After about four months he began to study with a flamboyant Hungarian immigrant, Professor Goldfarb (who was famed for having written the "Theodore Roosevelt March"). Many years later he said that he had three neighborhood teachers (he may have also counted his Aunt Kate as his first teacher).[3] With Goldfarb he ran through the standard instruction manual and was introduced to the light classics. If in fact he had mastered all of the exercises in Ferdinand Beyer's "Elementary Instruction Book for the Piano Forte," which Ira used, he would have been quite accomplished.

George was friendly with a young boy named Jack Miller, who belonged to the Beethoven Musical Society. It was an orchestra of young people from the East Side who played without pay, and was conducted by Henry Lefkowitz, who was described as a "twine salesman." George was not a member, as many writers mistakenly claim; he just happened to be there when a group picture was taken and published. Miller urged George to study more seriously with his own teacher, Charles Hambitzer. The lessons with Hambitzer apparently began sometime in 1912 (about two years after the piano arrived) when George was about to turn fourteen. Gershwin must have shown considerable talent, for Hambitzer recognized his ability immediately. He wrote his sister that his new student was a "genius, without a doubt." His new pupil was "crazy about music and can't wait until its time to take his lesson."[4]

Gershwin's abilities were indeed extraordinary. At the keyboard he far exceeded his contemporaries—Kern, Rodgers, Porter, and of course, Irving Berlin, who played only on the black keys. His friend Oscar Levant wrote of his ability: "He had such fluency at the piano and so steady a surge of ideas that any time he sat down just to amuse himself something came of it. Actually this is how he got most of his ideas—just by playing."[5]

Even before he began his more serious studies with Charles Hambitzer, Gershwin's interest in the classics was evident. His childhood scrapbook (preserved in the Library of Congress) is filled with the programs of concerts he attended at Carnegie Hall, Aeolian Hall, Cooper Union, and various other locales in Manhattan, including one lecture at the "People's Institute," titled "Shall We Exclude the Immigrant." This scrapbook was probably begun by late 1912; there is a program of a concert in December 1912 of the Beethoven Society at Cooper Union. Ira Gershwin commented that this scrapbook shows that George had more than a passing interest in the more serious side of music. George's scrapbook includes several pictures of composers pasted in the first pages; they are mainly Russian composers, pictures cut out of *Etude* magazines. There is also a page of pictures labeled "Great Pianists at the Keyboard."

The programs of concerts that he saved are instructive evidence of Gershwin's early interests. He attended a flurry of concerts in early 1913, almost every weekend, including eight concerts in ten weeks. The concert almost always featured a piano performance, for example, by Josef Lhevinne (a Russian-born pianist on tour who eventually settled in the United States), noted for his impressive technique. Gershwin also heard Leo Ornstein at Cooper Union in February 1913 and again at the Wannamaker Auditorium in April 1913. Ornstein had a reputation for his radical ideas; the programs George heard, however, were quite conventional—Bach, Mendelssohn, and Chopin. George never mentioned Ornstein as an influence.

The entire Gershwin family went to a concert that featured George's classmate, the violinist Max Rosenzweig, whose playing of "Humoresque" had so mesmerized George. There was one ironic occasion. Young student Gershwin attended a "farewell" concert of the great Leopold Godowsky at the new Aeolian Hall in March 1913. Neither Gershwin nor Godowsky could imagine that Godowsky's son would marry Gershwin's sister. Ira recalled a concert by the conductor Pierre Monteux. It was sold out and he and George sat on the stage behind the orchestra, where they could witness Monteux's every gesture. There was a buffet at intermission: Sandwiches were twenty-five cents and lemonade was a nickel.

These concerts did indeed make an indelible impression on the young boy. He went to the concerts, he said, and listened not only with his ears but with his nerves, mind, and heart. He listened so earnestly the he became saturated with music. Then he went home and listened in his memory and sat at the piano and played the motifs he had heard. In this process of absorbing music, an important event for Gershwin must have been a Sunday evening concert by the Waldorf-Astoria Orchestra that featured his teacher, Charles Hambitzer, in April 1913, playing Rubinstein's Concerto in D Minor. At the impressionable age of fourteen Gershwin was exposed to a wide variety of classical music. He must have savored the experiences, because he kept the programs and carefully pasted them into his scrapbook. His new teacher noted that Gershwin was intrigued by modern music, such as jazz, but wrote that he would see to it that Gershwin got a firm foundation in the standard music first.

After he began his studies with Hambitzer, he played on a program in March 1914 arranged by Ira for the Finley Club (a literary club) at the Christadora House on the Lower East Side. He was listed as "George Gershvin." Within months he left the High School of Commerce to become a song plugger with the publishing firm of Jerome H. Remick & Company. How this opening came his way is not clear. A family friend apparently touted him to Mose Gumble, the leader of Remick's popular music department (Gershwin returned the favor by recording piano rolls of some of Gumble's songs).

Remick's was not the leading publisher, but was moving smartly to the fore after being transplanted early in the decade from Detroit. Originally, it was Whitney Warner Music that was bought by Jerome Remick, a prominent business man and political leader in Detroit (Remick was a Michigan delegate to the Democratic convention that nominated Woodrow Wilson). Remick also bought out Shapiro, Bernstein, and in 1905 established his own company and became the largest-volume publisher. At first Remick's concentrated on classical music but later added a popular catalogue, featuring such songs as "Pretty Baby" (1916) and the wartime favorite "Smiles" (1918). Concentrating on ragtime, it soon outdistanced its competitors, which may explain the decision to hire Gershwin. Remick's was eventually bought out by Warner Brothers in 1929 (so too were Witmark and Harms; the three were then merged.)

Rose Gershwin is often portrayed as having opposed George's decision to become a professional musician, but that may be exaggerated (in the movie biography both parents are adamantly opposed; clearly this was not true of Morris).[6] Supposedly, Rose was finally persuaded by George's argument that he intended to be a composer, like Irving Berlin, a name Rose recognized. Thus, he left behind his boyhood and entered the professional world of popular music. He was fifteen.

Selling popular music was an active business in New York. There were no radios, so a song's popularity depended on live performances and "plugging" to sell sheet music. Publishers began to print "professional copies" and provide them free to performers, along with free orchestrations. They pushed their own songs by singing out from the balconies of the vaudeville shows to "help" a performer who seemed to conveniently forget the lyrics. Publishers hired songwriters and arrangers as well as pluggers to demonstrate their music in different locales.

In the evenings the song pluggers, plus some song-and-dance teams, would make the rounds of the various taverns, music halls, and cafes, hoping to persuade an entertainer to use the publisher's songs. George was one of this "fleet" of teams. It was highly competitive and required hustling to keep up with the other pluggers. On the whole, however, they were not a cutthroat band. At the end of an evening they might congregate in one of the late-night cafes for a round of stories and drinks. After hours many of the cafes, especially near the Lower East Side, were social gathering places. And in the European tradition, they were the center for lively discussions and debate. The *New York Tribune* described them in September 1900:

> Not every Russian cafe reaches this level of [intellectual center]. There are many which exist for the purpose of dispensing food and for that alone. Four of five, however, make this only a part of their business. At most hours of the day and night until three o'clock in the morning, these places are filled with men who have come there to sip Russian tea out of tumblers, meet their friends and discuss everything under heaven.[7]

One of the publishing firms that employed these pluggers was owned and operated by Harry von Tilzer, known mainly for having written a million-dollar-sales song, "A Bird in a Gilded Cage." It was supposedly in von Tilzer's office that the songwriter and news reporter Monroe Rosenfeld heard the musical din outside and called it "Tin Pan Alley."

Song plugging had evolved since the days when Irving Berlin was hired by von Tilzer as a "busker" who would plug a song by singing out in the balcony of a theater during intermission. By the time Gershwin began to ply this trade, it was a more organized and more remunerative business. Contemporary accounts suggest that the publisher's quarters were shabby, more of a "bower" than an office; several pianos were available for the professional song pluggers to run through the firm's latest creations for the singers and other performers. One observer, however, provided a glimpse into what was still a hectic existence: "The professional department of a popular publishing house is like an extra noisy hour at the psychopathic ward in Bellevue Hospital. . . . All around are cubicles, theoretically sound proof, each with a piano of uncertain vintage, and still more uncertain pitch."[8]

The performing "artists" would be conducted into one of these cubicles, where young pluggers like Gershwin would play the catalogue of the firm—perhaps sneaking in a tune of his own. He first met Fred and Adele Astaire at Remick's. Nevertheless, from the beginning George claimed that he was unhappy. Indeed, Isaac Goldberg's chapter about George's time at Remick's is entitled "Pluggers' Purgatory." Gershwin found it tedious work and the hapless song plugger was sometimes treated badly by the various condescending performers who were shopping the rounds.

At Remick's Gershwin met Herman Paley, also a Remick's songwriter, who introduced him into his circle of family and friends. It was there that he met Lou Paley, a high school English teacher, who would write an occasional lyric with George. At the Paleys' George also met Emily Strunsky and the Paleys' nice friend, Mabel Pleshette Schirmer; both would become George's lifelong friends. Lou Paley married Emily Strunsky in 1920 and George played at their wedding. The couple held open houses at their apartment on Saturday nights. The group would include playwright Sam Behrman, songwriters Phil Charig and Vincent Youmans, lyricist Buddy de Sylva, and actor Edward G. Robinson, as well as Dick Simon (of Simon and Schuster), the lyricist and future vice president of MGM, Howard Dietz, and many others, including Oscar Levant, who described the Paleys' as a "gathering place for people interested in newer and fresher ideas relating to the theatre, music and painting."[9]

Dietz and his wife lived in the apartment below, and one Saturday Dietz went upstairs to complain of the noise and celebration, but after being admitted he was intrigued by the music and joined the party from then on. Emily Paley said that their apartment was a testing ground for George's dates; if his lady friend didn't like the atmosphere, he dropped her. Ira became a regular after George took him to the Paleys'; he met Emily's sister Leonore, and eventually married her.[10]

Remick's was a strange interlude in Gershwin's career. Almost nothing is known of his activities there. He said little about it, except to complain some years later that the business got on his nerves; the tunes began to offend him and he was a most "unhappy lad." There are only a few notable anecdotes about Remick's relayed by others, but not by Gershwin. Why did he stay so long? The obvious reason is that he was getting paid reasonably well. He was also beginning to have an odd tune published and performed, and Remick's provided access to performers. Remick's discouraged independent song writing, however; they did not want their pluggers to become composers as well. Gershwin left in March 1917. While he may have been displeased, as he claimed, in fact he had stayed for almost three years.

Gershwin's introduction to popular music at Remick's came at a time of transition in musical styles. Ragtime was still a powerful influence. At first the rags were piano solos or instrumentals based on a strong rhythmic syncopation. Scott Joplin's "Maple Leaf Rag" was the classic example. Later there was a rash of songs with ragtime mainly in the title or lyrics. Thus, *Hullo Ragtime* was a popular revue in 1912 in London, featuring Irving Berlin as a performer. Shortly after Gershwin joined Remick's, Irving Berlin wrote the score for *Watch Your Step*, starring Vernon and Irene Castle ("Syncopated Walk" was the main theme for this show). Berlin was so bold as to proclaim that he wanted to write a ragtime opera. Ragtime was also the musical spine of Berlin's *Stop! Look! Listen!* There was even a song, "Everything in America is Ragtime," popularized by Gaby Deslys, one of the show's stars.

The older tradition of operettas was still a major musical force on Broadway. The main American stylist was Victor Herbert. His *Naughty Marietta* and *Sweethearts* were among his last big hit shows before World War I. That war cast a shadow over operettas that originated in Europe, especially Germany or Austria. Gradually, operettas were being supplanted by "musical comedies," as they were called. The leading practitioner was George M. Cohan. A prominent third musical strain was the revue, popularized by Florenz Ziegfeld's *Follies*, which first opened in 1907. Thus, Gershwin began his professional musical career at a time that one music historian characterized as the "most exciting in the history of the American Musical theater."[11]

One reason why this was an extraordinary period was the major innovation in musical theater that began the year before Gershwin joined Remick's. It started at the tiny Princess Theater on 39th Street. It was there that Jerome Kern, Guy Bolton, and later P.G. Wodehouse wrote a series of musicals that were different. Their aim was to create an integrated show tying together music, plot, and lyrics and dispensing with gags, comic plots, and novelty music. To a large extent they succeeded and set a new standard for American musicals. For Gershwin, these diverse influences were a fortunate break; they allowed him to pick and choose those musical strains that attracted him. In the company of Ira he saw many of Kern's early shows, including *Leave It to Jane* and *Rock-a-bye Baby*.

In one respect his work for Remick's was quite significant. It led to a part-time job recording piano rolls, beginning in late 1915. While he may well have thought song plugging for Remick's was a dead end, recording piano rolls widened his experiences considerably. They are the earliest surviving examples of his pianistic ability. A kaleidoscope of musical styles was reflected in Gershwin's early rolls; for example, in January 1916 he recorded "Bantam Steps (a Raggy Fox Trot)," and "When You're Dancing the Old Fashioned Waltz" by von Tilzer, as well as "I Gave My Heart and Hand to Someone in Dixie." He also recorded a roll of "Past Ragtime" by the ragtime composer Artie Matthews. He was not obligated to play only songs from Remick's catalogue and even recorded his own composition "Rialto Ripples (Rag)," released in September 1916. His co-author was Will Donaldson (not Walter Donaldson, the composer of "My Blue Heaven" and other hits). It was not really a rag in the Scott Joplin tradition, as some of his admirers wrote; it was more of a novelty along the lines of Zez Confrey's "Kitten on the Keys" or Felix Arndt's "Nola," though by no means up to those two vintage piano pieces. But it was not a bad effort for its time (George turned eighteen by the time it was released).

What the piano rolls prove is that Gershwin was not only a skillful ragtime pianist, but that he also had begun to develop a piano style of his own, more evident on other piano rolls recorded later in 1916 and 1917. Before leaving Remick's he wrote a novelty tune with the lyricist Murray Roth, entitled "When You Want 'Em You Can't Get 'Em, When You've Got 'Em, You Don't Want 'Em," which he recorded as a piano roll in September 1916; also with Roth he wrote "My Runaway Girl," which brought George into contact with Sigmund Romberg, who liked the song and inserted it into a revue called *The Passing Show of 1916*.

After he left Remick's he was temporarily out of work. Indeed, both he and Ira were not working steadily. George was going on nineteen and Ira was twenty-two; both lived at home and apparently took little responsibility for contributing to their family's support. Ira did work at some odd jobs for his father. George made the rounds looking for a job. He went to see his "good friend" Will Vodery, a black orchestrator who had been writing arrangements for Ziegfeld. This is an interesting sidelight on Gershwin's musical education. How did he come to know Vodery? Probably through Remick's; the interesting point is that he knew him well enough to ask for help in finding a job. This seems to confirm that Gershwin was already becoming acquainted with black musicians.

Gershwin picked up a number of odd jobs playing the piano. He related an incident that occurred while he was job-hunting. He was hired to play the piano in the pit for a vaudeville comedy act at the Fox City Theater on 14th Street. He had to sight-read the music and lost his place. This subjected him to endless ridicule from the comedian on stage. Gershwin promptly quit and asked for his money from the cashier, who refused him; he then "beat an ignominious retreat." Gershwin said that the affair left a "deep scar."[12] It seems likely that Gerswhin was at pains to recall this anecdote to emphasize the irony of the contrast between his humiliation in 1917 and how far he had come since then. How could he know, he told Goldberg, that a dozen years later he would sign a contract for $100,000 to write music for the very same Fox movies.

In October, Gershwin, probably on Vodery's recommendation, was hired as a rehearsal pianist for Charles Dillingham and Florenz Ziegfeld's new extravaganza *Miss 1917*, with music written by both Jerome Kern and Victor Herbert and sketches by Guy Bolton and P.G. Wodehouse. It was the successor to their earlier show *The Century Girl*. On paper, at least, it was a sure success. Its stars were the young Vivienne Segal, the veterans Bessie McCoy and Lew Fields, and the glamorous Vernon and Irene Castle. The score included a delightful new song by Kern, "The Land Where the Good Songs Go," which Gershwin would record as a piano roll, released in January 1918.

As the rehearsal pianist Gershwin was paid $35 per week, but more importantly, as Ira carefully noted, George was in contact with some of the major figures on Broadway. Kern and Herbert both befriended him, even though they were feuding over the score. Vivienne Segal, then at the beginning of an illustrious career, was caught in the middle when both composers insisted that she feature their songs. She performed during the special Sunday night shows staged by the cast and in those shows she introduced two Gershwin songs with lyrics by Irving Caesar: "There's More to a Kiss than XXX" (published later for the imported British comedy *Good Morning Judge*), and "You-oo, Just You." Ira records in his diary that he and his brother were slightly starstruck at the time. George met two of the Ziegfeld dancers—George White and Ann Pennington. White would soon launch his own revue and Ann Pennington would star in it. White would hire Gershwin to write the score for five versions of his *Scandals*.

Miss 1917 ran into difficulties and took more time to rehearse, which gave added weeks to Gershwin's salary. The show finally opened on November 5, 1917, but failed and closed quickly. Ira was at the opening and wrote in his diary: "A glorious show—entertaining every minute." But the critics disagreed and the show closed.

Gershwin, however, was gainfully employed as an accompanist to the long-time star Louise Dresser, whose specialty was singing "My Gal Sal," written by her mentor Paul Dresser, whose brother was the famous writer Theodore Dreiser.

She opened in February 1918 and, accompanied by Gershwin, toured Baltimore, Boston, and Washington. In March 1918, Gershwin witnessed a stirring patriotic parade and he and Dresser performed for an audience that included President Wilson. Gershwin was nineteen and of draft age; in anticipation of being inducted he began to practice the saxophone in the hope of joining an army band.

Before this tour with Dresser, Gershwin was briefly associated with Ziegfeld. On Sunday nights before prohibition Ziegfeld would stage new shows, in effect, a dinner theater on his theater roof garden, drawing on the cast of the current version of the *Follies*. They were called the *Frolics*. George was signed on as the rehearsal pianist, but that experience was not a particularly memorable one.

Throughout his career Gershwin was at the right place at the right time, and his natural talents did the rest. George came to the attention of the *Miss 1917*'s production manager Harry Askins, who in turn brought him to the attention of one of the giants of music publishing, Max Dreyfus. During his long career Dreyfus became a legend. He helped to establish T.B. Harms as a major music publisher and he discovered and encouraged many of the great songwriters of that era (failing only on Richard Rodgers and Larry Hart, whose "Manhattan" did not impress Dreyfus). But Gerswhin did impress him, and he decided to sign him in February 1918 for $35 a week, not to plug songs but simply to write them for the T.B. Harms publishing company.

The Harms connection was important. It offered access to Broadway productions and a chance to interpolate songs in various shows. Thus, Gershwin and Irving Caesar, who was also from the Lower East Side and became a lifelong friend, wrote "I Was So Young," which was interpolated into *Good Morning Judge*. It was a Schubert production of a British import based on a Pinero play, *The Boy*, and starred Charles and Mollie King. One reviewer wrote: "Any song that can be sung twelve times in succession in a show must be some melody— and that's the actual happening in "Good Morning Judge"—and the happy title is "I'm So Young and You're So Beautiful" (the actual title was "I Was So Young"). Gershwin received no credit in the program but a reviewer noted that "to some unknown native genius of syncopation belong several numbers that possibly appealed more to the audience."[13]

Gershwin was more fortunate in managing to get three songs inserted into another production—*Look Who's Here*, later renamed *Ladies First* and starring the legendary Nora Bayes. His songs were "Some Wonderful Sort of Someone," "Something about Love," and one of the first George and Ira Gershwin songs, "The Real American Folk Song Is a Rag," credited to another writer in the reviews.

George toured briefly with Nora Bayes (Dora Goldberg), who was a major star of vaudeville as a singer and comedienne. She wrote some of her own songs, produced her own shows, and eventually acquired her own theater. In 1902, she first caught on as the "Wurzburger Girl" for her rendition of "Down Where the Wurzburger Flows." She appeared in the first of Ziegfeld's *Follies* in 1907 and again in 1908. Along with her husband Jack Norworth, she wrote "Shine on,

Harvest Moon," and popularized "Has Anybody Here Seen Kelly?" George M. Cohan personally chose her to perform the premiere of his World War I song, "Over There." As a comedienne, Bayes satirized the suffragettes in *Ladies First*.

Gershwin thus was involved in the big-time vaudeville when he joined her company. The pre-Broadway tour of this show, however, did not go well for Gershwin. The songs used were constantly changing. When the tour reached Pittsburgh a young Oscar Levant was in the gallery (his uncle was the conductor). Levant was transfixed by George's playing: "I never heard such fresh, brisk, unstudied, completely free and inventive playing."[14] Nora Bayes, however, would not indulge the free-wheeling style of her traveling pianist. Many years later, when Levant reminded George of this tour, he said that Bayes was constantly complaining that his playing distracted her from what she was trying to do; she frequently threatened to fire him. Gershwin in turn found her difficult, especially when she insisted on changing one of his songs. Gershwin wrote a letter to Irving Caesar complaining that his songs were being misused. "The Folk Song," as he described it, "is ruined in its present condition. No fault of the songs but the singer." "So you see," Gerswhin wrote, "it's not merely having good songs that make hits." In any case, when the show opened in New York in October 1918, Gershwin and his songs were out.[15]

For another show, *The Lady in Red*, billed as a "melodious" musical comedy, with lyrics by Anne Caldwell and music by Robert Winterberg, two Gershwin songs were interpolated: "Something about Love," with lyrics by his friend Lou Paley and a revised version of "Some Wonderful Sort of Someone," with lyrics by Schuyler Green (a song plugger from Remick's). This show starred another well-known veteran, Adele Rowland. She had starred in George M. Cohan's *Hello Broadway* in 1914, introducing "Down By the Erie Canal." She had also appeared in one of Jerome Kern's Princess shows, *Have a Heart*, and introduced the popular wartime song "Pack Up Your Troubles in Your Old Kit Bag." After her tour with Gershwin her new show opened in New York in 1919 to mixed reviews. It "looked good enough" to stick for a profitable summer run, but in fact it closed after forty-eight performances. The two Gershwin songs, for which he did not receive credit in the notices, did, however, relieve "the dead level" of the show, according to one review.

Gershwin's songs were typical of the period, but with some unusual touches in the melodies. "Something about Love" starts with a customary eight-bar phrase, but the second eight bars do not simply repeat the first eight, as was usual in the Tin Pan Alley songs. Moreover, after returning to the opening phrase, Gershwin introduced a significant variant for a full sixteen bars. The harmony is not unusual, but another song, "Some Wonderful Sort of Someone," is more notable for its unexpected chromatics in the harmony and bass line.

Finally, Gershwin interpolated songs in Morris Gest's *Midnight Whirl*. It was one of the many late-night rooftop revues usually held after the show closed in the theater itself. This show was staged on the Century Roof. The star was the dancer Bessie McCoy who married the famous foreign correspondent Richard

Harding Davis. For McCoy Gershwin wrote "Limehouse Nights," an undistinguished effort to sound Chinese. The lyrics were by Buddy De Sylva, a new partner for Gershwin.

In late 1918, while in Cleveland with the Nora Bayes show, Gershwin began to speculate on doing a complete score. He wrote a friend: "Seriously I am thinking of writing a show. . . . In spite of what J.K. (Jerome Kern) told me." Kern had advised him to wait and to consult him first. Gershwin continued: "I am getting confidence & encouragement from this show." He added that he would make an attempt when he returned to New York; meanwhile he hoped that his name would be printed in the program: "I sorely need to get into that select circle of composers."[16]

He was only going on twenty, but obviously he was ambitious and eager to break into Broadway. Gershwin had already experienced a variety of musical productions. But there was still one grand failure yet to come. In late 1918, Dreyfus had put Gershwin in touch with an aspiring amateur producer named Edward Perkins, who gathered a cast, a book of sorts, wrote some lyrics, and directed a production called *Half Past Eight*. The show was built around the antics of vaudeville comic Joe Cook; there were other acts including various singers and a cyclist, but no chorus, which caused "hissing" from the audience that had expected a girly show. There were three songs listed in the program: "Cupid," "Hong Kong," and "Little Sunbeam," but whether Gershwin wrote them is unclear. One song, "There's Magic in the Air," had lyrics by Ira, but apparently was not used (later recycled for *La, La, Lucille*).

The production opened in December in Syracuse and promptly closed to murderous reviews in *Variety*: "2$ Show Not Worth War Tax." Perkins was taken "ill," and several members of the cast were never paid. A sidelight may be worth mentioning, however. The orchestra was the Clef Club Players, one of several black organizations created under the auspices of the influential ragtime and jazz bandleader James Reese Europe. They opened the show with "After You've Gone," and for the finale played a "Dixieland" medley and a "jazz" dance by Cook. At this early point in his career, George was exposed to the jazz style that was just barely emerging in such orchestras as James Reese Europe's Clef Club. Gershwin enjoyed reciting this futile episode, and for some strange reason a distorted version of this episode is mentioned prominently in the movie biography *Rhapsody in Blue*, apparently to prove that George was not always successful.

Rather than obtaining his own show, Gershwin, however, had to settle for more openings to insert songs in various productions. For one show, *The Sweetheart Shop*, he wrote a song with Ira. The show was a hit in Chicago, and as it was preparing for Broadway George heard that the producer wanted a new song for the leading lady, the young Helen Ford, not yet the star she would become on Broadway. A Pollyana song was needed so George and Ira wrote "Waiting for the Sun to Come Out," their first published song together (though Ira was then writing under the pseudonym of Arthur Francis). The producer,

Edgar MacGregor, bought it for $250. The show failed and he reneged on the promised payment. George pleaded for the lyricist, who was a "young college boy" who needed the money; MacGregor gave George a check for half ($125), made out to Arthur Francis.

In sum, Gershwin had written songs featured by three important Broadway stars—Nora Bayes, Adele Rowland, and Helen Ford. He was being noticed and his prospects for his own show were improving.

Isaac Goldberg pompously comments that these early songs "adumbrated the humor, the gracility [*sic*], the colloquialness of Gershwin's melodic line." In the song "Some Wonderful Sort of Someone," Gershwin showed "skill in the use of chromatics and in his shifting of keys"; in "You-oo, Just You," he revealed "expertness in the melodic adaption, to grace and humor, of the five note scale."[17] Alec Wilder, in his analysis of Gershwin in his great book *American Popular Song*, is far less enthusiastic, though he more or less agrees that "Some Wonderful Sort of Someone" was an example of "inventiveness."[18]

The partnership of the two Gershwin brothers became so dominant in later years that it is easy to forget that Gershwin collaborated with many different lyricists. These songs were, for the most part, quite conventional. Their structure was not unusual—mainly the standard thirty-two bars. There were only flashes of Gershwin's skill in his use of unusual harmonies, and there were only fleeting glimpses of the innovative style found in his later songs. To be sure, the songs with Irving Caesar were slightly better than the others. Gershwin recorded "I Was So Young" as a piano roll. "You-oo, Just You" was a Gershwin-Caesar song which they sold to Remick's for $500. When they hurried home to tell Rose Gershwin the news, she supposedly told Morris to send for a lawyer to help them. She was afraid the boys would be "eaten up alive."

Sometime during this period he met Irving Berlin, who sought him as a recording secretary to take down Berlin's song, "Revolutionary Rag." Gershwin toyed with joining Berlin, but the master himself advised him to seek his own fortune. All of this is according to Gershwin's recollection; Berlin did not remember the incident.

It was around this time that George and Irving Caesar deliberately sat down to write a popular song in the idiom of "Hindustan" and other current favorite two-steps. The result was "Swanee." The story of its creation has been told and retold endless times. Since there were dozens of songs with a "dixie" flavor, it is not surprising that they chose "Swanee," and they supposedly finished it in a few minutes, according to Caesar's version, but according to George it took most of the late afternoon and evening. It was published by Harms, and inserted in the *Capitol Revue*, produced by Ned Wayburn in October.

The song languished until Al Jolson heard Gershwin play it at a party. Jolson was one of the most important Broadway personalities; he had broken into stardom in 1913, and since then everything he touched had turned to gold. Audiences wanted to see and hear him, never mind the quality of the show. His Sunday night concerts were legendary. *Sinbad*, his latest show, opened in January 1918 and was a hit. The big song was "Rock-a-bye Your Baby with a Dixie Melody." Sometime later, Buddy De Sylva took George to a party also attended by Jolson. Inevitably, George began to play and Jolson was captivated by "Swanee." He decided to interpolate it into *Sinbad* and, more important, to record it on January 8, 1920 for Columbia.[19] Jolson also took out a full page ad in *Variety* in February, with the blazing headline "AL JOLSON'S GREATEST SONG SWANEE." Suddenly Gershwin and Caesar were the authors of a major hit, selling thousands of copies of sheet music, records, and piano rolls. Their royalties began to look like real money. "Swanee" earned $7,487 in the second quarter of 1920; Gershwin's share of the royalties was $1,848 for three months, a substantial sum considering that he was working for only $35 a week at Harms.

George Gershwin had finally made his mark. A few years later, when he went to England, the customs inspector who passed him through at Southampton asked if he was the composer of "Swanee." George gleefully reported this to Ira.

"Swanee" was written to order; a synthetic formula production, in a style unlike almost anything Gershwin wrote subsequently (except perhaps, "Liza"). But it revealed a significant side to his character. He was deeply ambitious and craved success, especially the recognition of that success. For songwriters, that recognition meant writing established "hits." Gershwin was highly conscious of commercial success. Writing hits was what he wanted. Many, many years later he vehemently denied a report relayed by his agent in Hollywood that his music was too "highbrow." He informed his agents that he was out to write "hits."

Even before "Swanee" became a hit for Al Jolson, Gershwin's next association was more satisfying and marked the beginning of a long business and personal relationship with Alex Aarons. He was the young son of Alfred Aarons, a well-known Broadway impresario. He turned to Max Dreyfus for help in putting on his own first production. An intermediary was Arthur Jackson, the lyricist who had already worked with Gershwin and Dreyfus, who also steered Aarons to Gershwin. Gershwin later commented that it was "brave" of Aarons to take him on, because Gershwin had yet to write a complete score. On the other hand, Aarons had yet to produce a successful show. It was the beginning of a happy partnership. Alex Aarons together with Vinton Freedly would produce most of the shows written by the two Gershwin brothers, well into the 1930s. Thus it was that Gershwin first wrote his own score for a successful comedy *La, La, Lucille* that opened in May 1919, (the credits list Alfred Aarons the elder as the producer, but that may have been pro forma to help his son).

A Broadway production was not the massive undertaking it would become in the decades after World War II. In the early 1920s a production could be funded for $10,000, though the average had begun to creep upward. There were seventy theaters and the number of productions each year grew from about 127 in 1917 to over 200 by 1927. It required about two hundred performances for a show to break even; top price for a good orchestra seat in the 1920s was

$5.50. A composer received about 1/2 cent per copy of sheet music, as a starting royalty. Often a song was bought outright, and the composer would never receive any money even if the song became a major hit.

The book for *Lucille* by Arthur Jackson was naturally a comedy. An aged aunt dies, leaving her nephew an inheritance provided he divorces his wife, Lucille. The nephew, John, decides on a sham divorce from Lucille, and then, after inheriting the money, to remarry her. He arranges a rendezvous with the janitor's "frowsy" but "pure" wife, Fanny, to create a fake scene to provide grounds for the divorce. Fanny's husband, uninitiated into the farce, arrives and trouble begins. In the end the aunt reappears, alive after all, and announces she has only been testing John and Lucille. Naturally, a happy ending follows.

The show was favorably reviewed. The show was "packing 'em in" at the Henry Miller Theatre and the indications were that it was going to keep right on doing it all through the summer. Heywood Hale Broun, writing in the *Daily Mail*, called it a farce with bed and music. Gershwin's music was "spirited." Burns Mantle found it the best of the recent musical plays. It combined the bedroom with the school of farce comedy set to tunes. He noted that Gershwin had composed the score and picked out "Tee Oddle-Um-Bum-Bo" for special praise. The *Times* found the production the "incarnation of jazz" but failed to mention Gershwin. The *Globe* mentioned him but in a mixed review—the songs by a new composer George Gershwin were "tuneful," but "negative" and slowed down the action. Another review (*Washington Times*, April 28, 1919) when the show was out of town in Washington stated that the "music is possible [*sic*] the most commendable element of the production." The review noted that Gershwin was responsible for the score and had written at least two songs of promise: "Tee Oddle Um Bum Bo" and "From Now On."

"Tee-Oddle" was a ragtime novelty, but "From Now On" was much more interesting. Its refrain fluctuated between a liquid melody and a ragtime rhythmic figure; the smooth melody alternating with the jerky one created quite an unusual effect. Even the eight-bar bridge was a variant on this formula, and foreshadowed the Gershwin of the mid-1920s. It is seldom heard, however. The more enduring number in the score was "Nobody but You" (lyrics by Buddy De Sylva and Arthur Jackson), one of Gershwin's favorites which he included in his *Song-Book* in 1932. It has pianistic frills that probably appealed to his style. He probably wrote it while he was a student of Edward Kilenyi, and his exercise book suggests he was experimenting with its harmony. The harmony is not radical, but it does demonstrate a Gershwin trademark: repeating the same melodic phrase, but each time with a different harmony. This same formula was evident in one of Gershwin's first songs, "Come to the Moon," with lyrics by Lou Paley. The show also interpolated "There's More to a Kiss than the XXX."[20]

Some critics have noted the continuing influence of Jerome Kern on Gershwin in this show; this is true of the bright "Somehow It Seldom Comes True," an echo of the old Princess shows; but one can also hear the residual effect of ragtime, especially in Gershwin's own piano solo recording of "Tee-Oddle," and the early foreshadowing of a jazz influence in "Nobody but You," that was never present in Kern.

Unfortunately, *La, La, Lucille* opened in the spring of 1919, a tumultuous period of labor strikes that spread to Broadway. For years Broadway was in the grip of a monopoly called the Syndicate, a group of theater owners who combined to allow performers and houses to work only with the Syndicate or not at all. Working conditions and pay scale were set by the producers. The Shubert brothers challenged the Syndicate, allowing theaters and productions to book with them and anyone else they chose. As soon as the Shuberts were strong enough, however, they too shut the door, just like the Syndicate had.

This monopoly was one aspect of the noose drawn around the actors. For the performers there was no minimum wage, rehearsals were unpaid and without any time limits, and the number of performances in a week was up to the theater owners and producers. Performers and others began to organize. The stage hands' union (the National Alliance of Theatrical Stage Employees) was recognized in 1910, and the Dramatists' Guild was formed in 1912, as a bargaining agent for playwrights. In 1913, the Actors' Equity Association was organized and attempted to arbitrate differences with the Managing Producer's Association. After an initial compromise in 1917, limiting unpaid rehearsals to four weeks, Actors' Equity got nowhere and in 1919 the Manager's Association refused further negotiations, fearing that if they recognized Equity as the sole bargaining agent, the union would join the more powerful A.F.L. The producers were convinced that the actors couldn't afford to cause any real trouble and that a strike was out of the question.

While Gershwin's show *Lucille* was still running, Equity called the first strike in the history of the American theater. It lasted thirty days, spread to eight cities, closed thirty-seven plays, prevented the opening of sixteen others, and cost millions of dollars. Chorus performers joined in the fight along with the actors. Five days after the strike began, Chorus Equity was formed. Hollywood screen star Marie Dressler, who began her career in the chorus at $8 per week, was instrumental in forming the chorus union, and was elected its first president. Equity was making inroads. Comedian Ed Wynn, who was starring in a Shubert production called *Gaieties of 1919*, left the theater and gathered a group of theatergoers around him on the street to listen to an impassioned plea for better treatment for his fellow performers. The crowd soon picked him up and began a march down Broadway. Prominent actors held shows to raise money to finance the strike. Ed Wynn came out of the audience to announce that he had been forbidden to perform his act by a judge; whereupon he demonstrated exactly what he could not do.[21]

There was strong resistance led by George M. Cohan who donated $100,000 to create an alternative union called the Actors' Fidelity League (derisively called "Fido"). Being both an actor and a producer, Cohan was caught in the middle. Producers never thought that "their" stars would participate in a strike action, but they were wrong. The Barrymores were highly visible; Marie Dressler led a picket line; Lillian Russell was an ardent supporter. When stagehands and musicians refused to cross picket lines, the strike was complete. Equity won the fight and the strike was settled exactly one month after it had begun. The producers signed a five-year contract that included most of Equity's demands.

The strike forced the closing of Gershwin's show in August 1919; nevertheless, his reputation as a Broadway composer was established. As *La, La, Lucille* ended so did George White's first production of his *Scandals*; it was somewhere between a success and a failure, but White had learned a lesson, and in his next outing he recruited both Gershwin and B.G. "Buddy" De Sylva. George signed his contract with White on February 27, 1920, for $75 a week. It was the start of a long association; Gershwin would write five *Scandals* through 1924–25. Curiously, with some exceptions, his music for White was not particularly distinguished when compared to his later work.

Most of the songs Gershwin wrote in this period both for George White's *Scandals* and for other shows, were pedestrian, often trite, and rarely inspired. Of course, they were dictated by the schemes of the revues. Thus, Gershwin wrote such unmemorable songs as "Night Time in Araby," "Cinderelatives," "Kongo Kate," and many others. Alec Wilder speculates—correctly—that such songs must have bored Gershwin to death. Nevertheless, writing under duress was a valuable experience. For four years Gershwin was forced to experiment with a variety of styles, melodic twists, and harmonic innovations to accommodate the wide range of programs thrown up by each new production.

The musical revue was a natural outgrowth of vaudeville, but the two modes were competitive for years. By the time Gershwin left Remick's, the revue was triumphant and vaudeville had begun its painful decline. Indeed, Gershwin was involved on the periphery of several revues, adding a song or two. The dominant force was the Ziegfeld *Follies*, which first opened in 1906 (not yet called the *Ziegfeld Follies*). The *Follies* became increasingly extravagant performances, with lavish costumes, handsome scenery, and well-known headliners. A critic in Philadelphia wrote: "Why ask if it's good? Why ask how it compared with last year, or the year before. . . . It's the typical Follies—colorful, tuneful, dazzling, alternately excruciatingly funny and satisfyingly beautiful—and there you are."[22] On its tenth anniversary the show adopted a Shakespeare theme for its satire in two acts with thirteen scenes in the first act and six in the second. Ina Claire starred as Juliet in one sketch called the "Travesty of Romeo and Juliet." In another sketch Juliet was played by Marion Davies; Ann Pennington danced (Ziegfeld advertised her "dimpled knees"). The comedy was supplied by W.C. Fields and Fanny Brice. Bert Williams closed the show with his specialties. The music was by Jerome Kern, Louis Hirsch, and Ziegfeld's standby, Dave Stamper.

None of Ziegfeld's competitors could hope to match his array of costumes, settings, and talent. They were more or less forced to experiment in other directions, more fast-paced, less elaborate, but gaudier productions, including scanty costumes. Although George White and Ann Pennington were Ziegfeld graduates, White's *Scandals* were quite different. One Broadway history described the essence of a George White show:

> The *Scandals* captured the fundamental flavor and texture of the roaring twenties. In their jazz-colored music, their raucous comedy and high-kicking dances, in their frequent move away from the soft material and hues of the past for their settings and costumes they mirrored the essence of a happy, carefree and careless age.[23]

The historian of the musical theater, Ethan Mordden, described Ziegfeld's role as essentially a "traffic manager," but White performed as a "racing car." White would have none of the stunning Ziegfeld tableau. White's idea of a Big Revue was "some crazy ukulele guy like Tom Patricola singing a Charleston number, then zipping offstage as sixty girls raced on and danced the tune to pieces."[24] White also had a keen ear, and thus hired Gershwin, who was enjoying the celebrity of Jolson's recording of "Swanee."

Gershwin's first George White show (June 7, 1920 at the Globe Theater) was the "talk of the town as a summer revue." It starred the producer and Ann Pennington, with comedy supplied by the vaudeville comic Lou Holtz. One review found the music not only superior to the previous year but "easily one of the most tuneful now being played on Broadway. Its colorful melodies and piquant jazz strains will not fail of popular renditions in the various cafes and places where orchestra held forth." According to another authority, however, the show possessed "all the subtely of a dinosaur charge"; it did not work as a satire, but the audiences liked it and it lasted for 318 performances (compared to 157 for Ziegfeld's *Follies*).[25] Gershwin recorded three songs from the score as piano rolls: "On My Mind the Whole Night Long," "Scandal Walk," and "Idle Dreams." The virtue of these rolls is not so much the melodies (they were originally music for elaborate dance numbers) but the amalgamation of blues, ragtime, and jazz in his improvisations around the melodic line.

All of these *Scandals* were mixed bags for Gershwin. For example, in the *Scandals* of 1921, he wrote "Drifting Along with the Tide," a very pleasant melody with little jazz influence, which he also recorded as a piano roll. Alec Wilder notes that it, along with "Some Wonderful Sort of Someone," showed Gershwin's effort to break out of songwriting conventions. One review of the *Scandals* compared Gershwin to the music by Victor Herbert and Rudolf Friml in the *Follies* for that year, commenting that Gershwin "gave us our thrill." It was less successful than the preceding year, but left for a national tour and made a profit.

The *Scandals* were primarily a dancing show, although there were comedy routines, including one by another graduate of the *Follies*, W.C. Fields. One of the elaborate dance routines was performed in the 1922 version to one of Gershwin's best songs—"I'll Build a Stairway to Paradise." It was a smart and spectacular number that closed the first act. George recalled two circular staircases surrounded by Paul Whiteman's orchestra on the stage, leading high up into theatrical paradise and fifty beautiful girls in a black patent-leather material which brilliantly reflected the spotlight. Gershwin's song was a nearly perfect example of stage music. Starting with a strong verse that was built up by ascending half-tones, it created a growing sense of tension until relieved by the onset of the refrain, which was introduced by the punch of an octave jump. The melody then led the listeners almost literally up that stairway. Almost every musical device was employed with good effect to give the song a jazzy feeling, with an undertone of the blues, all the while sustaining the rhythm so that the listener senses the ascent up those imaginary stairs. The lyrics were supplied in part by Ira Gershwin and without a doubt they add to the overall ambience of the melody.

Gershwin was impressed by the Paul Whiteman orchestra's performance of this song, recorded in September 1922: Whiteman's version "almost floored me . . . there was no stopping "Stairway to Paradise" once Whiteman got his brass into it."[26] This version that Gershwin liked so much featured a so-called "hot" trumpet solo, probably by Henry Busse. The "brasses" that impressed Gershwin played the final refrain with flutter-tongue and wha-wha mutes. "Stairway" has remained a standard in the Gershwin literature, the subject of a memorable performance in the motion picture *An American in Paris*, where the French singer Georges Guetary does in fact ascend a stairway, presumably to paradise.

While Alec Wilder found the song "stiffly contrived and synthetic," the musicologist Steven E. Gilbert notes that although "Stairway" seemed a bit dated, it was nonetheless "remarkable, not only for its verve and sustained energy, but for the structural soundness of its pitch material."[27] Critics liked other songs from this 1922 show, like "I Found a Four Leaf Clover," but Whiteman's recording reveals an ordinary melody. This 1922 version of the *Scandals* was also notable for the production of the so-called jazz opera *Blue Monday* (but this belongs to a different story, leading ultimately to *Porgy and Bess*). This version was the first to carry the producer's name, and was hereafter *George White's Scandals*. Ann Pennington had returned to Ziegfeld, while W.C. Fields had come over from Ziegfeld. Nevertheless, the show had a shorter run than the two previous versions.

The 1923 version demonstrated that White was becoming more "sure-handed." This version was a substantial and frequently excellent revue. W.C. Fields and Paul Whiteman's orchestra were gone, but many from the previous year's cast were back. Gershwin contributed "Throw Her in High (gear, that is)," part of a spoof on prohibition that closed the first act. The love song, "Let's Be Lonesome Together," once again featured Gershwin's emphasis on repeated notes, not as striking in a slow ballad as in his faster numbers. "The Life of a Rose" was among the better Gershwin melodies, adopting a pseudo-Latin flavor. (It too was recorded by Paul Whiteman.)

Gershwin began to display an affinity for blue notes. He even wrote a song titled "Yankee Doodle Blues," but he never wrote a classical blues, that is, the twelve-bar structure adopted by jazz musicians. He did favor two simple melodic devices: the flatted third and the flatted seventh. Both of these "blue" notes transform a straightforward sound into a melancholy one. This penchant emerged to good effect in Gershwin's last *Scandals*, in July 1924. "Somebody Loves Me," was sung by the "breezy and bewitching" Winnie Lightner. Years later Gershwin's secretary, Nanette Kuttner, recalled the last rehearsal: Bill Daly was the conductor, "an indomitable guardian," of Gershwin's score, as Winnie Lightner came "bouncing across a bare stage, orchid chiffon skirt swaying in the rhythm of her new song." The refrain, with Buddy De Sylva's lyrics, starts simply enough; but in the fourth bar, on the word "who," Gershwin uses a blue note, so that the simple question—"I wonder who"—takes on a different meaning and suggests that the answer to the question will be an unhappy one. The same pattern was used in the earlier "I'll Build a Stairway to Paradise," when the phrase ends on the words "to paradise." It is the twist of the blue note that gives both songs a distinct character. Professor Allen Forte in his extensive analysis of "Somebody Loves Me," comments: "In general, the harmony and voice leading of this song are wonderfully innovative and reflect in obvious ways, Gershwin's immediate contact with the keyboard at the time he first improvised the melody and its accompaniment."[28]

In the original version of "Somebody Loves Me," unearthed among the discoveries in the Warner Brothers warehouse in Secaucus, New Jersey in the 1980s, it turned out that after the refrain there was a half-spoken patter. It elaborated on a list of "perfect lovers," including Romeo, Marc Anthony, and "big Bill Hart" (the star of westerns in silent films), and Jackie Coogan, then a child star, to whom, when Coogan was grown up, the performer intended to croon "Somebody Loves Me."[29] This version of the *Scandals*, in 1924, was George's last. He insisted on a raise in salary, but White refused and George left.

It may have been slightly embarrassing for Gershwin that the next two versions of the *Scandals* were successes, with scores by Lew Brown, Ray Henderson, and De Sylva. The 1926 version ran for a record 426 shows; Ann Pennington returned to introduce the famous "Black Bottom" and Harry Richman introduced "The Birth of the Blues." It was the "high point in Twenties Broadway revues, and was remembered fondly as everything a revue should be but seldom was."[30] The *Scandals* continued into the 1939-40 season; the last show featured the dancing of Ann Miller and the comedy of the Three Stooges, with a score by Sammy Fain and Jack Yellen.

In between the annual George White shows, Gershwin also wrote six songs with Ira for their first major collaboration, *A Dangerous Maid*. This assignment grew out of their song "Waiting for the Sun to Come Out," written for the *Sweetheart Shop*. The producer, Edgar MacGregor, was impressed by the Gershwins. He turned to them for the score of his new musical, *A Dangerous Maid*. The show opened in Atlantic City in March 1921 and closed five weeks later out of town in Pittsburgh. The cast included Vivienne Segal, as well as Vinton Freedley, who would eventually become a producer, along with Alex Aarons, of Gershwin shows. Frank Saddler did the orchestrations. The music, according to one reviewer, was "dainty music—nothing great you understand." The score included "Boy Wanted," which became an important Gershwin song. After *Dangerous Maid* closed, "Boy Wanted" was used again in the London Show *Primrose* (1924), and revived decades later with rewritten lyrics for Ella Fitzgerald, and also revived again for the Broadway show *My One and Only*. Other songs in *A Dangerous Maid* included "Dancing Shoes," a reasonably good melody, and "Some Rain Must Fall," not nearly so good. This show was notable for the extended cooperation between George and Ira, but since it failed out of town it is virtually unknown. In this period Gershwin contributed a song to a show starring Ed Wynn, famous as the Perfect Fool; the song, "Oh, How I Love to Be Loved by You," is suspiciously similar to "Love Walked In," written two decades later.

Of course, there were occasionally other notable songs, especially "Do It Again." It was the result of Buddy De Sylva's prodding George to write another "hit." Gershwin, seated at the piano in the office of Max Dreyfus, began to play a melody, and De Sylva exclaimed, "do it again"—at least that is the story. Described as "innocently sensual," George began playing it at parties. The petite, coquettish French chanteuse Irene Bordoni heard it and demanded that she sing it in her show. She interpolated it in the *French Doll*, not really a musical, but a romantic comedy. In the show her mother warns her against her first kiss; when kissed she pretends to hate it, but then she sings, "Do It Again." Alan Dale, reviewing the Bordoni show in the *New York American* (February 1922) wrote: "Yevette in her prime and her long black gloves never warbled anything as deliciously taquiante [*sic*] and tantalizing as 'Do It Again,' as Irene Bordoni manipulated it at the Lyceum last night in the 'French Doll.' " Unfortunately, she never recorded it. However, from a British show, *Mayfair and Montmartre*, another French singer named Alice Delysia sang "Do It Again" with an inevitable French accent and later recorded it. In November 1923, Bordoni recorded another Gershwin song, "I Won't Say I Will, But I Won't Say I Won't," with lyrics by De Sylva and "Arthur Francis" (i.e., Ira Gershwin). She interpolated it into her show *Little Miss Bluebird*. It is a good example of her style, which was a pale foreshadowing of Edith Piaf. "Do It Again" achieved "a quite un-Tin Pan Alley harmonic distinction by subtly changing from bar to bar with each phrase repetition, an effect that was to become a part of the Gershwin style."[31]

It is interesting to compare the inventive harmony of this song with some others of the same period. For example, "We're Pals" and "My Lady" have similar structures, but in these two songs there is no effort to provide any spark. They illustrate the problem for the songwriter. For "We're Pals," Gershwin had to write a sentimental song for a sentimental show (*Dere Mable*) about wartime letters from a soldier to his sweetheart. "My Lady" was a love song for his first *Scandals* show. But "Do It Again" was written without regard to any other circumstances. Of course, as De Sylva said, they wanted to write a "hit," and his risque lyrics probably helped ensure its success, but George was free to write the melody and harmony to his own liking.

There was no major Broadway show immediately forthcoming for Gershwin. In 1922, while still engaged in the *Scandals*, however, he collaborated with Bill Daly on a show called *Our Nell* (originally *Hayseed*), a comedy starring Helen Ford. It was set in New England, a laugh aimed at Broadway musical comedy, and Gershwin provided a captivating score. The text, lyrics, and music "abound in little effects that are delicious." In particular, the critics liked "Walking Home with Angeline." As the title suggests it was a light romantic song; it did use his trademark, repeated notes.[32]

George had invested some money in the show, but lost it when it closed early. The importance of this show for Gershwin was not so much the critical success, always welcome of course, but the comradeship he forged with William Daly, who would become his lifelong friend. For *Our Nell* they collaborated to write one of Gershwin's most scintillating songs, "Innocent Ingenue Baby."

The following season Gershwin at last found a full-scale book musical. Two new producers, Lawrence Schwab and Frank Mandel, were looking for a show. They contacted Max Dreyfus for advice. He suggested Rodgers and Hart, but they were unknowns, and the producers backed off. Then Dreyfus urged them to take Gershwin, who was much better known. They agreed, and started a show called *Perfect Lady*, later changed to *Sweet Little Devil*, starring Constance Binney, a diminutive singer and dancer who had starred in vaudeville. It was a success. The reviews, while favorable to Constance Binney, also praised the show's "vim and vigor," and Gershwin's score: "Not often has a production of like pretensions been graced by a better score." At the "slightest occasion everyone dances," wrote one reviewer, "to the artful syncopations and the polite jazz of Mr. Gershwin." Another review of the out-of-town tryouts commented that Gershwin was well-known in Boston because of his association with the Hasty Pudding theatricals at Harvard. Gershwin, who dropped out of the High School of Commerce, must have been surprised and probably pleased at his promotion to the Ivy League. *Sweet Little Devil* was completely overshadowed by *Rhapsody in Blue*, which followed almost immediately after its opening. Several songs were published, the most prominent being "Virginia." The score also included "Under a One-Man Top," and a lively dance number entitled "The Jijibo," which foreshadowed "Fascinating Rhythm," written a few months later for *Lady Be Good!*

Gershwin was still a 42nd Streeter; he was nowhere near the concert halls at Carnegie or the Aeolian—that is, until November 1923, when he was the beneficiary of an extraordinary concert given by the singer Eva Gauthier. She had planned a program, "Recital of Ancient and Modern Music for Voice," that included selections of Ancient, Modern Hungarian and German, Austrian, British, and French vocal music. Her friend Carl Van Vechten urged her to add some American songs, consisting of popular tunes, and he suggested that she choose as her accompanist George Gershwin. Van Vechten was an admirer of

Gershwin as a "jazz" artist and was particularly impressed by "Stairway to Paradise." Gauthier at first demurred, though she later said she had been thinking of it for some time. In any case, she saw the promotional value of including some American jazz, and she recruited Gershwin. Thus it was on the evening of November 1, 1923, that George Gershwin strode out onto the stage of Aeolian Hall, a bundle of "lurid colored" sheet music under his arm, and sat himself down before the Steinway. He was nervous and ill at ease in these unfamiliar surroundings and the audience at first was apprehensive. Then Gauthier belted out "Alexander's Rag Time Band," and the audience relaxed. A splash of Jerome Kern ("The Siren's Song") and Walter Donaldson ("Carolina in the Morning") followed, and then came Gershwin playing "Paradise," "Innocent Ingenue Baby," and "Swanee," and as an encore, "Do It Again." The audience howled, when he slyly interpolated a snatch from Scherazade in "Do It Again." They demanded another encore and she did it again. In his review in the *Literary Digest*, Deems Taylor found the audience began by being a trifle patronizing, but ended by surrendering completely to the alluring rhythms of folk music.

For Gershwin this was an important landmark. The program notes stated that he was a potential successor to Irving Berlin. He had just turned twenty-five in September 1923. Compared to Berlin, Kern, or Rodgers when they were that age, Gershwin's career was impressive although not that remarkable. He had already composed a highly successful hit, "Swanee," several popular songs, and two solid Broadway shows—*Lucille* and *Sweet Little Devil*. He was known among the professionals and the leading performers. He was an accomplished pianist much in demand even in the more fashionable quarters of New York. He was earning $125 a week with the *Scandals*. He had become a good songwriter, on the verge of being a great one. And now he had dipped into the rarefied atmosphere of the Aeolian Hall. He was becoming the personification of popular "jazz."

There were critics, of course, who disputed Gauthier's contention that she had presented representative American music—"viewed in this light—simply as music for voice and piano—it seemed to us that they came off rather badly." Though Gershwin could not know it, this particular strain of criticism would evolve into a major theme attacking his music. Nevertheless, the interesting question is how this young Jewish boy from the Lower East Side, caught up in the Jazz Age and "multicolored, eye filling" Broadway revues, could return three months later to that very hall to perform his own composition, one of the great classics of American music, *Rhapsody in Blue*.

NOTES

1. Quoted in Irving Howe, *World of Our Fathers* (New York: Simon and Schuster, 1976), p. 161.

2. Michael Feinstein, *Nice Work If You Can Get It* (New York: Hyperion, 1995), p. 56. The author was for several years the assistant to Ira Gershwin.

3. Deena Rosenberg, in her biography *Fascinating Rhythm* (New York: Dutton, 1991), gives a different version: she wrote that George's teacher was a man named von Zerly, who in fact was Goldfarb's teacher.

4. This letter from Hambitzer to his sister Olive is quoted in Isaac Goldberg (supplemented by Edith Garson), *George Gershwin: A Study in American Music* (New York: Frederick Ungar Publishing, 1958), but also printed in an article by Walter Monfried in the *Milwaukee Journal*, January 28, 1931.

5. Oscar Levant, *A Smattering of Ignorance* (New York: Doubleday, 1940), p. 160.

6. David Ewen, *The Story of George Gershwin* (New York: Henry Holt, 1943), p. 34. In this book for young people, Ewen creates an imaginary dialogue and argument between George and his mother, which finally ends with her acquiescence: "I won't stop you. Pop won't like your giving up school, and I don't know how I'll explain it to him. But do what you think is best. How can I be sure that I am right and you are wrong."

7. Quoted in Alan Schoener, *Portal to America* (New York: Holt, Rinehart & Winston, 1967), p. 132.

8. Henry O. Osgood, *So This Is Jazz* (Boston: Little, Brown, 1926), p. 174.

9. Oscar Levant, *The Memoirs of an Amnesiac* (New York: G.P. Putnam, 1965), p. 89.

10. Robert Kimball and Alfred Simon, *The Gershwins* (New York: Bonanza Books, 1973), pp. 15–16.

11. Gerald Bordman, *American Musical Theatre* (New York: Oxford University Press, 1986), p. 297.

12. Joan Peyser, *The Memory of All That* (New York: Simon and Schuster, 1993), p. 47. Ms. Peyser interprets the incident as an example of Gershwin "internalizing" his frustrations, because he did nothing about his rebuff. According to Peyser, when Gershwin was insulted he never responded with a counterattack: "Such internalization of hostility and aggression is not good for one's health." Charles Schwartz, *Gershwin: His Life and Music*, relates a truncated version of this incident but without comment.

13. Newspaper clippings of these reviews, dated but unidentified, are in the Gershwin Collection, Library of Congress.

14. Levant, *A Smattering of Ignorance*, p. 148.

15. Gershwin's letter to Max Abramson, September 12, 1918; Gershwin Collection, Library of Congress. "The Real American Folk Song (Is a Rag)" was never published, and was forgotten until Ella Fitzgerald recorded it in her "George and Ira Gershwin Song Book" collection in 1959. Her producer, Norman Granz, suggested including this very first all-Gershwin song, and Ira relented. It was again revived as a sparkling dance number in the modern musical *Crazy for You* in 1992.

16. Library of Congress: Gershwin Collection, Correspondence.

17. Goldberg, *George Gershwin*, p. 101.

18. Alec Wilder, *American Popular Song* (New York: Oxford University Press, 1972), p. 126.

19. Herbert G. Goldman, *Jolson* (New York: Oxford University Press, 1988), pp. 109–10.

20. Six songs were published: In addition to "From Now On," "Nobody but You," and "Tee-Oddle," there were "The Best of Everything," "The Love of a Wife," and "Somehow It Seldom Comes True." Gershwin recorded a piano roll of "Tee-Oddle." "There's More to a Kiss" is performed by Barbara Cook in Ben Bagley's CD *George Gershwin Revisited*.

21. Brooks Atkinson, *Broadway* (New York: Macmillan, 1970), pp. 187–88.

22. Richard Kislan, *The Musical*, rev. ed. (New York: Applause Books, 1995), p. 86.

23. Gerald Bordman, *American Musical Revue* (New York: Oxford University Press, 1985), p. 79.

24. Ethan Mordden, *Make Believe* (New York: Oxford University Press, 1997), p. 89.

25. Norbert Carnovale, *George Gershwin* (Westport, CT: Greenwood Press, 2000), p. 344; Lee Davis, *Scandals and Follies* (New York: Limelight Editions, 2000), p. 164.

26. Kimball and Simon, *The Gershwins*, p. 34.

27. Wilder, *American Popular Song*, p. 127; Steven E. Gilbert, *The Music of George Gershwin* (New Haven, CT: Yale University Press, 1995), p. 49.

28. Allen Forte, *The American Popular Ballad of the Golden Age, 1924–1950* (New Haven, CT: Yale University Press, 1995), pp. 149–53.

29. This original version has been recorded by Judy Blazer on "George and Ira Gershwin, Standards and Gems" (Nonesuch CD 79482–2, 1998). The orchestration is based on the original by Maurice B. de Packh.

30. Davis, *Scandals and Follies*, pp. 233–34.

31. Edward Jablonski and Lawrence Stewart, *The Gershwin Years* (New York: Doubleday & Company, 1958), p. 78.

32. Many Gershwin songs of this period have been published in the collection "Gershwin on Broadway" (Warner Brothers, 1987). Also some of the more obscure songs are contained in a collection, "Rediscovered Gershwin" (Warner Brothers, 1991).

Chapter 3

Musical Influences

Gershwin claimed that he was largely "self-taught." He told his first biographer, Isaac Goldberg, that when he wrote *Rhapsody in Blue* in 1924 his formal knowledge of harmony was about as much as could be found in a ten-cent manual. He explained that while ignorant of harmony, he always had an instinctive feeling for tonal "combinations" which he employed in his compositions without any particular attention to their theoretical structure. This must be taken with a grain of salt. Gershwin studied piano, harmony, theory, and orchestration from 1912 through 1921 and probably later.

First came his serious turn to a genuine professional piano teacher. Gershwin had been persuaded by a young friend to study piano with Charles Hambitzer— probably late in 1912, when George had just turned fourteen. Unfortunately, it is not clear just how long he studied with Hambitzer. Gershwin later said that he had four years of piano instruction, but not all with "celebrity teachers." Presumably this qualification ruled out a full four years with Hambitzer. On the other hand, he also once said he had studied for five years. If he began taking piano lessons from Ira's teacher, "Miss Green," in 1911 after the family acquired a piano, then the four- or five-year span ended about 1915 or 1916, after he began working as a song plugger for Remick's. According to H.O. Osgood, George studied with Hambitzer for "several years," even after he went to work at Remick's. Later Gershwin said he stopped when his teacher died, which would be as late as 1918. In any case, Gershwin evidently maintained some relationship with Hambitzer after he joined Remick's in 1914.

Charles Hambitzer was born in 1878 in Beloit, Wisconsin. His family was quite musical. His great grandfather was a court violinist for the Czar; his father operated a music store and music publishing business in Milwaukee; his two sisters were musicians. One was a skilled pianist and the other a professional concert singer and teacher. His sister said, however, that Charles was the real genius of the family. Young Hambitzer studied music and later taught at the Wisconsin Conservatory. He also was educated at Marquette University. He became musical director of a stock company that performed operettas at the Pabst Theater in Milwaukee. Before coming to New York in 1905, when he was twenty-seven, he taught violin, cello, and piano. He also arranged sheet music published by his father and created orchestrations for Pabst Theater productions.

In New York he became a member of the Waldorf-Astoria orchestra led by the conductor Joseph Knecht. Although Hambitzer played the viola as well as piano in the orchestra, he was a skilled solo pianist and teacher. He also created orchestrations for the Waldorf orchestra. Shortly before Gershwin began his studies, Hambitzer wrote a light operetta, *The Love Wager*, which Gershwin claimed to cherish, after discovering some old Hambitzer manuscripts. These manuscripts included several full orchestral scores and instrumental parts for various operettas; some are clearly for the Waldorf orchestra and some for a larger orchestra, probably from his career in Milwaukee.[1]

There was an obvious mutual admiration between student and teacher. Hambitzer was sufficiently impressed that he wrote his sister Olive that his new pupil was a "genius, without a doubt; he's just crazy about music and can't wait until it's time to take his lesson." According to Hambitzer, Gershwin wanted to go in for the "modern stuff, jazz and what not," but Hambitzer was determined not to let him: "I'll see that he gets a firm foundation in the standard music first."[2] Later, Gershwin told Goldberg, "I revere the man." He also said that Hambitzer was the first great influence on his music.

He credited Hambitzer with introducing him to Chopin, Liszt, and Debussy. While it is understandable that a piano instructor would emphasize Chopin and Liszt, the attention to Debussy was somewhat unusual. That Gershwin would mention this particular trio almost twenty years later also suggests he was especially impressed. Debussy's "Golliwogg's Cakewalk," from his *Children's Corner Suite*, must have been intriguing to a young man who was wrapped up in ragtime—a kissing cousin of the cakewalk. When he traveled to Europe in 1928 he bought a set of Debussy's piano music and orchestral scores. Most of Gershwin's exposure to piano music was nineteenth-century romantic, but also of particular note was Hambitzer's introduction of his young student to Arnold Schoenberg's work. This, too, was quite unusual. Perhaps because of Hambitzer's influence Gershwin and his brother attended the first performance of Schoenberg's *Pierrot lunaire* in the United States (February 4, 1923). It caused a sensation—severed lifelong friendships, according to one critic.

Hambitzer's talents were testified to by two Gershwin friends: the future conductor Nathaniel Shilkret, and Mabel Schirmer, who was recruited by Gershwin to study piano with Hambitzer. She described his careful solicitude for his students. He did not hover over them. There were two pianos in his studio; he would sit at one while his student sat at the other. He would demonstrate a piece, and then his student would take it home, learn it, and play it. Hambitzer would then listen to his student: "he was a very kind and sweet man—and an outstanding pianist." Similarly, Shilkret was awed by Hambitzer; he remembered him as

> mild, sweet-tempered, a little sloppy in appearance . . . relaxed, very likable and very charitable. Pupils of his who had talent, but no money he either taught free or lent them financial assistance. To him talent was most important. . . . He was one of the greatest pianists I ever heard. And I would say he was a genius.[3]

Student and teacher became quite close, but biographers go too far in attributing Gershwin's turn to ragtime to Hambitzer's untimely death; otherwise, they contend, Gershwin might have pursued a concert career. Gershwin did say of Hambitzer that with his death went his career as a pianist. But it should be noted that he said this in an interview in Milwaukee, Hambitzer's home town, in which he praised Hambitzer profusely. Indeed, by 1918 when Hambitzer died, Gershwin had already worked at Remick's for three years and for two years he had been recording piano rolls, displaying a considerable familiarity with ragtime. Some commentators allege that Gershwin's preference for popular music supposedly "wounded" Hambitzer and contributed to his early demise. This, too, is highly improbable, since Hambitzer died during an influenza epidemic in 1918, and Gershwin's definitive turn to popular music came in the spring of 1914, when he joined Remick's.

Gershwin did say that he was just beginning to learn the intricacies of harmony when Hambitzer died. On most occasions Gershwin only said that Hambitzer had made him "harmony conscious." In this same interview Gershwin added: "Thenceforward [after Hambitzer's death] he was forced to learn mainly by himself" (Gershwin seems conveniently to have forgotten four years of study with Edward Kilenyi).[4] But his exposure to Chopin might have had a lasting influence. There are many passages in Gershwin's popular songs that contain repeated notes, one of his trademarks, but accompanied by shifting harmony, a technique employed by Chopin. One observer has noted the similarity between Chopin and Gershwin songs, both of which use a fairly simple melody and a complex harmonic and bass line.[5] In this respect, his debt to Hambitzer may have been greater than Gershwin realized. In 1925, Carl Van Vechten (not a very reliable source) wrote that Gershwin was working on Chopin preludes when Hambitzer died. Gershwin never recorded any classical piano works (other than his own) by Chopin or any others.[6]

When he began his study with Hambitzer, Gershwin was relatively accomplished, but probably still somewhat crude. Mabel Schirmer, a longtime friend and confidant, and also a student of Hambitzer, vividly remembered that whenever Gershwin sat down at the piano he not only played what was written but was improvising all the time. It was Gershwin's conviction that it was his natural talent and not his teachers that contributed to his success. He told an interviewer that he never played like a beginner. He often cited famous pianists—Leopold Godowsky, and Sergei Rachmaninoff—who praised his playing. His piano rolls are evidence of Gershwin's progress as an accomplished pianist, perhaps due to Hambitzer's training.

At some point Hambitzer recommended that his colleague Edward Kilenyi take Gershwin as a student. Kilenyi was the second major influence on Gershwin, but for some reason his studies with Kilenyi are given short shrift. In the Goldberg biography Gershwin scarcely mentions Kilenyi, perhaps because Kilenyi was still alive and quite active as a musician and teacher. According to Kilenyi's recollections thirty-five years later, Hambitzer informed him that Gershwin wanted to study harmony "seriously." Hambitzer praised Gershwin as an exemplary student and urged Kilenyi to take him as a pupil. This was in 1917, the year before Hambitzer died.[7]

At that time, Kilenyi was giving lessons in theory, composition, harmony, and orchestration. He was a thoroughly trained musician, more so than Hambitzer. Born in 1884 in Hungary, he earned a degree from the Hungarian State College, and studied in Rome (1902–3) with the great opera composer Pietro Mascagni, who wrote the famous *Cavalleria Rusticana*. He also studied at the Cologne Conservatory (1904–7) before emigrating to the United States in 1908. Kilenyi continued his studies at Columbia University, under the conservative classicist Daniel Gregory Mason, in order to get his master's and doctor's degrees to teach composition. He was a prolific writer for academic musical journals, especially about harmony. For example, in 1915 he wrote an erudite article on Schoenberg's use of harmony. This was quite unusual, since Schoenberg was scarcely known outside of Europe.[8]

When Gershwin encountered him Kilenyi was playing violin in the Waldorf orchestras along with Hambitzer. It was a "symphonic ensemble" of twenty-three–twenty-six players. They played for ninety minutes each night; a smaller string group played in the afternoon in the hotel's tea room as well. Kilenyi was well-connected with the musical community of Hungary. He wrote a study of Hungarian music, and enrolled his son as a piano pupil in Budapest under the illustrious pianist and composer Ernst von Dohnányi; a fellow pupil was the future conductor Sir Georg Solti.

Gershwin's exercise books indicate that he had begun study with Kilenyi by 1919 and possibly earlier, and was still studying with him in late 1923.[9] These workbooks include a number of exercises in traditional harmony. Kilenyi commented that when Gershwin began his study he was preoccupied with his first Broadway show, which probably referred to *La, La, Lucille*, which opened in May 1919. Some examples in his notebooks include sketches of "Nobody but You" from *La, La, Lucille*. Gershwin wrote a few bars of the melody and then transposed it into different keys. It would not be surprising if Gershwin went over some of his song writing with Kilenyi. His notebooks, for example, include a sketch for "The Man I Love," and several bars of "Maybe" finished several years later for *Oh, Kay!*[10] These notebooks are not completely reliable as evidence, since Gershwin probably used them for more than Kilenyi's harmony exercises. In one book, for example, Gershwin wrote down a list of the songs for *Oh, Kay!* On the other hand, "The Man I Love" was sketched in 1923, when he was still a pupil of Kilenyi.

Kilenyi used a textbook by Percy Goetschius (*The Material Used in Musical Composition*). Goetschius was a renowned teacher from Harvard, and, later, at the Institute of Musical Art, the predecessor of Juilliard. (At the Institute Goetschius taught Richard Rodgers.) Kilenyi said that Gershwin never showed any impatience or touch of resentment when doing his assigned studies. Kilenyi also taught Gershwin how to analyze compositions and introduced him to annotated scores. Gershwin wrote a string quartet while studying with Kilenyi and later borrowed one of its themes for a song for his mini-opera *Blue Monday*.[11] Some sources claim that Gershwin also took a summer course at Columbia University in elements of orchestration.

Even though Gershwin liked to be regarded as a natural talent and frequently played down his instruction, his notebooks from his studies contain some evidence of his development as a composer. Kilenyi taught Gershwin harmony, theory, composition, and orchestration.[12] He learned instrumentation with Kilenyi, who brought in fellow musicians from the Waldorf orchestra to show Gershwin the capabilities of the various instruments. Gershwin's notebooks include some writing for different instruments. There is a waltz ("Valse Lente") scored for woodwinds and strings. Under Kilenyi's tutelage, he wrote a "Figured Choral" in July 1921, with orchestral notations. Moreover, he owned a copy of the standard text on orchestration by Cecil Forsyth; his copy includes some notations by Kilenyi.

Kilenyi's influence on Gershwin is badly underplayed. In his biography Charles Schwartz, for example, dismisses Kilenyi's instruction. He claimed that Gershwin was not a conscientious student, but supposedly assumed that he could pick up musical skills and knowledge "simply by association with top professionals instead of through the effort that extensive study requires."[13] Kilenyi would have strongly disagreed with this sweeping generalization. He commented many years later:

[Gershwin] had an extraordinary faculty for absorbing everything he observed and applying it to his own music in his own individual ways. He was the kind of student who did not have to work and labor mechanically . . . nor did [he] have to write pages and pages of his lessons, to show he assimilated them. . . . His way of working was musical not merely intellectual or mechanical.[14]

Gershwin learned a great deal from Kilenyi by the time their regular study tapered off in 1923–24. Moreover, Gershwin remained friendly with him for years after he stopped his formal study with him and consulted him from time to time. He instructed Gershwin in conducting in 1929. Kilenyi moved to Hollywood in 1930–31 where he wrote background music for the movies (*The Adventures of Chico* in 1937, *Ravaged Earth* in 1942, and *Belle Star's Daughter* in 1949, among others). He saw Gershwin the month before Gershwin died.[15]

Gershwin also studied very briefly with Rubin Goldmark, a well-known teacher of composition and mentor to young Aaron Copland. Copland was Goldmark's pupil for four years, 1917–21, but Gershwin did not begin his studies until 1923, and then for only a few lessons. Goldmark was a nephew of the prominent Viennese composer Karl Goldmark. Not surprisingly, Goldmark favored the German Romantic tradition and discouraged his pupils' interest in the advanced musical idioms of the day, according to Copland. Nevertheless, Copland said that he received a valuable basic training from him, a genial and vivid teacher, who impressed on Copland that a career as a composer was not to be embarked on lightly.

Gershwin did not get along with his new teacher, however, and related an anecdote about his experience. After only a few lessons, Gershwin decided to show Goldmark the string quartet "Lullaby" that he had written some time earlier for Kilenyi. Goldmark, after surveying the work, commented that it demonstrated how much Gershwin had already learned from him. This version, too, is faithfully repeated by Gershwin's biographers.

Some writers cite Gershwin's dismissal of Goldmark as further proof of Gershwin's unwillingness to extend himself. This is wrong: Gershwin's teachers note that he could complete his assigned exercises quickly and without error. Gershwin's own explanation suggests a different conclusion, namely, his propensity to build himself up at the expense of others. Since Goldmark was quite well-known among musicians, Gershwin needed a rationale for why he did not pursue his studies. A friend, Abram Chasins, a student of Goldmark's, urged Gershwin to continue with Goldmark in order to achieve some "basic training." That caused a major quarrel with Gershwin, who exploded, that Chasins was "just the kind of person who's keeping me from doing my great work."[16] For years, however, musical dictionaries continued not only to cite Goldmark as one of Gershwin's teachers, but to embellish their association into a serious interlude in Gershwin's career. Even Ira, after George died, cited Kilenyi and Goldmark as George's teachers.[17]

The composers Henry Cowell and Wallingford Riegger are also sometimes listed among Gershwin's mentors. The studies with Cowell were probably around 1927. Cowell's wife later said that Gershwin's studies with Cowell did not amount to anything substantial. Cowell wrote that Gershwin had signed up for a lesson once a week, but seldom kept to this schedule; the lessons were nearer to once in three weeks. Gershwin's study with Cowell is nevertheless intriguing. Cowell was an important American composer and pianist. He was famous for his "tone clusters," accomplished by striking the key board with his fist (this must have been fascinating to Gershwin). He was a prolific composer—and wrote more than twenty symphonies, as well as operas and ballets. Gershwin had already written the *Rhapsody* and his piano concerto before any study with Cowell. So Cowell's influence, if any, is not clear. According to Cowell: Gershwin could master the rules, but was exasperated by them. He could rattle off a perfect exercise but was diverted by "using a juicy ninth and altered chords that he liked better, and would insert these into the Palestrina-style motet." Their whole association lasted a little over two years.[18]

Wallingford Riegger is reputed to have taught Gershwin; and he too is cited in various Gershwin entries in musical dictionaries. Little is known of this relationship. Schwartz, however, dates Gershwin's study with Riegger in the last half of the 1920s and claims it lasted only for several months. Gershwin did not mention it, and his study with Riegger is not elaborated on in other biographies.

Gershwin was constantly searching for mechanical formulas for writing music. This reflected not only his ambition to write "hits," but his unease with his own technical competence. Despite innumerable anecdotes about his excessive self-esteem, he recognized his limitations and was aware that there were important dimensions to musical composition that eluded him, especially counterpoint and formal structure. When critics attacked his major compositions for a lack of "structure," he replied that they were not telling him anything he did not already know. Yet, he was amazingly successful in combining his natural talents with his formal training. Kilenyi's advice was that Gershwin should avoid thinking of technical details that would interrupt the natural flow of his compositions.

He did urge Gershwin to study Arnold Schoenberg's approach to melodic composition and harmony, which he called in German *stufenreichtum* or, literally, "stepwise," in voice leading, moving by whole- or half-tones. This approach began to show up in Gershwin's compositions. What this involved was close-knit harmonic progressions. Moving linearly, or stepwise chromatically or by whole tones, was designed to give a composition a thick richness that can indeed be heard in many of Gershwin's popular compositions. Gershwin had a capacity to take from the classical training—whether Chopin or Schoenberg—and apply it to the popular idiom, which helped to create his unique style. One can identify this style both in his early works (e.g., the bass line of "Do It Again") and in the harmonies of one of the very last songs he wrote—"Nice Work if You Can Get It." Kilenyi later wrote that he introduced Gershwin to the so-called "false cadence." The last few bars of "I Got Rhythm" are the most famous Gershwin example.

Kilenyi later wrote that "Notes on paper meant music to him."[19] This indeed was the other key to Gershwin—his fabulous ear for music. After composing and orchestrating his piano concerto, he hired an orchestra to play through the score; after listening to the run-through he commented that it was exactly as he expected. When his inherent ability was combined with his dexterity at the keyboard, the result was a profound talent that could move from the Broadway stage to the concert hall. His early training with Hambitzer and Kilenyi sharpened his natural talent, and thus eased his way.

Many songwriters were as talented as Gershwin in one dimension or another: Berlin and Rodgers were at least as good, if not better melodists. Kern and Rodgers had a better feel for the popular theater. Porter was better trained and even had classical inclinations, but none of them could make the happy marriage of the two idioms, the popular and the concert hall. It was this ability to shuttle between the two worlds that distinguished George Gershwin and made him unique in American music.

Most of the Broadway composers could write pleasant and often thrilling melodies, and the best often survived because of a charming simplicity. Gershwin went to extraordinary lengths to find novel changes of harmony. He once complemented Harold Arlen on his "Stormy Weather" because Gershwin had spent some time trying to invent new harmonies. His harmonies are one reason his songs proved so popular with jazz musicians. Gershwin's reputation for intriguing harmonies was somewhat deceptive, however. Alec Wilder, when he began his analysis of Gershwin, expected to be confronted by intricate harmonies, but he often found that the harmonies did not interfere with the outstanding melodies.[20] There was another characteristic of Gershwin that could not, however, be taught, even by a skilled teacher. This was his unusual feel for the blues. Early in his career he began to use "blue" notes to interrupt strong traditional harmony. The effect was electrifying.

Gershwin continued his search for more instruction, at least that is his version. He tells the story that he sought instruction from the famous French teacher Nadia Boulanger, in 1928 when he was in Paris. She turned him down on the grounds that there was nothing she could teach him, according to Gershwin's version. Mabel Schirmer accompanied him to his meeting with Boulanger. After Gershwin died, Boulanger let it be known that Gershwin's version of their meeting was inaccurate. She was also asked if she regretted not teaching him, and she replied: "No, not at all. He died famous."[21]

When he met Maurice Ravel, first in New York and then in Paris, he also sought instruction. Ravel, too, turned him down on the grounds that he was better off as a first-class Gershwin than a second-class Ravel; this, too, is basically Gershwin's version, although Eva Gauthier, the singer, was present at Gershwin's first encounter, at a birthday party she gave for Ravel in 1927. Ravel, she recalled, was impressed by Gershwin's genius for weaving complicated rhythms and his great gift for melody. During his trip to New York in March 1928, Ravel did write a letter to Nadia Boulanger, praising Gershwin: "A musician endowed with the most brilliant, the most captivating, perhaps the most profound qualities." He feared, however, that if they were to teach him it might "destroy him. Did she have the courage to take on this terrible responsibility?"[22] Finally, Gershwin met Igor Stravinsky, and once again suggested that he take lessons. Stravinsky asked how much Gershwin earned, and upon hearing the reply, said that perhaps he should take lessons from Gershwin.

These stories are spurious, but they became part of the Gershwin mythology. The Stravinsky anecdote was denied specifically, but nevertheless, simply floated around among the stories about Gershwin. In all of these anecdotes, of course, Gershwin comes off quite well.

His only sustained, serious study, many years after Kilenyi, was with the musicologist and theorist Joseph Schillinger in the early 1930s, but that story belongs to the creation of *Porgy and Bess*. Shortly before he died, Gershwin met Schoenberg and Ernst Toch in Hollywood and they became friendly (Schoenberg played tennis on Gershwin's court). He wrote to Schillinger asking which of the two composers he ought to study with. His friend in New York suggested both. Nothing came of it.

The one person who was clearly a direct influence on Gershwin was his friend Bill Daly. They first met when Gershwin was working on some songs for *Our Nell* in 1922. Daly was the conductor; indeed, he became one of the best-known Broadway conductors. He was a highly trained musician and a child prodigy as a pianist. He temporarily left music after graduating from Harvard, but later returned as a conductor, songwriter, and an orchestrator. Daly became Gershwin's favorite critic, guide, and advisor, especially in the writing of the first major orchestral works and many of the principal musical-comedy scores. In 1931, Gershwin described Daly as "the best friend I have."

Throughout his career Gershwin was subjected to suspicions that he did not write or orchestrate his own compositions. One reason was that it was well-known that Ferde Grofé orchestrated *Rhapsody in Blue* because, supposedly, in 1924 Gershwin did not have that skill. This is what Grofé said, and Gershwin never contradicted him. Decades later, however, manuscripts were unearthed for three songs that Gershwin had orchestrated for a British show, *Primrose*, only a few months *after Rhapsody in Blue*.[23] In any case, Grofé's prominent role caused speculation that he had even written a part of the *Rhapsody* as well as orchestrated it. Both Gershwin and Grofé stoutly denied it, and there is no evidence that Grofé composed any of the *Rhapsody*. Gershwin wrote to ASCAP denying the stories that Grofé had any hand in the composition, yet the rumors clearly galled Gershwin.

The close collaboration between Daly and Gershwin created a new controversy, this time over orchestration of his subsequent works. Even though most Broadway composers and songwriters handed over their compositions to skilled orchestrators like Robert Russell Bennett, Gershwin apparently was determined to learn this craft—at least for his concert hall creations, if not his Broadway shows. When he was accused by an American composer, Walter Kramer (writing in the September issue of *Singing*), of not orchestrating his piano concerto, Gershwin replied at length, and expressed his particular resentment over the accusation.

Current scholarship supports Gershwin. A careful examination of the original score of the piano concerto by the musicologist Wayne D. Shirley, demonstrates that the orchestration was, in fact, Gershwin's. He received some marginal help but that was limited to minor suggestions concerned with doubling. This would correspond with Daly's public insistence that the most he did was to offer suggestions about "reinforcing" the score.[24]

Later a public dispute erupted again, this time involving Bill Daly, over the orchestration of *An American in Paris*; it was sparked by public accusations from a viola player and sometime composer, Allan Langley; he had earlier played in an orchestra performing the piano concerto. He knew Gershwin, as well as Daly and Robert Russell Bennett (there is a group picture of them with Oscar Levant and Deems Taylor published in Bennett's memoirs). Langley participated in the rehearsals for a Gershwin concert in 1932; he was struck by Daly's obvious familiarity with the scores compared to Gershwin's. Thereupon he wrote an article in which he charged that "any member of the orchestra could testify that he [Daly] knew far more about the score of *An American in Paris* than Gershwin." Langley speculated that Daly was the real orchestrator if not composer of all of Gershwin's music. His charge was published in the *American Spectator*, December 1932.

Daly fired back (in a letter to the *New York Times* dated January 15, 1933) that he neither wrote *American* nor orchestrated it. "My only contribution consisted of a few suggestions about reinforcing the scoring here and there, and I'm not sure that Gershwin, probably with good reason, accepted them." Daly did acknowledge that he had orchestrated some of Gershwin's numbers for the theater, and had reduced some of his symphonic works for smaller orchestra for use on the radio. As for *An American in Paris*, the manuscript of the orchestration in Gershwin's hand does include a few markings by Daly, but they are incidental rather than major changes.[25] Gershwin never commented on the Langley affair, leaving the battle to Daly.

A person who was in a position to observe Daly's role was the orchestrator Robert Russell Bennett, who arranged many Gershwin shows (*Lady Be Good!, Girl Crazy, Funny Face*, and others). He first met Gershwin during the George White *Scandals*. He told Max Wilk that "Daly used to sit right down with George and actually taught George a lot more than George could ever learn from any kind of teacher. Because George was not talented as a student. He could not study." On the other hand, Bennett found Gershwin's orchestrations quite satisfactory.[26] The final word comes from Gershwin's friend, the songwriter-composer Vernon Duke: "I can vouch for the fact that, except for musical comedy scores, George orchestrated every note he wrote after the *Rhapsody*."

In sum, the idea that he was "self-taught" is misleading. Gershwin was reluctant to acknowledge his debt to others, and he repeated stories that famous composers and teachers believed that they could not really teach him anything, because of his own natural talent. Perhaps he was right.

The prime influence on his musical evolution was simply his love of playing the piano. His recordings of piano rolls are important evidence. In the beginning he played the songs of other writers. These transcriptions included arrangements of the sheet music of a collection of different songwriters. At first, there was little room of improvisation. But, eventually, he began to improvise, sometimes extensively, especially as he came to record his own songs. On some rolls, Gershwin recorded a second piano part that was added to the original recordings, thus producing a rich, full texture.

He soon established a reputation as a skilled pianist. A noted authority on his piano rolls, Artis Wodehouse wrote that "In his later and better rolls, Gershwin interjects original ideas in the introduction, breaks and riffs; enriches or alters harmonization and fleshes out bass lines beyond the published sheets." By 1920, he recorded some "blues" numbers of his own such as "On My Mind the Whole Night Long," from the *Scandals*, as well as "Idle Dreams" and "Scandal Walk." Artis Wodehouse writes, "His rolls demonstrate how well Gershwin had learned blues piano style from James P. Johnson and others."[27]

This conclusion is debatable. James P. Johnson was undoubtedly a great influence on all jazz pianists of that era. But Gershwin's "blues" songs were written for the 1920 *Scandals*, which opened in June 1920. Gershwin had probably written his songs well before, especially since "Scandal Walk" was an elaborate production number for Ann Pennington. He could not have been influenced very much by Johnson, whom he had only met at the Aeolian studio that spring. According to Johnson, Gershwin was recording "oriental numbers" at the time he met him; this could refer to "Limehouse Nights" and "Poppyland," both released in March 1920.

For some reason Gershwin never said much about his piano rolls. Perhaps he was embarrassed by the selection of trite songs. Recording also added to his income of $15 per week from Remick's. He earned $5 per roll, or $35 for six. He recorded about 140 rolls. Ira Gershwin, commenting on these piano rolls years later, said that the Gershwin household did not contain a pianola, so that George's rolls never really meant much to them, and were just a sideline. Nevertheless, Gershwin was absorbing a broad range of contemporary music. An average roll would include the verse, the chorus, a return to the verse, and finally two choruses.

Gershwin's piano rolls were a mixture of rags and popular songs. Once freed from the constraints of Remick's in 1917, he could record his own songs as well as those of other songwriters: Jerome Kern, Irving Berlin, Richard Whiting, Walter Donaldson, and his colleague at Remick's, Harry Ruby. As he began to work at various musical assignments, he added to his repertoire. A comparison of Gershwin's piano rolls from the early 1920s and his phonograph recordings in the late 1920s demonstrates the evolution of his skills at improvisation.

A further influence on Gershwin was the songwriting of Irving Berlin and Jerome Kern. Gershwin held up Kern as his first model and also cited Berlin. He said that he particularly admired "Alexander's Ragtime Band," published by Berlin in 1911. It is not surprising that Gershwin would cite Berlin as an inspiration. He was, after all, the most successful songwriter of the post–World

War I period, writing for both the Ziegfeld *Follies* and his own *Music Box Revues.*

A link between Gershwin and Berlin was established by the publicist and musical critic Gilbert Seldes in 1923, that is, before *Rhapsody in Blue* and *Lady Be Good!* Gershwin was, Seldes decided, one of Berlin's likely successors if Berlin chose to stop (Cole Porter was the other candidate in Seldes' review). Gershwin, he wrote, was in Berlin's tradition: "He has almost all of the older man's qualities as a composer." [28]

Gershwin's respect for Kern was a claim he made repeatedly. He related the following tale to Goldberg, a version picked up with garnishes by most biographers: At his aunt's wedding the orchestra had struck up a tune. George rushed to the leader, asking him what it was called. It was "You're Here and I'm Here," from Kern's *The Girl from Utah.*[29]

When the orchestra struck up another Kern tune: "They Didn't Believe Me" from *The Girl from Utah*, Gershwin was awestruck and again rushed to the bandstand. He claimed that after this exposure he tried to imitate Kern's style in his own songs, to the point that it was almost impossible to differentiate between the original and the Gershwin imitation. In these remarks in 1931 he was obviously paying homage to Kern, who had became a good friend. But, at the same time, of course, Gershwin's remarks elevated his songs to the same level as Kern's, who was then a highly regarded composer of American popular music.[30]

In any case, Gershwin remained at Remick's well after being inspired by Kern's examples of the superiority of theater music. He was still at Remick's when he and Ira attended Kern's show, *The Love o' Mike* (January 1917). In May 1917, Gershwin recorded a piano roll of a Kern song, "I Wonder Why," from this show.

There are obvious differences between Kern and Gershwin. Kern was quite eclectic and versatile, but he wrote little that smacked of the jazz vogue of the 1920s, which became Gershwin's trademark. Gershwin said at this time that it was Kern's melodies that convinced him most popular music was of inferior quality and that musical-comedy music was made of better material. Nothing could be further from the Kern style, however, than Gershwin's first hit song, "Swanee." On the other hand, George and Irving Caesar had already written "You-oo Just You," and "I Was So Young." Both have the flavor of Kern, but that was true of dozens of songs by other composers.

Gershwin himself suggests that he was in fact developing a style that was different from Kern's. He said that he would spend hours trying to change the harmonies and melodic lines to satisfy himself. At this time, in the early 1920s his striving for innovations paid off in two songs, "Stairway to Paradise" and "Do It Again." In both songs, as the musical scholar Deena Rosenberg observes, there was a musical technique that was becoming a Gershwin trademark: "starting a song with a striking melodic fragment and then repeating it with a different and unexpected harmony underneath."[31] The musicologist Professor Allen Forte is skeptical of Kern's influence on Gershwin's songs. The ballads that Gershwin was composing in the early 1920s, at the very beginning of his career, "are markedly different in style from those of the established composers, Jerome Kern and Irving Berlin."[32] But Professor Forte writes that Gershwin was an innovator and a catalyst among songwriters for the musical theater, not a skilled imitator.

It was probably fortunate that Gershwin did not persevere in his endless search for a new teacher who would disclose some secret of composition. Although he claimed to be troubled by his lack of "technique," when confronted with serious study Gershwin may have instinctively concluded that he should not go too far. Had Gershwin succumbed to the conventional pedagogy of that era, which was derived from European traditions, it is likely that his innate talents would have been weakened or diluted. The songwriter and Gershwin friend Abe Chasins, writing well after Gershwin's death, concluded that George "may have known that he could not submit to comprehensive discipline without a serious loss of inspiration." Indeed, it is probable that Gershwin sensed this threat to his natural talents, and this wariness combined with his restless nature made it difficult for him to sustain a course of study, regardless of the teacher.[33] In this very broad sense, then, he was, indeed, "self-taught."

NOTES

1. The Hambitzer manuscripts are in the Library of Congress, Gershwin Collection. They are all in the same handwriting and signed Ch. Hambitzer; some contain notes written in German. Titles include, for example, "The Bedouins," "Hamlet," "If I Were King," "Romeo and Juliet," and "Twelfth Night Suite." "The Bedouins" is in a folder of the Waldorf-Astoria orchestra. Most are undated, but one is dated January 1911. There are several manuscripts that appear to be part of a larger work, possibly the operetta *Love Wager*, with lyrics by Will Lawson.

2. This letter was discovered by Goldberg in Hambitzer's sister's possession and is quoted by nearly every biographer. Its date and authenticity cannot be established, but there is no reason to doubt it.

3. Quoted in Edward Jablonski, *Gershwin: A Biography* (New York: Doubleday, 1987), p. 10.

4. The interview was published in *The Milwaukee Journal*, January 28, 1931.

5. David Schiff, *Atlantic Monthly*, October 1998. He cites Chopin's Prelude in E Minor as an example of the similarity between Chopin and Gershwin.

6. Oscar Levant, quoting David Diamond, wrote that Gershwin could not "run through" a Chopin prelude. Sam Kashner and Nancy Schoenberger, *A Talent for Genius: The Life and Times of Oscar Levant* (New York: Villard Books, 1994), p. 98.

7. Deena Rosenberg, *Fascinating Rhythm* (New York: Dutton, 1991) dates this to 1915, which is much earlier than any existing notebooks or exercises from his study with Kilenyi. It is plausible that he started in 1917 or 1918 as Kilenyi said, but not on a regular basis: Kilenyi interview, Florida State University Press Release, May 1966, in the Library of Congress, Gershwin Collection.

8. Edward Kilenyi, "Arnold Schoenberg's Harmony," *The New Music Review*, Oc-

tober 1915; the text of this article is in the Kilenyi file, Library of Congress, Gershwin Collection. Schoenberg's text on harmony (*Harmonielehre*), published in 1911, was only available in German when Kilenyi reviewed it.

9. The notebooks of Gershwin's lessons with Kilenyi were not available to Goldberg; they were preserved by Ira Gershwin, however, and donated to the Library of Congress. It is conceivable that Gershwin kept other notebooks of his studies, but they may have been misplaced or lost.

10. When he was in his eighties, Kilenyi claimed that Gershwin brought him a rough draft of "Swanee," which would have been in 1919. He also claimed to have been invited to a rehearsal of *Rhapsody in Blue*.

11. Edward Kilenyi, *Etude*, October 1950.

12. Kilenyi wrote (*Etude*, October 1950) that Gershwin studied with him for "about six years," and that "we had taken up the study of orchestration."

13. Charles Schwartz, *Gershwin: His Life and Music* (Indianapolis: Bobbs-Merrill, 1973), p. 53.

14. Edward Kilenyi, *Etude*, October 1950.

15. Kilenyi died in 1968 in Tallahassee Florida, where his son, Edward Kilenyi Jr., a well-known concert pianist, was a professor at Florida State University.

16. Abram Chasins, *Saturday Review of Literature*, February 25, 1956.

17. *The New Oxford Dictionary of Music* (1974), p. 584, for example, states that Gershwin "studied music *seriously* with Rubin Goldmark, then the most esteemed teacher of composition in New York" (emphasis added).

18. Letter from Cowell to David Ewen, reprinted in David Ewen, *George Gershwin: His Journey to Greatness* (New York: The Ungar Publishing Company, 1970), p. 115.

19. Kilenyi's comments are in his article for *Etude*, October 1950.

20. Alec Wilder, *American Popular Song* (New York: Oxford University Press, 1972), p. 122.

21. Leonie Rosenstiel, *Nadia Boulanger* (New York: W.W. Norton, 1998), p. 217.

22. Quoted in Jerome Spycket, *Nadia Boulanger* (New York: Pendragon Press, 1992), pp. 71–73; the full text was posted on the Internet, Gershwin Fan.com Message Board, November 25, 2002. The author is indebted to R. Lewis for finding this source.

23. The orchestral scores for three songs are in the Gershwin Collection in the Library of Congress. They are clearly labeled "orchestrated by George Gershwin," but are not dated, except for "1924." Recordings by the original London cast presumably used these Gershwin orchestrations. ("The Ultimate George Gershwin," Vol. I, Pearl, LC # 1836; also "George Gershwin, An American in London," Monmouth Evergreen Records, MES/7071).

24. Wayne Shirley, "Scoring the Concerto in F: George Gershwin's First Orchestration," *American Music* (Fall 1985), pp. 277–98. Daly's reply to Langley is reprinted in *George Gershwin*, ed. Merle Armitage (New York: Da Capo, 1995), pp. 30–31.

25. A commemorative facsimile edition of the orchestration in Gershwin's hand was published by Warner Brothers in 1987. It includes annotations of those points added or changed by Daly. The notes are by Jeff Sultanof, aided by Wayne Shirley and Robert Kimball. Nevertheless, Joan Peyser persists in the idea that the "character and extent of aid" Gershwin received from Daly continues to remain mysterious: "The musical ideas were Gershwin's; the form and many details owe a debt to Daly." Joan Peyser, *The Memory of All That* (New York: Simon and Schuster, 1993), pp. 11–12.

26. Robert Russell Bennett, *The Broadway Sound*, ed. George J. Ferencz (Rochester, NY: University of Rochester Press, 2001), p. 117.

27. Artis Wodehouse's notes for "Gershwin Plays Gershwin, The Piano Rolls" (Elektra Nonesuch, CD 79287–2).

28. Gilbert Seldes, *The Seven Lively Arts*, reprinted in *Gershwin Remembered*, ed. Edward Jablonski (Portland, OR: Amadeus Press, 1992), pp. 111–12.

29. Isaac Goldberg (supplemented by Edith Garson), *George Gershwin: A Study in American Music* (New York: Frederick Ungar Publishing, 1958), pp. 80–81. David Ewen relates virtually the same anecdote, and Deena Rosenberg, *Fascinating Rhythm*, repeats it, but notes, correctly, that the song, "You're Here and I'm Here" was originally from *The Laughing Husband* (1914).

30. This story of his flash of inspiration is puzzling. His aunt's wedding is placed in 1914 by his biographers. If, in fact, his aunt, Kate Wolpin, was married in June 1916, as she herself recalled, then the two Kern songs cited by Gershwin would have been at least two years old. It is difficult to believe that he was "awestruck" in 1916, when he had been plugging for Remick's for almost two years and recording piano rolls of songs by many composers. If, on the other hand, his aunt's wedding came earlier than she remembered (she was over 100 when interviewed), in 1914, then Gershwin could well have been impressed by Kern's melodies.

31. Rosenberg, *Fascinating Rhythm*, pp. 45–46.

32. Allen Forte, *The American Popular Ballad of the Golden Era* (Princeton, NJ: Princeton University Press, 1995), p. 148.

33. John Warthen Struble, *The History of American Classical Music* (New York: Facts on File, 1995), p. 109.

Chapter 4

Rhapsody in Blue

If joining Remick's was the first turning point in Gershwin's career, then composing and performing *Rhapsody in Blue* was a far more important one. It changed the direction of his life; it made him famous; eventually it made him rich. It earned him a picture on the cover of the fledgling *Time* on July 20, 1925. The accompanying article noted that he had composed the "famed *Rhapsody in Blue* a jazz concerto constructed after Liszt." The journalist-writer, Burton Rascoe, was in the balcony for the first performance; later, he wrote there were two works that were most representative of the twenties: T.S. Eliot's *The Waste Land* and *Rhapsody in Blue*.

It was first performed by Paul Whiteman's orchestra with Gershwin as the solo pianist on the late afternoon of Lincoln's birthday in 1924 in Aeolian Hall. Ross Gorman played the long, sweeping clarinet glissando that opens the work. Fourteen minutes later, when George Gershwin crashed down the final chords, he had changed American music, and the young composer's life would never be the same.

This historic moment supposedly started out as something of an accident. It was a promotional news item in the *New York Tribune* of January 4, 1924, that caught the eye of Ira Gershwin. It described Paul Whiteman's plan to stage a concert of American music and reported: "George Gershwin is at work on a jazz concerto." Ira called this to the attention of his brother, who was playing billiards with the lyricist Buddy De Sylva at the time. Supposedly, it was the "first inkling" that Whiteman was serious when he had "casually" mentioned that someday he hoped to do a concert featuring a piece by George. Gershwin vaguely remembered this incidental conversation with Whiteman some time earlier, but apparently nothing had come of it. It would be surprising that a man-about-town like Gershwin would not have some idea what Whiteman was up to. He called Whiteman the next morning and, according to Whiteman, Gershwin tried to beg off; he complained that Whiteman's schedule was too compressed; but Whiteman insisted and offered to have his arranger, Ferde Grofé, do the orchestration.

How reluctant was Gershwin? Probably not as much as he or Ira appeared to be. Indeed, there is reason to believe that he had given some thought to his so-called "concerto." Goldberg writes that the news item set George to thinking and to reconsidering his refusal. This is a titillating comment; it invites speculation that Gershwin had earlier considered writing something for Whiteman.

Gershwin, of course, knew Whiteman and Grofé from the *Scandals* in 1922. Gershwin and De Sylva had written *Blue Monday* for that production, and Whiteman conducted the pit orchestra for the ill-fated performances of Gershwin's so-called "jazz opera" (discussed in the context of *Porgy and Bess*). Consequently, Whiteman remembered Gershwin as a more serious composer than the other songwriters around Broadway. Gershwin's reputation may have also been enhanced by his appearance at a concert given by the singer Eva Gauthier in November.

It was probably around this time, in early November 1923, that Whiteman and Gershwin did in fact discuss the possibility of Gershwin writing a longer work for Whiteman's orchestra. It is quite possible that Whiteman, noting the publicity of Gauthier's concert, conceived for his own commercial reasons the idea of staging a program that would prove to the "highbrows" that jazz could be sophisticated enough for the concert hall. Fearful that another orchestra leader, Vincent Lopez, would perform a similar concert first, Whiteman's publicist rushed into print without bothering to call Gershwin.

Paul Whiteman was known as the King of Jazz. In August 1923, when the orchestra returned from its first tour of England, a reception was held at the dock in which Whiteman was crowned "King of Jazz." The August 14 issue of the *New York Times* called him "Jazz King of America." There is no question that his was the most popular dance band of the decade.

It was an ironic title since his background and training were in the traditional classical mode. He had been a violinist and violist with the Denver Symphony Orchestra. After World War I he organized a dance band, playing in San Francisco's Fairmont Hotel. The original eight-piece band included trumpeter Henry Busse and banjoist Mike Pingatore. By the time the orchestra reached the East Coast, Ferde Grofé had become the piano player and arranger. Whiteman began recording for Victor in 1920, including, especially, "The Japanese Sandman," and perhaps his most famous record, "Whispering," both recorded in August 1920. For four years the orchestra was featured almost exclusively in Manhattan at the Palais Royal at 48th and Broadway. It was there that his orchestra and Gershwin rehearsed for the Aeolian Hall concert.

The story of the actual construction of the *Rhapsody* grew in the telling and retelling.[1] For example, in 1926 Gershwin said that he wrote the *Rhapsody* in ten days, but later, in 1930, he expanded that to three weeks—which seems more accurate. According to Gershwin, at first he thought of a simple, short, regulation blues but then suddenly an idea occurred to him.

> There had been so much chatter about the limitations of jazz, not to speak of the manifest misunderstanding of its function. Jazz, they said, has to be in strict time. . . . I resolved, if possible, to kill that misconception with one sturdy blow. Inspired by this aim I set to work composing with un-wonted rapidity. No set plan was in my mind—no structure to which my music would conform. The rhapsody, as you see, began as a purpose, not a plan.[2]

In fact, he had started writing the piece that would become the *Rhapsody* within two days of talking to Whiteman. Indeed, he told Goldberg that when he was summoned to Boston to work on the out-of-town tryouts for *Sweet Little Devil*, "I had already done some work on the Rhapsody." Gershwin's manuscript score was dated January 7, and written in Gershwin's hand across the top of the music paper was the full title "RHAPSODY IN BLUE" and below it "FOR JAZZ BAND AND PIANO." This score was for two pianos, the second being the part for jazz band, or "J.B." in Gershwin's handwriting. At first George thought that the title might be *American Rhapsody*, but there are no surviving written sketches under this title. It seems likely that *An American Rhapsody* was a casual reference in conversations with Ira. It was Ira who claimed credit for the actual title. He had visited a museum showing a display of art in shades of color; hence his suggestion for the name. But blue was meant to evoke the musical blues rather than the color. Deena Rosenberg wrote, more accurately, that Ira's choice reflected his deep sensitivity to George's use of the blue notes.

During his trip to Boston to help with the out-of-town try-out of *Sweet Little Devil* (called *A Perfect Lady*, in Boston), Gershwin claimed he was inspired by the "steely rhythms" of the rails—suddenly he heard and even saw on paper the complete construction of the *Rhapsody*. No new themes came to him, but, he heard it as a sort of "musical kaleidoscope" of America. By the time he reached Boston he had a definite plot of the piece.[3]

Later, he reiterated much the same story in an article written after the pre-miere: *Rhapsody in Blue* reflected "the vivid panorama of American life swept through my mind—its feverishness, its vulgarity, its welter of love, marriage, and divorce, and its basic solidity in the character of the people. All of the emotional reactions excited by contemplating the American scene, with all its mixtures of races . . . were stuffed into the first outline of the *Rhapsody*.[4]

Gershwin's explanation of the origins are consistent with the original, tenta-tive title, *American Rhapsody*. Indeed, from early in his career, Gershwin was determined to put his compositions in an American setting; it became a recurring theme; hence his allusions to the "great melting pot" and the "vast panorama" of American life in describing the *Rhapsody*.

Gershwin was scheduled to go Boston again in this period to accompany Eva

Gauthier in a repeat of the jazz section of her concert of November 1923. That concert in Boston took place on January 29, 1924. Just before that trip, Carl Van Vechten, an acquaintance of Gauthier, encountered Gershwin at a rehearsal in New York for Gauthier's Boston performance. Gershwin explained to him about Whiteman's plan and told him that he was writing a concerto in "fantasia form." This version is supported by a story from Eva Gauthier. She asserts that at her final rehearsal in New York for her Boston concert she asked Gershwin to play something from his "new work." He did, and explained that it was for Paul Whiteman's concert in a few days, if he finished it in time. Many years later Gauthier claimed that this was the first performance of *Rhapsody in Blue*. Van Vechten, however, recalls that Gershwin had only made some "preliminary sketches," and had not yet decided on the slow theme. What he played for Gauthier was the "jazz theme," to be announced by the full orchestra, accompanied by figurations on the piano, and "the ingenious passage, not thematic, which ushers in the finale."[5]

It is likely that by this late date Gershwin had selected the themes for his composition and begun to stitch them together. A week after his return from Boston (the first time) he said he had completed the *Rhapsody*. Gershwin gave the date as January 25, 1924 (i.e., closer to three weeks than to ten days). This coincides with the Gauthier-Van Vechten version that they heard most of it before going to Boston for her concert, probably around January 27 or 28.

Under the pressure of a deadline for Whiteman to rehearse before the concert, Ferde Grofé, Whiteman's orchestrator, stopped by each day at the Gershwins' apartment at 110th and Amsterdam Avenue on New York's West Side. While George composed on an old upright in a back room, Grofé drank Russian tea with Rose, as he waited to pick up the new manuscript pages. Grofé had orchestrated Gershwin songs for George White's *Scandals*. The two discussed the orchestration, and the handwritten score has some notations (by Gershwin or Grofé) as to which soloists in the Whiteman orchestra could perform which passages; thus on the clarinet part is written "Ross" for Ross Gorman, and on the line for the trumpet parts was written "Busse Siegrist" meaning Henry Busse and Frank Siegrist. Though Busse became famous for his muted version of "Hot Lips," it was Siegrist who played the muted "wah-wah" solo in the first part of the *Rhapsody*.

Gershwin's partisans claimed that he could have done the orchestration but ran out of time. Grofé himself, however, said that Gershwin did not know orchestration at the time. This impression has lingered, but the notebooks Gershwin kept from his studies with Kilenyi show a number of experiments with orchestration. As already noted, some manuscripts discovered in the Warner Brothers warehouse in Secaucus, New Jersey, in the 1980s included the score from the British show *Primrose*; there were orchestrations in Gershwin's hand for three songs; this was shortly after the *Rhapsody*.[6]

Orchestration was an art often neglected by composers. Gershwin forced himself to learn it, but others—Kern, Rodgers, and Berlin—and even those who were trained, such as Vernon Duke, usually left the work to others. It was too time-consuming and the songwriter for a Broadway show was usually needed during the rehearsals and out-of-town performances. Moreover, there were skilled professional orchestrators available. The composer had to pay for the arrangements, however. The piano arrangement of the *Rhapsody* makes it clear that Gershwin wrote the entire composition, leaving only one gap for his own piano cadenza. In Grofé's orchestral score for the conductor there is a hand-written notation "wait for nod," apparently meaning that Gershwin would nod to Whiteman when he had finished his cadenza. The cadenza, therefore, was improvised and the original is forever lost, although subsequent early recordings by Gershwin are probably quite similar.

The construction of the separate musical themes for the *Rhapsody* is also a little confusing and encrusted with anecdotes of questionable validity. Some accounts claim that the opening clarinet glissando, or "smear," was clarinetist Ross Gorman's idea. In one account he and Gershwin supposedly worked for an hour to get it right. Another version claimed that Gorman supposedly ex-perimented with different clarinet reeds before he mastered the sound. One writer even claimed that this achievement was impossible before the *Rhapsody*.

All of this is nonsense. The glissando was similar to an exercise written in Gershwin's notebooks from his studies with Kilenyi. There are also examples in the standard text on orchestration by Cecil Forsyth, which Gershwin owned. Even a cursory acquaintance with the jazz clarinetists of the day would dem-onstrate the very same techniques. Such a phrase in the key of concert B-flat (C for a clarinet) is not that difficult. However, Gorman's interpretation of the opening bars, in the first Whiteman recordings is puzzling (the clarinet part in the recording may be by Chester Hazlitt). Gorman or Hazlitt played the passage more as a burlesque, with honking and slurring that sounded very similar to the "Livery Stable Blues," a classic of the Original Dixieland Jazz Band that opened the Whiteman program. Presumably this was intentional; in subsequent record-ings the clarinet part became much smoother. In any case, Gershwin had already decided it would be suitable as an opening, when he agreed to "chance it" and accept Whiteman's offer. Nevertheless, critics liked the beginning, particularly— "with a flutter-tongued, drunken whoop of an introduction that had the audience rocking."

Although Gershwin claimed that the whole composition "from beginning to end" was in his mind, the origin of the slow theme is also confusing. George gave a dramatic version. After he had returned to New York, the middle theme came to him suddenly, at the home of a friend: "All at once I heard myself playing a theme that must have been haunting me inside, seeking an outlet."[7]

But Ferde Grofé recounts a different version. He did not like the first melody for the slow or love theme, and when, at Ira's behest, Gershwin reluctantly played the one ultimately used, Grofé was enthusiastic. It borrowed from a melody written sometime earlier. George objected that it was too sweet, but finally gave in. This is puzzling because the melody becomes the basis for variants in the last section, supposedly already written. The critical reactions to this theme proved to be mixed; some thought it merely a Tin Pan Alley tune, but others were enthusiastic about its echo of Tchaikovsky (an "emotional and moving tune," wrote Henry Osgood; later he amended his praise to a "noble, dignified tune").

Grofé finished his orchestration on February 4, 1924. The score is signed by Grofé and initialed by Gershwin. A comparison of Gershwin's original piano version and Grofé's handwritten orchestration indicates that Gershwin owed a great debt to Grofé. There are passages in which Gershwin sketched in the melody line and little else; Grofé supplied the harmony, as played by the instrumentalists. Gershwin no doubt concurred, but the inspiration in many cases was Grofé's. However, the manuscript of the orchestration in the Grofé archives seems all of one piece; it is possible that the separate sheets Gershwin supposedly was handing over to Grofé every day, were discarded—if they ever existed.[8]

Whatever the details, the composition was a remarkable achievement. With no particular background or experience in writing longer forms, Gershwin assembled a masterpiece in a very short time. There are three parts, though not identified as such. The first is bright and fast and the longest; then comes a slow or love theme, and then a rousing finale. The *Rhapsody* was in essence a series of skirmishes between the piano and the orchestra. The piano echoed Gershwin's ragtime background with the use of grace notes and the thumping of strong triplets. The orchestra was more jazzy, with clarinet slurs, muted trumpets and trombones, and saxophone leads, probably influenced by Grofé. The orchestra introduces the themes forcefully but in a straightforward manner, while the piano uses various devices and embellishments. There is also a strong sense of Tin Pan Alley; many of the themes could be eight-bar phrases from a popular song. The musicologist David Schiff, in his important study of the *Rhapsody*, has analyzed the score and identifies five clear themes, which he believes probably were derived from trunk songs or sketches of melodies. He notes that at some point each of the major themes is played as a piano solo, which would be typical of Gershwin. The one exception is the so-called train theme. Oddly enough, this theme, which Gershwin talked about a great deal as his original inspiration, is repeated only twice by the orchestra (trumpets) and then abandoned.[9]

There were at least two rehearsals with the orchestra. The first was held before the orchestration was completely finished. Whiteman always had his eye on public relations. Thus, three music critics—Pitts Sanborn, Henry Osgood, and Leonard Liebling—were invited to the (second) full dress rehearsal. Whiteman brought George over to the group and introduced him. After the first run-through Liebling was impressed, as was Osgood, but Sanborn—who had never heard of Gershwin—was puzzled, though impressed by the "zip and punch." There was a gaggle of others—"curious persons" and "large unclassified elements, Rialtoites and musical comedy friends of Gershiwn," according to Osgood; they seemed to have dropped in to observe. Music historian John Tasker Howard described one dress rehearsal in the mid-afternoon at the Palais Royal: "the heavy drapes looked gloomy and the tables bare." Henry Osgood wrote the same thing in his review for the *Musical Courier* (February 21, 1924): there was "over the whole scene a tawdry shabbiness that positively depresses the sensitive soul." One rehearsal was attended by Victor Herbert, who had also written a "Suite for Strings" for the concert. Herbert made one suggestion to Gershwin to precede the opening passage of the slow theme, and it was incorporated by Gershwin.[10]

The Whiteman concert was well-publicized and drew a distinguished audience, including Walter Damrosch, Jascha Heifitz, Fritz Kreisler, and a full set of critics. The program stated that Paul Whiteman and his Palais Royal Orchestra would offer "An Experiment in Modern Music, assisted by Zez Confrey and George Gershwin."[11] The concert was scheduled for 3:00 P.M. on February 12, 1924; tickets were priced from $.55 to $2.20.

Whiteman's orchestra was arranged in a semicircle, in three steps. Behind the orchestra was an elaborate display of colorful Japanese screens. The printed program explained that the object of the concert would be purely "educational," to point out the tremendous strides made in popular music since the days of "discordant jazz" (illustrated in the program by the first number, "Livery Stable Blues," a classic of the Original Dixieland Jazz Band). This older instrumental served Whiteman's purpose: it was a raucous number, more a novelty than genuine jazz. According to the program the great strides in popular music since then were possible through the new art of "scoring" so that the arranger would be able to present the "melodies, harmony and rhythms which agitate the throbbing emotional resources of this young restless age." This was from the pen of Gilbert Seldes, who had become Whiteman's public relations man.

Gershwin was described in the program notes as capable of everything, "delicacy, even dreaminess is a quality he alone brings into jazz music. Gershwin's sense of variations in rhythms in shifting accents, of emphasis and color is faultless." He was "one of the brightest hopes of our popular music" (this rhetoric was lifted from an earlier Gilbert Seldes article praising Gershwin). As for the *Rhapsody* itself, the program notes were quite ecstatic: "Gershwin is a close student of music and a listener; yet there is not a derivative phrase in his work. He has composed a rhapsody and has chosen to build it out of materials known to him: the rhythms of popular American music, the harmonies produced by American jazz bands." The program assured the audience that the material was all new, that it had been completed only recently, though in the mind of the composer for some time."[12]

The Whiteman orchestra included eight violins; a brass section of two trumpets, two trombones, and two French horns; a piano and celesta, tuba and string bass, drums and tympani; and three men, whose collections of instruments included saxophones, oboes, bass clarinets, flutes, and even an octavian and one heckaphone. And, of course, Mike Pingatore played the banjo; he was Whiteman's longtime sideman, who earlier in the program played his rendition of "Whispering" in stop-time. The program was divided into sections with such titles as "The True Form of Jazz ("The Livery Stable Blues"), or "Legitimate Scoring vs. Jazzing" (two versions of "Whispering"). Later in the afternoon, Zez Confrey played his own popular "Kitten on the Keys" and other compositions on the piano. After the intermission, Whiteman conducted the four short pieces by Victor Herbert, a suite in four parts in the style of Spanish, Chinese, Cuban and Oriental music. After a brief selection of dance tunes came Gershwin and the *Rhapsody*.

Gershwin has left no precise recollection of that afternoon. Others described him as nervous but eager to start. Some recalled that people were starting to leave, but everyone agrees that the beginning, Gorman's clarinet glissando, was "electrifying."

The critical reaction was "divided," to borrow Whiteman's phrase.[13] Olin Downes of the *New York Times* was critical of Gershwin's lack of technical competence to structure such a work, but he found it "fresh and new, full of future promise." Gilbert Gabriel of the *New York Sun* found the beginning and ending "stunning." But he concluded that the title of *Rhapsody* was suitable to cover a "degree of formlessness to which the middle section of the work, relying too steadily on tort and retort of the piano itself, seemed to sag." The "grand old man" of New York criticism, W.J. Henderson, who wrote mainly for the *New York Sun*, found it a "highly ingenious work." Deems Taylor (in the *World*) noted the shortcomings in form but claimed that Gershwin had a "latent ability . . . to say something of considerable interest in his chosen idiom." Writing a week later Taylor decided that Gershwin was a "link between the jazz camp and the intellectuals." It was crude "but hinted at something new." Gershwin will bear watching, Taylor concluded.

On the other hand, one reviewer wrote that some of the instruments were quite "grotesque"; the clarinetist almost "burst his instrument and his veins indulging in tonal contortions and somersaults of the most grotesque and vulgar kind." Another reviewer, referring to the "Livery Stable Blues," commented that "the instruments made odd, unseemly bushman sounds." More serious criticism came from the likes of Lawrence Gilman who would become one of Gershwin's inveterate critics; he wrote for the *New York Tribune*: "Recall the most ambitious piece, the Rhapsody, and weep over the lifelessness of its melody and harmony, so derivative, so stale, so inexpressive."[14] Pitts Sanborn, who had attended the rehearsal, wrote: "Although to some ears this *Rhapsody* begins with a promising theme well stated, it soon runs off into empty passage work and meaningless repetition." On the other hand, several critics praised the orchestrations and concluded that they had heard something "new." Leonard Liebling, who had also attended the rehearsal, was polite, but noncommittal: Gershwin's "jazz concerto" made an "enormous hit with the composers' winning ways at the instrument to help put it over." A strong rejection came later from the modernist Paul Rosenfeld, who made a practice of attacking Gershwin, dismissing him as: "A gifted composer of the lower, unpretentious order; his compositions drowse one in a pink world of received ideas and sentiments. *Rhapsody in Blue* is circus-music, pre-eminent in the sphere of tinsel and fustian."[15]

Henry Osgood, a champion of Gershwin, wrote the opposite: "America is at least getting to the point where it can produce something which—be it good or bad—is at least original, without foreign earmarks of any sort." This must have pleased Gershwin who emphasized time and again that his music was not a European derivative. While not yet "pure gold," the result, Osgood concluded, was "something absolutely original . . . something really new in music."[16]

Thus near the very beginning of Gershwin's crossover from Broadway the issue of his proper place in American music was joined: had George Gershwin created a legitimate link between jazz and the concert hall? For decades both the jazz world and the concert hall camps would debate this question, leaving George Gershwin suspended between the two worlds.

The stature and popularity of the *Rhapsody* grew both in the concert hall and in the popular recognition of Gershwin as the composer of genuinely new American music. Whiteman did his part, immediately scheduling more concerts, including one at the prestigious Carnegie Hall (November 10, 1924). Olin Downes' review of this concert (*New York Times*, November 21, 1924) was more critical: "[it] suffers from a rather flimsy and unduly extended form, from unnecessary repetitions, and a piano style dictated by reminiscences of Liszt. But it has ideas, it has impudence, the swagger and tiff of Broadway . . . the orchestration is novel and of a kind peculiar to American dance orchestras."

Gershwin participated in part of the Whiteman tour until May and recorded a cut-down version in June 1924. The tour was Gershwin's opportunity to gain recognition outside the confines of New York. At every stop there were large enthusiastic crowds and ovations for George. In Boston he displayed himself as a skilled pianist and composer. After George left the tour a reviewer of the Indianapolis concert was disappointed: "little removed from the blatantly obvious, with no thematic development of any kind." There was also a fall tour, without George. Chicago found the *Rhapsody* even better than expected, but not as "thrilling" as Victor Herbert's "Spanish Serenade." Some years later Whiteman made a movie entitled "King of Jazz," in which his entire orchestra slowly rose from a gigantic piano. Gershwin's fee of $40,000 for the use of the *Rhapsody* probably soothed any resentment over Whiteman's saccharine interpretations.

For many decades, musicologists banished Gershwin to a sort of limbo. They were prone to classify music rigidly, according to European traditions; they established a hierarchy in which Gershwin was merely a commercial enterprise. Gershwin did not fit into the "conceptual framework adopted by so many Western music historians and critics."[17]

Young composers, including some important Americans, who were Gershwin's competitors, came down on the side of criticism.[18] Aaron Copland virtually ignored the *Rhapsody*, claiming that Gershwin was regarded in "everybody's book" as a composer of popular songs. The composer Virgil Thomson was also a Gershwin critic. Thomson acknowledged Gershwin's popularity and the charm of his music, but added that "Rhapsodies, however, are not very difficult to write, if one can think up enough tunes." Moreover, Thomson contended that "it is clear by now that Gershwin hasn't learned his business. At least he hasn't learned the business of being a serious composer, which one has long gathered to be the business he wanted to learn."[19]

Much later, Leonard Bernstein was also surprisingly critical, even though he made a reputation as an interpreter and performer of Gershwin. He found the *Rhapsody* formless: "the *Rhapsody* is not a composition at all." It was a "string of separate paragraphs stuck together—with thin paste of flour and water." He praised the "God-given" tunes, "perfectly harmonized, ideally proportioned, songful, clear, rich, moving." However, he said "one could cut out parts of it without affecting the whole in any way. . . . You can't just put four tunes together, God given though they may be and call them a composition."[20]

Bernstein's mentor, Serge Koussevitsky, however, in a memorial after Gershwin's death, wrote that "Whoever heard Gershwin in a performance of his *Rhapsody in Blue* shall not forget the experience. The sweeping brilliance, virtuosity and rhythmic precision of his playing were incredible, his perfect poise and ease beyond belief, his dynamic influence on the orchestra and the on the audience electrifying." Bernstein's colleague, the composer Ned Rorem, also disagreed with him. He argued that melody is indeed the heart of music. The musicologist Richard Crawford, responding to the criticism of the *Rhapsody* for lacking a more organic form, wrote: "it is precisely in the way the stylistic references are juxtaposed almost as if Gershwin were a film director, cutting from one scene to another that the work's eclectic essence shines through."[21]

There was also a whiff of anti-Semitism in some of the criticism. Professor David Schiff concluded in his study of the *Rhapsody*:

> In their fear of cultural leveling, modernists joined hands with reactionaries of both New England and the Bible Belt in rejecting Jewish influence. Gershwin, the dark handsome product of the lower East Side, Mr. Nobody from nowhere (as Tom Buchanan calls Gatsby) suddenly taking the music world by storm, would serve as one symbol of the cultural subversion of the Jazz Age, alongside the jungle goddesses, Bessie Smith and Josephine Baker. [22]

Over the years there have been seemingly endless versions of the *Rhapsody*. In addition to the early recording by Paul Whiteman with Gershwin at the piano, and another version in 1927 using a new Grofé orchestration, Gershwin also recorded unaccompanied piano roll solos in 1925 and 1927. The original *Rhapsody* was lively and bouncy, far more "jazzy" when played at Gershwin's own tempo (three minutes faster than modern performances) and with Grofé's original instrumentation. "Gershwin's first recording of the Rhapsody, made five months after its premiere, crackles with Jazz Age insouciance," according to musicologist David Schiff. Whiteman's sidemen were jazz musicians; if not in the superstar category of Armstrong or Benny Goodman, they were quite conscious of jazz music that they heard from Fletcher Henderson's orchestra playing a few blocks away at Roseland. They gave the *Rhapsody* a distinctive feeling.

Comparisons of the originals and later renditions are striking reminders of the increasingly sweet treatment given the *Rhapsody*. Most later versions came to be based on the new Grofé arrangement for a larger symphonic orchestra. Grofé even altered the instrumentation of major themes. The slow theme, for example, played by three saxophones in the original, was transformed by adding a larger string section.

Gradually, over the years the tempos became slower and more dramatic and the instrumental parts played by symphony musicians became wooden and uninspired. In most recordings there were cuts, some of them quite extensive. The pianist Earl Wild established himself as a major interpreter of Gershwin; but in his 1945 recording of the *Rhapsody* with Paul Whiteman, a sixteen-member vocal chorus was added! The musicologist and composer Gunther Schuller, commenting on the misinterpretation of Beethoven's Fifth Symphony, wrote about the *Rhapsody* that "certainly no famous work has been more mishandled, bowdlerized, dismembered and misinterpreted."[23]

The current consensus seems to be that Oscar Levant's recording of the *Rhapsody* is the closest in style to Gershwin's intentions. Leonard Bernstein, however, went in the wrong direction: Gershwin's close friend Kay Swift found his version "too sentimental" and lacking in the brashness and impetus that the piece required. She found Andre Previn's performance with the London Symphony to be "excellent."[24]

The *Rhapsody* gradually drifted into the "pops" category and faded from the classical repertory of the major orchestras. Its popularity made it suspect. Even in its own niche the *Rhapsody* was transformed into what Schiff calls the "Hollywood-Bowl-style." It lost its Jazz Age "brashness."

Then came the renewed interest in the original text as written by Gershwin and Grofé. The *Rhapsody* gradually made a comeback. The enterprising conductor Michael Tilson Thomas developed an ingenious idea. He adapted Gershwin's original piano roll and combined it with his orchestra, the Los Angeles Philharmonic, as an accompaniment (CD MK 39699). The melding is not smooth, although it does allow the listener to savor some of what might have been the ambience of that late Tuesday afternoon in February 1924.

Some musicologists have come to have a higher regard for Gershwin and the *Rhapsody*. Professor Richard Crawford, after years of dismissing the *Rhapsody* in his classes, came around to a different conclusion after reexamining it. He wrote in 1998: "The *Rhapsody* is an emblem of its time *and* a work with an enduring presence; a composition that has never gone out of style."[25] Steven E. Gilbert, in his detailed analysis of Gershwin's music, concluded: "it turns out to be a better written piece than anyone could first imagine it to be . . . a work of achievement and promise."[26]

Finally, on the sixtieth anniversary of the Aeolian Hall concert the entire program was recreated and recorded under the leadership and baton of Maurice Peress.[27] This time the critics found that the *Rhapsody* with Ivan Davis as soloist sounded as "fresh and original" as it had sixty years ago; it was "unwittingly such a shining evocation of New York." Francis Davis wrote that Whiteman eroded the boundaries between the highbrow and the lowbrow. His Aeolian Hall concert was a landmark event in American music. "So, in its own way, is Peress's loving re-creation—and not merely for its lustrous, slightly antic *Rhapsody in Blue*."[28]

NOTES

1. Gershwin's biographer, Edward Jablonski, acknowledged that the precise chronology of the *Rhapsody* is somewhat "misty." Edward Jablonski, *Gershwin: A Biography* (New York: Doubleday, 1987), p. 65.

2. Isaac Goldberg (supplemented by Edith Garson), *George Gershwin: A Study in American Music* (New York: Frederick Ungar Publishing, 1958), p. 139.

3. Ibid. Every writer seems to have repeated the story of the "steely" rhythm of the rails.

4. Goldberg, *Gershwin*, p. 139; also quoted in Erma Taylor in *George Gershwin*, ed. Merle Armitage (New York: Longmans, Green, 1938), p. 188.

5. Carl Van Vechten, "An American Composer Who is Writing Notable Music in the Jazz Idiom," *Vanity Fair*, March 1925, printed in *Gershwin in His Time: A Biographical Scrapbook, 1919–1937*, ed. Gregory R. Suriano (New York: Gramercy Books, 1998).

6. These orchestrations are housed in the Library of Congress, Gershwin Collection; one page of "Naughty Baby" is on display in the Gershwin exhibition. The orchestrations are for a full pit orchestra—strings, brass, and woodwinds.

7. Erma Taylor, "George Gershwin, A Lament," *Jones Magazine*, November 1937; quoted in *George Gershwin*, ed. Armitage, p. 188.

8. Ferde Grofé Collection, *Rhapsody in Blue*, "Gershwin Two Piano" holograph on microfilm, Library of Congress. The original is on display in the Gershwin Room in the Jefferson Building of the Library of Congress. There is also in Gershwin's hand a clean copy in pen, but not of the complete *Rhapsody*. A commemorative facsimile of Grofé's handwritten orchestration was published by Warner Brothers in 1987.

9. David Schiff, *Gershwin: Rhapsody in Blue* (Cambridge: Cambridge University Press, 1997), pp. 12–29.

10. Descriptions of the rehearsal are in Henry O. Osgood, *So This Is Jazz* (Boston: Little, Brown, 1926), pp. 133–35. Victor Herbert's suggestions, mentioned by several authors, are a trifle mysterious; the slow theme follows immediately at the end of the piano cadenza. As printed the cadenza includes, at the end an additional four bars of an ascending chromatic figure ending with an arpeggio that may well have been Herbert's suggestion. Something along this line would have been necessary because the key changes. But it is not written in Grofé's original orchestration.

11. The text of the program is printed with the CD "The Birth of the Rhapsody in Blue," Music Masters CD 601137.

12. The program is reprinted in the booklet accompanying the new recording of the entire concert conducted by Maurice Peress.

13. Excerpts from critical reviews are printed in Goldberg, *George Gershwin*, pp. 148–52.

14. Lawrence Gilman quoted in *Gershwin Remembered*, ed. Edward Jablonski (Portland, OR: Amadeus Press, 1992), p. 30. Winthrop Sargeant described Gilman as a "suave, sensitive and rather morose gentleman of extremely aesthetic appearance"; he eventually became dean of the New York critics. He was succeeded at the *New York Herald Tribune* by Virgil Thomson. Mark N. Grant, *Maestro of the Pen* (Boston: Northeastern University Press, 1998), pp. 275–76.

15. Paul Rosenfeld's critique of Gershwin's works is printed in his collection, *Discoveries of A Music Critic* (New York: Vienna House, 1972), pp. 264–72. Rosenfeld was a prolific writer, with strong opinions. [He] "was one of the prime agenda-setters of modernist American music of the early twentieth century." Grant, *Maestro of the Pen*, p. 291. See other reviews in Jablonski, *Gershwin Remembered*, pp. 30–32.

16. Osgood, *So This Is Jazz*. He provides an extensive musical analysis of the *Rhapsody*, pp. 196–203.

17. Carol J. Oja, "Gershwin and American Modernists in the 1920s," *Musical Quarterly*, 78/4 (1994); Charles Hamm, "Towards a New Reading of Gershwin," in *The Gershwin Style*, ed. Wayne Schneider (New York: Oxford University Press, 1999); Richard Crawford, "Rethinking the Rhapsody," *Institute for the Study of American Music (ISAM) Newsletter*, 28/1 (1998).

18. Richard Crawford, *America's Musical Life* (New York: W.W. Norton, 2001), pp. 578–79; Professor Crawford also presents a cogent musical analysis of the *Rhapsody*, pp. 575–78.

19. Virgil Thomson, *A Virgil Thomson Reader* (Boston: Houghton Mifflin, 1981), pp. 23–24.

20. Leonard Bernstein, *The Joy of Music* (New York: Simon and Schuster, 1959), p. 57.

21. Serge Koussevitsky in Armitage, *George Gershwin*, p. 113. Crawford, "Rethinking the Rhapsody."

22. Schiff, *Gershwin*, p. 92.

23. Gunther Schuller, *The Compleat Conductor* (New York: Oxford University Press, 1997), p. 109.

24. Schiff, *Rhapsody in Blue*, p. 67, argues that Earl Wild plays the *Rhapsody* as a classical concerto, while Bernstein ponderously drags it out "to the point of (intended?) parody."

25. Richard Crawford, "Rethinking the Rhapsody."

26. Steven E. Gilbert, *The Music of George Gershwin* (New Haven, CT: Yale University Press, 1995), p. 71.

27. "Gershwin: The Birth of Rhapsody in Blue" (Music Masters, MMD 60113T).

28. Francis Davis, commenting on the brilliance of this particular recording, noted that the *Rhapsody* "we have come to love or detest" is a "pale echo" of what was played that night in 1924. Francis Davis, *Outcats* (New York: Oxford University Press, 1990), pp. 188–89.

Chapter 5

Jazz

The program notes for the Whiteman concert described the *Rhapsody* as genuine jazz music, not only in its scoring but in its idiom. Gershwin was thus a link between the jazz camp and the intellectuals. Thereafter, until the end of his life, Gershwin was identified closely with jazz. Decades after his death his reputation could not escape the original conclusion—that he had forged a link between jazz and the concert hall. *The Oxford Dictionary of Music* (1985) wrote: "In 1924 he enjoyed success in a new genre, that of applying jazz idioms to concert works."

At first he was reluctant to acknowledge that *Rhapsody in Blue* was a "jazz concerto" as critics described it. For Gershwin that was a vast oversimplification. He wanted his creation to be taken as "serious" music. He never conceived of the *Rhapsody* as an example of what was later called "symphonic jazz." He wrote that "An entire composition written in jazz, could not live." Many observers agreed with him; they argued that the *Rhapsody* not only was *not* jazz, but not even jazz "dolled-up."[1]

In the strict sense of the term, of course, Gershwin's music was not jazz as it had developed by the mid-1920s. The *Rhapsody* was not in the category of the improvised jazz of Louis Armstrong, Jelly Roll Morton, or many other musicians, both white and black. This is not surprising. During Gershwin's formative years, when he was a young song plugger, he could not have been aware of the jazz style mainly imported from New Orleans. King Oliver and his Creole Jazz Band remained ensconced in Chicago and did not even begin recording until 1923. Gershwin's earliest exposure to that particular style of jazz might have been when the fabled Original Dixieland Jazz Band opened in 1917 in New York. They created a sensation—"as a new form of music it was revolutionary. It shocked, frightened, confused and finally captivated the listener."[2]

They recorded "Livery Stable Blues" in February. After a European tour the band returned to New York in 1920 for another engagement and more recordings. There is no evidence one way or the other that Gershwin heard this band. He may well have heard their records; over one million copies of the group's Victor recording of "Livery Stable Blues" were sold. Its popularity, of course, is one reason why Whiteman chose it as the opening number on his Aeolian concert to illustrate the older, "cruder" jazz. This was primarily instrumental music and Gershwin was far more intrigued by piano styles.

Along the way Gershwin absorbed some measure of authentic jazz. For example, Paul Whiteman was playing at the Palais Royal on 47th Street. Only a few blocks north on 51st Street was the Roseland ballroom, where Fletcher Henderson alternated with other bands. By October 1924 he was starring the young Louis Armstrong on trumpet. And in the same neighborhood, at the Hollywood Inn (also known as the Kentucky Club), was young Edward Kennedy Ellington and a small band. Ellington's sidemen claimed that Whiteman and Gershwin as well as Whiteman's players would drop by late in the evening. Grofé's orchestral style was influenced by Ellington. Gershwin, of course, was well-acquainted with Grofé and Whiteman's sidemen who frequented the various jazz locales.

At first Gershwin was wary of being too closely associated with "jazz" for several reasons. The very term had obscene connotations, especially when Gershwin was young. An opinion magazine in 1918 wrote that "one touch of jazz makes savages of us all." Moreover, his early exposure was to music that he found quite crude. Some early jazz bands in New York were little more than comic or novelty acts. He later wrote that jazz had evolved: "The blatant jazz of ten years ago, crude, vulgar and unadorned is passing. Jazz was gradually freeing itself and moving toward a higher plane."

Eventually, Gershwin became a defender of jazz. While he admitted that he employed jazz, he claimed that he had used it "incidentally," just as he employed syncopation. But he also went further, writing that jazz suggested to him something "vital" in American life, although it expressed "only one element." To express the full richness of American life, the composer had to use melody, harmony, counterpoint "as employed by the great composers of the past." His turnaround came, in part, because he was determined to link his music to genuine American folk art, which made jazz respectable:

> Jazz I regard as an American folk music; not the only one but a very powerful one which is probably in the blood and feeling of the American people more than any other style of folk music. I believe that it can be made the basis of serious symphonic works of lasting value, in the hands of a composer with talent for both jazz and symphonic music.[3]

Gershwin was obviously referring to himself as a "composer with talent for both jazz and symphonic music," but this was written in 1933, when Gershwin had established himself on Broadway and in the concert hall. While defending jazz, his definition was eclectic: it had a bit of ragtime, the blues, classicism, and spirituals. Basically, it is a matter of rhythm. Jazz already had an enduring value for America, in the sense that it was an original American achievement. Earlier he had written that every musician who studied modern music knew that jazz already had made a real contribution to the art."

These comments provide an insight into Gershwin, namely, his determination to be regarded as an American composer writing genuine American music, reflecting the spirit of the country. That his music was the embodiment of Americana is exactly what he was striving for.[4] He would define all of his major compositions in this broad sense, whether the Concerto in F, *An American in Paris*, or *Porgy and Bess*. One of Gershwin's later biographers stressed Gershwin's Americanism:

> In the American renaissance of the twenties, George Gershwin played a dual role. Like Fitzgerald and Hemingway and Faulkner and Dreiser, like the modernists and the men who made the movies, he chronicled the conflict of old values and new. But he also personified these conflicts and changes. . . . The art of the twenties deals with the rise of the new America; Gershwin not only dealt with it, he and his work embodied it.[5]

It is clear, however, that Gershwin's appreciation of jazz was derived from popular music as played by Paul Whiteman and other similar orchestras. Well after writing the *Rhapsody* he offered a list of those jazz songs that deserved to be "studied" by singers and performers. His list included "Japanese Sandman," "Carolina in the Morning," "I Want to Be Happy," among others, and three of his own songs including "Swanee," as well as W.C. Handy's "St. Louis Blues." It is difficult to believe that Gershwin—or anyone for that matter—would consider such a popular, mundane song as "Carolina in the Morning" as jazz music.

His limited perspective may be explained by what the musicologist Charles Hamm describes as the considerable "conceptual confusion" in the early 1920s between popular music that was "jazzed" and the authentic music being pioneered by black musicians. The music as played by Paul Whiteman and, indeed, by Gershwin himself, belonged to a common category—white music played by white men, within the social context of white culture. This was the dominant concept of jazz in the 1920s.[6]

Some writers of the period, including those extolling Gershwin (Henry Osgood in *So This Is Jazz*), restricted their analysis of jazz to music being played by white bands and written by composers from Tin Pan Alley. Osgood wrote: "very rarely are the best black players as good as the best white virtuosos."[7] While acknowledging the many good "negro jazz bands," Osgood concluded that none of them are as good as the "best white bands."[8] Gershwin was described by Osgood as the "Great White Hope," a phrase borrowed from the days of the black heavyweight champion Jack Johnson—it was probably not meant to be racial in Gershwin's case. It had come to mean any important challenger.

On the other hand, there was no lack of harsh criticism. Rabbi Stephen Wise said, "When America regains its soul, jazz will go, not before." The composer Amy Beach dismissed jazz as "vulgar or debasing." British critics were especially hard. In January 1921, Clive Bell proclaimed that "Jazz is dead." The respected British critic Ernest Newman was weary with jazz; even Paul Whiteman's orchestra left him "dead cold." He concluded that the only hope for jazz was to be taken up by some composer who "can really compose." This suggested Gershwin, but Newman was critical of *Rhapsody in Blue*.[9]

After Gershwin died, a generation of jazz critics were determined to reject any link between Gershwin and "real" jazz. They persistently disparaged his contribution. Rudi Blesh, in his history of jazz, *Shining Trumpets*, wrote: "Even less jazz is the Gershwin *Rhapsody in Blue* that treats quasi-blues harmonies and certain jazz instrumental traits in a symphonic manner." The prominent jazz authority, Dave Dexter, in his book *Jazz Cavalcade* (1946), wrote that "The *Rhapsody*, of course, was and always will remain nothing more than *ersatz* jazz." The French jazz critic Andre Hodier wrote: "It is no longer possible . . . to confuse authentic jazz with cheap dance music or pretentious pieces like *Rhapsody in Blue*." The well-known jazz critic Leonard Feather, in *An Encyclopedia of Jazz* (1960), wrote that "Gershwin's symphonic works made only superficial use of jazz devices, and are not now generally considered to be an important part of jazz history." Barry Ulanov, writing in his *History of Jazz in America* (1972), sarcastically dismissed Gershwin as the man who succeeded in making Whiteman King of Jazz and who was "just as synthetic a jazz musician." (This is stupidly unfair to Whiteman, whose orchestra housed Bix Beiderbecke, Bunny Berigan, Frank Trumbauer, Eddie Lang, and Joe Venuti).

Another critic, Richard Sudhalter, made a more relevant and cogent point. He pointed out that Gershwin was writing from "outside the hot music circles: while in 1924 the *Rhapsody in Blue* was considered a great leap forward, it was manifestly the work of a musician approaching the language from an external point." In the context of 1924, as defined by King Oliver and the New Orleans Rhythm Kings, "the raggy working vocabulary of *Rhapsody in Blue* already seems an anachronism."[10]

That Gershwin was an outsider and that he was white are important points in the canon of jazz criticism of Gershwin. Invoking race, however, is unfair, since Gershwin was closer than most popular composers to the world of black music. It is ironic that this relationship led to a stubborn resistance to accepting Gershwin at face value. Many writers decided that his compositions did not reflect his own innate talents, but were "appropriated" from black music and musicians. Sociologists have elaborated this into a general theory—that the work of Jewish songwriters, dating back to ragtime, was produced by "Negro culture." This was the view of Ann Douglas in her widely acclaimed study *Terrible Honesty*.[11]

Gershwin's biographers have not gone quite this far but they support the idea that his music was derived from his exposure to the influence of black musicians. Joan Peyser, for example, argues that Gershwin appropriated from the blacks a drive and syncopation then unknown to white players. This appropriation of drive and syncopation unknown to white players would have been news to such white players as Bix Beiderbecke, Jack Teagarden, or Benny Goodman. Peyser also asserted that Gershwin appropriated black jazz and incorporated it into European forms: "the influence of blacks on Gershwin became seminal." Gershwin "not only responded to the music the blacks made; he felt as though he were one of them."[12]

Gershwin's view was the exact opposite. He certainly did not consider himself "one of them." Gershwin wrote in August 1925, after a Whiteman concert:

There is one superstition that must be destroyed. This is the superstition that jazz is essentially Negro. The Negroes, of course, take to jazz, but in its essence it is no more Negro than syncopation, which exists in the music of all nations. *Jazz is not Negro but American.* It is the spontaneous expression of the nervous energy of modern American life.[13] (emphasis added)

Later in 1932, he said:

Harlem is a sort of breeding place for musical ideas, but most of them are left in a kind of germinal state. You can find new rhythm, even richer harmonies there, but the germs are left for *outsiders* to pick up and develop.[14] (emphasis added)

Isaac Goldberg, in his biography of Gershwin, echoed Gershwin's views; he wrote that "jazz was traceable to the negro" but was "developed commercially and artistically by the Jew."

After Gershwin achieved a certain fame, black pianists boasted of influencing or even teaching him. Eubie Blake, for example, a well-known black songwriter, claimed that he heard about Gershwin in 1916 [*sic*] from two stride pianists, James P. Johnson and Luckey Roberts, who told him of a "very talented ofay [white] piano player at Remick's . . . good enough to learn some of those terribly difficult tricks that only a few of us could master."[15] This is truly fanciful; neither Roberts nor Johnson knew Gershwin in 1916, and it is doubtful that Eubie Blake had heard of him at that time.

It was over five years after he went to work at Remick's that Gershwin became acquainted with James P. Johnson, who was considered the "dean" of Harlem stride pianists. He was a fellow recording artist for Aeolian piano rolls in 1920–21—several years after Gershwin had begun making piano rolls. Johnson said that he first met Gershwin in 1920 when Gershwin was recording some "oriental" music rolls. According to Johnson's biographer, "the two men exchanged ideas and spoke about their mutual interest in the blues and other indigenous American music. We had lots of talks about our ambitions to do great music on American themes."[16] Their paths may have crossed again in London in 1923 when an all-black show, *Plantation Days*, with some music by Johnson, was cut down in size and inserted in an abortive revue, *Rainbow*, written by Gershwin.[17]

Contact with Johnson, through his piano rolls, could have been an important influence for Gershwin. According to Gunther Schuller, Johnson transformed the ragtime style into jazz "by the infusion of the blues, by the introduction of a more swinging rhythmic conception, and, lastly, through the concept of improvisation." Johnson was particularly well-known for his stride composition "Carolina Shout," which was the litmus test for aspiring jazz pianists. Both Duke Ellington and Fats Waller memorized it by slowing down the piano roll. Johnson explained why the New York style, presumably including Gershwin's, was special:

> The other sections of the country never developed the piano as far as the New York boys did. . . . The people in New York were used to hearing good piano played in concerts and cafes. The ragtime player had to live up to that standard. They had to get orchestral effects, sound harmonies, chords and all the techniques of European concert pianists who were playing their music all over the city.[18]

Johnson also wrote some serious concert music that was not appreciated until decades later. His *Yamekraw: A Negro Rhapsody*, published in 1927, however, reflected the clear influence of Gershwin's *Rhapsody in Blue*.

Gershwin did come to know Fats Waller, a protégé of James P. Johnson, and urged him to study with Frances Gershwin's father-in-law, the renowned Leopold Godowsky. Waller's biographer, Ed Kirkeby, however, embellishes the myth that Gershwin went uptown "incessantly, making the rounds and drinking in all there was to be seen and heard. Gershwin wrote down the jazz forms that came at him . . . penetrating even the lowest of the low-down clubs. He invaded the rent-parties and socials and was often to be seen sitting on the floor, agape at the dazzling virtuosity and limitless improvisation that clamoured around him."[19]

This has to be an invention. It is inconceivable that Gershwin was ever "agape" at any one else's virtuosity (many years later, he marvelled at Art Tatum's dexterity, but he was not alone in admiring Tatum). It is equally inconceivable that Gershwin would write down what he heard; after all, he had one of the best ears for music and could remember note for note what he heard. Yet, the myth has persisted.

Moreover, it is very unlikely that Gershwin frequented black bars, night clubs, cafes, or rent-parties in Harlem prior to composing the *Rhapsody*. Neither Ira in his diaries, nor George in his reminisces mentioned going to Harlem bars in the 1920s. Gershwin did not begin to "frequent" Harlem until *after* 1925, sometimes in the company of the controversial writer, jazz enthusiast, and avid student of black culture, Carl Van Vechten. According to Van Vechten, Gershwin first heard Bessie Smith during one of Van Vechten's parties. If so, this had to be after mid-1925, because Bessie Smith had not attended a Van Vechten party before June 1925, when he wrote a letter to Langston Hughes saying she had promised him an evening soon. If Gershwin had not heard Bessie Smith before mid-1925, then he certainly was not frequenting Harlem jazz clubs.[20]

Gershwin's links to ragtime also obviously pre-dated his meetings with any of the Harlem stride pianists. Indeed, in the preface to his *Song-Book* (1932), Gershwin acknowledged his indebtedness to several ragtime pianists: "some of the effects I use in my transcriptions derive from their style of playing the piano." He mentioned pianists Mike Bernard, Les Copeland, Lucky Roberts, and Zez Confrey, as well as Arden and Ohman, who played in some Gershwin shows. He cites in particular some "stunts" such as the left-hand style of Copeland, "thumping" chords that slid into a regular chord, and Bernard's habit of playing the melody in the left hand while weaving a "filigree of counterpoint with the right." (Gershwin employs this style in the *Song-Book* version of "Somebody Loves Me.") While he mentioned the stride pianist Lucky Roberts, Johnson is notably missing from Gershwin's list. He credits only Confrey with a "permanent contribution," that made its way into "serious composition." Gershwin knew Confrey, and his piano rolls probably were a "potent influence" on Gershwin; they both appeared on the Paul Whiteman program that introduced *Rhapsody in Blue* when Confrey played his most famous novelty, "Kitten on the Keys."[21]

Of course, Gershwin was acquainted with black musicians other than the stride pianists. He knew the outstanding black arranger of the era, Will Vodery. After Gershwin left Remick's, he sought out Vodery for advice, describing him as a "good friend." It was Vodery, an orchestrator for the Ziegfeld *Follies*, who did the arrangements for Gershwin's mini-opera *Blue Monday*. Some years later Vodery recommended Duke Ellington's band for an onstage role in *Show Girl*, a 1927 musical with a Gershwin score. It is a safe assumption that Gershwin either concurred in, or himself recommended, hiring Ellington's band.

Some of Gershwin's primitive notions of what constituted jazz may be explained by his familiarity with the music of James Reese Europe's Clef Club Players performing at Barron's, a popular "black and tan" restaurant and night club. Gershwin made a point of mentioning that he heard Europe's music. Gershwin was probably influenced by Europe's style, which was basically a popularized version of ragtime. Gunther Schuller describes Europe as the most important transitional figure in the pre-history of jazz on the East Coast. His music was "relentlessly rhythmic." No doubt Gershwin—always conscious of rhythm—was impressed by Europe's rough "swing."

The same is true of his appreciation of Paul Whiteman's orchestra. An interesting comparison is Whiteman's recording of "Whispering" and Gershwin's piano roll of the same song in September 1919: their respective breaks and fill-ins show that Gershwin was much more advanced toward "jazz" than White-man's orchestrators (probably Ferde Grofé).

In 1924, when Gershwin wrote the *Rhapsody* and *Lady Be Good!*, he had moved from ragtime to something approaching jazz, both in his piano style and his appreciation of the sounds of a jazz band. The jazz authority, Martin Williams, wrote: "anyone who has heard Gershwin the pianist on a piece like his *'I Got Rhythm' Variations* knows that there is more jazz in him than we generally suppose."[22] The modern jazz pianist Dick Hyman wrote: "Gershwin certainly was playing jazz piano—however obsolete our ears perceived his style to have been."[23] Ample proof of Hyman's assertion can be found in Gershwin's piano rolls. His evolution is obvious: the piano roll of his own first song, "When You Want 'Em, You Can't Get 'Em," demonstrates the strong hold of ragtime on Gershwin in 1916. But three years later, in his rolls of three songs he wrote for the *Scandals*—"Idle Dreams," "On My Mind the Whole Night Long," and "Scandal Walk"—there are only faint echoes of ragtime, but the style of these recordings can only be described as jazz.

Gershwin's growing appreciation of "hot" music was evident by the late 1920s. Bix Beiderbecke and Frank Trumbauer had joined Whiteman by 1927 when Gershwin was still performing with Whiteman from time to time. The trumpet solo in the slow, second movement of Whiteman's recording of the Gershwin's piano concerto was played by Beiderbecke. In 1929, Gershwin secured the services of the jazz cornetist Red Nichols and his "Five Pennies" for a role in the second version of *Strike Up the Band*. In 1930, Gershwin repeated this endeavor, hiring Nichols to put together a jazz band for *Girl Crazy*. Nichols in turn hired Benny Goodman, Glenn Miller, and Charlie Teagarden (trumpet), and the drummer Gene Krupa, as well as other jazz musicians. It is believed that Gershwin used Glenn Miller to orchestrate the final "ride-out" chorus of "I Got Rhythm." Nichols' band also played a hot number during intermission.

The ultimate irony is that while Gershwin was dismissed by jazz critics, the actual performers adopted and adapted many of Gershwin's songs; "I Got Rhythm" was especially valued for its melody and harmonic structure.[24] The legendary Charlie Parker recorded "Embraceable You" in a version that is considered a jazz classic. The major jazz vocalists, Ella Fitzgerald, Billie Holiday, and Sarah Vaughan, all emphasized Gershwin's songs in their recorded works. Similarly, Miles Davis, supported by Gil Evans, recorded a collection from *Porgy and Bess*. These links to Gershwin's music guarantee that in one odd respect, at least, he will always be associated with jazz.

NOTES

1. Robert Kimball and Alfred Simon, *The Gershwins* (New York: Bonanza Books, 1963), p. 30.

2. William G. Hyland, *The Song Is Ended* (New York: Oxford University Press, 1995), p. 80.

3. George Gershwin, "The Relation of Jazz to American Life," included in *Gershwin in His Time: A Biographical Scrapbook, 1919–1937*, ed. Gregory R. Suriano (New York: Gramercy Books, 1998), p. 97.

4. In this determination to identify with America, he was vindicated long after his death. *The New Grove Dictionary of Music* (1980) concluded: "his music has had a wide impact on international audiences who have accepted it as the embodiment of musical Americana."

5. Deena Rosenberg, *Fascinating Rhythm* (New York: Dutton, 1991), p. 127. One authority, however, suggests that Gershwin's equating of folk music with jazz and jazz with genuine American music is too nationalistic; he argues that true American music is defined by its inclusivity and plurality. David Nicholls, "Defining American Music," *ISAM Newsletter*, Spring 1999.

6. Charles Hamm, "Toward a New Reading of Gershwin," included in *The Gershwin Style*, ed. Wayne Schneider (New York: Oxford University Press, 1999), p. 6.

7. Henry O. Osgood, *So This Is Jazz* (Boston: Little, Brown, 1926), p. 103.

8. Ibid.

9. Bell and Newman are quoted in Stanley Coben, *Rebellion against Victorianism* (New York: Oxford University Press, 1991), pp. 76–77.

10. Richard M. Sudhalter, *Lost Chords* (New York: Oxford University Press, 1999), p. 428.

11. Ann Douglas, *Terrible Honesty* (New York: Farrar, Straus and Giroux, 1995). She writes, "George Gershwin, Jewish composer and egocentric genius, had *sprung direct from black music*" (emphasis added). Picking up from Gershwin's biographers, she also wrote, "Gershwin could also be seen at Harlem parties and night spots, patently at ease," p. 102; C. Andre Barbera, "George Gershwin and Jazz," in Schneider, *The Gershwin Style*, p. 202.

12. Joan Peyser, *The Memory of All That* (New York: Simon and Schuster, 1993), pp. 35–36. Deena Rosenberg makes much the same point, that beginning in his "early teens" Gershwin sought out black pianists mainly in Harlem night spots, the others in midtown clubs or vaudeville theaters.

13. George Gershwin, "Our New National Anthem," *Theatre Magazine*, August 1925, included in Suriano, *Gershwin in His Time*, p. 27.

14. Gershwin's comments in the *New York Times*, September 25, 1932.

15. Blake is quoted in Peyser, *The Memory of All That*, pp. 41–42.

16. Tom Davin, "Conversations with James P. Johnson," p. 177, included in *Ragtime: Its History, Composers, and Music*, ed. John Edward Hasse (New York: Schirmer Books, 1985); Scott E. Pross and Robert Hilbert, *James P. Johnson* (Metuchen, NJ: Scarecrow Press, 1986), p. 112; Richard Hadlock, *Jazz Masters of the 20s* (New York: Macmillan Publishing, 1972; reprint, New York: Da Capo, 1988).

17. There is some confusion about Johnson's relationship to *Plantation Days*; the original music was written by another composer named Johnson, but when it toured in England, James P. seems to have been traveling with it. Davin, p. 177, "Conversation with James P. Johnson," in Hasse, *Ragtime*; Pross and Hilbert, *James P. Johnson*, p. 112.

18. Davin, "Conversations," p. 168; Ted Gioia, *The History of Jazz* (New York: Oxford University Press, 1999), p. 97.

19. W.T. Kirkeby, *Ain't Misbehavin': The Story of Fats Waller* (New York: Da Capo, 1996), p. 53.

20. Langston Hughes, *Remember Me to Harlem*, ed. Emily Bernard (New York: Alfred A. Knopf, 2001), p. 17.

21. Gershwin's references to other pianists appeared in his Introduction to *George Gershwin's Song-Book*, rev. ed. (New York: Simon and Schuster, 1941). An evaluation of Zez Confrey's influence is argued by Artis Wodehouse, "Time to Remember Zez Confrey," *ISAM Newsletter*, Fall 1998. Confrey published an instruction book on novelty techniques; some students of Confrey's work believe that Gershwin adopted some of his ideas from this book to include in *Rhapsody in Blue*; Ronald Riddle, "Novelty Piano Music," in Hasse, *Ragtime*, p. 286.

22. Martin Williams, *Jazz Heritage* (New York: Oxford University Press, 1985), p. 70. The various versions of "I Got Rhythm" are ample proof of Gershwin's ability to improvise. His piano solo versions of that song on radio shows in the 1930s, for example, are quite different from his earlier recordings.

23. Quoted in Sudhalter, *Lost Chords*, p. 429.

24. Professor Richard Crawford devotes a chapter to a survey of jazz versions of "I Got Rhythm" in his *The American Musical Landscape* (Berkeley: University of California Press, 1993), pp. 213–36. He notes eighty separate recordings between 1930 and 1942. There have been almost twenty versions by Charlie Parker, improvising around the harmony.

Chapter 6

Broadway

The Jazz Age officially began on January 16, 1920, when the Volstead Act, enforcing the Eighteenth Amendment to the Constitution, prohibiting interstate commerce in alcoholic beverages, went into effect. It was the beginning of what the historian Frederick Lewis Allen called a "revolution" in manners and morals. F. Scott Fitzgerald took credit for christening the era, but he dated it from May Day 1919. Indeed, he wrote a novelette entitled "May Day" that featured a segment about the "riots" in New York City, which in fact were little more than a brawl. It was the "general hysteria of that spring" of 1919 which "inaugurated the Age of Jazz," he wrote in the introduction to *May Day*, published in 1920. Scott and Zelda Fitzgerald led lives that personifed the Jazz Age. He wrote "America was going on the greatest gaudiest spree in history and there was going to be plenty to tell about it." Three months after the beginning of official prohibition Fitzgerald's daring first novel, *This Side of Paradise*, was published by Charles Scribner's.

Viewed from a musical perspective, one could argue that the Jazz Age began with the opening performance of the Original Dixieland Jasz [*sic*] Band on a cold winter's night at a restaurant on Columbus Circle in New York in January 1917. Another way of looking at it would be to date the era to the time when the red light district of Storyville in New Orleans (1917) was closed and black musicians left and began their trek up the Mississippi, winding up in Chicago.

But the era was much more than jazz music. The 1920s were a chaotic decade. There was a growing sense of disillusionment produced by the horrors of the Great War and the failure of the statesmen to produce a genuine peace at the Versailles Peace Conference. One writer in the *Atlantic Monthly* in 1920 complained that "the older generation had certainly pretty well ruined this world before passing it on to us. They gave us this thing knocked to pieces, leaky, red-hot, threatening to blow up; and then they are surprised that we don't accept it with the same attitude of pretty, decorous enthusiasm with which they received it, way back in the eighties."[1] Indeed, there was a pervasive cynicism, rebellion, and radicalism that infected almost every phase of life. There was a growing sense of fatalism that inevitably gave way to a gay abandon, to frivolity and fadism, and other means of escape—"a whole race going hedonistic, deciding on pleasure," wrote Fitzgerald. It was a prosperous time and a belief that the good times would continue indefinitely. Frederick Lewis Allen summed it up:

> [T]he country felt that it ought to be enjoying itself more than it was, and that life was futile and nothing mattered much. But in the meantime it might as well play—follow the crowd, take up the new toys that were amusing the crowd, go in for the new fads, savor the amusing scandals and trivialities of life. By 1921 the new toys and fads and scandals were forthcoming, and the country seized upon them feverishly.[2]

These attitudes were fueled by Prohibition. It was the culmination of a long-fought, perennial campaign against "demon rum." Prohibition, as it was usually called, passed into a federal law, even though it was widely predicted that it could not be enforced. And, indeed, it was not enforced. The flouting of the law created a subculture of manufacture of illegal liquor (bathtub gin), speakeasies, and gangsterism. The atmosphere of contempt for order encouraged extremism in dress, especially among women; loose pubic morals; vulgarization of language; but also a new literature and a new music.

There was also the darker side. There was the infamous Red Scare. There was the spectacle of the KKK's cross burnings. There were lynchings in the South and race riots in the north. Henry Ford discovered the conspiracy of "international Jewry." Sacco and Vanzetti were tried, found guilty, and executed. The rebellion of youth was matched by a growing rebellion of labor against management, culminating in the violent steel strike.

Not surprisingly, Broadway held a mirror to the frivolity of the Jazz Age. The most typical composer was not Gershwin, or Irving Berlin, but Vincent Youmans. He was semi-officially adopted by the Fitzgeralds, largely because of his song "Tea for Two." In Zelda's novel *Save Me the Last Waltz*, she wrote:

> Vincent Youmans wrote the [songs] for those twilights just after the war. They were wonderful. They hung above the city like an indigo wash, forming themselves from asphalt dust and sooty shadows under the cornices and limp gusts of air exhaled from closing windows. They lay above the streets like a white fog off a swamp. Through the gloom, the whole world went to tea.[3]

It was poetic justice that Youmans became one of the symbols of the Jazz Age, for he hated jazz music and especially hot versions of "Tea for Two."

Nevertheless, on Broadway the musical plots became zanier, capturing the increasing absurdity of society. Until the end of World War I the Broadway shows were dominated by operettas, mostly foreign imports, as well as the home-grown variety of Victor Herbert. There was also still the pseudo-vaudeville of George M. Cohan and Irving Berlin's *Music Box Revues*. But the new era was bound to create new trends on Broadway. The new type of show, inaugurated at the Princess Theater, binding together plot, music, and lyrics had not really caught on; they were out of step with the Jazz Age and even its composer, Jerome Kern, had moved on. His big hit of 1920 was *Sally*, introducing Ziegfeld's star Marilyn Miller. A far cry from the Princess, it was a Cinderella show that included one of Kern's most memorable, "Look for the Silver Lining." In contrast, Gershwin's *La, La, Lucille* was in itself a minor landmark, not because it was particularly good but because its songs seemed to herald a "jazzy" age ("Tee-Oodle-Um-Bum-Bo" and "Nobody But You").

George was an avowed admirer of Kern. (As noted, he claimed that Kern's songs overawed him and convinced him that the musical theater was his objective.) Although George was the rehearsal pianist for a Kern-Herbert show *Miss 1917*, his own first show was not another copy of the Princess series. *La, La, Lucille* was billed as a new "up-to-the minute Musical Comedy of Class and Distinction." Though produced in 1919, it was a precursor of the roaring twenties to come. "There was a hustle to *La, La, Lucille* that the Princess style missed." On the other hand, there was an innocence in the Princess style that *Lucille* missed. "But this was the 1920s; innocence was over."[4]

The season that the Gershwins collaborated for their first great success (*Lady Be Good!*) was the beginning of what would later be seen as the Golden Age of the American musical. Brilliant songwriters and clever lyricists began to take charge. Their scores were clearly superior to the hodgepodge that preceded the new era. First-rate teams emerged—especially Rodgers and Hart; Cole Porter finally returned to Broadway from France; Bert Kalmar and Harry Ruby scored important successes as did Vincent Youmans and Irving Caesar. The historian of the American musical theater, Gerald Bordman, characterized the most notable achievement as "the enthralling outpouring of magnificent melody," as well as the unique sophistication of the lyricists. Only the librettos were relatively uninspired, but were nevertheless marked by professional craftsmanship.[5]

This period, beginning with the 1924–25 season, lasted until the bubble burst on Wall Street. But over these five years the results were remarkable. First of all, the old operettas were by no means finished. The longest-running show was *Rose Marie* (Friml, Hammerstein, and Harbach), which made more money than any show until *Oklahoma!* In this same season came *The Student Prince* by Sigmund Romberg and Dorothy Donnelly, and in the following year *The Vagabond King*, again by Rudolf Friml. The revues were not to be outdone. For his *Music Box Revues*, Irving Berlin wrote "All Alone" and "Say It with Music" among other hits. Ziegfeld did not falter, propped up by Eddie Cantor, and from his grand new theater came one of the big successes of this era—*Rio Rita*.

It was the book musical that distinguished this era. Two shows were quite popular, *Good News* and *No, No, Nanette*. Both established hit songs that would echo for decades—"Tea for Two" from Youmans and Caesar and the "Best Things in Life Are Free," by Henderson, Brown, and De Sylva. Other shows were not so successful, but they yielded fine songs. Kalmar and Ruby scored with *The Ramblers* (1926), featuring "All Alone Monday" and then the *Five O'Clock Girl*, offering the beautiful "Thinking of You." Cole Porter established himself as a sophisticate with "Let's Do It" from *Paris*. Vincent Youmans returned with *Hit the Deck*, that contained some of his best—"Hallelujah" and "Sometimes I'm Happy."

But it was Rodgers and Hart that created a storm of hit shows and outstanding songs, beginning with the *Garrick Gaieties* in 1925; this was the show that introduced "Manhattan." Then came their first book show, *Dearest Enemy*, followed by *The Girl Friend*; the title song of this show came as close as any to becoming the theme song of the twenties; but there was also "Blue Room," which survived for decades. Not for several years did they falter with the bizarre *Chee-Chee*, a story about the grand eunuch of Peking, but before that there was *A Connecticut Yankee*, that captured "My Heart Stood Still" and "Thou Swell."

The Jazz Age especially dictated the settings for the new musicals. Gone were the days of exotic foreign locales and stories of princesses incognito (well, not quite considering *The Student Prince*). The new themes had to be quite contemporary—which meant frivolous—*Good News* and *No, No, Nanette*. The books for Gershwin shows picked up the new themes—society parties in the Hamptons (*Lady Be Good!*); Florida real estate confidence men (*Tip Toes*), and bootleggers (*Oh, Kay!*). The librettos were "not only ineffectual and silly but were expected to be." Thus Alan Dale, reviewing *Lady Be Good!*, wrote that the characters had been "jellied" into some sort of plot which eluded him, but he advised the audiences not to worry about the plots: "Let 'em go, I say. Why worry with plots." In a review of the Gershwin show *Tell Me More*, the critic wrote: "the Story isn't much but that doesn't matter."[6]

There had to be more room for the new dances. The dances too followed the spirit of innovation and radicalism (e.g., the Charleston, Black Bottom, and the Bunny Hug). In this sense the Gershwins were the musical incarnation of the Jazz Age, summed up by the title of their first showstopper from *Lady Be Good!*—"Fascinating Rhythm." It was this slightly offbeat, pulsating rhythm that caught the popular fancy. Never mind that Gershwin's best work included many dreamy love songs; after all, it was George Gershwin who said that a musical thrives on 2/4 rhythm as an army travels on its stomach. "Fascinating Rhythm" was indeed the big moment for the Astaires in *Lady Be Good!* For the British version George added a new novelty number for the Astaires, "I'd Rather Charleston." Irving Berlin seemed to sum it up best in his song "Everyone in the World is Doing the Charleston."

Much of the Jazz Age would have bypassed the rural areas of the country had it not been for the invention of the phonograph and radio. These mass media, along with movies, amplified all of the elements of gaiety. *Our Dancing Daughters* (1928) made a star of Joan Crawford dancing the Charleston to hot jazz bands, even though the movie was silent! Popular music began to spread. Chicago, Los Angeles, and New York could listen to the same phonograph recording by the bands of Paul Whiteman or Vincent Lopez. National radio broadcasting began in 1920 and expanded rapidly. There was music on the radio almost any night sponsored by various companies. Broadcast music had to feature colorful orchestras; their "color" had to substitute for in-person performances. On Sunday night one could hear the Chase and Sanborn Orchestra with pianists Arden and Ohman (direct from the pit of Gershwin musicals), or the Old Gold orchestra led by Paul Whiteman. On Saturdays New York's WEAF featured the General Electric Symphony led by Walter Damrosch.

By the late 1920s, a trip to Harlem to Connie's Inn or Small's Paradise might take in Bessie Smith or Louis Armstrong, or of course Duke Ellington at the legendary Cotton Club, where Harold Arlen was writing the music for the elaborate revues. Hot jazz was recorded, but the songs that became quickly and truly popular throughout the entire country were light and airy if not a little silly as dictated by the era. Thus, "Kiss Me Again" and "After the Ball" gave way to the obviously unsentimental "Ain't She Sweet" or "Baby Face" or "Yes Sir! That's My Baby." For the college crowd there was "Betty Coed" and "Collegiate." Perhaps it all was summed up by "Runnin' Wild." A big favorite was "Yes, We Have No Bananas," extracted from the punch line of a vaudeville routine. At the top of the list of best-selling Victor records for the decade was "The Prisoner's Song." Irving Berlin's "Blue Skies" only placed eighth, and neither Gershwin nor Kern were in the top ten. George Gershwin commented that songs died when they were sung and played too much in the era of the phonograph and radio, but he was wrong.

What the public heard from the leading songwriters, including the Gershwins, was often filtered through the popular styles of dance orchestras. Paul Whiteman was probably the best known. Then came the inevitable imitations all playing the popular "hits" most often at ballrooms or the large hotels. The "sweet" bands in particular tended to reduce every song to the same dance tempo, and despite a few gimmicks the sound of the orchestras was becoming more or less standard.[7] These popular versions were on the whole faster in tempo; even the love songs bounced along. Whiteman's arrangements by Ferde Grofé and Bill Challis tilted toward jazz, especially in allowing a spot for individual soloists.

This was the musical atmosphere in which the Gershwin brothers became a major force in American popular music. A dozen new musicals flowed from their fertile talents, featuring over two hundred songs, ranging from such lovely ballads as "Someone to Watch Over Me" to the "hot" tunes such as "I Got Rhythm."

The spark for the Gershwins was the fact that they were working together; they had collaborated on individual songs and the unfortunate *A Dangerous Maid*, but in 1924, for the first time in their careers they were working together on an entire score for a Broadway show. Indeed, it is the music and lyrics, not the librettos from this period that have survived so well. The scripts were witty enough and entertaining but easy to forget. The plots were usually too topical, as were the themes, jokes, puns, and punch lines. They had no special value, social significance, or messages.

Indeed, Guy Bolton, the outstanding librettist of this era, would have been appalled by the suggestion that he try to give his plots a serious turn. This was, after all, musical comedy. George Gershwin once wrote that good music could not rescue a bad play. But if the music was by George Gershwin, it was easy to overlook the weaknesses of the plot and characters. In the end, even with an acceptable book, it would be the words and music that would decide whether a good musical would endure.

Guy Bolton still had the good business sense to write scenarios that allowed ample room for star turns. And the Gershwins' producers were fortunate enough to enlist genuine stage attractions; indeed, it is difficult to think of a more impressive roster: the Astaires for two shows, Gertrude Lawrence twice, Marilyn Miller for one Ziegfeld show, and Ethel Merman and Ginger Rogers in the same show. Stars of this caliber could sustain a weak production, provided they had material that they could exploit to perform their specialties, and that is what the Gershwins gave them. The Gershwins were not immune from interventions by specialty entertainers like Ukelele Ike (Cliff Edwards) in *Lady Be Good!*; he not only introduced "Fascinating Rhythm" on his ukelele but had a solo spot, for which the Gershwins wrote "Little Jazz Bird" and "Singin' Pete," but "Ike" sometimes interpolated other songs of his choosing.

The collaboration of George and Ira enhanced the talents of both. Until then, when working separately, neither was particularly brilliant. The bulk of Gershwin's popular music before 1924 was not nearly as inspired as his later work with his brother. One reason, of course, was their proximity. As adults they either lived together or close by, even after Ira was married. George liked to work at odd hours, and Ira was always available. Ira, in turn, liked to work among familiar surroundings, with his books and reference materials. So it was an ideal match.

The perennial question: Which came first, the words or the music? is easily answered in the case of the Gershwins. It was George's music. This was true of many composers like Jerome Kern, Richard Rodgers, and Vincent Youmans. Cole Porter and Irving Berlin wrote their own lyrics. In effect, the composer was always composing. Almost all melody writers kept tune books in which they would set down ideas, sometimes complete melodies.[8] Even the Russian classical composer Sergei Prokofiev kept song books, with different-colored covers to distinguish categories of ideas.

These song books, or "trunk" songs, as they were often called, make it difficult to trace the evolution of a songwriter's art. A great song might have been several years old before it publicly surfaced. An unused song from one production was apt to reappear in a new show, albeit usually in a different guise.

"Embraceable You" was dropped from an abortive Ziegfeld show, *East Is West*, which was to have had a Chinese motif. The show never opened, but "Embraceable You" reemerged eighteen months later in another show about the wild west (*Girl Crazy*).

The best-known Gershwin example of a song's metamorphosis is "The Man I Love." It began as a verse to another song, which was never completed. Ira liked it and suggested changing it to a refrain. He wrote the words for it, and it was put into *Lady Be Good!* But shortly before the Broadway opening, it was dropped because a more lively song was needed. It was too late to call off the publication of the sheet music, however. So the song began to be played, especially in England, where it became a favorite of dance bands. It was revived for *Strike Up the Band*, but again, inexplicably, it was dropped; by then it was becoming popular. In the end it was one of the most durable of all Gershwin songs, yet it was never produced on Broadway.

The Gershwin tune books and some unpublished manuscripts also indicate that he saved some parts—say a verse or a release from a song—and used them in an entirely different song. "Wait A Bit, Susie" from *Primrose* became "Beautiful Gypsy" in *Rosalie* four years later, but it was dropped and replaced by "Say So," which was recycled music from *Funny Face* the preceding year.

Until the mid- to late 1920s, the lyrics were as simple as much of the music. Highly repetitive musical refrains called for repetitive lyrics, such as "yes sir, that's my baby." Gradually, however, this approach was broken, first by Ira Gershwin and then by Lorenz Hart, and to a different degree by Oscar Hammerstein and Jerome Kern, and finally and most definitively, by Cole Porter.[9] Composers might pay little attention to the libretto, but they were usually sensitive to lyrics. Ira Gershwin related several long, friendly arguments he had with his brother over one word or even one syllable.

Ira Gershwin was one of the most skilled craftsmen in modern popular music. In the 1920s he easily fitted into the Jazz Age, offering clever lyrics that adopted the tone of the era. "The Babbitt and the Bromide" skewered the jaded upper classes, while "These Charming People" parodied the sophisticated rich. Even as late as 1930, one of his heroines out west (*Girl Crazy*) dismissed her eastern suitor, telling him to go back to "flappers" and "high-ball lappers."

He demonstrated his skills by writing spectacularly with a variety of artists who had quite different styles such as Vincent Youmans and Vernon Duke ("I Can't Get Started") while George was still alive, and after his death with Jerome Kern ("Long Ago and Far Away"), Harold Arlen ("The Man that Got Away"), and Kurt Weill ("Jenny"). He described his craft thus: "Since most of the lyrics . . . were arrived at by fitting words mosaically to music already composed, any resemblance to actual poetry, living or dead is highly improbable."[10] He was of course much too modest.

The music and lyrics had to be brought together with the libretto and put in some order. On Broadway, as opposed to films, the libretto was usually finished before the songwriters attacked the project, but not always. Even so, usually a dozen or so songs were written and many then discarded. Perhaps nine or ten songs would survive to the opening in New York, and even after the show opened substitutions were made.

The Broadway shows gradually assumed a standard format: two acts and several scenes. The first act was the key. The major songs had to be introduced during this act so that they could be and usually were reprised, sometimes in both the first and second acts. The show would usually open with a fast-paced dance number—the so-called ice-breaker—employing all of the chorus but also introducing the principals early in the scene. Rarely were these memorable moments. The first love song would have to emerge soon enough so that it might be repeated in the first act. In *Lady Be Good!* the first love song was "So Am I."

The star performers were of course important to any musical. A new generation of stars was emerging. The Astaires were an obvious example. If the show had major dancers like the Astaires the task was easy: "Fascinating Rhythm" was their vehicle in *Lady Be Good!*, and it quickly became the highlight. Their appearance on Broadway was always enthusiastically anticipated. The stars could influence the production. Once they were involved, new numbers might be constructed around them.

In 1924 the Astaires were eager to return to Broadway. Two years earlier they had starred in a musical produced by Alex Aarons, *For Goodness Sake*. The score was by George's new friend Bill Daly, but included three Gershwin songs with lyrics by Ira, still writing under his paper-thin pseudonym Arthur Francis. One song, "Tra-La-La," faded away; but this light number written for Fred Astaire was revived by another great dancer, Gene Kelly, in the movie *An American in Paris*, some thirty years later. *For Goodness Sake* was a success, mainly because of the Astaires. Reviewer Robert Benchley wrote that when the Astaires danced everything seemed brighter. For this show the Astaires introduced their famous runaround; it started as a leisurely shoulder-to-shoulder walk in a circle, then increased to a trot and finally a fast runaround and a flying exit. It was the running exit that Fred believed caught the audience. After a show that failed, the Astaires traveled to London with *For Goodness Sake* (renamed *Stop Flirting*), where it finally settled in for a major success (May 1923). Suddenly, the Astaires were the toast of the social set. The Prince of Wales attended several performances.

After basking in this glamorous setting for almost two years, Alex Aarons approached them with the opportunity to return to Broadway in a new show with an entire score by the Gershwins. They eagerly agreed even though no one liked the tentative title *Black-Eyed Susan*. The title was derived from Adele Astaire's character, Susan Trevor, sister of Dick Trevor, played by Fred Astaire of course. They were supposed to be two young people of social prominence but down on their luck, which they hoped to retrieve by profitable marriages. No one ever doubted that in fact true love would break through before the

11:00 P.M. curtain. The show's name was changed to *Lady Be Good!* after the producers heard the Gershwin song of that name.

While Alex Aarons was in London getting ready for *Lady Be Good!*, George was also in London involved in a British show called *Primrose*. The previous year he had gone to London for *The Rainbow Revue*, or simply *The Rainbow* (April 3, 1923) which Gershwin thought was his weakest score. He was under great pressure to write his score, and an obnoxious producer kept badgering him to write "hits." No hits emerged except "Innocent Lonesome Baby," which was in fact simply taken over from *Our Nell*. *Rainbow* ran for 113 performances, not all that bad. Nevertheless, when offered a new British show Gershwin leaped at the chance to redeem himself.

The new show was scheduled for the Wintergarden Theater, which usually featured a show by Jerome Kern. Although Kern was occupied, the producers, George Grossmith and J.A.E. Malone, still preferred an American composer, and George's triumph in Whiteman's Aeolian concert made him their choice. For the book the producers turned once again to their standby, Kern's old colleague Guy Bolton. But the usual lyricist, P.G. Wodehouse, was not available, so they recruited a new British lyric writer, Desmond Carter. Although he did not go to London with George, Ira collaborated on some of the lyrics with Carter. It appears from Ira's lyrics that the score was partly written in New York. Some of George's music was also reworked from earlier shows. One fine song, "Boy Wanted," was transferred from *A Dangerous Maid* and "Some Far-Away Someone" was originally introduced in *Niftes of 1923*.

Primrose was an unusual opportunity for Gershwin. The Wintergarden shows were major events, and for this show there were some outstanding British performers available—the comedians Leslie Henson and Heather Thatcher and a prominent leading man, Percy Hemming. Originally the cast was to include the well-known producer George Grossmith, but Gershwin objected to the fact that he could not sing.

The plot was about Hillary Vane (Percy Hemming), a novelist who falls in love with a young lady who reminds him of one of the characters in his novels named Primrose. Hillary's friend is Toby Mopham (Leslie Henson), who finds himself in an embarrassing fix with another young lady (Heather Thatcher). Toby uses Hillary to extricate himself, but Hillary manages to make his own girlfriend jealous, and she in turn retaliates and makes Hillary jealous by flirting with another man. Of course, after the usual mix-ups all ends well: "It was all quite perfect for the Winter Garden, bright, light and modern . . . and Gershwin's music fitted the mood of the piece nicely," wrote one reviewer. George was captivated by the chance to write in the spirit of a Gilbert and Sullivan show. Accordingly, his music took on a decidedly British aura ("Wasn't It Terrible What They Did to Mary, Queen of Scots," as well as "That New Fangled Mother of Mine"). He wrote home that after writing one song, "Berkeley Square and Kew," the producers told him that they had not heard such a British song since the famous Paul Ruebens. Not quite as British were "Wait a Bit, Susie," the most popular song according to the reviews, and the sprightly duet "Naughty Baby." The *London Times* summed up: "Gershwin's music is always tuneful."[11] The show never made it to New York, as Gershwin had hoped; his music was a passable British score, including a ballet; light and pleasant, though not much more. Most of the orchestrations were by others, but three songs including "Naughty Baby" were orchestrated by George—a fact not discovered for many years.[12] *Primrose* opened to good notices in September 1924. It enjoyed a reasonable run of the season for seven months, to be replaced by another Gershwin show from Broadway, *Tell Me More.* He was becoming a fixture in the West End. His reputation in London was made, and he remained an Anglophile for the rest of his days. He repaid his debt to the city a decade later when he celebrated London and its fog in one of his finest songs.

In London George shared the "cheeriest flat" overlooking the Devonshire Gardens with Alex Aarons and his wife. Gershwin was beginning to live the good life of the roaring twenties: watching a tennis match at Wimbledon, playing a round of golf with Guy Bolton, dining with wealthy Americans from New York who were visiting London, and circulating in London society with Lord Berners, Prince George, Otto Kahn, and the Earl of Latham among others. When he sailed for home on the *Majestic*, Otto Kahn, the Wall Street mogul and patron of music was on board. He made a practice of not investing in Broadway shows, but during the voyage George played "The Man I Love," which was then intended for the Astaire show. Kahn offered $10,000 on the spot (he made money on the show), but the song was cut.

For his new show Alex Aarons wanted to recreate the ambience of the old Princess Theater shows. After closing the deal with the Astaires, Aarons recruited the author of the Princess series, Guy Bolton, but his cohort P.G. Wodehouse begged off because he assumed that the lyrics would be written by Ira. (Later Ira and Wodehouse became close friends.) Bolton was a new partner for the Gershwins, but the Astaires had known them for several years. Astaire was fond of recalling that he first met Gershwin at Remick's, when Fred and his sister Adele were still in vaudeville. Astaire remembered that George mused that it would be great if he would write a hit musical and they would star in it. Their working relationship became close enough that during rehearsals Gershwin suggested a dance step to the Astaires, which they adopted to Gershwin's immense satisfaction. He was inordinately proud of his dancing, and showed off for his sister Frances, who admitted that he was quite graceful.

During the out-of-town tryouts in Philadelphia, Ira Gershwin wrote to friends that *Lady Be Good!* needed a "lot of fixing," that the first act was too slow, but nevertheless Ira thought that it would run for a few months on Broadway. The show was much too long; the Gershwins wrote over twenty numbers but only half survived. The show was surrounded by considerable turmoil, mainly in trying to tie the music and dancing into a flimsy plot. For example, "The Man I Love" was intended to open the show as a sort of prologue, but was moved to the second act during the Philadelphia tryouts (the verse was different from the verse eventually published). The song lasted long enough to be incorporated into early drafts of the overture and was mentioned in the Philadelphia reviews, indicating that it was not cut until the show reached New York, perhaps reflecting Ira's comment that the first act was too slow. Then "The Man I Love" was scrapped altogether.

Everyone thought that the major love song would be "So Am I"; it replaced a song entitled "Will You Remember Me?", which was not used at all. "So Am I" was a good, though repetitive melody, a "very cute number," commented Ira Gershwin. The song that endured was "Oh, Lady Be Good!", but it was assigned to the comic character played by Walter Catlett; it was also moved about.

The opening chorus written for the second act was dropped. At one point the second act opened with "Half of It, Dearie, Blues," but it too was moved. Several different orchestrators were involved; Robert Russell Bennett called it a Sears and Roebuck score. In addition to Bennett, there were Paul Lanin, Charles P. Grant and S.P. Jones, and Max Steiner (of later Hollywood fame). Bill Daly wrote an overture that was not used. In the end the show was closer to a revue than a book musical. All of this probably accounts for Ira's complaint that the show needed a lot of fixing, but he was too pessimistic.

Featuring Fred and Adele Astaire paid off. The dancing of the Astaires was the centerpiece, and the show was built around their specialties. In Philadelphia the reception was enthusiastic: "smart, classy, clean and entertaining," the show "seems to be headed for a long run in New York." Gershwin's score was applauded as the most original and tuneful heard in Philadelphia in years. As predicted in Philadelphia, the show went on to become a major hit (December 1, 1924). It was widely heralded as the first truly Jazz Age musical. The *New York Times* review was ecstatic over Adele: "as charming and entertaining a musical comedy actress as the town had seen on display in many a moon." George shared in the praise: "George Gershwin's score is excellent. It contains as might have been expected, many happy hints for wise orchestra leaders of the dancing Winter that lies ahead and a number of tunes that the unmusical and serious-minded will find hard to get rid of." The other reviewers concurred.

Lady Be Good! was an interesting commentary on George's abilities; for weeks he had been immersed in a Gilbert and Sullivan atmosphere in the London show *Primrose*. Shortly after he plunged into *Lady Be Good!*, which was almost the complete opposite. While in London George was writing about the very British "Berkeley Square and Kew," but he also found time to compose eight bars of "Fascinating Rhythm." Its original title was "Syncopated City" which was the title written on George's early drafts, but then crossed out. He brought it back from London for Ira to wrestle with devising a lyric for this intricate rhythm.

There were four songs that clinched the title of the typical Jazz Age musical: the opening duet "Hang on to Me" set the tone, and the high point was "Fascinating Rhythm," which was woven into other numbers. The "Little Jazz Bird" was dependent on the whim of Cliff Edwards, but it too captured the spirit of the era; and finally, "Half of It, Dearie, Blues" dispelled any doubt that this was a product of the Jazz Age.

When the curtain rises, Fred and Adele (Dick and Susie) are on the street having been evicted from their apartment. They try to convince themselves (in song) that it might be fun to set up their furniture on the sidewalk ("Hang on to Me"). It begins to rain, and they sprout umbrellas and go into their dance. It is a highly syncopated song that repeats the same musical pattern in the refrain and the bridge. It is close to the Tin Pan Alley formula, but in the first cadence George even throws in a blue note that reinforces the "jazz" character of the melody (but it was, in fact, written earlier, in December 1922).

The Trevors then proceed to a party—"A Wonderful Party" sung by the ensemble. In this melody Gershwin still seems to have been under the lingering influence of his British experience. The secondary leads, Daisy and Bertie, appear at the party and sing to explain their presence, since they are feuding ("We're Here"). This is another lively and syncopated melody with a British music hall flavor. Unexpectedly, Dick's engagement to a socialite, Jo, is announced by her, provoking an argument with Susie. Their argument is interrupted by Jeff, who is played by Cliff Edwards (popularly known as Ukulele Ike), who introduces "Fascinating Rhythm," which is taken over by Fred and Adele who sing a chorus and then launch into what George Gershwin called a "miraculous dance." The orchestration featured the piano duo of Arden and Ohman in the pit. Of this particular moment, the *New York Herald Tribune* review concluded:

> When at 9:15 they sang and danced "Fascinating Rhythm" the callous Broadwayites cheered them as if their favorite halfback had planted the ball behind the goal posts after an 80-yard run. Seldom has it been our pleasure to witness such a heartfelt, spontaneous and so deserved a tribute.[13]

Ira's lyrics were scintillating and clever, laced with current slang. "Half of It, Dearie, Blues," now little known, was a good example of the Gershwin style. It is only sixteen bars, and the first four bars were repeated three times with only a four-bar bridge. Yet by sustaining one note in the third and fourth bars for a full seven counts, Gershwin provided space for the pianist, other instrumentalists, or tap dancers to improvise; this became Fred Astaire's very first tap dance solo. In his version George Gershwin interpolated a phrase from *Rhapsody in Blue* in the breaks.

The plot thickens. Susie falls in love with a young man who appears to be a hobo ("So Am I"), but he is in fact the wealthy Jack Robinson. Walter Catlett, playing a shady lawyer, Watty Watkins, persuades Adele to impersonate Jack Robinson's wife, a Mexican dancer in order to claim Jack Robinson's large inheritance. The so-called wife cannot appear because she is doing five years in "canto, canto," which Catlett explains is Mexican for Sing-Sing. His song "Oh,

Lady Be Good!" thus is not a love song, but a plea for Adele to join his nefarious scheme. She finally agrees and is forced to imitate a Mexican dancer in "Juanita." Jack, the hobo, then reveals his true identity, and sings a clever version of "Oh, wife be good, to me." She and Watty are exposed and arrested, but saved by Jack. Dick returns to his true love, who's miffed by his previous announcement of his engagement to Jo; she warns him she may get married ("Half of It, Dearie, Blues"). Of course they reconcile as do Dick and Susie. The entire company assembles for a rousing finale, a menage of most of the songs, beginning with "Oh, Lady Be Good!", now finally a love song.

Eventually, the Astaires and their show traveled to London, turning the British production of *Lady Be Good!* into another sensation. The London production had to be adjusted for British audiences. For example, London audiences were notorious for arriving late. The producers therefore put in a "prologue" ("Buy a Little Button") so that the Astaires would make their entrance later, rather than in the original opening scene. An old song, "Something about Love," from *Lady in Red* was revived, and a new song, "I'd Rather Charleston," was written with lyrics by Desmond Carter. It gave the Astaires another chance to dance, and of course solidified the idea that this was a true Jazz Age musical even in distant London.

British shows traditionally went out of town for an extended period, playing in outlying provinces before finally settling in London. Rodgers and Hart were driven to distraction by the long delays while their show *Lido Lady* ambled around the countryside for weeks. They finally threw up their hands and left. American shows opened "cold" compared to this leisurely practice. (*Lady Be Good!* played for two weeks in Liverpool.) Even rehearsals in London were different; they were permitted only in the daytime. Sunday rehearsals were allowed only in an emergency, and then only if the cast agreed. In any case, the Astaires were acclaimed in London, but Gershwin did not fare quite as well. The august *London Times* described Gershwin's score as "ugly and cacophonous [as] jazz can be." Jazz, however defined, was not all that well received in Britain. The noted writer Arnold Bennett, commenting on dance bands, said that they played bad music well, and Aldous Huxley added that modern popular music was more barbarous than any folk art had been for many years.

Nevertheless, the title song, "Oh, Lady Be Good!", gradually became a standard. In the 1940s the song was appropriated for a movie. Only the title and a few songs remained, and a new plot was invented for Robert Young and Ann Sothern, who played the roles of songwriters. Of course, they composed "Oh, Lady Be Good!" on the screen in about two minutes. A high point was Eleanor Powell's dance to an elaborate version of "Fascinating Rhythm." In that movie, a new Jerome Kern/Oscar Hammerstein song, "The Last Time I Saw Paris," was interpolated and won an academy award, although it was not composed for that film.[14]

Fifty years after the Broadway opening, a revival by the Goodspeed Opera House in East Haddam, Connecticut in 1974 evoked everyone's fantasy of Jazz

Age style—of haughty naughty flappers and their debonair beaus all madly
kicking. The plot was "thin" but rescued by a "grand" Gershwin score (adding
"Somebody Loves Me" and "The Man I Love" probably helped). It was revived
again in 1987, again by the Goodspeed Opera House and benefitted from the
discovery of the cache of Gershwin's original orchestrations. But it was marred
by a too-faithful restoration of the original plot. Of course, any revival of an
original dance musical that starred the Astaires was hazardous. The *New York
Times* reviewer Frank Rich found the plot "little more than a giddy period
piece," but he added, it "succeeds in creating a delightfully engrossing dream
of Jazz Age pleasure."

While basking in their new glory, the Gershwins quickly turned to their next
project, also produced by Aarons: *Tell Me More*. Songwriters had limited control
over their choice of shows. The Gershwins were more or less indifferent to the
books for their shows, according to Edward Jablonski. Once tied into a producer,
in the Gershwins' case Alex Aarons, they were likely to remain with that producer for several shows. Major stars like Marilyn Miller might move from Ziegfeld to Dillingham and back, but they were the exception. There were no
guarantees: Often one show would be a tremendous hit, only to be followed by
a moderate success or even a failure by the same team.

Tell Me More began life entitled *My Fair Lady* [*sic*]! Years later Ira would
tease Alan Jay Lerner that the Gershwins had thought of it first. The title was
changed to *Tell Me More*, apparently because the producers, once again, liked
the Gershwins' new song by that name. This show too was a romantic comedy.
Aarons had hoped that *Lady Be Good!* would pick up the tradition of the old
Princess shows, but it veered into a Jazz Age revue. Now Aarons returned to
his original plan. *Tell Me More* was described as the Princess show that Kern
never wrote. Given the intentionally modest plot, the Gershwins responded with
a restrained score. Indeed, the show was the most unlikely of Jazz Age musicals.
It relied on charm, modesty, and an impish sense of humor.[15]

The story involved the complicated interaction of three separate couples. Kenneth (Alexander Gray) is a member of high society; at a masquerade ball he
spies Peggy from afar and falls in love with her when they meet accidentally
("Tell Me More"). She is a working girl in a fashionable Fifth Avenue millinery
shop (Peggy was played by a relative newcomer Phyllis Cleveland). In fact she
too belongs to a "good" family. Kenneth shows up at Peggy's shop, accompanied by his sidekick Billy (played by the comic Andrew Tombes), who becomes
involved with Peggy's co-worker Bonnie, played by the dancer Emma Haig. It
turns out that Billy is in fact Peggy's estranged brother, but she does not know
this. Monty (played by the Yiddish comic Lou Holtz, whom the Gershwins knew
from the *Scandals*), had been involved for sometime secretly with Jane, a
wealthy heiress, who is a friend of Peggy. He proposes and she accepts; they
sing "Why Do I Love You." All three couples wind up at a resort—Viewport.
Before leaving Kenneth promises Peggy when he returns they will wed; his love
is expressed in "Three Times a Day." Peggy decides to accompany Jane to

Viewport, where Monty will pose as her brother. The cast assembles to celebrate in the finale of the first act by singing and dancing "Kickin' the Clouds Away" followed by a medley of the songs, similar to the finale of *Lady Be Good!*

Of course, everything is finally worked out. Even without the Astaires the show had its share of lively dancing directed by one of Broadway's rising stars, choreographer Sammy Lee. He was a veteran of the Earl Carroll *Vanities*, and had joined the Gershwins for *Sweet Little Devil* and then guided the Astaires in *Lady Be Good!* All-in-all an impressive line-up: "in a word, an inspiring show," with the same "whirl wind pace" as *Lady Be Good!*, wrote the critic Alan Dale. George's score was praised, even as an improvement over *Lady Be Good!*: "Gershwin's music in 'Tell Me More' is, I think more consistently beautiful than in 'Lady Be Good!'," wrote one reviewer. Alexander Woollcott disagreed: the new Gershwin score seemed to him "less eventful and distinguished" than the one he wrote for *Lady Be Good!*, but "nevertheless it is gay." Another review concluded that there were three or four "admirably harmonized numbers." Other reviewers thought well of the score. "Its music by George Gershwin IS music. It isn't treacle, sugar and those awful airs that elevator boys blow into your tympanum on the way to your office" (Alan Dale). Unlike most shows in the 1920s, the show opened with a romantic ballad "Tell Me More." This song was a pleasant slower melody, not like Gershwin songs of that era (and very, very similar to another song by Burton Lane and Frank Loesser called "Fall In Love," written in 1938!). It is based on a three-note phrase, repeated over and over but cleverly manipulated by George. It has no intervening bridge or middle section, but adds an eight-bar phrase, leading to the final cadence. The harmony is traditional but well-suited to the smooth melody.

This musical also had some famous titles: "Why Do I Love You?" was described by a reviewer as one of the "prettiest" melodies George Gershwin ever composed; "My Fair Lady" also stands up well. "Baby!" was a sharper rhythm song, a melody that had been recycled several times. "In Sardinia," a comic number sung by Lou Holtz, was sharply attacked by one reviewer. The melody that enjoyed some popularity was "Three Times a Day," a smooth love song, but the most popular song was the very lively "Kickin' the Clouds Away," described as Mr. Gershwin's inimitable piece of jazz, in which the ensemble went "daffy."[16]

The *Times* review called it, a first-class Gershwin score, adequate comedy, intelligent lyrics, an appealing heroine, and fast and furious dancing by a personable chorus. Yet, it did not do well. It was overshadowed by *Lady Be Good!* which was still running when *Tell Me More* opened. Despite some good reviews, the show only ran for one hundred performances. It was criticized mainly for its lack of "individuality," apparently meaning that it did not differ from many other shows. For some reason, *Tell Me More* did better in London than in New York—perhaps because the British cast starred Leslie Henson and Heather Thatcher.

Before *Tell Me More* closed, there came the announcement (May 12, 1925) that George Gershwin would write a new concerto for the New York Symphony Society. Woollcott noted that George was sailing for Europe to perform the *Rhapsody* in London, where the London Symphony would have to borrow some "heathenish instruments" from the Savoy Jazz Band.

Gershwin was still smarting under the criticism that the *Rhapsody* was a "happy accident." Gershwin told Isaac Goldberg that he went out, for one thing, to show them that there was plenty more where that had come from. "I made up my mind to do a piece of absolute music." This led to his next milestone, the *Concerto in F*.

In the wake of the success of the *Rhapsody*, Walter Damrosch decided to commission another, longer Gerswhin work for the New York Philharmonic— this time it was to be a traditional piano concerto. Damrosch said, after George died, that Gershwin's Broadway productions showed such originality both of melodic invention and harmonic progressions that he had in him the possibility of development on more serious lines. Later Damrosch confessed that he did indeed try to "wean" George from Broadway. A little more than a year after the *Rhapsody* Gershwin signed a contract on April 17, 1925, looking toward a performance by December. Compared to the highly intensive schedule for the *Rhapsody*, Gershwin allowed himself roughly seven months for his concerto. He later claimed he had to buy some books to find out just what a concerto really was. This was of course "tongue-in-cheek." He had analyzed concertos with Kilenyi, and had heard concertos in the concerts he attended over the years. First he made a crude list of the pattern the concerto would follow: (1) rhythm; (2) melody blues; (3) more rhythm. He also wrote down the development of the first movement: charleston, first theme, effects for piano, effects for brass, double charleston. His first title was *New York Concerto*.

Gershwin accomplished one thing that was extraordinary. After the *Rhapsody* he taught himself orchestration—at least to the extent that he had not already mastered it.[17] He would orchestrate all of his subsequent concert works. Twenty years later, Ira Gershwin called the piano concerto the bravest thing George ever did, not only because he wrote in an unfamiliar form but he also orchestrated it. Besieged by the various demands on his time and energy, that summer he retreated to the Chautauqua Institute where his friend, the eminent piano teacher Ernest Hutcheson, held a summer camp for aspiring piano students. Gershwin had already started work during a visit to London. By July he had completed the composition, but he was sidetracked by work on his next musical, *Tip Toes*. He did not begin the orchestration until October and completed it on November 10.

Beforehand, Olin Downes wrote that the concerto would be a test for Gershwin: to see how far he had progressed in the art of composition and to determine the availability of jazz as "symphonic material." At first Gershwin made a "trial" orchestration of the opening movement, apparently as requested by Damrosch. This draft contains some minor revisions in various hands, perhaps by Damrosch or Bill Daly.[18] Later Gershwin hired a large orchestra conducted by Bill Daly to play the score: "You can imagine my delight when it sounded just as I had planned." He subsequently said that it was not the actual performance that was his greatest thrill, but hearing this performance, listening to his orchestration for the first time. A leading authority on the orchestration summed it up: "These (including *An American in Paris*) are great orchestrations, and they are all unaided Gershwin."[19]

Nevertheless, he was apprehensive, much more so than before the *Rhapsody*. Olin Downes had raised the question of whether "dance rhythms" could be translated into three movements of a concerto, and whether Gershwin had the technical ability to do it. In an effort to anticipate and to counter criticism, Gershwin provided his own analytical description of the concerto:

> The first movement employs the Charleston rhythm. It is quick and pulsating, *representing the young enthusiastic spirit of American life* (emphasis added). It begins with a rhythmic motif given out by the kettle drums, supported by other percussion instruments, and with a Charleston motif introduced by bassoons, horns, clarinets, and violins. The principal theme is announced by the bassoon. Later a second theme is introduced by the piano.
>
> The second movement has a poetic, nocturnal tone. It utilizes the atmosphere of what has come to be referred to as the American blues, but in a purer form than that in which they are usually treated.
>
> The final movement reverts to the style of the first. It is an orgy of rhythm starting violently and keeping to the same pace throughout.[20]

In advance of the concerto's premiere, he provided a defense that played down his concert work on the one hand, but stressed his innovations at the same time:

> I have only written three opuses so far [the *Rhapsody*, *Blue Monday* and the Concerto] . . . they are not my regular work. They are experiments— laboratory work in American music. I tell you that it requires real bravery to write works like those and know that one is breaking rules and set forms that much adverse comment will probably be aroused.[21]

The *Concerto in F* had its premiere on December 3, 1926, at Carnegie Hall. Shortly before, Gershwin told *Washington Times* news reporters during the try-outs for *Tip Toes*: "You know, we can't follow the old forms in music and call them an expression of America. You've got to feel the tempo of our life, the animation, the zest of New York" (which explains why he originally thought of naming it the *New York Concerto*).

Damrosch was enthusiastic, musing about the transformation of Lady Jazz. He said that while other composers had been walking around jazz "like a cat around a plate of hot soup," it was George Gershwin who accomplished the miracle. "He has done it boldly by dressing this extremely independent and up-to-date young lady [jazz] in the classic garb of a concerto. Yet he has not detracted one whit from her fascinating personality."

Inevitably, the concerto was compared to the *Rhapsody*. Downes concluded that the concerto was more ambitious and less original than the *Rhapsody*. Downes was right. The concerto was more complex musically than the *Rhapsody*. There was, for example, more counterpoint than in the *Rhapsody*, and the various themes were developed and interwoven throughout the three movements. John Tasker Howard later noted an ambivalence in the reaction to Gershwin: some felt that the concerto was Gershwin's finest orchestral work, but others believed that he was a little too mindful of his musical manners: "His desire to compose a real symphonic work took away much of the natural charm and exuberance of the *Rhapsody in Blue*."[22]

Time magazine, not exactly a fount of musical wisdom, had featured Gershwin on its cover in July, but then published a caustic review in its then super-cute purple prose style: "[The audience] heard pinguid platitudes of the symphonic concert hall resuscitated; they heard discreet echoes of Tchaikovsky, of Stravinsky, of Rachmaninov; [Gershwin] has become an earnest aspirant of musical respectability."[23]

Henry Osgood, writing in the *Musical Courier*, (December 10, 1925) found the concerto a musical advance over the *Rhapsody*: "Gershwin is working a new medium which he invented and of which he himself is not complete master." The *New Yorker* (December 12, 1925), however, found it "about the most important new work that has been aired in this hamlet." The magazine, too, decided that the concerto was an advance over the *Rhapsody*, even though it "springs from the same musical impulses. . . . However, the concerto has in it something that might be called nobility, and that is what we shall call it." Carl Engel (*Musical Quarterly*, April 1926) found it both very courageous and very creditable. The concerto's merit was chiefly in its general tenor, which was "unquestionably new of a newness to be found nowhere except in the United States."

Other critics were more perplexed. They could not decide what was the proper standard by which to evaluate the concerto: was it jazz or was it an extension or a perversion of the European tradition? Olin Downes conceded that what was "astonishing" was that a composer of Gershwin's limited experience and superficial craftsmanship accomplished as much as he did. Hearing the concerto again a year later, Downes conceded that it stood up well. Another critic, Charles Buchanan, who originally thought the concerto was too self-conscious, changed his mind upon a second hearing over a year later; he wrote, "I am now inclined to assert that this work can hold its own with the finest examples of this form of composition that we have."[24]

As for the musical substance, Gershwin's supporter Henry Osgood found the first movement the least effective, but concluded that the second movement was one of the best and most original things Gershwin had done. It was unique in orchestral literature. Downes was also enthusiastic about the second movement.

Steven Gilbert, in his analysis, calls the theme of the second movement played by a muted solo trumpet one of Gershwin's longest and grandest melodies. Gershwin said about this movement that it was almost "Mozartian" in it simplicity—which was certainly stretching things. Osgood, again, was impressed with the last movement: "exciting in its headlong dash to the finish. . . . Breathless is a good adjective to apply to this last movement. It had the rhythmic persistence of Stravinsky."[25] Gershwin's themes for the concerto were so striking that once again he was subjected to criticism for composing compelling "jazz" melodies. To some extent this was true: the first movement introduces a secondary theme that has overtones of "jazz," while the second movement is built around a stunning blues theme played by a solo trumpet, which Gershwin acknowledged as the American blues, but in a "purer form." Walter Damrosch wrote: "I still think that the second movement of this concerto, with its dreamy atmosphere of a summer night in a garden in our South, reaches a high water mark of his talent."[26] Sigmund Spaeth concurred that the theme was completely original even though the concerto was harmonized in the French style.

W.J. Henderson's review stated that the concerto reflected Gershwin's "convictions backed by courage." On a second hearing a year later, Henderson noted that the audience manifested a "riotous delight in the typically American product." Gershwin must have been proud to read that he was regarded as an American composer who "unlike the vast majority, appeared to have something important to say" (*Outlook*, December 16, 1925). In his own subsequent comments Gershwin went out of his way to note that the pianists who heard the concerto, including Rachmaninoff and Josef Hoffman, congratulated him on his piano performance. Of course, there was a touch of ego-building in these remarks, but it also must have been genuinely gratifying: it was only a decade earlier that he and Ira were making the rounds of the concert halls listening to these very same pianists.

Of course there were sour notes. Gershwin's nemesis, Lawrence Gilman, reacted as expected: "We need not discuss the question whether his Concerto in F is good jazz or not; this seems to us relatively unimportant beside the question whether it is good music or not; and we think it is only fairish music—conventional, trite, at its worst a little dull." [27]

It was two years before the concerto was performed abroad, in Paris, with Dimitri Tiomkin, the future Hollywood composer, as the soloist. Oscar Levant was amused to discover that Tiomkin had his assistant play the solo part in rehearsal. That concert was attended by George, the ballet impresario Diaghilev, and the Russian composer Sergei Prokofiev. Diaghilev muttered to Vernon Duke, "good jazz, bad Liszt." The following day Vernon Duke took George to Prokofiev's apartment where George played some of the concerto. According to Duke's recollection, Prokofiev liked the melodies and embellishments, but thought little of the concerto which he said consisted of 32-bar choruses ineptly bridged together. He thought highly of George's gifts as a composer, however, and suggested he could go far if he gave up "dollars and dinners."

Prokofiev aside, the concerto is extraordinary. Before this he had written only one other concert piece. The concerto was much longer, divided into three traditional movements, confined by certain time-honored "rules." The *Rhapsody* had been given its tone and color by the arrangement of Ferde Grofé. But now Gershwin had learned to orchestrate, not for Paul Whiteman's Jazz Band of a dozen or so musicians, but for the New York Symphony Society's orchestra of over fifty. In 1928, Paul Whiteman recorded the concerto but in a new arrangement by Ferde Grofé, cut down especially for Whiteman's orchestra. The piano part was played by Roy Bargy. This version is a significant distortion of Gershwin's original orchestration, and it was rumored that he was displeased by both the orchestration and the recording. However, this recording was redeemed by the great jazz artist Bix Beiderbecke who played the trumpet solo in the second movement. After George died, Kay Swift commented that she had forgotten how moving the concerto was, because there had been so many bad recordings.[28]

From the winter of 1924 through the end of 1925 was an extraordinary period, a high point for Gershwin. *Sweet Little Devil* opened on January 21, 1924. The *Rhapsody* followed on February 12. The 1924 version of the *Scandals* had its premiere on June 30. His British show *Primrose* opened in September, and *Lady Be Good!* opened on December 1, 1924, followed by *Tell Me More*, opening on April 13, 1925. He performed his concerto at Carnegie Hall on December 2, 1925, and finally his new show, *Tip Toes*, opened at the Liberty Theater on December 28, 1925; two days later came Arthur Hammerstein's *Song of the Flame*, which included several Gershwin songs. All of this occurred as he was squeezing in a trip to London and Paris.

At this time, as Gershwin left for Europe, Alexander Woollcott wrote, "Gershwin is twenty-six years old, the world lies before him. Bon Voyage."

NOTES

1. Quoted in Richard Sudhalter, *Lost Chords* (New York: Oxford University Press, 1999), p. 19.

2. Frederick Lewis Allen, *Only Yesterday* (New York: Perennial Library classics, 2000), p. 67.

3. Zelda Fitzgerald, *The Collected Writings*, ed. Matthew Bruccoli (New York: Scribners, 1991), p. 46.

4. Ethan Mordden, *Make Believe* (New York: Oxford University Press, 1997), p. 25.

5. Gerald Bordman, *American Musical Theatre* (New York: Oxford University Press, expanded edition, 1986), p. 388.

6. Lehman Engel, *The American Musical Theater*, rev. ed. (New York: Macmillan Publishing, 1975), pp. 37–38.

7. Paul Whiteman recorded most of Gershwin's better-known songs, including "Somebody Loves Me," "I'll Build a Stairway to Paradise," and shortly after its opening the title song from *Lady Be Good!* ("Paul Whiteman's Gershwin," 1998 Efrem Productions, CD Nac 4002). The entire original score for *Lady Be Good!* has been recreated and recorded, conducted by Eric Stern: Electra Nonesuch CD 79308–2, Roxbury Re-

cordings; with excellent notes on the original production by Tommy Krasker, John Mueller, and Deena Rosenberg. This project of recording the entire scores of Gershwin musicals was sponsored by the late Leonore Gershwin.

8. Some of George Gershwin's tune books are held in the Gershwin Collection of the Library of Congress.

9. Phillip Furia, *The Poets of Tin Pan Alley* (New York: Oxford University Press, 1990). An outstanding survey and analysis of the major lyricists of the Golden Age.

10. Ira Gershwin, *Lyrics on Several Occasions* (New York: Alfred Knopf, 1959), p. ix.

11. Most of the score was recorded by the principals and released as an LP, "George Gershwin, An American in London," Monmouth Evergreen Records, MES/7071; reissued as a CD: "The Ultimate George Gershwin," GEM 0113, Pavillion Records. There was a concert version performed at the Library of Congress in May 1987. The reviewer for the *Washington Post*, Lon Tuck, wrote that "no one is writing stuff this good these days— 'Les Miserables' very much included."

12. Three orchestrations in George's hand were unearthed in a cache of music in the Warner Brothers storehouse in Secaucus, New Jersey; the Gershwin orchestrations were deposited in the Library of Congress. One is on display in the Gershwin exhibition in the Jefferson Building.

13. Quoted in Bill Adler, *Fred Astaire: A Wonderful Life* (New York: Carroll and Graf, 1987), p. 47.

14. The Gershwins, including George's estate, were paid $20,000 for this movie. "Oh, Lady Be Good!" the song, became closely identified with Ella Fitzgerald, who performed and recorded a famous "scat" version.

15. Liner notes by Tommy Krasker for *Tell Me More/Tip Toes*, New World Records, CD 80598–2. This recording in 2001 was a reconstruction of the original, based on piano-vocal scores discovered in the Warner Brothers warehouse in Secaucus, New Jersey. The original orchestrations have not been found.

16. Paul Whiteman recorded "Tell Me More," "Baby," "Why Do I Love You?", and "Kickin' the Clouds Away." His tempos are livelier than the stage version. "Three Times A Day" was recorded in the collection *Ben Bagley's George Gershwin Revisited*" (Painted Smiles Records). "Kickin' the Clouds Away" was revived to good effect in *My One and Only*.

17. Gershwin may have learned some orchestration from his friend, the songwriter Milton Ager ("Happy Days Are Here Again"). They were good friends in the early 1920s, but had a falling out later, perhaps over George's attentions to Ager's wife Cecelia, according to the Ager's daughter, the writer Shana Alexander: *Happy Days* (New York: Doubleday, 1995), pp. 292–93.

18. Wayne Shirley, "Scoring the Concerto in F," in *American Music*, Fall 1985. The author has compared the different orchestral and piano versions for discrepancies. Over-all, however, he agrees with the "basic truth" of Vernon Duke's claim that Gershwin orchestrated every note he wrote, except for musical comedies, after the *Rhapsody*. As for the *Concerto in F*, Shirley concludes that while Gershwin's technique is a "bit shaky . . . it does win through, in fact, much of the piece is quite beautiful."

19. Ibid.

20. Quoted in Edward Jablonski and Lawrence Stewart, *The Gershwin Years* (New York: Doubleday & Company, 1958), p. 105.

21. Interview with George Gershwin, no date, probably December 1925, located in the Gershwin Collection, Library of Congress.

22. John Tasker Howard, *Our American Music*, 4th ed. (New York: Thomas Crowell, 1965), p. 427.

23. *Time*, December 14, printed in *Time Capsule 1925*, p. 167.

24. Charles L. Buchanan, "Gershwin and Musical Snobbery," *The Outlook*, February 2, 1927; printed in *Gershwin In His Time: A Biographical Scrapbook, 1919–1937*, ed. Gregory R. Suriano (New York: Gramercy Books, 1998), p. 44.

25. Henry O. Osgood, *So This Is Jazz* (Boston: Little, Brown, 1926), pp. 215–16.

26. Walter Damrosch in *George Gershwin*, ed. Merle Armitage (New York: Longmans, Green, 1938), p. 32.

27. Gershwin's critics were persistent. More than a decade later Virgil Thomson, reviewing a performance by Byron Janis, wrote, "George Gershwin's *Concerto in F* is not an ugly piece . . . but it is a pretty empty one."

28. Jablonski and Stewart, *The Gershwin Years*, p. 365. The concerto is analyzed by Steven E. Gilbert, *The Music of George Gershwin* (New Haven, CT: Yale University Press, 1995), pp. 90–109; his analysis is highly technical but he is obviously impressed with Gershwin's progress after the *Rhapsody*.

Chapter 7

Oh, Kay!

While nervously anticipating the premiere of his concerto, Gershwin was in Washington, D.C., supervising the out-of-town tryout of his new show *Tip Toes*. It was the true successor to *Lady Be Good!* The new show was produced by the same team as *Lady Be Good!*, was written by the same authors (Fred Thompson and Guy Bolton), and opened at the same theater (the Liberty on December 28, 1925). Even though *Tip Toes* was without the Astaires, it was a more spirited Jazz Age romp than *Tell Me More*. It too was a hit.

This time the characters were stranded vaudevillians in Palm Beach. It was an ideal setting for musical comedy. George Kaufman devised *Cocoanuts*, set in Florida for the Marx Brothers, with a score by Irving Berlin. After the end of World War I, Florida suddenly began enjoying an enormous real estate boom. The Atlantic coast from Palm Beach southward was being developed into an "American Riviera." The population of Miami and other cities and towns exploded, as did the prices for building lots. Investors were flocking to Florida, both the east and west coasts: "Everybody was making money on land, prices were climbing to incredible heights, and those who came to scoff remained to speculate."[1] One wily promoter hired the Great Commoner William Jennings Bryan to sit on the beach under an umbrella and lecture on the virtues of Florida's climate. Along with land-hungry speculators came outright crooks and charlatans. Real estate lots advertised in New York as waterfront turned out to be miles inland and located in a swamp. Still the trains carried people in great numbers before the bubble burst in the late 1920s.

This was the spirit of the opening scene of *Tip Toes*—a railroad platform where the entire chorus sang the rewards of speculating in Florida real estate options, which they urged people to grab while they were "hot." Two men disembark from the train; they are Al and Hen Kaye, and hidden in their trunk (to avoid paying her fare) is their niece, Tip Toes. They are the three "Komical Kayes."

Also at the station are the socialite Rollo and his wife Sylvia; they are planning a big party. They sing "Nice Baby," a cutesy love duet. Then Rollo discovers to his horror that one of the Kayes is Tip Toes, with whom he had unsuccessfully flirted some time ago. Rollo quickly pays them off, and the Kayes are inspired to hatch a plot: Tip Toes, posing as a high society lady named van Renssalaer, would enchant some rich man who would pay blackmail rather than be exposed as linked to a common dancer. The Kayes spot their intended victim, Sylvia's brother Steve, the glue king, played by the perennial leading man Alan Kearns. They all adjourn to the Surf Club; but Steve is bored and sings "When Do We Dance?" The Kayes then rehearse their new roles in high society, but begin to argue. Tip Toes intervenes to remind them of their elevated new social position; they sing "These Charming People," a clever song that was a particular favorite of Ira's. He complained that he had not written any comic lyrics for *Lady Be Good!*, but *Tip Toes* gave him a new opportunity to ridicule the rich.

Tip Toes was played by Queenie Smith and her uncles by Andrew Tombes and Harry Watson, Jr. A young, undiscovered Jeannette MacDonald had the role of Sylvia. When she appeared at the office of Alex Aarons to audition, she was surprised to encounter George Gershwin. After they discussed their mutual admiration for Jerome Kern, Gershwin offered to accompany her; she sang Kern's "Left All Alone Again Blues"; she got the job, and drew favorable notices. Many years later Ira commented that her voice was too good for musical comedy.

Queenie Smith did not elicit the raves of Adele Astaire, but she was charming—a pert little blue-eyed blonde, a thing of beauty and joy. She was, in fact, an experienced dancer with strong Broadway credits. Years later she went on to star as "Ellie" in the movie version of *Show Boat*. She could not only dance but sing as well, introducing "Looking for a Boy" as a solo number "in one" before the curtain during a scene change.

Tip Toes appeals to Steve, of course, and he announces his enchantment with "That Certain Feeling." This song was both rhythmic and romantic, a hybrid category that the Gershwins were polishing. Alec Wilder called this number "neat as a pin" and "mint Gershwin."[2] In its unexpected use of a quarter-note rest in the first bar and an eighth-note rest in the third bar to "kick" the melody, the listener once again encounters Gershwin's deft use of rhythm. Ira Gershwin complained, however, that few singers abided by the way the song was actually written; they ignored the rest in the first beat of the first measure thus losing the "kick." Ira complained that rather than singing it as written singers would perform it too evenly. George and Ira's device works if the tempo is brisk, but not if sung as a slow romantic ballad. It was obviously one of George's favorites, for he included it in his *Song-Book*.[3] "Looking for a Boy" holds up better as a love song.

Inevitably, Tip Toes' deception is uncovered, and she has to convince Steve that she is truly in love. Of course, she wins him over, singing and dancing along the way.

When the show was still out of town in Philadelphia, one reviewer wrote that only a "mummy or a moron could conceivably remain immune to the merriment of this red letter musical comedy." Another Philadelphia reviewer opined that Gershwin had "turned out a score which equals, if not surpasses his music in 'Lady Be Good.' " The Gershwins were clearly hitting their stride: mixing hot numbers, jazzy specialty dances, and poignant love songs (i.e., "Looking for a Boy"). Ira thought the show contained "longer openings, [and] many of the songs had crisp lines," more so than *Lady Be Good!* He particularly enjoyed doing the more sophisticated, urbane lyrics of "These Charming People," a witty parody of the upper classes which he thought amused the audiences. Lorenz Hart wrote to Ira: "Your lyrics gave me as much pleasure as Mr. George Gershwin's music . . . I have heard none so good this many a day."[4]

Tip Toes suffers an accident that causes temporary amnesia. She believes that she is truly Roberta van Renssalaer, and to the dismay of her uncles begins spending money lavishly. At this point came the show's big moment, a punchy rhythm song, "Sweet and Low Down." It was a jazzy number according to Ira, a production number for the entire ensemble, who were supplied with miniature toy trombones and kazoos. It employed an ascending musical figure that gave the song a strong rhythmic impetus. It was a worthy successor to "Fascinating Rhythm" and "Kickin' the Clouds Away." Indeed, these three numbers are distinctly Gershwin. They harken back to his days as a piano-pounding song plugger at Remick's. "Sweet and Low Down" closed the first act, lasting four or five minutes.

The second act begins on Steve's yacht. He and Tip Toes reprise "Looking for a Boy." He is happy and excited and sings "It's a Great Little World," but then he learns of the deception perpetrated by Tip Toes and her uncles. As Tip Toes emerges from her amnesia Steve slyly lets it be known that he is in fact quite broke. His guests depart his yacht, except for Tip Toes who confesses she does not care about his money because she loves him. They spend the night on board, but not together, and they sing "Nightie-Night!" The next morning back at the Everglades Inn, Steve reveals the truth, that he is truly quite rich.[5] Everyone celebrates to a reprise of "Sweet and Low Down." The song and dance was a "truly rollicking affair" according to one reviewer: the audience went "quite mad."[6]

Tip Toes, wrote Alexander Woollcott, was "Gershwin's evening so sweet and sassy are the melodies he has poured out . . . so fresh and unstinted the gay, young blood of his invention." Woollcott, usually friendly to Gershwin shows, outdid himself: "all told, the best score he has written in his days in the theater."[7] Like its predecessors, *Tip Toes* traveled to London where it was moderately successful.[8]

The show was revived in 1978 by the Brooklyn Academy of Music and was described as "exhilarating"; Gershwin's score was considered one of his finest, "brimming with the distinctive melodic, harmonic and rhythmic vitality of the young and seasoned composer." One reviewer even claimed that "Others have written great melodies, but the harmonies and rhythms of our theatre are Gershwin's own."[9]

Tip Toes perfectly captured the gay abandon of the Jazz Age. Vincent Youmans may have been the choice of Zelda Fitzgerald, but Osbert Sitwell, of the famous English literary family, recalled in his memoir, *Laughter in the Next Room*, that the 1920s lived and expired to [George Gershwin's] ingenious tunes, "so expert of their kind, and no chronicle of the epoch could fail to mention them and their pervasive influence."

On July 20, 1925, *Time* featured George on its cover. *Time* was still a fledgling magazine, not yet the prestigious journal it would become. But Gershwin was in good company; other subjects for the covers were Churchill, Trotsky, Ford, and Chaplin. The accompanying article described his apartment—old newspapers lying about in crumpled disorder, but two clippings were circled, with news that he had returned from Europe and that he would write a new musical comedy after finishing his concerto for Walter Damrosch. The telephone rang and he abruptly dismissed the caller because he was leaving for the weekend. All the new attention was a nuisance, but he could not honestly pretend that it bored him, this growing interest in his movements, his past, his plans.

Simultaneously with the production of *Tip Toes*, George, but without Ira, was briefly involved with a show entitled *Song of the Flame*, produced by Arthur Hammerstein. Originally the music was to have been written by Rudolf Friml, but when he withdrew Hammerstein prevailed on Gershwin. He shared the music with Herbert Stothart, one of Ziegfeld's staff composers. It was described as a "romantic opera," featuring attractive Russian costumes and backdrops—the Russian equivalent of *Rose Marie*. The book and lyrics were by Otto Harbach and Oscar Hammerstein II, which explains why Ira was excluded. The show, opening on December 30, 1925, enjoyed a respectable run. Some of the reviews were enthusiastic, calling it an operetta that featured princes and peasants in the throes of lyrical love, naughty old counts, waggish bumpkins and more chorus girls than one would think probable. The columnist Walter Winchell found it to be a spectacular production. Percy Hammond thought it a large, beautiful, and serious feast. And he was no doubt right. Photographs of the finale show about fifty young ladies in pseudo-Cossack costumes brandishing sabres, surrounding the leading lady. Little wonder that Otto Kahn wanted to move it to the Metropolitan.

This show was an "oddity" for Gershwin, according to Ethan Mordden, since Gershwin was perceived as an expert in Aaron-Freedly "razzle-dazzle," not the romantic opera of *Song of the Flame*; for Gershwin it was "pseudo-Slavic" rather than "Manhattan smart." [10] In any case, most of the music was uninteresting if not outright awful. A big number for the heroine was "Midnight Bells." It was like nothing Gershwin had written before—or after, fortunately. The star, Tessa Kosta, played Aunita, a Russian revolutionary in October 1917, known as The

Flame; hence the title song. She has to flee Russia to Paris where she meets another émigré, Volodya. They fall in love and vow to return to Russia.

Kosta, who had a strong voice, complained that Stothart, conducting the orchestra, drowned her out. Arthur Hammerstein protested that if he could not hear Kosta, he could not hear anybody. Kosta said that she and the cast had little contact with Gershwin during rehearsals, but that he was very attractive, easy to work with, and cooperative in every way.[11] The orchestrations were written by Robert Russell Bennett. He too noted that Gershwin was not much in evidence—testimony to the fact that he did not think much of the show. Gershwin was still full of "youthful fun," and when he did show up in his fur coat smoking a very large black cigar, according to Bennett, he needed only a beard to "look like Johannes Brahms."[12] One song attributed to Gershwin, Stothart, Harbach, and Hammerstein prompted Cole Porter's acerbic comment: "It took four men to write *that*?"[13]

After a busy winter, by the spring of 1926 Gershwin had no new productions in the works, nor did he have a concert piece. During this period he first met Kay Swift who would play an important part in his life.

She was a vivacious, highly attractive young woman, and a well-educated musician, having studied at the Institute of Musical Art (the future Juilliard), and was continuing to study composition with Charles Loeffler and harmony and orchestration with Percy Goetschius. Her father was a music critic who died when she was young, and she helped her mother by playing professionally with the Edith Rubel Trio. She played at a social affair given by the Lewisohns where she met Bettina Warburg, who could hardly wait to tell her brother Jimmy about this ravishing young lady: "with her brown laughing eyes, delicate nose, and fine jaw, the petite Katharine would be irresistible to him. She was quick, she was game, and she had musical talent besides." [14] The Warburgs were a distinguished Jewish family with deep roots in German banking, and best known in the financial world of New York for their attachment to Kuhn, Loeb. Their Hamburg bank, M.M. Warburg, was the largest private bank in Europe.

Kay married James P. "Jimmy" Warburg in 1918. His parents were reconciled to his marriage outside the Jewish religion, but his uncle Jacob Schiff strenuously objected. Jimmy was a relatively free spirit who had no qualms about defying his prestigious and influential uncle. Their marriage was free and open and they enjoyed the "high life" of New York society. Jimmy was quite attractive and had his share of dalliances, but they had three children between 1919 and 1924.

She was a self-admitted musical snob who had no time for popular music. But she was awed by Gershwin, whom she first met at a party for Jascha Heifetz at her apartment in early 1926. He came as the escort of Pauline Heifetz. He played, of course, but at some point he jumped up and said "I've got to go to Europe." Kay found this charming.

After the spring of 1926 their friendship gradually blossomed. At first Jimmy Warburg was tolerant. He was often in Germany on the family's banking business, and George and Kay began seeing each other in public. George was a frequent guest at the Warburg farm in Connecticut. Kay Swift's granddaughter, the novelist Katharine Weber, wrote: "Kay and George were a glamorous couple when they were together at parties or the theater. They wafted through those years, flouting convention, having a good time, breaking all the rules." But she adds that their romance caused "tremendous pain" for her husband and her three daughters, and she was "a truly terrible mother."[15] Indeed, Jimmy Warburg was increasingly upset by the open flaunting of her affair. He later said that he liked Gershwin, but resented the way in which our "whole life was taken over by this completely self-centered but charming genius."[16]

As they became closer, George got Kay a job as the rehearsal pianist for Rodgers and Hart's *A Connecticut Yankee*. He also urged her to try her hand at composing for the musical theater, which she did successfully in the late 1920s. When she began to write popular songs her husband wrote lyrics under the pseudonym of Paul James, so as not to completely embarrass his banking business, but also to join Kay in her new life, in a sense to compete with Gershwin. She wrote one important hit, "Can't We Be Friends" (1929) for *The Little Show*, introduced by Libby Holman, who also sang "Moanin' Low" in the same show. She also wrote the score for *Fine and Dandy* (1930); the title song became an outstanding jazz classic.

She was mesmerized by Gershwin's music, by him, and by the strong quality of excitement that prevailed when he played. It was plain to everyone, she said, that when he played something important was happening. On the other hand, she thought that his Broadway shows were more of a headache for him because there were so many changes. He was anxious for his shows to succeed, because he was a good showman who realized there was no use in having a great score if the show failed.

How can the Gershwin-Swift love affair be explained? It lasted ten years, much longer than Gershwin's frequent flirtations. She had a prominent husband, three children, and an advantageous social position. Gershwin's talent turned her head, and she became increasingly passionate, though she preferred that they not live together. One suspects that at first Gershwin was restless and lonely. He was still a young man, only twenty-seven, but most of his friends were married, including his brother Ira. When he met her Gershwin was escorting Pauline Heifetz, and carrying on flirtations with Rosamond Walling and Aileen Pringle in Hollywood. Kay Swift was not only appealing but, unlike most of his women friends, a highly talented musician. The combination was probably irresistible.

As Gershwin had exclaimed at Kay Swift's party, he did indeed sail for Europe, stopping first in London and then Paris. There was no special mission for this trip. Ostensibly he was to rework his scores for the London version of *Lady Be Good!* and *Tip Toes*. Most of his time in London was spent in socializing. A British writer interviewed him there, and was overwhelmed as George played "the music of intoxication"—one of the most singular occasions in the

writer's experience. George played much of the concerto, and the writer, Beverley Nichols, was enthralled by the various rhythms "fighting" each other. He
was intrigued by how George joined all of it together, and Gershwin's explanation was characteristic: "I feel things, and then I work them out—that's all."[17]
Meanwhile, during the interview George was "dabbling" at the piano and suddenly a rather fascinating phrase came out. He worked it over and over again
until he said: "Well, at any rate, that's a beginning." The melody turned out to
be "I'd Rather Charleston," to be inserted into the London version of *Lady Be
Good*! (This was probably staged for Nichols' benefit; the song had already
been written in New York).

Paris was next, where he was the house guest of his old friends Mabel and
Bob Schirmer. The Schirmers wrote to Emily Paley that their days consisted of
breakfast together, then lying around the house, playing the piano, the Victrola,
and "our vocal chords till about 2 or 3 p.m." Of course, there was socializing
in the evening, diversions to a Steeplechase, a prize fight, and a French musical
comedy, which put George to sleep.[18] There was a dinner with the composer
George Anthiel; his compositions were so exotic (i.e., for sixteen pianos) that
he found he could not play them properly for George. One important result of
his visit to Paris was the inspiration for a new composition, which turned out
to be *An American In Paris*. In his thank-you note to the Schirmers, inscribed
with the usual bits of music, there were the first bars of the famous walking
scene from *An American in Paris*. This was April 1926, two years before he
actually wrote it. Again it seems as if he was restless, straining to start something
new.

After a "splendid week" they returned to London for a Whiteman concert,
including the *Rhapsody*. George thought Whiteman "murdered it," playing a lot
of "crazy" tempos. They also attended a ballet of the *Rhapsody* which they
liked, even though the pianist "stumbled" through the solo passages, the clarinet
player "cracked" on the high note of the opening glissando, and the trombonist
blew some "sour notes." Next they attended the British opening of *Lady Be
Good!* "It was a triumph," Mabel wrote. Afterward there was a fashionable party
at the Embassy Club given by Lord and Lady Butt; he was the managing director
of the Empire Theatre. The Astaires came and so did many other prominent
people. The Schirmers left around 2:00 A.M., but George remained until eight
that morning. "Some evening," Mabel Schirmer wrote to Emily Paley.

Sometime during this period Gershwin began writing some piano preludes. It
appears that Gershwin may have begun to compose some of these preludes—
how many is still a mystery—in early 1925. In March 1925 Carl Van Vechten
referred in an article to a cycle of twenty-four piano preludes Gershwin was
undertaking, but this large project, if it ever existed, was abandoned. One fragment for a prelude in G-major exists, dated "Jan. 1925," but an earlier version
is dated August 1923. Gershwin mentioned in a published article in July 1926
that he was working on two or three jazz preludes which would be heard for
the first time at the concert of Mme. D'Alvarez's "very dignified and sedate

program." He did in fact perform some of them at a concert given by the Peruvian contralto Marguriete d'Alvarez. Her concert took place in December 1926 at the Roosevelt Hotel. It was not so "sedate": with George at the piano Mme. Alvarez sang "The Man I Love" and "Nashville Nightingale." One review of the program claimed that Gershwin's preludes proved to be skillfully written, with the flavor of Broadway combined with various European flavors. Three of the preludes he performed were published and a fragment of a fourth was incorporated into the Concerto in F.

Prelude I is a sprightly piece. According to Kay Swift, Gershwin ran through this prelude, and as he played it she transcribed it. The other two preludes came later, she said.[19] The second prelude is subtitled "Blue Lullaby," and it is notable for its moving bass line, often used by jazz pianists. The melody, however, is somewhat reminiscent of the *Rhapsody* and also foreshadows a figure used in *Porgy and Bess*.[20] The third prelude is called "The Spanish" and while not in Latin rhythm, it stresses the rhythm rather than the melody. In this period, in addition to the three published preludes Gershwin wrote a duet for violin and piano entitled "Short Story," which he performed with the violinist Samuel Dushkin. Finally, there is one other composition that seems to fall in this same category of short piano pieces written around this time; it is called "Sleepless Night," a favorite of Kay Swift and Ira, which they intended to turn into a song, but decided against. (Kay Swift rewrote the original as a 32-bar song, which was published as a "prelude").[21]

He seems to have composed these preludes and other short pieces as a diversion. They are predominantly piano pieces and very characteristic of Gershwin's style. He recorded three of the published preludes, interpreting them quite differently from the published version. Legato passages, for example, in the second prelude are not played by Gershwin smoothly as written, but with a carefully marked emphasis on each note. Subsequent performers of course have followed the written text, either unaware of or ignoring Gershwin's interpretation. After George died Kay Swift commented that it's very easy to ruin the preludes. They were not foolproof at all. She said the fast preludes are taken too fast by most performers and the slow ones, too slow.[22]

The Gershwins were about to embark on one of their greatest purely musical achievements, *Oh, Kay!* It was again a typical 1920s plot: bootleggers cavorting around the Hamptons together with mistaken identities and zany deceptions abound. Of course, the plot provided usual opportunities for the principals and chorus to burst into song and dance.

The book was by Guy Bolton and P.G. Wodehouse. This made it inevitable that it would find echoes of the Princess shows. And indeed, some of the characters are derivatives of old Princess shows, and even the title sounds like one of those shows (*Oh, Boy!*). The opening scene takes place on the beach where the bootleggers discuss their opportunities in "When Our Ship Comes Sailing In," an appropriate Gershwin song to start off the festivities, but later cut. The problem for the bootleggers is that their hiding place for the booze is a beach house thought to be vacant, but soon to be occupied by the return of its owner Jimmy Winter. The bootleggers split up to take on various assignments. Shorty (played by Victor Moore) is off to the house, but he runs into Kay, the sister of Duke, one of the other bootleggers. She has come ashore from their yacht searching for a young man she met at this very place a year before, when she rescued him from drowning. She (Gertrude Lawrence) sings "Someone to Watch Over Me." Obviously, this was one of the show's high points. During the tryouts the song was moved to later in the first act; Kay had already met Jimmy, so the original lyrics are incongruous at this later point; she was no longer looking everywhere. This famous song was moved, much like "The Man I Love," because it slowed the action too early in the show.[23]

In any case, this was the most memorable moment for the show and for Gertrude Lawrence. The staging was her idea, a spontaneous bit of theater: she sang this lament caressing a rag doll supposedly bought for her by George Gershwin.[24] The pedigree of this famous Gershwin love song is something of a mystery. It apparently began life as a fast number, in which the descending melody and chord changes in the third and fourth bar were highly syncopated and therefore very "jazzy." Ira wrote that if it had remained as a rhythm number, as originally conceived by George, this tune would not be around much. While noodling around one day, George played the melody slowly, and both he and Ira had the same reaction: it was not a rhythm song but a rather a wistful and warm one. Then Ira supplied a romantic lyric.[25] While it clearly became a slow, romantic love song, George Gershwin's piano recording is at a relatively fast pace.[26]

The plot continues: Jimmy arrives with his new wife, but she leaves outraged to learn that his divorce is not yet final. Jimmy consoles himself and his friends, singing "Dear Little Girl," and retires for the evening when Kay bursts through the french doors, trying to escape an immigration officer and a revenue agent. Jimmy recognizes her and defends her, claiming she is his wife. Kay persuades Jimmy to let her stay ("Maybe"). Kay's brother is frantic at her disappearance; his friends cheer him up with the rollicking "Clap Yo' Hands." The revenue officer returns to check up on Jimmy and Kay; they pretend they are still newlyweds, and sing "Do, Do, Do." As was often the case, the second act was spotty. Jimmy finally escapes from his intended bride, and everything falls into place. The show closes with a spirited song and dance led by Gertrude Lawrence to the song "Oh, Kay!", a brisk melody and lyrics typical of the Gershwins in this era.

What made all of this special was Gertrude Lawrence. She was a British import who had made her entrance on the American scene in the London transplant *Charlot's Revue*, produced by Andre Charlot, which also featured Jack Buchanan and Beatrice Lillie. The first *Charlot's Revue* was a great success as was the second version in late 1925. Beatrice Lillie established herself as one of the best comediennes in the West End and Broadway:

Gertrude Lawrence drew good notices for her singing and comedy: Lawrence was a looker and she split the difference between airy and earthy. If her singing was uneven (but lovely) and her dancing derivative, she had spontaneity. . . . She was quicksilver, unpredictable, even unprofessional: that spontaneity was real.[27]

She was eager for a starring vehicle on Broadway, and was recruited by Alex Aarons and Guy Bolton who promised her a book musical. They suggested that the score would be written by George Gershwin. And, in fact, Gershwin's music would launch her on a long and brilliant Broadway career that lasted until her death twenty years later when she was starring in *The King and I*. One of her biographers wrote:

She may not have always been the best, but she was certainly the brightest. Others of her generation were better singers, better dancers, better actresses; Gertrude Lawrence was a better star. For a brief but memorable time she was First Lady of the musical comedy stage on Broadway and in the West End.[28]

The book for *Oh, Kay!* was originally titled *Mayfair*, then *Miss Mayfair*, then *Cheerio*, and finally *Oh, Kay!* It was said that Gershwin renamed this 1926 musical for Kay Swift; the two leading characters are indeed Kay and Jimmy; Kay Swift was at the time still married to Jimmy Warburg; she was usually known as Katharine, but George began calling her Kay. The authors, Bolton and Wodehouse, worked on it over the summer. At first Wodehouse was uneasy working with the Gershwins; he did not really know them and he usually wrote the lyrics for the shows he worked on with Bolton and Kern. But he came to admire Ira as a fine lyricist. It was Bolton and Wodehouse's idea to hire Victor Moore as the butler/bootlegger. The producers were skeptical; they even offered to pay Moore ten thousand dollars to withdraw, but on opening night of the previews Moore charmed the audiences. The scene in which Lawrence poses as a maid and Moore poses as a butler and they serve tea was regarded as some of the best comedy on Broadway.

During the preparation of *Oh, Kay!*, Ira Gershwin was taken ill with appendicitis and was out for six weeks. His substitute was the very able young lyricist Howard Dietz, a friend of both brothers. P.G. Wodehouse was working on the book with Guy Bolton, but for some reason he was not asked to do the lyrics for the ailing Ira. He volunteered a lyric that was not used. Some writers believe that Wodehouse was passed over because his lyrics would give the show too much of a British flavor, especially since Gertrude Lawrence was the lead. They were probably right; subsequent revivals of the show with added lyrics by Wodehouse are very, very British. In any case, Dietz supplied the title and some of the lyrics to "Someone to Watch Over Me." It is a little uncertain how much he contributed. Some of the musical manuscripts include his name along with

Ira's, but the published versions drop him. In his memoirs, Dietz rather archly speculated that he was chosen by George Gershwin to save money, since Dietz was willing to work for less, and thus Ira's share of the royalties would remain largely intact.[29] The orchestra was conducted by Gershwin's good friend William Daly. Gershwin wrote a musical sketch for an overture, with some marking for the orchestrations, but it does not seem to have been used.

The musical score for *Oh, Kay!* surpassed its predecessors. It included several outstanding songs. Some of Gershwin's manuscripts suggest that he wrote songs early in the preparations. His music sheets for "Someone to Watch Over Me," as well as "Maybe" and "Do, Do, Do" are labeled "Cheerio," one of the show's original titles. "Maybe" is a much neglected song: a simple melodic line, with an innovative twist in the second eight bars, leading back to the original line. It had long lines that permitted it to be sung as a duet, with the boy echoing the girl and vice versa. On the other hand, "Fidgety Feet" in the second act was a rhythmic comic song, not unlike a "Little Jazz Bird" in *Lady Be Good!* George cited it as an example of misleading inspiration. He thought of the melody one evening as he fell asleep, but immediately wrote it down. The next morning he was not as impressed, but nevertheless, decided to work on it. It is an interesting gloss on Gershwin's talent that the lovely, slow "Maybe" has the same opening musical phrase as the lively "Clap Yo' Hands." This song was in an old-fashioned revival camp meeting style, a shouting and stomping revel.

When the show opened on November 8, 1926, at the Imperial Theater, the critic Percy Hammond wrote, "All of us floated away on the canoodling notes of 'Maybe' and were brought back to Broadway by such flesh and bony anthems as 'Fidgety Feet' and 'Clap Yo Hands.' " He might well have added "Do, Do, Do." Ira had an idea that do, do, do, and done, done, done might form the spine of a song. George went up to his lair on the fifth floor at 103rd street and came down a half hour later with the melody for the refrain. It became, in Ira's description, a catchy song about a kiss—and nothing else. Maybe so, but it is still rather suggestive.

The score also included another beautiful love song, "Dear Little Girl," which was badly overshadowed by "Someone to Watch Over Me." It was singled out for special praise by Alec Wilder in his study of the American popular song. Thus, there were three appealing ballads—"Someone to Watch Over Me," "Dear Little Girl," and "Maybe," refuting the notion that the Gershwins were only hot rhythm writers. Nevertheless, the Gershwins were type-cast. When the show was out of town in Philadelphia a critic described the score as having a "jazzical lilt" which was typical of Gershwin.

While playing in Philadelphia, the show's reviews were favorable. Gershwin's score was given credit—just as lilting and a bit more attractive than the score of *Lady Be Good!* But it was Lawrence who was singled out. She ran away with the show, according to one review. Once in New York on Broadway (November 8, 1926, at the Imperial) the critics found the show to be the third hit after *Lady Be Good!* and *Tip Toes* (conveniently leaving out *Tell Me More*).

The drama critic Burns Mantle attributed the show's success to Aarons and Freedley's determination to stick to a policy of placing quality and cleanliness first: "there is good fun, good music, adult humor, a handsome setting and a gifted company" (*New York Daily News*, November 9, 1926). The book by Bolton and Wodehouse was praised, though Alan Dale found it "sad to the verge of tears." Dale also complained that Gertrude Lawrence's talents were submerged by too many funnymen, choruses, and a "stupid" plot. Dale did credit Gershwin with "some really nice and clever and unusual music." Brooks Atkinson, by then the *New York Times* reviewer, wrote: "Musical comedy seldom proves more intensely delightful than "Oh, Kay!" . . . [an] excellent blending of all the creative arts of musical entertainment" (November 9, 1926). Finally, Percy Hammond of the *New York Tribune* wrote that "Miss Lawrence, of course, was the greatest influence in the prevailing happiness."

Like its predecessors, *Oh, Kay!* also moved to London and enjoyed a long run, with Gertrude Lawrence again in the starring role. While the British reviews were not as enthusiastic as the American ones, Gertrude Lawrence was warmly welcomed back home by the venerable *London Times*: "a brilliant and happy girl, combining in the most remarkable manner a variety of talents. She has looks, grace, humour, voice dignity, acting ability and immense charm."

Revivals of *Oh, Kay!* have been enhanced by the addition of songs borrowed from different Gershwin productions, and in one instance some entirely new lyrics by Wodehouse (with Ira Gershwin's permission).[30] The revival produced by David Merrick in the 1980s did not fare well. It closed, but then shortly thereafter an innovative and extensively revised and updated version reopened. It had an all-black cast and the plot and action were modernized and transferred from the Hamptons to Harlem, though still set during prohibition. It too added songs from other Gershwin scores. Edith Oliver for *The New Yorker* thought it was one of the most joyous performances to be seen locally in years. In the face of some hostile reviews Merrick had the wit simply to reprint the original reviews for this "Champagne Musical," as it had been called in 1926.

While in London before the opening of *Oh, Kay!*, George began recording phonograph records. He accompanied Fred Astaire on some songs from *Lady Be Good!* In London he also recorded the slow movement from *Rhapsody in Blue* as a piano solo, and began to record his highly stylized versions of songs from his shows. These recordings are of interest for his improvisations as well as for the tempos he adopted, some quite different from the tempos that became standard. Once at the piano Gershwin tended to select tempos that suited his lively style. As noted, he played "Someone to Watch Over Me" at a faster tempo than sung by Gertrude Lawrence but played "Sweet and Low Down" at a slower tempo than the pace of the show. It may well also be that Gershwin was dissatisfied with the decision to slow down "Someone to Watch Over Me." In any case, it is surprisingly omitted from his 1932 *Song-Book*. The sheet music is marked "Scherzando" ("playful").

Gershwin's continuing success on Broadway was producing a strange backlash. He was more and more resented by the classical musical community. His Broadway successes were cited as proof that he belonged to Tin Pan Alley, not the concert hall. The writer Charles L. Buchanan called attention to the snobbery of the intelligentsia in Gershwin's case. In writing about Gershwin's concerto, he said that on the one hand the intelligentsia complained of the sterility of American art, but when a new and vital sound appeared they brought out the "old deadly steamroller" that squashes the achievement and extinguishes it.[31]

Without realizing it, Gershwin would soon become the subject of a rancorous debate. Some American composers, including Aaron Copland and Virgil Thomson, dismissed his concert works as unimportant. According to the musicologist Francis Davis, this was a typical attitude of the "Europhile classical music establishment." It regarded any "serious" work indebted to American popular music as a "bastard offspring."[32] Another observer, Professor David Schiff, commented:

> They relegated Gershwin to a lesser realm, even though his works often shared programs with theirs. . . . Copland, whose modernistically jazzy Piano Concerto of 1927 was dismissed as a "harrowing horror" by one Boston critic and never achieved the success of Gershwin's "Concerto in F," later drew a clear line between himself and Gershwin.[33]

Gershwin had his supporters—Deems Taylor and E.B. Hill; it was even rumored that the eminent conductor Willem Mengelberg was favorable toward Gershwin. The composer E.B. Hill, then at Harvard, wrote about *Rhapsody in Blue*: "That Gershwin is uneasy in a piece of this length is obvious, but despite its defects it is better than the illusory jazz of some 'high brow' composers." Nevertheless, in the later 1920s the "modernists" felt threatened. Their most vocal and prominent spokesman, the critic Paul Rosenfeld, saw Gershwin as a "dark horse galloping in to usurp a position for which he [Rosenfeld] had very different plans," and he worked hard to fend off Gershwin in the process.[34]

Gershwin's works came at about the same time as Copland's and were an opportunity for critics to skewer Gershwin while elevating Copland. Thus Copland's jazz-based *Piano Concerto* was praised while Gershwin's *Concerto in F* was dismissed by Paul Rosenfeld as a "hash derivative." While Edmund Wilson found Copland had a gift similar to Stravinsky's, he found Gershwin "mechanical and unsatisfactory." Even Gershwin's sometime teacher Henry Cowell joined the fray denouncing Gershwin for failing to create "anything worthy in this idiom."[35]

Gershwin did not help matters in some of his comments: Just before the premiere of the concerto he said in an interview in Washington, D.C. that he studied harmony but not counterpoint:

> I don't think it is necessary for one who aims to write really American music to study too closely and pattern after the fugues and other forms

that were original with the old German masters. We need American forms
for American music.[36]

The concerto was in that particular form, Gershwin explained, because Damrosch wanted it in a form his orchestra could play. It was condescending comments such as these that led some to claim that Gershwin was too self-confident
to pay attention to his critics. This is doubtful. He and his brother meticulously
clipped every mention of their works in the newspapers, especially the reviews,
and pasted them in fat notebooks.

Gershwin obviously had an amazing ability to shift his focus from a popular
score to a serious concert work. Sam Behrman wrote that he saw Gershwin
working on the score of his concerto in a room in which there must have been
six other people talking among themselves, having tea, and playing checkers.
Apparently, Gershwin concentrated on developing themes and later brought
them into a broader context.

After *Oh, Kay!* came an interesting experiment that eventually failed, and
failed so badly that it even closed out of town. This was an unusual setback for
the Gershwins; they had not experienced an out-of-town closing since *A Dangerous Maid* in 1921. The unfortunate show was *Strike Up the Band*, a satire
on war written by the highly admired playwright George Kaufman. It was the
beginning of a fateful association for the Gershwins. They would be involved
in four political musicals: one would fail, then succeed as a revised version; one
would win a Pulitzer Prize, and the final one would open in New York but close
quickly, bringing the Gershwins' Broadway career to an end.

The producer Edgar Selwyn approached the Gershwins in the fall of 1926 to
interest them in Kaufman's political lampoon, which had not yet been written.
Composers too often paid little attention to the book, but it is still somewhat
puzzling that the Gershwins agreed to do an avowedly political musical. Ira, if
not George, probably was attracted by the chance to work with Kaufman and
to write satiric political lyrics. Both Gershwins had to be impressed by Kaufman's reputation. Perhaps they were taken with the title, *Strike Up the Band*, a
song to which George Gershwin would devote an inordinate amount of time in
writing.

George Gershwin was not particularly political. But his brother was politically
sensitive; along with most New York intellectuals, Ira was well to the left of
center, as were Kaufman and his collaborator Morrie Ryskind. It was Ryskind,
expelled from Columbia University for pacifist agitation during World War I,
who prodded Kaufman to write the original version of *Strike Up the Band*, and
then helped with some rewrites.

The Gershwins did not lack for assignments: *Funny Face* was in the works
or, more exactly, in difficulty. George was working on the preliminaries of *An
American in Paris* and there were negotiations with Ziegfeld for another musical.

Strike Up the Band was unveiled at the Shubert Theater in Philadelphia in
September 1927. It was a debatable time for still another attack on the horrors

of war, even as seen through the comedic lense of George Kaufman. By 1927 the peace movement was dominant. The Kellogg-Briand pact outlawing war was under negotiation, peace committees in the United States were offering huge sums of money for the best "peace plan." The public concern over a glorification of war, which motivated Kaufman, was still evident but it was questionable whether musical comedy audiences were ready for a play that ended with the threat of another war, however preposterous and humorous the dialogue and plot.

Kaufman's script for *Strike Up the Band* was not only an attack on war, but on the League of Nations, patriotism, all politicians, and especially American businessmen. It was a humorous satire, but it was Kaufman who said, famously, that satire is a show that closes on Saturday night. The Kaufman script was ambivalent: its targets kept moving from war itself to the venality of an American business man, embodied in a character named Horace P. Fletcher. He was the cheese king who wanted to make war against Switzerland because that country was protesting against the new outrageous tariffs on imported cheese. War does ensue, after Fletcher offers to pay for it, but only if it is named in his honor. The United States wins a battle by means of a yodel that tricks a Swiss general. Fletcher's aide is exposed as a spy who has been diluting the cheese with grade B milk.

The tone was too bitter. It was, after all, 1927, the year of Lindy's flight, Babe Ruth's home run record, the Dempsey–Tunney fight. The country was not in the mood for harsh satire. The show failed. It was too dark for musical comedy, and yet too frivolous to be taken more seriously. Kaufman was superb as a collaborator, especially later with Moss Hart, but when he wrote alone the results were often below his standard. During the woeful out-of-town tryouts, Kaufman and Ira Gershwin were in the lobby when two well-dressed gentlemen alighted from a taxi and entered the theater. "Gilbert and Sullivan coming to fix the play," Ira commented.

Kaufman always claimed that he knew little of music. He admired good lyricists, especially Ira. The title song, "Strike Up the Band," he claimed was his favorite musical number from Broadway. But he also liked to chide George. When he heard that Gershwin was playing songs from Kaufman's musical yet to be completed, he commented that Gershwin played his songs so often beforehand, that the first-night audience thought they were attending a revival.

Kaufman manfully took credit (or blame) for the failure of *Strike Up the Band*. Oddly enough the initial reviews were favorable—"a rollicking show, a veritable geyser of spontaneous comedy," wrote one Philadelphia newspaper. "Characteristically smart and snappy," wrote the *Philadelphia Ledger*. "A sophisticated, ornamental and richly musical piece," wrote still another (*Evening Ledger*). But there were warning signs as well. Philadelphia reviewers noted that when the show reached New York—and even assuming a slow second act was fixed—it would cause a furor, but also might have difficulty drawing audiences, because satirical musicals were not usually successful and Americans did not like to be laughed at. *Variety* (September 7, 1927) concluded that the "masses still believed in patriotism." This may well be why, despite the favorable reviews, the preview audiences in Philadelphia dwindled down. There were also numerous cast changes, especially among the principals. The producer Edgar Selwyn finally decided to close it, vowing to revive it after some further work.[37]

"The Man I Love" once again was inserted and would have probably remained had the show gone on to New York. The song was earning its reputation as a standard, however, largely through individual performances and recordings over the years, beginning with a version by Helen Morgan. But in *Strike Up the Band* it was not the torch song it became. It fit appropriately into the setting of soldiers returning home. It came after a Gershwin melody that disappeared with the failure of the show—"Homeward Bound"—one of George's most plaintive melodies. Ironically, the love songs, like the show itself, may have been counterproductive: they reminded audiences of the doughboys who did not return from the War.[38]

The music was a mixed bag. For some strange reason, perhaps because of the political satire, the Gershwins decided to tilt toward Gilbert and Sullivan. With some exceptions the score was permeated with a kind of tongue-in-cheek version of the great English masters. It is difficult to tell how much was outright parody of Gilbert and Sullivan and how much was intended to re-create their spirit. Almost every review noted the show's indebtedness to Gilbert and Sullivan. Gershwin got credit for a "full-bodied score," but without any haunting melodies. Even though the music was original, the "pattering" songs were too reminiscent of Gilbert and Sullivan. The culprit was not only Kaufman and his bitter comedy, but Ira's obsessively clever lyrics—the show was more Gilbert than Sullivan noted one review. *Variety* commented that the lyrics were good-humored kidding, but also mordant, bitter, and stinging.[39]

Almost sixty years later in 1984 an approximation of the original version was "reconstructed" and presented in Philadelphia where the original had closed. While retaining the original Kaufman book, it was also fleshed out with some of the melodies from the second, more successful version. The *New York Times* critic, Frank Rich, found that "the book's acerbic point of view holds up amazingly well, it's the writing that does not." After the discovery of some original materials, there was a subsequent revival as a concert version; it was well received in New York. The reviewer wrote that "Gershwin wrote a score as sweet and varied as a chocolate sampler." It restored "The Man I Love" and a song borrowed from the second 1930 version, "I've Got a Crush on You," which no doubt helped the show's appeal. The *New York Times* review by Ben Brantley concluded the show "demonstrates that Manhattan musicals once had sass, wit and sex appeal." In Los Angeles, however, the revival was panned as an odd form of ancient ancestor worship.

After the closing in Philadelphia, Selwyn frequently beseeched Kaufman to rewrite it, but he refused and finally suggested that Selwyn turn to Morrie Ryskind. Ryskind agreed to redo the plot and the Gershwins again amicably agreed to participate with an almost completely new score. One can only wonder why. Perhaps they felt obligated to Selwyn in light of the first failure.

Ryskind proceeded to drain most of the venom from the plot, turning the cheese war into a dispute over chocolate and reducing the entire war itself to a dream. The comedy was enhanced by the team of Bobby Clark and Paul McCullough. Everyone enjoyed the war so much that a tariff was imposed on caviar and America prepared for a war with Russia. Indeed, Horace Fletcher, the war's sponsor, foreshadowing the sentiment of the Cold War, demanded, "we can't let Russia tell us what to do."

It was after all still the roaring twenties, when the original was produced. But the revised version opened (January 14, 1930) after the stock market crash, and a lighter fantasy, through still satirical finally seemed to strike a more favorable chord. The Gershwins' score was a distinct improvement over the first version; it included the inventive "Soon," a scintillating dance number "Hanging around with You," and one of the great Gershwin standards, "I've Got Crush on You." Unfortunately, "The Man I Love" had become too popular to be included as intended.

Fortunately, the Gershwins had more or less shaken off their Gilbert and Sullivan trance and returned to more standard fare. Accordingly, there was one new song, "Soon," elaborated from part of a melody in the earlier version, that would endure, and of course the title song, "Strike Up the Band," has surely endured (many years later Ira Gershwin agreed that the UCLA marching band could adopt it as the school's song). Still, their penchant for a British flavor broke through now and then. In one song there is the phrase "I am a typical self-made American," the echo of "He is an Englishman" from *Pinafore* is unmistakable.

This time both the critics and public liked it; Brooks Atkinson (*New York Times*) wrote that although the fun gradually trickled out, Gershwin's satiric score was "an original contribution to the comic musical stage." Kaufman and Ryskind sheepishly admitted that it lacked the edge they had hoped for, so they decided to write still another political satire. Again they enlisted the Gershwins, who by that time were on their way to Hollywood.

The bad luck of the original *Strike Up the Band* was compounded for a time by the travails of *Funny Face*, originally titled *Smarty*. As with many shows, it had looked perfect on paper: Gershwin lyrics and music, a book by Robert Benchley and Fred Thompson, and starring roles for Adele and Fred Astaire. But things began to go wrong. In his autobiography, Astaire recalled that it was terrible because in Washington they were playing one version while rehearsing another. The Gershwin show happened to be trying out in Philadelphia when Rodgers and Hart's *A Connecticut Yankee* was there. Richard Rodgers saw *Funny Face* and wrote his future wife: "God will have to do miracles if it's to be fixed." The score was a terrible disappointment, but the book was worse.

The Astaires wanted to junk the entire project, but producers Aarons and Freedley believed, correctly, that it could be salvaged.

The book proved a major problem, especially after Robert Benchley quit because of some acid out-of-town reviews that pointed out that it was the very kind of "turkey" that he had so uproariously attacked as a critic. He was replaced by Paul Gerard Smith, noted as a play doctor. The score was rewritten in places. One casualty was an excellent song, one of the Gershwins' best, "How Long Has This Been Going On?" The harmony is quite innovative, as were the lyrics. It was replaced by another good song, "He Loves and She Loves," a brighter more optimistic statement, perhaps better for the show, but musically far less exciting. "Your Eyes, Your Smile" was discarded to reappear many years later as "You've Got What Gets Me." According to Ira everyone worked day and night, recasting, rewriting, rehearsing recriminating—but "of rejoicing there was none."

The comic talent of the reliable Victor Moore was added to the cast, and Ira composed the lyrics to the very witty commentary on the jaded upper classes, "The Babbitt and the Bromide." It was performed by Adele and Fred Astaire, playing two world-weary sophisticates who meet and can think of nothing to say except to repeat the most inane cliches. They meet ten years later and go through the same routine; twenty years later they meet again, this time in heaven, but go through the same trite exchange. It ended with the Astaires' famous runaround dance, and Ira believed this helped to save the show. Ira relished telling the story that Fred Astaire took him aside and said he knew what a babbitt was, but what was a bromide? Then the producer, Vinton Freedly, sheepishly admitted he knew a bromide, but what was a babbitt? The song was revived by Fred Astaire and Gene Kelly in their only joint performance for the film *Ziegfeld Follies* in 1946.

Funny Face was also notable for Fred Astaire's first appearance in black tie and top hat as a solo tap dancer supported by a large chorus. This would become his trademark image in the movies. But he began it with the number "High Hat" on the stage of the new Alvin Theater in that autumn of 1927. Again, the astute Alexander Woollcott captured the significance:

> I do not know whether George Gershwin was born into this world to write rhythms for Fred Astaire's feet or whether Fred Astaire was born into this world to show how the Gershwin music should really be danced. But surely they were written in the same key, those two.[40]

Despite the problems, when the show finally opened at Aarons and Freedley's newly constructed Alvin Theater the reviews were solid. The return of the Astaires of course was welcomed, and they came in for most of the applause. However, in his review Burns Mantle (*New York Daily News*) found the book "flat," a little stale and fairly unprofitable, a criticism echoed by others: the story is engagingly slight but never meant to be taken very seriously. Burns Mantle also found the Gershwin score only average Gershwin, not the superior Gershwin for which he had hoped. But the *New York Times'* Brooks Atkinson found the score to be one of Gershwin's best. He singled out several good songs: the best were the title song as well as " 'S Wonderful" and "Let's Kiss and Make Up." Woollcott (*New York World*), as expected, wrote that Gershwin had written a clever, sparkling, teasing score.

Ira Gershwin's maturity was evident in the unusual lyrics for " 'S Wonderful." Dropping part of the first word was an inspired innovation. Among the many other hits of this show was "My One and Only." A critic wrote that this song was "an odd melody in despairing Polish minors." For this number Fred Astaire and Gertrude McDonald danced a soft shoe—the highlight of the evening. The title song, "Funny Face," was an unusual melody, highly rated by Alec Wilder, who described it as a "backward" song; that is, its harmony reversed the traditional harmonic progression in the first few bars.[41] Indeed, the score—if only in retrospect—is stunning: not only "Funny Face" and " 'S Wonderful," but "My One and Only," as well as "He Loves and She Loves," which replaced "How Long Has This Been Going On?"—five major songs!

Funny Face was also transported to London, with the Astaires again in their leading roles and the comic role was taken by Leslie Henson. There was a huge advance sale. Critics thought that judging from the applause on opening night the show would have an unlimited run, largely because of the Astaires, who showed their best. The Gershwins were becoming a pillar of West End musicals.

By then George Gershwin was deep into the production of *Rosalie*, working for the first time for Florenz Ziegfeld on "a colossal combination of musical comedy, operetta, and extravaganza that served as sumptuous salute to the Main Stem's most radiant star, Marilyn Miller."[42] The score was to have been written by Sigmund Romberg, but when Ziegfeld wanted a faster schedule, Gershwin was enlisted to help out. Gershwin's contribution included a number of recycled melodies: "Beautiful Gypsy," the music for "Wait a Bit Susie" from *Primrose*. This was replaced by "Say So," which had been cut from *Funny Face*. "Show Me the Town" was lifted from *Oh, Kay!* and Gershwin's principal contribution was to salvage "How Long Has This Been Going On," discarded from *Funny Face* a few weeks earlier. It became one of his most durable ballads among sophisticated songstresses. In the original *Rosalie*, however, it was rejected by Marilyn Miller as too melancholy, and thus sung by the ingenue Bobbe Arnst. Miller also turned down a chance to sing "The Man I Love," which still had not found a home.

Rosalie opened at Ziegfeld's New Amsterdam Theater on January 10, 1928. It was more of an operetta than a Broadway book musical. The setting was the military academy at West Point. Marilyn Miller played a princess of "Romanza." She is visiting West Point, but incognito at first. The show benefitted from the publicity given the visit of a genuine queen, the glamorous Marie of Romania, a few months before. It had two sets of music. Romberg wrote the European part, naturally, and P.G. Wodehouse supplied the lyrics. Gershwin did the American segments, and George and Ira wrote a bouncing score: "Yankee Doodle Rhythm," as well as "Oh Gee! Oh Joy!" and "Say So!" both delightful, which one review described as "smash hits." They contrasted with the more romantic ballads of Romberg. The score served its purpose, wrote Brooks Atkinson, but scarcely added to the lustre of either Gershwin or Romberg. To be sure, the title song "Rosalie" is trite and surprisingly bad for George Gershwin.

Both Guy Bolton and P.G. Wodehouse worked on the book. Wodehouse commented that while he did not much like the show the presence of Marilyn Miller and Jack Donahue guaranteed a success. And he was right. *Rosalie* enjoyed a quite respectable run of 335 performances. It was a blend of an old-fashioned operetta and a 1920s musical. On the other hand, while the "radiant" Marilyn Miller was engaging, the new show did not match her *Sunny* or the "perfection" of *Show Boat*, wrote Brooks Atkinson. Alexander Woollcott caught the appeal of the show and Marilyn Miller:

> Down in the orchestra pit the violins chitter with excitement and the brasses blare. The spotlight turns white with expectation. Fifty beautiful girls in simple peasant costumes of satin and chiffon rush pellmell onto the stage, all squealing simple peasant outcries of "Here she comes!" Fifty hussars in fatigue uniforms of ivory white and tomato bisque march on in columns of four and kneel to express an emotion too strong for words. . . . The house holds its breath and on walks Marilyn Miller.[43]

Rosalie opened a few days after *Show Boat*. Comparisons were inevitable. It is rather amazing that a seasoned critic like Gilbert Gabriel wrote that *Rosalie* was "immensely livelier entertainment" than *Show Boat*. This seminal show's inspiration was Jerome Kern's. In the fall of 1926 he had read about one-half of the new best-seller by Edna Ferber. He was so excited that he telephoned Oscar Hammerstein, his collaborator on *Sunny* and urged him to read the novel. It had a "million dollar" title, Kern exclaimed. Hammerstein agreed that *Show Boat* was an attractive project—even though the plot centered around an extremely sensitive issue—miscegenation.

Show Boat became a slice of Americana, brought to life by the music that drew on both a genuine American voice and the European tradition. Kern was the ideal composer to combine these elements. It was not, however, a dividing line as its admirers are wont to claim. *Show Boat* did not become a model because it was the culmination of an era rather than a new breakout. It was in the tradition of Herbert or even Lehar, basically a bittersweet romance but set in the new world, much as Herbert had tried to do. It was what Kern had been striving for over a decade. In retrospect, but only in retrospect, it was unique in its time. If the "perfection" of *Show Boat* marked the beginning of a new era in the American musical, few, including the Gershwins, realized it, although Gershwin was quite impressed; he would say later that it was the finest light opera achievement in American music. Nevertheless, its successor would not come until Oscar Hammerstein and Richard Rodgers created *Oklahoma!* in 1943, sixteen years later.

Most of the musicals that followed were in the current popular mode of revues or romantic comedies. A most popular new show was *Good News*, a daffy college romp with jazzy lyrics and songs by De Sylva and Lew Brown (lyrics) and Ray Henderson (music). As for the Gershwins, one historian of the musical stage concluded that *Oh, Kay!* and *Funny Face* together represent the "summit" of what a Gershwin show meant in the 1920s:

> All the elements introduced in *Lady Be Good!* were in place—the duo pianists Phil Ohman and Victor Arden superintending the Gershwin autograph sound in the pit; silly stories as thin as clothesline on which to hang songs, dance and comedy for the maximum effect; first class Aarons and Freedley productions—not spectacles but sound fully fleshed presentations; astonishingly tune-filled, even hit-filled scores.[44]

It may well be that the Gershwins had reached their summit, but they still had major triumphs to register. The 1920s were still roaring, and few if any saw that the Jazz Age was approaching its end.

Meanwhile, the Gershwins had moved to New York's upper West Side, at 103rd and Riverside Drive. It was a spacious apartment house with five floors. George occupied the top floor, accessible by an elevator. The playwright Sam Behrman characterized the top floor as "sacrosanct" and a symbol of George's new dignity (decorated by Kay Swift). Still, the atmosphere was slightly chaotic: the lower floors would be occupied by groups playing ping pong, playing cards, chattering, and smoking. When Behrman asked Ira the identity of these groups, Ira confessed he did not know them, probably friends of Arthur's. When asked about George, Ira also confessed that George had taken his old rooms at the hotel around the corner to work on *Funny Face*. Indeed, in the tumult of the older house at 110th Street, George used to mutter that he needed privacy. Behrman wrote that nevertheless he had long come to the conclusion that George did not in fact need privacy. His talent was so prodigal that he did not have to dig and prod for his music.

NOTES

1. Frederick Lewis Allen, *Only Yesterday* (New York: Harper Collins, Perennial Classics, 2000; originally published in 1931), p. 236.

2. Alec Wilder, *American Popular Song The Great Innovators 1900–1950*, ed. James T. Maher (New York: Oxford University Press, 1972), pp. 132–33.

3. Gershwin cut a piano roll of "That Certain Feeling" in April 1926 and a record in July 1926 in London; his tempo is on the fast side. Paul Whiteman recorded a version earlier, in December 1925. It too attempts a "hot" tempo, with a bevy of jazzy flourishes.

In the Gershwin *Song-Book* the melody is marked "moderato simplice," but the piano improvisation that follows is marked "ardently."

4. Frederick Nolan, *Lorenz Hart* (New York: Oxford University Press, 1994), pp. 72–73.

5. A synopsis of the plot is included in the liner notes by Mark Trent Goldberg for the New World Records CD of *Tip Toes* and *Tell Me More*, CD 85598–2. *Tip Toes* was performed in a concert version at Carnegie Hall, and then recorded under the music direction of Rob Fisher.

6. "Sweet and Low Down" is usually played "hot"; for example, in the Paul Whiteman recording of December 1925, which features a jazz trombone solo. The original music, however, is marked "moderato," and Gershwin's piano improvisation is marked "Slow (in a jazzy manner)." This is more or less how George Gershwin played it in his piano roll of April 1926 and his recording of July 1926. Without any accompaniment, he maintains a strong, steady tempo. ("Gershwin Plays Gershwin, The Piano Rolls," Elektra Nonesuch 9 79287–2; "Gershwin Plays Gershwin" Nostalgia, Naxos, 8.120512.) At the suggestion of the great trumpet player Bunny Berigan, the vocalist Lee Wiley recorded "Sweet and Low Down" in 1939. Her tempo is moderate, slightly slower than the Gershwin recordings, but she and her accompanists gave it a "swing" rhythm. "Sweet and Low Down" was revived as a special dance number in the 1980s musical *My One and Only*, performed by Tommy Tune and the late Honey Coles. They sang and danced it into a genuine show stopper.

7. Alexander Woollcott, "Mr. Gershwin's Latest," *New York World*, December 29, 1925, printed in *Gershwin in His Time: A Biographical Scrapbook, 1919–1937*, ed. Gregory R. Suriano (New York: Gramercy Books, 1998), p. 35.

8. A recording of most of the original score by the British cast is contained in a long playing record, "George and Ira Gershwin's Tip Toes," Monmouth Evergreen Records, MES/7052. Dorothy Dickson played Tip Toes.

9. A complete restoration of the score was undertaken in 1998, and performed at Carnegie's Weill Recital Hall and then recorded. The score was restored by Rob Fisher, and the role of Tip Toes was sung by Emily Loesser; "Tip Toes," New World Records CD 80598–2.

10. Ethan Mordden, *Make Believe* (New York: Oxford University Press, 1997), p. 110; the title number, "Song of the Flame," sounds more like Friml or Romberg than Gershwin.

11. Robert Kimball and Alfred Simon, *The Gershwins* (New York: Baonanza Books, 1963), p. 59. Tessa Kosta recorded the title song, attributed to Gershwin and Hammerstein in 1926; it is a dramatic song, with a pseudo-Russian tone; her voice could pass for Jeannette MacDonald.

12. Robert Russell Bennett, *The Broadway Sound*, ed. George J. Ferencz (Rochester: The Rochester University Press, 2001), pp. 78–79.

13. Mordden, *Make Believe*, pp. 110–11.

14. Nicholas Fox Weber, *Patron Saints* (New York: Knopf, 1992; reprint, New Haven, CT: Yale University Press, 1995), p. 247. The author was Kay Swift's grandson by marriage.

15. Katharine Weber, "The Memory of All That," in *A Few Thousand Words about Love*, ed. Mickey Pearlman (New York: St. Martin's Press, 1998), p. 23.

16. Ron Chernow, *The Warburgs* (New York: Random House, Vintage Books edition, 1994), p. 333.

17. Beverley Nichols printed in *George Gershwin*, ed. Merle Armitage (New York: Longmans, Green, 1938), p. 231.

18. Kimball and Simon, *The Gershwins*, p. 63.

19. Robert Wyatt, "The Seven Jazz Preludes of George Gershwin: A Historical Narrative," *American Music*, Spring 1989. The original manuscripts are in the Library of Congress, Gershwin Collection.

20. Steven Gilbert, *The Music of George Gershwin* (New Haven, CT: Yale University Press, 1995), p. 151.

21. These piano pieces are included in "The Complete Gershwin Keyboard Works" (Warner Brothers, 1996). They are edited by Alicia Zizzo. There are minor discrepancies between these versions and the manuscripts in the Library of Congress' Gershwin Collection. Gershwin's written metronome markings of tempo have been eliminated.

22. The *Three Preludes* were recorded by Gershwin in June 1928 in London. Gershwin's interpretations are not as brisk for the first and third, as well as not as slow for the second, as versions that came to be the standard. Oscar Levant's recordings, not surprisingly, came closest to Gershwin's original version.

23. In the modern reconstruction of this show, recorded in the Roxbury Recordings series of Gershwin shows; the man in charge of the reconstruction, Tommy Krasker, relates the story about moving this song; in the recording he supervised the song comes early as originally intended.

24. Gertrude Lawrence's original rendition of this song is available on a CD in the Smithsonian collection, *The American Musical Theater*, Vol I. She also recorded the same song, and "Do, Do, Do" with only a piano accompaniment shortly after the show opened. Her comical bent is evident in "Do, Do, Do." Interestingly, both Lawrence and Adele Astaire sound very much alike, in contrast to other popular singers of that day, like Helen Morgan and Ruth Etting, who have less tremolo.

25. Quoting Ira Gershwin, *Lyrics on Several Occasions*, in *The Complete Lyrics of Ira Gershwin*, ed. Robert Kimball (New York: Knopf, 1993), pp. 80–83.

26. Almost all of Gershwin's recordings of his music are taken at a faster pace than modern versions; one reason was that his piano style was not well-suited to slow tempos. His ability to maintain a fast tempo throughout, even including the verses, is quite extraordinary, and his flourishes, including changing keys, give his melodies a special flavor. The original tempos are probably better reflected in the vocal versions by Adele Astaire or Gertrude Lawrence.

27. Ethan Mordden, *Make Believe*, p. 155.

28. Sheridan Morley, *A Bright Particular Star* (New York: Pavillion Books, 1986), p. 1.

29. Dietz's role is somewhat clouded. In the published songs, Dietz's name along with Ira's appears on "Heaven on Earth" and Oh, Kay! Ira said that Dietz collaborated on two lyrics and helped out with a "couple" of other songs. But Dietz had some role in providing the title for "Someone to Watch Over Me," and it is likely that he wrote some lyrics for this song. In the vocal selections from the show, this song is in the key of C; but in other publications it is in E-flat.

30. *Oh, Kay!* was re-created in the series sponsored by Leonore Gershwin: Nonesuch Records, Roxbury Recordings, 79361. The Orchestra of St. Luke's was conducted by Eric Stern. Tommy Krasker was in charge of the restoration, and he and Lee Davis contributed excellent short essays for the accompanying pamphlet. Dawn Upshaw sang the role of Gertrude Lawrence.

31. Charles L. Buchanan, "Gershwin and Musical Snobbery," *The Outlook*, February 2, 1927, printed in Suriano, *Gershwin in His Time*, p. 44.

32. Francis Davis, *Outcats* (New York: Oxford University Press, 1990), p. 187.

33. David Schiff, "Misunderstanding Gershwin," *Atlantic Monthly*, October 1998, p. 104.

34. Carol J. Oja, "Gershwin and American Modernists of the 1920s," *Musical Quarterly*, 78/4 (1994), pp. 654–55; the quotation from E.B. Hill is on p. 654.

35. Carol J. Oja, *Making Music Modern* (New York: Oxford University Press, 2000), p. 353–55. Professor Oja writes that the appearance of Copland's *Piano Concerto* one year after Gershwin's *Concerto in F* resulted in an "undeclared contest that pitted Copland against Gershwin."

36. Undated clipping of an interview, probably November 1925; located in the Gershwin Collection, Library of Congress.

37. Joan Pirie, "Winning the Battle and Losing the War: The 1927 *Strike Up the Band*," in *Musical Theater in America*, ed. Glenn Loney (Westport, CT: Greenwood Press, 1984).

38. The entire score was reconstructed by the musicologist Tommy Krasker and recorded by John Mauceri as conductor; it is in the series sponsored by the late Leonore Gershwin: Roxbury Recordings, Elektra Nonesuch CD 79273–2, on two compact discs entitled "Strike Up the Band."

39. Kay Swift was a great fan of Gilbert and Sullivan, and perhaps she urged the Gershwins in that direction.

40. Edward Jablonski, *Gershwin: A Biography* (New York: Doubleday, 1987), p. 146.

41. "My One and Only" was the title adopted for a revival based on *Funny Face* in the 1980s, featuring Tommy Tune and Twiggy. It was a solid hit, running for several years. The librettists Peter Stone and Timothy S. Mayer tried to refurbish the original, but found it too dated. A new plot, with the twang of the twenties, was concocted, and the producers claimed that Ira Gershwin even helped with some new lyrics (not true according to Michael Feinstein). Most of the score for *Funny Face* was incorporated, with some additions from other Gershwin shows, especially "Sweet and Low Down" and "How Long Has This Been Going On?" *Funny Face* also became a movie, but many years after the Broadway version, with Fred Astaire and Audrey Hepburn, with a much altered plot but many of the original songs.

42. Robert Kimball, ed., "Introduction," in *The Complete Lyrics of Ira Gershwin* (New York: Knopf, 1993), p. xi.

43. Quoted in William G. Hyland, *The Song Is Ended* (New York: Oxford University Press, 1995), p. 44.

44. Mordden, *Make Believe*, p. 110.

Grandpa Bruskin. (© Library of Congress, Music Division)

Grandma Bruskin. (© Library of Congress, Music Division)

Morris and Rose Gershovitz around the time of their marriage, July 1895. (© Library of Congress, Music Division)

Rose Gershwin (right), Prospect Park, Brooklyn, circa 1901, with a maid and her sons: Arthur, George, and Ira. (© Library of Congress, Music Division)

(Left to right) Deems Taylor, Ferde Grofé, Paul Whiteman, Blossom Seely, and George Gershwin discussing concert of "135th Street," 1925. (© Library of Congress, Music Division)

George Gershwin in a rented house in Beverly Hills, late 1930. (© Library of Congress, Music Division)

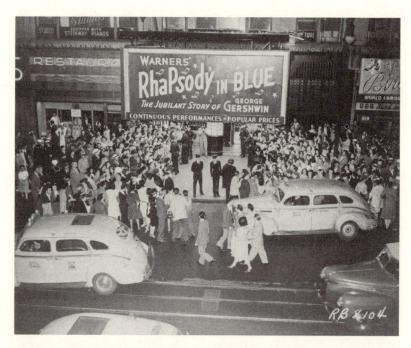

Premiere of the movie *Rhapsody in Blue*. (© Library of Congress, Music Division)

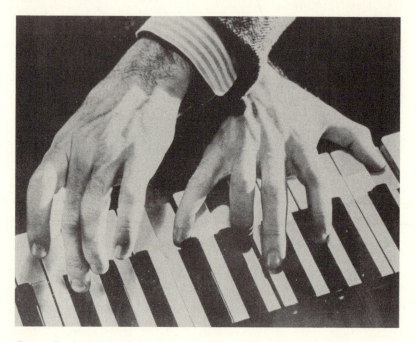

George Gershwin's hands in crossover, playing *Rhapsody in Blue*. (© Museum of the City of New York)

Bill Daly, in a photo taken by Gershwin. (© Library of Congress, Music Division)

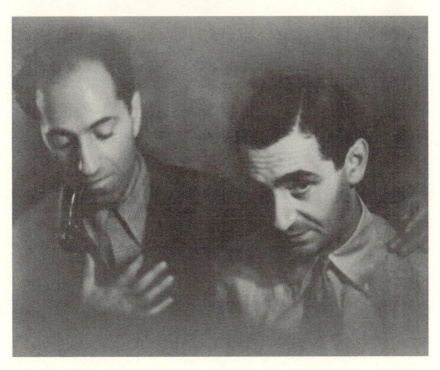

George Gershwin with Irving Berlin, in a photo taken by Gershwin. (© Library of Congress, Music Division)

George Gershwin and Jerome Kern in a broadcasting studio, June 1933. (© Library of Congress, Music Division)

George Gershwin, DuBose Heyward, and Ira Gershwin working on *Porgy and Bess*. (© Library of Congress, Music Division)

Boston premiere of *Porgy and Bess*, 1935. (© Library of Congress, Music Division)

George and Ira Gershwin boarding a plane for Hollywood, August 1936. (© Library of Congress, Music Division)

George Gershwin painting a portrait of composer Arnold Schoenberg, December 1936. (© Library of Congress, Music Division)

George Gershwin at the piano in his 72nd Street apartment, in front of a portrait that he painted of his valet Paul's daughter. (© Museum of the City of New York)

George Gershwin demonstrating songs for *Shall We Dance*. Fred Astaire and Ginger Rogers are seated to his right; behind him are Ira Gershwin and musical director Nathaniel Shilkret. Standing behind Rogers and Astaire are dance director Hermes Pan and director Mark Sandrich. (© Library of Congress, Music Division)

George Gershwin conducting a rehearsal for an All-Gershwin Concert in Los Angeles in February 1937, during which he first showed signs of his fatal illness. (© Library of Congress, Music Division)

Almost immediately after completing the *Shall We Dance* songs, the Gershwins went to work on *A Damsel in Distress*, which starred Astaire without Rogers. Photo was taken in the spring of 1937. (© Library of Congress, Music Division)

The last known photo of George Gershwin, performing at the RKO Radio Picture Convention, June 19, 1937. (© Museum of the City of New York)

Chapter 8

An American in Paris

In the spring of 1928 the Gershwins—George, Ira, Lee, and Frances—embarked on a grand tour, stopping first in London, then to Paris, on to Vienna, a side trip to Budapest, and back to Paris. It was sightseeing for a change. George had no concerts scheduled, though nothing could prevent his performance at parties, including on shipboard. Before leaving he wrote to Mabel Schirmer, who lived in Paris, that he wanted to do some work, perhaps in the south of France. He was looking forward to the trip, he wrote, more than any other, because for the first time he did not have to perform.

They sailed on March 10, 1928, after discussing with Flo Ziegfeld a new show he was planning, tentatively titled *East Is West*. The night before sailing they all gathered for a going away party given by Kay Swift Warburg and her husband. The celebration lasted until five in the morning. The trip was pleasant. Ira kept a diary, noting that George played in the lounge of the restaurant to a crowd of about thirty passengers. On board was the well-known violinist and composer Albert Spalding. In London, George and Ira almost immediately began to encounter friends. While visiting an auto showroom, they ran into Vincent Youmans and Max Dreyfus, and were soon joined by Jerome Kern and Robert Russell Bennett. The Gershwins had already signed a contract to do Ziegfeld's *East Is West* (they received an advance of $1,500; $1,000 for George and $500 for Ira) and were surprised to learn from Youmans that he was going to write it—typical Ziegfeld chicanery. In the end no one wrote it. George began his round of socializing: Lady Mountbatten's for dinner, chatting with the Prince of Wales at the Embassy Club; a Gershwin evening at the Kit Kat Club; drinks and dinner with Noel Coward, Lady Mountbatten, Andre Charlot, Jerome Kern, and Guy Bolton. And then the Gershwins attended the final performance of *Oh,*

Kay! Despite some clowning by Gertrude Lawrence, the show was an agreeable surprise, especially since Jerome Kern had warned them that it was poor.[1]

In Paris they settled in for four weeks at the Majestic Hotel. One writer who interviewed Ira described the Gershwins' stop in Paris as a "series of soirees." When she visited their suite at the Majestic she found the rooms in great disarray; strewn about were a Victrola, a collection of taxi horns, and other "noise producing objects." George was sleeping, but Ira sat there calm and sphinx-like, while his wife adjusted the cufflinks and studs in his dress shirt. Ira ventured the view that there were more musicians in London determined to play loud enough to drown out the words. He attributed this to lower wages in Britain.

The Gershwins attended a performance of *Rhapsody in Blue* on March 31. It was so bad that George quietly adjourned to the bar next door. Ira had to retrieve him when the audience demanded to see him. An encore was demanded, and the two featured concert pianists played "Do, Do, Do" to Ira's astonishment. Later the conductor apologized to George for the performance saying they had had little time to prepare. Dimitri Tiomkin, the future Hollywood composer, dropped by; he was preparing to play Gershwin's *Concerto in F* with Vladimir Golschman conducting. George, with Mabel Schirmer in tow, went shopping for French taxi horns.

During the trip George made several musical contacts. In Berlin he met Kurt Weill, who hosted a small reception. He also had lunch with Franz Lehar and attended a performance of Krenek's anti-war "opera" *Jonny Spielt Auf*. A friend, Lester Donahue, commented rather loudly in the lobby that if a jazz opera was to be written it should be by George Gershwin. Someone commented "Oh, Yeah," and Donahue turned to encounter the Gershwins. Donahue said that Gershwin was very fair in his comments about Krenek. He said it was a "worthy effort" (this does not seems very favorable).

In Vienna he was hosted for lunch at the famous Sacher's restaurant by the acclaimed operetta composer Emmerich Kalman (*Countess Maritza*). Perhaps most important in terms of musical influence was a meeting in Vienna with Alban Berg, the student of Arnold Schoenberg. Along with Berg, Gershwin attended a private performance of Berg's *Lyric Suite*. Berg gave him an autographed photo with a sketch of a few measures from the *Lyric Suite*. Although Gershwin became a good friend to Schoenberg in New York and Hollywood and admired Berg's opera *Wozzeck*, he showed no tendency to write in the twelve-tone system devised by Schoenberg. What intrigued Gershwin was the studied use of dissonance, which he adopted sparingly but to good effect. In Paris he met Arthur Honneger, and visited Nadia Boulanger in her studio.

Despite the incompatible surroundings or distractions, Gershwin's ability to focus on his compositions was again evident. Throughout this tour, he worked on *An American in Paris*. Its precise origins are murky. Oscar Levant commented that Gershwin never wrote a score in strict musical form. He could not accustom himself to such restraints as the sonata form, or a rondo, or any of the other classical modes: "The thematic fluency, the easy going rhythmic freedom of the rhapsody or unrestricted fantasy was his natural genre." Even the concerto, Levant said, was a "Lisztian mantle draped loosely on the skeleton of the sonata form."[2]

In light of such comments it is no surprise that George's next major work was a fantasy of sorts, *An American in Paris*. As noted, he must have had the basic concept as early as the spring of 1926 when he had visited Paris. By then he had conceived of the opening "walking" theme. For a time, however, he was "stuck," according to Mabel Schirmer. Nevertheless, before his European trip he apparently had composed the slow movement based on a blues theme. In the Gershwin collection there is a separate pencil sketch of the blues theme in a different key than the final version, but without a date. The two-piano version he wrote is dated January 1, 1928, presumably the date he began, roughly two months before leaving for Europe; on the orchestral score is written "Begun in early 1928." He must have made considerable progress during his stay in Paris. One afternoon in Paris, two young pianists visited him and he put them to work playing the taxi horns in rhythm while he played the beginning passages. While in Vienna on April 29, Richard Simon, the publisher and brother of Alfred Simon and a sometime Gershwin rehearsal pianist, heard Gershwin play quite a large portion of *An American in Paris*. Simon was enthusiastic: "boy if the slow movement isn't going to throw the public for a row of W.C.'s then I'm just tone deaf." This encounter, probably May 1, suggests that George had completed the blues theme.[3] By May 22, Ira wrote in his diary that *An American in Paris* was "getting along nicely."

After Tiomkin's concert, there was a reception given by Tiomkin for three hundred guests in Gershwin's honor—"one of the most remarkable receptions staged here this season," commented a French newspaper. The concerto played by Tiomkin drew a thunderous ovation, and George was compelled to come to the front of his box to acknowledge the audience—"the greatest manifestation of enthusiasm seen at the Paris Opera for a long time past." (The French reviews of the concerto were not so kind.) Before the Gershwins left for home, George went back to London briefly by himself to discuss a new show with Gertrude Lawrence, to be produced by Alex Aarons (this would become *Treasure Girl*).

The trip was an inspiration for George. After he returned to New York, he wrote a lady friend he had met in Paris that for the first time in his life he was in a "real musical atmosphere." He decided, he wrote, that he would like to spend the rest of his life working mornings in New York, and then spending his evenings in Paris.[4] All of them returned to New York on June 18. Among the friends welcoming them was a young college student, a relative of the Strunskys named Rosamond Walling. George was smitten with her and they struck up a romantic relationship, even though she was a student at Swarthmore. For two years they conducted an affectionate correspondence and romance that lasted until George left for Hollywood and Rosamond left for Geneva where she eventually married a diplomat.

When he arrived in New York he brought back a nearly finished "sketch" of

An American in Paris. He had embarked on his new composition without any commitments for a performance, but eventually he agreed to a New York Philharmonic premiere. Accordingly, Walter Damrosch pestered him for a schedule, which George had to dodge for a time. In early August, he told Damrosch that he had finished the "first sketch," and hoped to complete a two-piano arrangement within a few days. In fact, he had finished more than just a first sketch but he faced the orchestration, which was not completed until November 18, 1928. He wrote some of the orchestration at Kay Swift's guest cottage at her farm in Connecticut. But he still had to evade a precise commitment to a date for the first performance. He cited the new show with Gertrude Lawrence as an excuse. He was, in fact, working on the score for *Treasure Girl*, which opened on November 8.

Thus he was writing the score for a musical while completing his concert work. It is interesting that there are no similarities. He could compartmentalize, apparently quite easily. *An American in Paris* is programmatic music: "really a rhapsodic ballet, [that] is written very freely and is the most modern music I've yet attempted," Gershwin wrote. "The opening part will be developed in typical French style, in the manner of Debussy and the Six, though the tunes are all original."[5] According to elaborate program notes issued for the New York Philharmonic premiere, written by Deems Taylor, each segment represented some facet of an American experiencing life in Paris. Starting by walking down the Champs-Élyseés, but overtaken by homesickness (the blues theme) he then encounters another American (the Charleston theme), but finally returns to the pleasures of Paris, with a second "walking" theme" and the finale.

The premiere performance was at Carnegie Hall, December 13, 1928. The influence of his visit to Europe was evident more in the orchestration than in the composition. It is in the orchestral transformation that the influence of the French, especially Debussy, is most obvious. Gershwin used such novelties as a xylophone and celesta, as well as three saxophones. Vernon Duke objected to the sweetness of the blues, once again played by a solo trumpet as in the concerto. When Duke first heard it in Paris he thought the composition was too sentimental and argued against it, but the British composer William Walton reassured George, who probably would have left it alone in any case.

There is a similarity between the blues themes in the concerto and *An American in Paris.* Both are introduced by a solo trumpet; both begin with a long sustained note and consist of three eight-bar phrases; both drop down an octave. *American* is marked "Tempo Blues" at this point in the piano score, while Gershwin called the passage in the concerto a "pure blues." In both cases the blues aura is embedded more in the accompanying harmony than the melody of the trumpet theme. Although *American* uses a blue note, the concerto does not.

The reception of his new composition was becoming a pattern. Just as the concerto was compared with the *Rhapsody*, *American* was compared to both. George was competing with himself. The partisanship on each side was growing meaner and sharper. Olin Downes concluded that in *American* there was a material gain in workmanship and structure over the two earlier pieces. Moreover, in *American*, Gershwin had returned to his "native vein" which he had forsaken in his more serious *Concerto in F*. Lawrence Gilman, as expected, was indifferent, devoting his entire review to a sarcastic commentary on the program notes of what the imaginary American was doing strolling around Paris. Herbert Peyser's review in the *New York Telegram* (December 14, 1928) tore it to shreds: "nauseous clap trap, so dull patchy, thin, vulgar long winded and inane. . . . Even as honest jazz the whole cheap and silly affair seemed pitifully futile and inept." Leonard Leibling countered that it was "merrily, rollicking appealing music. . . . Anyone who dislikes this piece is not an American." Once again Gershwin's melodies were so striking that the critics focused on them and dismissed the development and transitions as "filler" (Leonard Bernstein's phrase many years later). Downes made this same point, that it contained "too much material, too many ideas for its best good." More recently Steven E. Gilbert, in his extensive analysis, wrote: "The piece is far more advanced than its predecessor, not only harmonically and contrapuntally but also rhythmically."[6]

Forty-five years after its premiere, *An American in Paris* was performed under the baton of Gunther Schuller and the New England Conservatory orchestra. The review in the *Boston Globe* commented (December 11, 1973): "It is an enshrinement of two cliches, but it is funny and touching, the big slow tune in the middle is a lovely indulgent squeeze, it is all put together neatly and without strain, and the sound has a captivating flash and richness to it. . . . Gershwin extracts astonishingly varied and vivid colors."

As he had told Damrosch, Gershwin had been preoccupied with the new show for Gertrude Lawrence. At first there was talk with Ziegfeld of another show to succeed *Rosalie*, again with Marilyn Miller. But Ziegfeld was unreliable, and the Gershwins preferred to try their hand in another Aarons-Freedley show, *Treasure Girl*. It should have been a hit since it was almost the same group that presented *Lady Be Good!*, *Tip Toes*, and *Oh, Kay!* Once again the producers were Aarons and Freedley. Fred Thompson, Bolton's collaborator from *Lady Be Good!*, and one of the authors of *Funny Face*, wrote the book. In addition to Gertrude Lawrence the cast included the comedian Walter Catlett, also from *Lady Be Good!*, and Clifton Webb (then a debonair young leading man). The conductor was the Gershwins' friend Alfred Newman, and the orchestrations were by Bill Daly. Lawrence was so confident that she brought her daughter, her maid, and two automobiles from London.

Surprisingly, the show folded soon after its opening (68 performances). It is an interesting commentary on the delicate balance of musical comedies; virtually the same team created two major hits, and then a dismal failure, all within a few years. Again the plot was the culprit. Ira Gershwin blamed the book for making Gertrude Lawrence's character too conniving. She played a money-grabbing adventuress looking for a $100,000 treasure, betraying various people in the quest. It was not an appropriate part for Gertrude Lawrence, whose image was that of the "poor little rich girl." Brooks Atkinson wrote that the show was not merely an "innocuous pastiche," but an "evil thing," presenting Gertrude Lawrence in a disagreeable light, portraying her as a "malicious liar and a spoiled child." This was unfortunate because Atkinson found that Gertrude Lawrence:

> embodies most of the qualities that make for versatility and splendor in musical comedy stars—slender, fresh beauty, a lilting style of dancing, fullness and sweetness of voice, infectious mirth, a trick or two of clowning, subtle coquetry and a gift for dramatic acting . . . when she sings, when she dances she is irresistible.[7]

The score was loaded with gems that included "I've Got a Crush on You," and also featured "I Don't Think I'll Fall in Love Today" and "Feeling I'm Falling," as well as "Oh, So Nice" and "Where's the Boy? Here's The Girl!" Unfortunately, much of the score was forgotten after the show folded. One of the best songs, "Got a Rainbow," for example, is virtually unknown. Moreover, "I've Got a Crush on You" gained little attention. On stage it had been a brightly paced dance number; one of the fastest, Ira recalled. Some years later the jazz vocalist Lee Wiley rediscovered it and slowed down the tempo turning it into a plaintive ballad. Ira Gershwin was perplexed when he first heard this slow version, but came to like it. In any case, this interpretation then became a standard, and all subsequent renditions, including Frank Sinatra's, have been at the ballad tempo. The reviews found that the bright spot was the music, even though Gershwin had done better. The listeners had grown to expect too much, and were disappointed when all of his tunes were not as original and gifted as his best ones.

The tension between the book on the one hand, and the music and lyrics on the other was not an unusual problem. It happened to all composers, not just the Gershwins. In any case, *Treasure Girl* folded, taken to "Cain's warehouse" as Ira put it (Cain's was the warehouse where used scenery was stored).

Meanwhile, Ziegfeld's plans for something new for Marilyn Miller were progressing. At first he wanted to revive a straight drama, *East Is West*, produced many years earlier, and turn it into a musical, tentatively titled *Ming Toy*. The Gershwins began work on a score, even though there was no book. The original was the story of an Asian girl, Ming Toy, who fell in love with a European. P.G. Wodehouse worked on it for a time. He hated it and described it to a friend: it was about a Chinese girl who goes around saying "Me love Chlistian god velly much." Despite some work done by the Gershwins, the entire project collapsed. Marilyn Miller turned it down because the subject of racial intermarriage in Asia was too serious for her image.

Without Marilyn Miller, Ziegfeld lost interest in the show. For this abortive outing George wrote one of his finest melodies, "Embraceable You." For a ballet sequence of Chinese girls, they had written "In the Mandarin's Orchid Garden." Although there were lyrics it was more an instrumental, and eventually it became an "art song." The Gershwins also finished "Lady of the Moon," which was not used, but for *Show Girl* a year later it reemerged with new lyrics; again it was discarded. Finally it was salvaged for the Gershwins' movie score *Delicious*. Thus the same melody went through three iterations. For the final one for the movie *Delicious*, to the very same melody Ira wrote a new version, a parody of love songs entitled "Blah, Blah, Blah."

After *East Is West* was abandoned, its place was taken by yet another Ziegfeld project, tentatively entitled *Show Girl*. The story line was about a young aspiring dancer, Dixie Dugan, who meets Ziegfeld (on stage, that is), and he encourages her career. Once again Marilyn Miller opted out, and the part went to a young dancer named Ruby Keeler, who had gained fame by marrying Al Jolson. Ziegfeld demanded a rush job, the fastest Gershwin had done, George said afterwards. In April and May the Gershwins were working on this show, and it went into rehearsal although 75 percent of the music and lyrics were still to be written. Nevertheless, George said they were "miles ahead of the book." The last scene was rehearsed on the train to Boston. Bill Daly conducted the orchestra; orchestrations were by Maurice de Packh and Daly. The score was not particularly distinguished. One of the better songs, "Feeling Sentimental," was dropped after opening. The mildly risque "Do What You Do" attracted some attention, but the Gershwins' major contribution was "Liza."

On opening night in New York, July 2, 1929, in the second act, as Ruby Keeler began to descend a stairway set up on the stage of the Ziegfeld Theater, surrounded by eighty chorus girls, to sing and dance to "Liza," suddenly a voice arose from the aisle of the second row. It was her new husband belting out the opening bars. It created a sensation. In his movie biography, *The Jolson Story*, this incident is dramatically portrayed. In that version, Ruby Keeler supposedly falters at the top of the steps, and Jolson rises to her rescue. His unexpected presence in the audience was a welcome surprise; she regained her confidence and went on to stardom. This happened, in fact, not in the Broadway opening but in the dress rehearsal. At the Broadway opening Ruby Keeler knew Jolson was there because he had continued to intervene in the out-of-town previews (to the surprise of all concerned, including the Gershwins). Jolson was not above exploiting their recent marriage for a little publicity. He had attended every rehearsal and overwhelmed his new wife with advice. Fifty years later, Keeler admitted that she still had no idea why Jolson did it. Of course, it gave "Liza" a "great start," Ira commented.

One can only wonder whether this whole episode was a setup by Ziegfeld. The Gershwins were told by Ziegfeld to write a minstrel number for Ruby Keeler to dance and sing backed by a huge chorus. So the Gershwins wrote "Liza" with a melody and lyrics not ideally suited to Ruby Keeler, but perfect for Al Jolson.

The song evoked near adulation from Gershwin's first biographer, Isaac Goldberg: "I should call it one of the happiest touches in our contemporary music." He was referring to the first four bars, in which the melody and underlying harmonies mirror the growing "anxiety" of the lyric. Supposedly, Gershwin did not realize, until pointed out by Goldberg, that the refrain begins with half notes, continues with quarter notes, and "dissolves into eights." Goldberg adds that this is a Gershwin characteristic: starting on a long note, then letting it "spatter into shorter ones." He cites the blues theme of *An American in Paris*, and the refrain of "Soon" in *Strike Up the Band*—not very impressive evidence, but a point worth noting.[8]

Show Girl was a hodgepodge of talents. It was virtually a revue. Clayton, Jackson, and Durante performed some of their specialties, as did Nick Lucas. Duke Ellington's orchestra played two numbers, recommended by Gershwin. Ellington wrote favorably of Gershwin's willingness, dressed like a stagehand, to pitch in and help put the show in shape. In his memoirs Ellington noted that Oscar Levant told him that Gershwin said he wished he had written the bridge to "Sophisticated Lady." That made Ellington very "proud."[9] The second act opened with a long ballet sequence danced to *An American in Paris* by Harriet Hoctor and the Albertina Rasch troupe, which one reviewer thought was the high point.

The lyrics were credited to both Ira and Gus Kahn, whom Ziegfeld asked to be added to the credits because Ziegfeld owed him a favor. In fact, Kahn did help Ira with the words. The critics, however, were not enthusiastic. Brooks Atkinson of the *New York Times* wrote: "Although Mr. Gershwin's spray of notes does not result in a first rate score, it has moments of vividness." Another reviewer admitted that it was hard for Gershwin to come up to expectations; the result was a show that was "only fair." Keeler got good reviews, but once Jolson stopped his interventions, ticket sales declined and Keeler left the cast, replaced by Dorothy Stone. When Brooks Atkinson saw the show again he thought it had improved; on a second hearing he was especially impressed by the *An American in Paris* ballet. Gershwin, unlike most popular songwriters, Atkinson wrote, "composes with most flexibility when he is serious and ambitious. His heart is in his best work." Nevertheless, the show closed after 111 performances. Ziegfeld and the Gershwins had a dispute over money. The Gershwins had to threaten to sue for the money due them from the aborted *East Is West* as well as from *Show Girl*. (Rodgers and Hart had a similar experience.) The Gershwins and Ziegfeld "made up" later in October.[10]

The year was far from a washout. Gershwin received $50,000 for the use of the *Rhapsody* in a Paul Whiteman movie, *Jazz King*, with Bing Crosby in a small part. Gershwin performed the *Rhapsody* live at the Roxy for thirty-two performances. He ended with a lame back, sore fingers, and tired arms, but nevertheless he had great fun. In August it was reported that the Gershwins had been "won over" by the talkies, but for some reason Gershwin denied it, perhaps to improve his bargaining leverage. In fact, they signed a contract on September 22, 1930, for $100,000 from Fox studios ($70,000 for George and $30,000 for Ira). It was reported that George was skeptical, but had made a study of the talkies and concluded that they were a good vehicle for jazz and other forms of modern music.

Before Hollywood, and after a vacation in Florida, the Gershwins had yet another show that became memorable in the annals of Broadway for several reasons. The show was *Girl Crazy* (produced again by Aarons and Freedley), which opened on October 14, 1930, at the Alvin Theater. It had a fine score with some of the Gershwins' most enduring songs. The cast included Ginger Rogers in the lead role and introduced Ethel Merman to Broadway. Also in the cast were the leading man Allen Kearns and the comedian Willie Howard.

The story was about a young playboy from Manhattan, sent West by his father to settle down. He arrives in Arizona by taxi, and decides to start a dude ranch and gambling casino in Custerville. He employs a slinky lady named Kate, wife of Slick, a gambler. But he meets a local girl, Molly Gray, falls in love with her, but is rejected until he proves himself worthy in the code of the West. *Girl Crazy* was not only simply another frivolous comedy by the inevitable Guy Bolton. The score lifted it beyond the ordinary. It included: "I'm Biding My Time," "Embraceable You," "But Not for Me," and "I Got Rhythm." The performance of "I Got Rhythm" was one of those rare Broadway moments that was truly historic. The song was belted out by newcomer Ethel Merman playing Kate. She had been discovered by Freedley, who had her audition for Gershwin. She sang "Little White Lies," Gershwin hired her, and then played a selection from *Girl Crazy*: "Sam and Delilah," and "Boy What Love Has Done to Me." He asked Merman if she wanted any changes, and she replied, "No, they'll do nicely."

The highlight of her sensational debut was her astounding rendition of "I Got Rhythm." In this particular number she held one high note on the word "more" for an entire sixteen bars, a feat all of her successors and imitators in this role have felt compelled to emulate, with varying degrees of success. She stopped the show three times. At the opening night intermission Gershwin rushed to her dressing room and urged her never to take singing lessons or change her delivery in any way. They remained friends after Merman's career took off. She kept her autographed picture of Gershwin on her piano throughout her life. The headline of one review read, "Unbilled Singer Steals Honors of 'Girl Crazy.' " The review itself said that Ethel Merman "just rolled it up and took it away." Another reviewer, Robert Garland, wrote that Ethel Merman was the outstanding personality on the stage.

Ginger Rogers played Molly, the romantic lead. She was only nineteen, and she sang "Embraceable You," and "But Not for Me." It is difficult to think of a star blessed with two better numbers for her debut as a leading lady. It was during rehearsals that she first met Fred Astaire, who helped her with one of her numbers; they went out together, briefly. "Cute" was one critic's description of Ginger Rogers. She got $1,500 a week, and Merman $375.

George Gershwin conducted the opening night and received as much applause as the cast. The pit band, in addition to the usual complement, also included a small ensemble led by the jazz cornetist Red Nichols. His "orchestra" also included Glenn Miller and Benny Goodman. Gershwin wrote a clarinet part into the score for Goodman, because he was so impressed with his playing. And Glenn Miller helped out with some of the orchestrations.

It was a lively and "expert" show, wrote the *New York Times* reviewer. This was an astute observation, for by this time, the fall of 1930, the Gershwins and Guy Bolton had mastered all of the necessary techniques—indeed, they were all truly "expert."[11] *Girl Crazy* was craftsmanship, not inspiration. The plot was still trite, but it was a better and more sophisticated musical comedy than *Lady Be Good!*, six years earlier. The Gershwins had become quite adept at their trade. Ira had mastered the tricks and techniques of his profession and had added his own genuine inspiration. He seemed especially proud of his unusual rhymes such as coupling embraceable you with irreplaceable you, or a trick rhyme: lining glorify love with Encore! If I love.

"Embraceable You" was also one of George Gershwin's most inventive melodies. It has a simple line for the first eight bars, the same figure repeated but played out over a complex chord structure, which gives the melody an impetus as it goes up by the interval of a fourth. Then the composer breaks the traditional AABA formula and introduces a completely different eight bars before returning to the first themes. But once again the melody takes off in a new direction after eight more bars. The final eight bars are an innovative variant on the major theme and the ending is an unexpected melodic and harmonic turn.

One critic noted that in light of the uninspiring scores in *Show Girl* and *Strike Up the Band* there had been speculation that Gershwin had grown stale. But *Girl Crazy* dissipated any such belief: "fresh, ingenious . . . a rich delight, as well as gratifying proof that the composer hasn't started being patronizing towards musical comedy."[12] Another critic wrote that not since *Oh, Kay!* had Gershwin "run so true to form." Ira wrote that one might imagine that writing lyrics for *Girl Crazy* would flow more easily after his years of experience. But this was not so, because there was so much one could not repeat when trying to set reasonable ideas to unreasonable rhythms.

The show was turned into a movie in 1932 (after George and Ira had completed their stint in Hollywood); they were paid $7,050 for the rights. It conformed more or less to the show's original plot, but was transformed into a comedy vehicle for two vaudeville comics, Wheeler and Woolsey, who managed to revive every gag in vaudeville history. Some of the score was retained, and one good new song was added, "You've Got What Gets Me."

Six decades later, the freshness of both the music and the lyrics of *Girl Crazy* were evident in a new show, *Crazy for You*, which demonstrated why the Gershwins were so successful at their craft.[13]

After launching *Girl Crazy*, the Gershwins went to Hollywood and underwent roughly the same thoughtless treatment as the other New York writers. Nevertheless, Hollywood provided a welcome interlude and diversion, to say nothing of a large sum of money; George used the interval to continue his more serious compositions, but it was on Broadway and not in the movies that the Gershwins would score their next major triumph, one that would bring them an enduring niche in the American musical theater. On their way to Hollywood they carried in their luggage an outline for a new show, tentatively titled *Tweedledee*, but later to become famous as *Of Thee I Sing*.

Once talking pictures had exploded in Hollywood, there was a flurry of musicals. Many were adapted from Broadway shows, for example, *Sally, No, No, Nanette, The Desert Song*, and *Rio Rita*; oddly, *Rio Rita* was the most successful. Broadway songwriters were therefore in great demand, and they were more plentiful than other artists, except for the new sound technicians. But after the luminaries of the Great White Way arrived, the studios did not know what to do with them, or how to use their music. Jerome Kern composed songs for a film about flying. After he left, all of his music was abandoned and the show became a melodrama. Irving Berlin was assigned to one of the first all-black movies on the theory that he knew how to write black music (i.e., jazz). Rodgers and Hart were more fortunate at first, writing for a very good film called *Love Me Tonight* with Jeannette MacDonald and Maurice Chevalier. But then they were diverted to some truly bad films. Hollywood filmed Cole Porter's *Paris*, but cut most of his music.

Unfortunately, the Gershwins arrived as the first wave of enthusiasm for both musicals and for Broadway composers was waning. Audiences wanted more than trite stories sung by performers who were frozen like statues or photographed in long shots that made them look like characters out of *Gulliver*. Busby Berkeley had not yet arrived to create a new concept of Hollywood musicals; nor had the major Broadway performers settled in Hollywood. The results were second rate at best. At theaters signs were posted proclaiming: This Is Not a Musical. *Billboard* featured a headline in August 1930—MUSICAL FILMS ARE TABOO: "Songwriters returning East in Great Numbers."[14]

Nevertheless, George was enthusiastic. He wrote that they all were very excited about it and expected to like it immensely. The Gershwins were to write for a movie scripted by their old colleague Guy Bolton. The picture went slowly, although the Gershwins completed their songs before the production began. While Ira relaxed George used the time to start work on a longer, serious piece that began as background music for a dream sequence in the movie. There was the usual round of parties. Ira wrote to friends in the East that since they had arrived there had not been a dozen meals without two or more guests, or in which they themselves were the guests.[15] At a party given by Myrna Loy, the movie actress, both Richard Rodgers and Gershwin played, but George outlasted everyone and did not leave until sunrise, which he watched while chatting with his hostess. P.G. Wodehouse was in Hollywood and along with Guy Bolton, the Gershwins hosted their share of parties.

Their picture was titled *Delicious* which was a sequel to *Sunny Side Up*, an earlier picture with Janet Gaynor and Charles Farrell, who had starred in silent films. The music as well as the story and dialogue for their first musical had been supplied by the team of Ray Henderson, Lew Brown, and their old comrade Buddy De Sylva. They wrote the title song as well as "If I Had a Talking Picture of You," both very successful. Despite mediocre reviews, the movie did well at the box office. So, the studio naturally decided on a second version.

The repeat had lost whatever novelty there was in the first vehicle. Neither Gaynor nor Farrell were singers, and the acting was vintage early talkies. Guy Bolton was assisted by Sonya Lieven, who would later write the script for George's movie biography in 1945. The plot concerned a Scotch immigrant, a young girl who imagines her new country in a fantasy sequence. On the boat to America she falls in love with a wealthy young man played by Charles Farrell. She is pursued by immigration officers through a series of absurd situations, including a dream sequence in New York, with dark shadows and ominous scenes. This dream sequence had background music by George, which he first entitled "New York Rhapsody." In the end the dream rhapsody was greatly reduced in the film.

The reviews in Hollywood were favorable, except for one critic who concluded, "George Gershwin is said to have written the music involved but you'd never know it. . . . Civilization hasn't had such a setback since the Dark Ages."[16] On the other hand, most agreed that Gershwin's music was "grand." The "New York Rhapsody" was "real Gershwin stuff." The New York reviewers were not so kind: "a simple and conventional little musical comedy but by no means a fresh and attractive one." The *New York Sun* pointed out that in the silent movies Janet Gaynor had a "wistful Cinderella quality, but in the talkies her "slightly adenoidal intonation removes that touch forcibly and renders her consistently less interesting." The New Yorkers agreed, however, that the best item in the film was Gershwin's "New York Rhapsody" as background music while Gaynor stumbles around a nightmarish city—"George Gershwin's finest contribution to the picture." A student of these early movies concluded that what really mattered was that audiences liked Janet Gaynor: "Although Gershwin's name brought Fox some pleasing P.R. in big cities, *Delicious* would have been a success with music by anybody, or by nobody at all."[17]

Gershwin found Hollywood "o.k." but was bored by all of the "picture talk." The Hollywood pattern that bedeviled other New York songwriters reappeared. Thus, the final version of *Delicious* dropped some Gershwin songs, but kept a miniature version of the longer "Rhapsody." Ira contributed "Blah, Blah, Blah," the much recycled melody from *East Is West*, but transformed into a clever parody of the standard love songs. Its sophistication was not suited for a movie audience, though Ira was inordinately pleased by it. One wonders whether Ira was carried away by Hollywood. Another of his songs called "Katinkitschka" was cute but trite. On the other hand, "Somebody from Somewhere" is quite good, despite an awful performance by Janet Gaynor. The movie was not released until December 1931, almost a year after the Gershwins had left. The title song was of course one their best, but entitled "Delishious," Ira's clever play on words.

He was "very disappointed," George commented when the movie was re-leased. He mused over the problems of the Hollywood musical. It was practically impossible, he said, to transpose Broadway musical hits to film versions, because it was difficult to find a personality with the ability to act and sing on the screen. Hollywood musicals were an entirely different medium than the stage, but Hollywood was only beginning to realize it. Nevertheless, a song in a picture could have an unusual effect if put in the right place. (Gershwin might well have added this was true of Broadway as well.) He concluded that he expected to spend his time between Broadway and Hollywood, and would return to the film capital that summer to work on the music in *Delicious*. The studio, however, discouraged him from returning, and the production was completed without his or Ira's participation. This too was a doleful Hollywood practice. Irving Berlin always complained that on Broadway the songwriter knew the next morning whether he had a hit, but in Hollywood he had to wait for months before anyone heard his music. Ironically, while the movie *Delicious* failed, the song "Deli-shious"[*sic*] caught on.

For most of the time George concentrated on developing a longer piece; his first outline was titled *New York Rhapsody*, then tentatively *Manhattan Rhapsody*, and because of the pounding rhythm of the first theme, renamed *Rhapsody in Rivets*, and finally, more simply, the *Second Rhapsody*. Isaac Goldberg wrote that the *Second Rhapsody* was redolent of the aphrodisiac atmosphere of orange blossoms and Beverly Hills. In fact, Gershwin composed it at a beach cottage in Santa Monica, loaned to him by the comely movie star Aileen Pringle. When he left Hollywood he said that nearly everybody brought back a tan and movie-picture money, but he also came back with a serious composition.

Once again he hired an orchestra for a trial run at the NBC studio. He wrote to Aileen Pringle, still in Santa Monica, that "every part came through as I expected." For the premiere, however, this time the orchestra was the Boston Symphony conducted by Koussevitsky. It premiered on January 29, 1932, in Boston, where the reception was tremendous, and was repeated a few days later at Carnegie Hall. George played the piano part. The reviews in Boston noted that while a few pages were too bombastic, as a whole the composition was a "fine work, a characteristically American work, of which Americans may well be proud." Predictably, the *Second Rhapsody* was compared with *Rhapsody in Blue*, the latter coming off better. The composer Marc Blitzstein, in *Modern Music*, dismissed it as "no better and no worse than his earlier one," but said that it was a repetition in rather more "pretentious terms." Blitzstein wrote that "there was the same evidence of thinking from one four-measure phrase to another."[18] According to the *New York Times* critic Olin Downes (February 6, 1932) the *Second Rhapsody* was "imitative" in many ways; many sections were "direct derivatives." While the *Second Rhapsody* was "full of youth and reck-lessness," most music lovers were likely to prefer the first rhapsody, since it expressed America and its musical inclinations even better than the second, according to Walter J. Henderson's review (*New York Sun*, February 6, 1932).

Gershwin himself drew a parallel between the two rhapsodies. For the first he had only exactly five weeks, so he wrote it in three; he was composing page after page and handing them in to the orchestra, feeling that it was not as good as he would have liked. But for this new rhapsody, he said in an interview with the *Boston Evening Transcript* that he had seven weeks in California. He had the chance to do some serious work; seven weeks of "a most uninterrupted opportunity to write the best music I could possibly think of! What a chance." The studio had asked that he not release his composition until after the premiere of the picture (December 1931), so he had more time to revise and polish.

When asked in Boston for his interpretation of the second, slower theme, he responded, "I wanted to write a broad flowing melody, the same as Bach, Brahms or Wagner have done." The new rhapsody was not a continuation of the first, not so sentimental as the first, he said, and would not be as popular. The idea, Gershwin explained, was to write music that would express a composer's first emotional reaction to New York City. Hence, a view of the skyscrapers under construction was expressed as a "rivets" theme, but then the music develops into a "broad, flowing movement that is almost religious in effect."[19]

As for the change from the New York Symphony to the Boston under Koussevitsky, Gershwin was understandably pleased. Koussevitsky brought out things "that I hardly knew were there. . . . You know, he does things with pianissimo that I had not suspected. I guess I have never had a chance to know about pianissimo (laughter from the bystanders)."[20]

Koussevitsky returned the compliments. He was impressed when Gershwin brought him the orchestration: "I was amazed at his talent. . . . It is a masterful orchestration. Finished—complete. It is not jazz, it is symphonic—a new development that has come from jazz. Very interesting, the boy's talent does not stop with composition—his talent to orchestrate is what amazed me."

The Gershwins had reached a turning point. Hollywood was clearly not the answer—at least not then, and even the highly successful *Girl Crazy* was a pre–*Show Boat* throwback, another product of the roaring twenties. The Gershwins were comfortable in the social and musical climate of that period, but that era was disappearing with the onset of the Great Depression. Broadway discovered that one way to cope with the new, gloomier atmosphere was to poke fun at it, namely through political satire—"who cares if banks fail in Yonkers" Ira wrote. It was George Kaufman who would lead the Gershwins to explore this very frontier of combining political satire and music.

Gershwin found himself in two vastly different worlds. In the concert hall he had earned a great deal of fame, but not as much critical acclaim. The critics who had made allowances for *Rhapsody in Blue* were holding him up to more rigorous standards; the *Concerto in F* and the *Second Rhapsody*, and even *An American in Paris* were treated more roughly, while his Broadway vehicles were still enthusiastically praised. Kaufman's intervention relieved Gershwin of having to choose his future path. Kaufman offered something different when Gershwin was also searching for something new.

NOTES

1. Robert Kimball and Alfred Simon, *The Gershwins* (New York: Bonanza Books, 1963), p. 95.

2. Oscar Levant, *A Smattering of Ignorance* (New York: Doubleday, 1940), p. 182.

3. Ibid., pp. 98–99.

4. Library of Congress, Gershwin Collection.

5. Hyman Sandow, "Gershwin Presents a New Work," *Musical Courier*, August 18, 1928, reprinted in *Gershwin in His Time: A Biographical Scrapbook, 1919–1937*, ed. Gregory R. Suriano (New York: Gramercy Books, 1998), p. 58.

6. Steven Gilbert, *The Music of George Gershwin* (New Haven, CT: Yale University Press, 1995), pp. 112, 120.

7. *New York Times*, November 10, 1928.

8. Isaac Goldberg (supplemented by Edith Garson), *George Gershwin: A Study in American Music* (New York: Frederick Ungar Publishing, 1958), p. 253.

9. A.H. Lawrence, *Duke Ellington and His World* (New York: Routledge, 2001), p. 146.

10. One unused song was "Tonight's the Night." It was discovered in 1982 in the Secaucus warehouse and used in the Broadway musical *Crazy for You* in 1992. Robert Kimball, ed., *The Complete Lyrics of Ira Gershwin* (New York: Alfred Knopf, 1993), p. 145.

11. The entire score of *Girl Crazy* was revived for a modern recording using most of the original orchestrations (Electra Nonesuch CD 979250–2), conducted by John Mauceri. This two-CD set includes an informative booklet by Tommy Krasker. Lorna Luft, Judy Garland's daughter, sings the part of Ethel Merman.

12. Richard Watts, *New York Herald Tribune*, October 29, 1930.

13. Many of the songs, plus a large number of other Gershwin songs, were revived in 1992 for a new show loosely based on the original, but retitled *Crazy for You*. The score, though in modern orchestrations and performances, was nevertheless a stunning reprise of Gershwiniana.

14. Richard Barrios, *A Song in the Dark* (New York: Oxford University Press, 1995), p. 341.

15. Kimball and Simon, *The Gershwins*, p. 152.

16. Quoted in Lee Davis, *Bolton and Wodehouse and Kern* (New York: James Heineman, 1993), p. 324. A slightly different version is quoted in Edward Jablonski and Lawrence Stewart, *The Gershwin Years* (New York: Doubleday & Company, 1958), p. 163.

17. Barrios, *A Song in the Dark*, p. 352.

18. Marc Blitzstein, "Premiers and Experiments," *Modern Music*, March/April 1932, p. 122.

19. *Boston Evening Transcript*, January 28, 1932.

20. Ibid.

Why do these arrogant immigrants
insist on lecturing America?

Without America — and our military—
George, Ira, etc would have been
performing at Austwic or Bergen Belsen—
and then marched into the gas chamber.

To hell with Ira and Kaufman's
obvious commie politics.

Chapter 9

Of Thee I Sing

The late 1920s may well have been the high point of the Golden Age of American popular music. Certainly it was for the Gershwins. In 1926, one could have bought a ticket to the highly successful *Oh, Kay!* or *Show Girl*. The following year came *Funny Face* and *Rosalie*. Sandwiched in between was the controversial *Strike Up the Band*.

Two major developments were to threaten this era of good feelings: One was competition from talking pictures (*The Jazz Singer* with Al Jolson premiered in October 1927). Two years later came the collapse of the stock market in October 1929. It would take some time before either event would have its full impact on Broadway, but gradually the atmosphere changed.

The Wall Street crash badly dampened business, and Broadway was no exception. The number of shows declined from sixty-two in 1928 to thirty-four in 1931. In early 1931 the top ten shows were still earning about $360,000 in a week, but the gross had dropped drastically to $170,000 by May. The Gershwins' *Girl Crazy* was a critical and commercial success, grossing over $1 million, but even its weekly gross dropped from $37,000 to $20,000, and it closed in the summer of 1931 after thirty-four weeks.

By July 1931 the number of first-run shows had declined to eleven. There were thirty-two new musicals produced in 1930 but only ten in 1935. Long runs proved more and more difficult to achieve. Throughout the 1930s only four musicals ran for more than four hundred performances. The critic Burns Mantle, in his annual review, lamented that the theater was surviving on "half rations." The 1932–33 season was described figuratively as the season in which the Depression held the theater in its power.

There were precious few musical successes: Jerome Kern's *Music in the Air*, Cole Porter's *Gay Divorce* starring Fred Astaire, Irving Berlin's *As Thousands*

Cheer (September 1933), and Cole Porter's *Anything Goes* (November 1934). No more than half the theaters in New York were in use, something less than half the actors were employed, and virtually all "bankrolls were in hiding," as described by Burns Mantle's colorful phrase. As the Depression deepened, top ticket prices dropped from around $6.50 to $3.30. Falling ticket prices meant declines in royalties and salaries.

George Gershwin suffered from the Depression along with the rest of the country. In 1932 he sold his stocks, valued at $81,000, for $19,000; accordingly, his net income for that year was only about $4,700. His losses on stocks were paper losses, however, and his income from royalties was over $65,000. Nonetheless, even royalties declined in the 1930s, and the Gershwins were kept afloat by their ASCAP earnings. On the other hand, their prospects were potentially quite bright. George and Ira were about to burst forth with a major Broadway achievement, *Of Thee I Sing*, written by George Kaufman and Morrie Ryskind.

It was a sharply pointed satire about the sterility of political parties and their handpicked candidates. At first the main theme was to be a political competition for a new national anthem. There would be two conflicting anthems and the show's title would be *Tweedledee*. George Gershwin was delighted and commented that he would handle the competing anthems "contrapuntally." This of course baffled Kaufman, who later commented that Gershwin's counterpoint was giving him acid indigestion.

An initial version was written and sent to the Gershwins in Hollywood, with precise instructions for integrating the music. Kaufman's attentiveness in itself was a change from the usual carefree construction of musicals. Ira said: "We liked him tremendously. Kaufman was certainly one of the most experienced showmen alive. The Gershwins wouldn't argue with him. If he didn't like it we'd write something new."[1] In turn, the often irascible Kaufman liked the Gershwins, although he chided George occasionally. At one rehearsal Kaufman predicted to George that the show was likely to fail. Astonished, Gershwin asked why, and Kaufman said it was because during rehearsals the balcony was only half full of Gershwin's fans.

Meanwhile, the plot changed from a competition for a new national anthem to the conduct of a political campaign for the presidency, with one ticket headed by John P. Wintergreen, played by William "Billy" Gaxton, and his hapless vice president Alexander Throttlebottom, played by the incomparable Victor Moore.

After receiving Kaufman's draft for the first act, Gershwin commented in a letter that it was "very satirical." Whether the public would like it he didn't know, but it was "surely worth the gamble." He also wrote: "It's most amusing and we are looking forward to writing a score for it." Later he wrote that he had a lot of "fun" writing the show, which was "different from anything we've done." From such comments it is clear that what intrigued Gershwin was the chance for something new. Whether he was impressed by the message or tone of the satire he did not say. It was a sharp departure from the usual Broadway musical. There were occasional political satires, such as *Strike Up the Band* and sketches in revues. The Depression stimulated more topical subjects including politics.[2]

The idea of embarking on something that would be regarded as an innovation impressed Gershwin, especially after the failure of his movie venture. *Of Thee I Sing* turned out to be the show he was most proud of—which was quite an admission. Gershwin said it was one of those rare shows in which everything clicked just right. There was little or no fixing to do. Not only was it a satire on politics; it was also not the traditional scene-song-scene-song show, but a highly integrated story told in many instances in music and lyrics. In some scenes, several songs or fragments of songs ran together and the entire scene was performed in music, with only occasional spoken interventions, as in the Finale of Act One. In some cases, the Gershwins reversed their usual practice and Ira wrote out the lyrics first and George then supplied music.

To be sure, there were 32-bar Tin Pan Alley songs, but they were also integrated with the story much more so than usual in Broadway shows. Some of the songs were written while the Gershwins were still in Hollywood. When one of Kaufman's friends in New York congratulated him on the songs for his new musical he was surprised, since he was still writing the script. He asked what music? And his friend said that in Hollywood he had heard Gershwin play "Who Cares" and "Of Thee I Sing, Baby." Kaufman remonstrated Gershwin, warning him that if he continued to preview the score, the audience would think they were attending a revival.

Of Thee I Sing opened with one of the most clever and rousing Broadway ice-breakers, "Wintergreen for President." It is a march of campaign workers who carry around the usual political signs, except these proclaim such slogans as "Vote for Prosperity and See What You Get," or "The Full Dinner Jacket," or "He Kept Us Out of Jail." The basic musical theme is in a minor key but it is interrupted by snatches of various famous campaign songs, such as "Hail, Hail, the Gang's All Here" and "Tammany." The musical effect is startling: these interpolations are in a major key in contrast to the main theme, but they strike a cynical note because they are so hackneyed and each fragment is quoted but then descends back into the main theme in the minor key. The best touch is Ira Gershwin's lyric for Wintergreen for President, perhaps the shortest of any Broadway play. Wintergreen was the man the people should choose, because he loved the Irish and the Jews.

A blackout follows, and the next scene opens in a hotel room where the cynical campaign managers are gathered to search for a new theme for their candidate: they ask a hotel chamber maid what she cares about more than anything else and she answers, "money, I guess." The managers are horrified and reject this, but then she volunteers that her second choice is love. They argue: some claim that people will kill for love, but will they vote for it? Thus is born Wintergreen's campaign theme and the Gershwin song "Love is Sweeping the County." In keeping with the theme of love, the campaign then turns into a contest for the girl who will marry Wintergreen if and when he is elected.

Complications emerge when Wintergreen falls in love with "plain" Mary Turner and rejects the contest winner, Miss Diana Devereaux. She turns out to be, in Ira's words, "the illegitimate daughter of an illegitimate son of a nephew of Napoleon." Kaufman and Ryskind often deferred to Ira; they simply wrote that she had to have a French title, the rest was Ira's creation.

France is outraged at this rebuff. The French government presents a note of protest (when the ambassador enters, the orchestra strikes up a few bars of *An American in Paris*). America's answer to the protest note is that "we have a lot of notes from France, some due 10 years ago." (This provoked a real-life letter of rebuke from a Franco-American friendship society; Kaufman answered that if they could think of a joke that would get more laughs he would put it in.) The Supreme Court is asked to decide which is more important: justice for Diana Devereaux and France, or corn muffins, Mary Turner's specialty. The answer is obvious. Nevertheless, impeachment proceedings begin in the Senate against Wintergreen—the roll call of senators is in rhyme. Just as the Senate is about to vote for impeachment, Mary Turner suddenly announces she is with child. An expectant father cannot be impeached, intones Throttlebottom. This prompts the song "Of Thee I Sing—Baby." George Kaufman hated the word "baby" but George and Ira insisted. Throttlebottom is relieved: Wintergreen can still be president, and he, Throttlebottom, can go back to "vice."

The threat of a war with France is averted when Wintergreen remembers that the Constitution holds that whenever the president is unable to fulfill his duties, his obligations are assumed by the vice president. Throttlebottom exclaims, "I get her!" The French are placated. Mary's baby is born, and the Supreme Court is called on to decide its gender. In fact there are twins and Wintergreen announces that he is both a father and a mother. The ensemble sings "Of Thee I Sing, Baby."

The score was an extraordinary achievement for George. Almost everything is musicalized—even the Senate roll call of impeachment. It all comes off very well and seems almost effortless. There is an inevitable tinge of Gilbert and Sullivan, but not enough to matter. "Of Thee I Sing" and "Love is Sweeping the Country" are the best-known songs, but the finest one may well have been "Who Cares?", introduced first as a bright, carefree ramble at a presidential press conference but then reprised later as a love song at a slower tempo. It displayed one of Ira Gershwin's finest lyrics. Amid the Great Depression Ira dismissed bank failures in Yonkers and stocks and bonds. The harmony for this song is unusual, especially in the first four bars. A similar unusual harmonic progression would reappear five years later in "Nice Work if You Can Get It."

The critics were enthralled. Even in Boston, with Mayor Curley in the audience, there was a tumultuous reception. The much respected Boston critic H.T. Parker caught the importance of George's music to the whole production (December 22, 1931): "Never before has Mr. Gershwin written a music that so continuously expresses the text; characters the personages, sharpens the pervading humor. Seldom has he been more fertile with apt device. One more piece now affirms him the distinctive composer of our musical pieces."[3]

When the show was still in Boston, a reporter witnessed a rehearsal. George was telling the violins how a number should be played. He whistled, sang, gestured, and then suddenly they got it, and he sang enthusiastically with them.

Nevertheless, Kaufman was pessimistic and wrote a note to George to please make all possible musical cuts. According to Alfred Simon, the rehearsal pianist, the original score was scarcely changed. He described the Gershwins around this time: Ira, reticent by nature, preferred to leave most decisions to his brother, while George was always up on the stage, in the orchestra pit, or in the back of the theater listening.[4] A little more than a year later, Kaufman and Moss Hart wrote a new play, *Merrily We Roll Along.* One of the characters, Max Frankl, was obviously modelled on Gershwin. He is cocky and arrogant; at one point he announces that "those old hacks [Kern and Berlin] were "washed up ten years ago." When asked if he resented Kaufman and Hart's portrayal of him as a character, Gershwin replied that his character was the only sane one in the play.

Of Thee I Sing opened in New York to highly favorable reviews on December 26, 1931, at the Music Box Theater, our best "raves," according to George. Brooks Atkinson in the *New York Times* wrote (December 28) that the show was "funnier than the government, and not nearly so dangerous." He added that "Best of all there is Mr. Gershwin's score." On the other hand, he wrote in his review that the book was too long and complicated, and being in "one strident key" grew tiresome. Some of the critics came to the opening night party given by Kay Swift and read their reviews. John Anderson in the *New York Journal* concluded that "It is grand fun." Burns Mantle in the *Daily News* found it "The newest, maddest and brightest of musical satire." Only Robert Benchley, Kaufman's friend from the Algonquin Round Table, held out against the tide, writing in *The New Yorker*: "dull, musically, repetitious, and not particularly fresh satirically . . . reminiscent of an old Hasty Pudding spoof." When told that Benchley had left early, Kaufman was apoplectic. But Benchley's was a minority vote. Although Marc Blitzstein (*Modern Music*, May/June 1932) did comment that while "Gershwin's music is good," it was not up to his standard, nor was his style unified: he was evidently getting ambitious, "in a misguided attempt to approach 'art.' "

The real verdict would come in May 1932, when the Pulitzer Prize Committee announced that *Of Thee I Sing* had won the prize for best drama of 1931. The announcement read: "This award may seem unusual, but the play is unusual. Not only is it coherent and well knit enough to class as a play, aside from the music, but it is a biting and true satire on American politics and the public attitude toward them." George Gershwin's father offered a succinct summary: "That Pulitzer must be a smart man."

The award, however, led to controversy. Brooks Atkinson thought it trivialized the value of the prize to give it to a musical. And it turned out that infighting within the committee was partly responsible for this minor revolt against convention. In 1932, however, it was a mark of great respect. Even such jaded veterans as George Jean Nathan were fascinated by the new mode. He wrote that whereas older musicals were caught in routine and rusty tracks *Of Thee I Sing* was the most successful native music-stage lampoon that had come in the American theater.

The Pulitzer award went to the writers, Kaufman and Ryskind, and Ira Gershwin. Since there was no category for music, George Gershwin was omitted. Over the years it turned out to be an ironic touch. The score and music have held up better than the plot. The critic Howard Taubman wrote for the *New York Times* that at the time he would have predicted it would become a classic, but when it was revived two decades later, "alas, it had aged . . . after a devastating war, its satire was altogether too scattered and pallid. Only the score retained its luster." By 1990, however, critics found a revival in New York more pleasing because of the contrast with the contemporary politics. *Of Thee I Sing* was marked by an absence of anger. Stephen Holden wrote in the *New York Times* (April 1990): "How fresh the show seems nearly 60 years after it first opened on Broadway. In many ways its satire of Presidential politics and media manipulation more than half a century ago seems as apt today as ever." This evaluation was not far from Brooks Atkinson's original *New York Times* review in 1931, that began by stating: "What little dignity there may have been in politics and government has been laughed out of court by 'Of Thee I Sing.' "

After the opening George, Ira, and Lee and some friends went to Cuba for a vacation. "Ira and Lee loved it," George wrote home. As for George, his friend Bennett Cerf reported that he was most indignant after a "lovely Cuban miss" stood him up and failed to show up for a rendezvous. When he accosted her later, she explained that she could not call him because she could not remember his name. Cerf claimed that "George did not recover for days."[5] In Havana there was a sixteen-piece Cuban band that serenaded George one evening until four in the morning, whereupon he vowed to write a rhumba of his own and he did so.

At first it was entitled *Rhumba*, but later was changed to *Cuban Overture*. He completed the composition in July 1932. On the score he drew pictures of the Latin instruments to be used (e.g., bongos, maracas, gourds, and "Cuban sticks"). There was no piano part, however. When he came back to New York, he went to his friend Emil Mosbacher's country house in Westchester, Connecticut, to finish the composition and orchestration. Kay Swift would come over to visit and help with the orchestration. She worked "day and night," according to Mosbacher. They both talked to Mosbacher separately about marriage, but he wisely avoided giving any advice. Nevertheless, George was "nuts about her," he said.[6] The *Rhumba* was premiered at a summer concert in Lewisohn Stadium on August 16, 1932, and again in November at the Metropolitan Opera House, with the more formal title *Cuban Overture*. The premiere at the Lewisohn Stadium was an all-Gershwin program, including *Rhapsody in Blue*, the *Second Rhapsody*, with George at the piano; also *An American in Paris*, the *Concerto in F* played by Oscar Levant, and a medley from *Of Thee I Sing*; thousands were turned away. The *New York Times* review, however, was far from kind:

> Mr. Gershwin did his cause more harm than good in allowing so revealing a program to be presented. For if he has any pretensions to being considered a truly gifted composer, the almost unvarying sameness or formlessness of this body of music did not help him . . . the "Rumba" despite the addition of maracas, gourd, bongo and other Cuban instruments was merely old Gershwin in recognizable form.[7]

The *Cuban Overture* has been overshadowed by Gershwin's better-known work and thus played less often.[8] Its "technical complexity" exceeds Aaron Copland's *El Salon Mexico*, according to one authority.[9] The orchestration is particularly brilliant, not only for its use of Latin rhythms but for the alternating of themes from one section of the orchestra to another. In this case, he may have benefitted from Kay Swift's advice and help.

During this period Gershwin also worked with Kay Swift on his *Song-Book*, a collection of eighteen songs. Each song was first printed as in the published sheet music, but then each was followed by an elaborate Gershwin improvisation. Kay Swift apparently helped to transcribe his variations and the book is dedicated to her.[10] It was a grand compilation; reviewers pointed out that it was not for the novice. The improvised versions were not necessarily the ones Gershwin himself played in various recordings; some are more complicated.[11]

On the occasion of its publication by Simon and Schuster, Gershwin gave an interview at Richard Simon's apartment. He said some foolish things. For example, he said "jazz" was old: "There are passages of jazz in Bach, and, I understand, in Beethoven." This is simply baffling; perhaps he was referring to syncopation. As for his own new book of songs, he claimed that he always kept in mind that the persons who most often would play them were "young girls with small hands." This, of course, was also ridiculous; few girls with large or small hands could play his improvisations in the *Song-Book*. He did defend his "Rhumba"; he said that people were expecting something like the "Peanut Vendor," but his composition was a "serious work," which he intended to rename *Cuban Overture*.[12]

Had the successful team of Kaufman, Ryskind, and the Gershwins rested with their Pulitzer Prize, all would have been well. But Beatrice Kaufman, George's wife, suggested a sequel in which Wintergreen would be defeated for reelection. Kaufman and Ryskind were intrigued and began to sketch out ideas, and the same principals (Gaxton and Moore) were recruited for the cast. Probably they were influenced by the success of another political spoof, *Face the Music*, which Kaufman had directed. Moss Hart wrote the script for what amounted to a revue; the music was by Irving Berlin. His music was almost the opposite of Gershwin's. George's songs had been "sharp edged, satirical," while Berlin's music was "optimistic and romantic," for example, "Let's Have Another Cup O' Coffee."[13] *"Let's Face the music and dance" is brilliant!*

In any case, the Gershwins also agreed to another Kaufman and Ryskind show, in part because in the interim they had become involved in a failure, *Pardon My English.* That book was nominally by Herbert Fields but doctored by five or six others. Its production was chaotic; it stayed out of town for weeks in a vain attempt to fix the plot. One of the stars, the suave British dancer-singer Jack Buchanan, finally quit. In the end the plot was rebuilt around the randy comedy of the remaining star, the vaudeville comic Jack Pearl, famous as Baron Munchausen on the radio. The score was not bad, but some of it was lost for decades, only to be recovered in Warner Brothers' warehouse in Secaucus, New Jersey.

The Gershwins agreed to the show out of loyalty to Alex Aarons, who was broke. According to Ira, he told them that if the Gershwins did not do the score his financial backers would pull out. Nevertheless, the show was a headache from start to finish, Ira said. The setting in Germany was an uneasy topic when Hitler was on the verge of power. Ira disliked the plot, but felt they were lucky to be working when the Great Depression was at its deepest. They were living off the profits from *Of Thee I Sing.* (This is stretching things; royalties from other shows and songs were still considerable.) George Kaufman wrote to his wife that he was sorry to hear of the troubles of the Gershwin show [*Pardon My English*], but of course it was inevitable: It might be patched together, but not for more than a few months. The score was not exactly as brilliant as the Gershwins' partisans claimed. After every flop, however, Ira commented there were those who said there were some good things in it. Ira agreed and pointed to a "couple of pretty good songs." Indeed, this was the show that yielded the delightful and amusing "Lorelei," as well as some of the Gershwins' best: "My Cousin in Milwaukee" was one of Ira's most inventive and humorous lyrics, and perhaps their best song was "Isn't It a Pity?" This particular song was not as easily forgotten, and several different performers would revive it over the years. One song, "Tonight," was not published but reworked as a piano piece, "Two Waltzes in C."

By this time Rosamond Walling had gone to Europe, and in a strange barbed intervention, Lee Gershwin, her cousin, wrote to tell her that George had found a new girl who was right for him, but Rosamond was not to know. Lee added that George spoke of Rosamond wistfully, but was a little resigned. The lady in question was Roberta Robinson, then in the cast of *Pardon My English.* George needled Rosamond, divulging his new relationship with Roberta to Rosamond shortly after Lee's intervention: "I've seen her a few times lately." In any case, the Gershwin-Walling romance was over. In May 1932 she wrote George that she would soon marry the diplomat Rifat Tirana. On the other hand, George's romance with Roberta Robinson did not last and did not save her from being let out of *Pardon My English* during its chaotic tryouts.[14]

While still in Philadelphia, one critic found the show "smartly and luxuriously produced," while another thought that George's score had "unbent a little from the cryptogrammic [*sic*] music of 'Of Thee I Sing' and other recent shows." As feared, however, in New York the reviews turned out to be hostile, especially since some of the comedy bordered on smut. Brooks Atkinson wrote for the *New York Times* that the show enjoys "rolling around the gutter. The smugness with which the dirt is sprinkled around draws attention to its odor." It closed after only forty-six performances on February 27, 1933. It was the Gershwins' worst humiliation. It was also the end of the highly successful Aarons-Freedley productions. Aarons collapsed during the tryouts and left for Hollywood. Freedley fled the country to avoid his creditors. It was an ironic end. The Gershwins had undertaken this abortive show to help Aarons and Freedley who had been badly hit by the stock market crash.

The Gershwins were not alone: one after another of Broadway's giants fell. Sigmund Romberg fared only slightly better than the Gershwins with his *Melody*. Kurt Weill's *Three Penny Opera* closed after two weeks. It was no consolation to the Gershwins that Irving Berlin had the only major hit of the season, *As Thousands Cheer*; it made fun of recent headlines, but included one serious scene about a lynching down south. Ethel Waters sang "Supper Time" against that headline. In the increasing drought along Broadway the huge success of Berlin's show may have encouraged the Gershwins to risk another satire. By the spring of 1933 the Gershwins were free to begin their new collaboration with Kaufman and Ryskind. The new show's title was borrowed from Marie Antoinette's infamous line, *Let 'Em Eat Cake*.

The plot centered around a revolution, staged by Wintergreen and his new political party, the Blue Shirts. After being defeated for reelection by Tweedledee, Wintergreen moves to New York and sets up a factory making blue shirts. The business is a success, and he and Mary sing "Mine." Meanwhile, on Union Square, the traditional locale for radical protests, a malcontent named Kruger advocates the elimination of majorities as well as minorities. Wintergreen is inspired to overthrow the government and retake the White House. Even Throttlebottom joins in. The revolution succeeds, and Wintergreen proclaims his dictatorship. The new administration starts to paint the White House blue, the song is "Blue, Blue, Blue," an intriguing Gershwin melody. There is still the problem of collecting the foreign war debts. Wintergreen proposes that the dispute be settled by a baseball game. At one point in the show, however, the guileless Throttlebottom (Victor Moore) is even threatened with execution by the prosecutor Kruger. He and Wintergreen are saved by a fashion show staged by Mary Turner, Wintergreen's wife. There is of course a happy ending. Wintergreen announces a new Republic and Throttlebottom becomes president.

Ira liked the show for its satire of nearly everything, both the extreme left and extreme right. He wrote later that it was "at times wonderfully witty—and at other times unrelentingly realistic in its criticism of the then American scene." Presumably, Ira was remembering the right-wing movement of that period (e.g.,

Huey Long and Father Coughlin, as well as the Veterans March on Washington, routed by the American Army under General MacArthur). In the Kaufman show a general is the key to overthrowing the government, but forgets to appear at the crucial moment because he has to go to a party.

As in *Of Thee I Sing*, the music was tightly integrated into the plot. But this time the comedy was often bitter and the songs were not as effective. The opener starts out the same as *Of Thee I Sing*, with a campaign rally to the same music as before, but then the opposition appears. Their song is also a march, but with interpolations of patriotic melodies, "Dixie," "The Battle Hymn of the Republic," and "Over There." The two campaign marches begin to intertwine in Gershwin's counterpoint. It is a brilliant musical introduction. While the music is integral to the plot, as before, the Tin Pan Alley songs are less impressive. Only one important melody emerged, "Mine." In this song there was a musical counterpoint theme set against the main melody. Gershwin was already beginning to study with the musical theorist Joseph Schillinger, and "Mine" was probably a result of Schillinger's influence. Indeed, Schillinger claimed credit for it.

The impact of Schillinger was unfortunate, at least for the Kaufman-Ryskind show. The plot was too often disconcerting and the score needed to provide a lift. Instead the music was often too complex and difficult to follow. Irving Kolodin described it as a "curious melange of ersatz Sullivan, shabby imitations of opera recitative and but a limited amount of good old-fashioned Gershwin."[15] Even the musical innovation—"Blue, Blue, Blue" with its interesting chromatic devices—was a song about the fascist blue shirts.

During rehearsals Kaufman became more and more apprehensive, but that was always his mood and his edginess was discounted. The Boston tryout was not well received by the critics. The venerable critic H.T. Parker suggested that extensive cuts were necessary, and the cuts began immediately after the Boston opening night. Parker thought that Gershwin had written a "more or less satirical music, built up into long scenes, shary-rythmed [*sic*] and modernist enough for a musical play. In recent years he has done nothing better." Once again Boston Mayor James Curley attended although he was the epitome of the kind of politician being satirized. Nevertheless, he thanked the four principals after the closing curtain. After the opening in Boston there were extensive revisions. However, the critics were not kind when the play opened in New York on October 21, 1933, at the Imperial, attended by Al Smith and Jimmy Walker. The reviewer from *Time* summed it up: "Sequels Are Not Equals." When this line was quoted to Kaufman, he was asked whether he wished he had said it? He replied that he wished no one had said it. However, H.T. Parker pointed out that the show was not so much a sequel as an independent piece. Brooks Atkinson found it a "brilliant, technical job, but a lampooning of general ideas that makes no intelligent point . . . the extravagance of the story tries the imagination." The venerable Percy Hammond liked it, but as he admitted, he was in the minority. Stanley Green summed it up: "The mood was excessively sour, the plotting contrived and much of the satire had an uncertain point of view."[16]

Variety dismissed it: "unfunny, verbose and unwieldy." George's score was praised, but was also considered too "intricate," and failed to recapture the vibrant mood of its predecessor, *Of Thee I Sing*. After ninety performances it folded and the road company also failed.

Once again the Gershwins were victims of a questionable book. This should have been even more obvious than the first version of *Strike Up the Band. Let 'Em Eat Cake* would have had to have been one of the great comedies to overcome the subject. Some authorities, looking back on the show, felt that it was too close to *Of Thee I Sing*, and audiences felt they were not seeing anything really new.[17] Moreover, Blue Shirts in America was not very humorous in an era when there were Brown Shirts in Germany. For some people the danger of a fascist coup was not as far-fetched in 1933 as Kaufman and Ryskind imagined. The audiences sensed this and the failure followed. Years later, Morrie Ryskind commented that times had changed; international affairs were no laughing matter. It was a mistake, he thought, to test the public's sympathy for their characters with an unsympathetic book: "The over-all mood of the show was unpleasant."[18]

For a time there was talk of a new production with Kaufman. This was the end, however, of the Gershwin team on Broadway, at least for musical comedy. The Gershwins were not alone. After his success in *As Thousands Cheer* (1933), Berlin did not write another Broadway show until 1940. He spent much of his time in Hollywood in the mid-1930s. Jerome Kern, despite his success with *Roberta* (1933), also did not write for Broadway for six years; he also was in Hollywood where he settled down to live.

Not surprisingly, George was still active. On a vacation in Palm Beach he began a new composition, a set of variations on the melody of "I Got Rhythm." Kay Swift said that George wrote this partly because he had become rather sick of playing the *Rhapsody* or the concerto. Perhaps so, but this composition was also highly influenced by his study with his new teacher, the pedagogue Joseph Schillinger. He was a brilliant but highly opinionated savant, who developed elaborate rules for composition. Of course, Gershwin was fascinated with the possibility of a new avenue to composition. Schillinger was born in Kharkov in the Ukraine in 1895 and studied at the Kharkov Conservatory before emigrating to the United States in 1928. He had worked out an elaborate system of composition and orchestration. The composer Henry Cowell wrote in the introduction to Schillinger's book, "the idea behind the Schillinger system is simple and inevitable; it undertakes the application of mathematical logic to all the materials of music and to their function."[19]

George was introduced to him by the violinist Joseph Achron. At least at first, Gershwin was intrigued. After a lesson, he would drop by the apartment of Kitty Carlisle and her mother, and proceed to spread sheets of paper all over the floor, explaining the contents of his lessons. Gershwin's fascination with Schillinger is not too surprising. He was always intrigued by the prospects of a formula for writing music. After George died, Schillinger asserted that he had exclaimed to Schillinger: "You don't have to compose music any more—it's all here."[20]

Schillinger's various claims about Gershwin are dubious. For example, Schillinger claimed that when Gershwin met him, his resources, not his abilities, were completely exhausted. When they did meet, Gershwin supposedly said: Here is my problem: I have written about seven hundred songs. I can't write anything new any more. I am repeating myself. Can you help me? Schillinger replied in the affirmative, and a "day later, Gershwin became a sort of Alice in Wonderland."[21] According to Schillinger, Gershwin studied with him for four and a half years. There are three notebooks (in the Library of Congress) from Gershwin's studies with Schillinger, but they are mostly exercises written by Schillinger. After Schillinger died his widow published his two volumes explaining his method. At that time, in 1943, she repeated the claim that Gershwin had come to Schillinger because he had writer's block and was bereft of ideas.[22] Ira vehemently denied this claim in an open letter to *Newsweek*.

In any case, George's new variations on "I Got Rhythm" clearly reflected the Schillinger method. This composition was introduced by a clarinet passage of six bars that is somewhat reminiscent of *Rhapsody in Blue*. The variations proper start with the piano playing the simple theme, followed by the first variation, a complicated version, played by the piano and the orchestra. While still indebted to Schillinger, one can feel an authentic Gershwin straining to break through, which he does in the piano parts that become more and more predominant. The next variation is a waltz (unusual for Gershwin); then comes a Chinese variation, played by "out-of-tune, as Chinese instruments invariably were," George said in a narrative when introducing the piece on the radio. Next, the piano plays the melody "upside down," an obvious Schillingerism, and finally there is a rousing ending described as "hot" or jazzy. It is a technical tour de force. Indeed, it may be that Schillinger himself wrote out some of the variations. After he died, his book was published in which he took credit for the ideas underlying one of the variations, which he cited as an example.[23] The entire piece was composed quickly and orchestrated for a smaller orchestra to be led by Leo Reisman. Kay Swift commented that it was the "best-orchestrated" of all of Gershwin's compositions.[24]

Its premiere was in Boston on January 14, 1934, with Leo Reisman's orchestra. It was the first of a series of concerts on a multi-city national tour that lasted through February 10, 1934, to celebrate the anniversary of *Rhapsody in Blue*. Charles Previn conducted (Reisman became ill) and the tour included songs by the tenor James Melton. The program usually included the concerto, a medley of Gershwin's popular songs, *Rhapsody in Blue*, *An American in Paris*, and the *Variations on I Got Rhythm*, with a bang-up finale of "Fascinating Rhythm," "Liza," and "I Got Rhythm." A grueling show, but Ira noted that George never complained and probably enjoyed it. Indeed, his valet Paul Mueller kept a diary and recorded the many parties and receptions in Gershwin's honor. Everywhere there were enthusiastic reviews. In Madison, the capital of

Wisconsin, reviewer Frank Schroeder wrote: "With a galaxy of blue notes and sparkling rhythm George Gershwin, composer and pianist, played triumphantly before an appreciative audience." In Milwaukee, the home town of his piano teacher Charles Hambitzer, the reviewer wrote: "It was one of the most stimulating evenings unveiled in Milwaukee in many a round moon." In Omaha Nebraska, his "sensuous melodies" and "tanglefooted rhythms" were praised. (Mueller commented that the "worst women" on the trip were in Omaha.)

It was a grueling schedule, venturing as far as Sioux Falls, South Dakota, where the audience wore overalls. Finally they returned to Brooklyn on February 10, 1934. One member of the Reisman orchestra believes that George suffered an unusual incident during the tour; he claimed to smell "burning rubber," but no one else did; the same sensation reappeared shortly before he died, so this incident in early 1934 could have been a possible symptom of the illness that would eventually kill him. But there is no other incident than on this one occasion.[25]

At the end of the tour George gave an interview in which he praised the value of the radio as an element of democracy that raised the people to a level where their tastes were more cosmopolitan as well as more discriminating. In less than a week after his return, George began a series of fifteen-minute radio broadcasts, "Music By Gershwin" at 7:30 on Mondays and Fridays.[26] There is some suggestion that George was mildly depressed around this time. Harold Arlen, the songwriter, had become a good friend, and he recalled that when George was doing his radio broadcasts he exclaimed to Arlen: "What do they want me to do? What are they criticizing me for?"[27] Apparently, Gershwin was reacting to the failure of his last Broadway shows and to the deeper criticism from musicologists. He was also irritated by carping that he was prostituting himself by endorsing products (i.e., Arrow shirts and Gillette razors). A member of the Reisman orchestra, the future conductor Mitch Miller, recalled over fifty years later that Gershwin was not a happy man. His serious works had been "clobbered by the critics" and the Reisman tour was a financial failure. But Miller gave a favorable description:

> Gershwin was always sweet. He never raised his voice. He did not have a commanding personality. He was the consummate craftsman. Gershwin had a poker face. It was impossible to judge his reaction. He never looked exultant or distressed.[28]

After the end of the tour Gershwin offered some remarks that were quite unusual for him. Whereas he had claimed that repetition of songs on the radio would kill them, now he was in awe of the power of the medium. Radio had not only raised the standards of taste but had made the average listener music conscious. Its effect had been "tremendous, and is constantly opening up undreamed vistas" (*New York Times*, March 4, 1934.) Of course, he was embarking on his own radio series and was not above a little promotion.

The failure of the Gershwins' last two Broadway outings had an unanticipated result. Had they been successful, the temptation would have been to continue in the same vein—another Kaufman satire, perhaps, or a more conventional book musical. In any event, Gershwin was suddenly liberated, and this would prove to be a significant turning point.

> Gershwin's musical abilities had undergone an evolution. There was a full decade between the *Rhapsody in Blue*, and the *Variations on I Got Rhythm*. Each of his "serious" compositions represented a gain in technical competence and, especially, in form and orchestration. His popular style, also reflected an advance in sophistication, without losing his feel for melodies: Gershwin was an innovator and, in the context of his time, a catalyst among songwriters for the musical theater, for motion pictures, and for the popular song market as cultivated by the Tin Pan Alley publishers. It is difficult, for example, to imagine a Harold Arlen (1905–86) without Gershwin's influence. And the ballads that Gershwin was composing in the early 1920s at the very beginning of his career are markedly different in style from those of the established composers.[29]

The influence of Jerome Kern, if it ever really had an impact, had long since been dissipated. (Richard Rodgers doubts that Kern had much influence on Gershwin.) The great ballads, "Someone to Watch Over Me," "How Long Has This Been Going On?", and "Embraceable You" are pure Gershwin. It is ironic that as Gershwin became popularly identified with "jazz" his own writing became softer and more complex. A new sophistication marked his writing for the controversial satires *Of Thee I Sing* and *Let 'Em Eat Cake*. The number of "hit" tunes in these productions declined. "Who Cares" from *Of Thee I Sing* and "Mine" from *Let 'Em Eat Cake* were not his ordinary Tin Pan Alley songs. Deena Rosenberg, in her biography, notes these two songs:

> In "Who Cares?" [and later in "Mine"] George used blue notes and harmonies to do more than augment, undermine, and make more poignant. In these two songs, a whole rich substratum of modern, elusive, jazz and blue-note-sprinkled harmonies is continuously audible, capturing the more complex demands of the dramatic situation and the more somber tone of the period.[30]

Long after he died a noted authority concluded that international audiences accepted his music as "the embodiment of musical Americana."[31] And that, of course, is exactly what Gershwin wanted. Yet, he had one more mountain to scale. In March 1932, he wrote again to DuBose Heyward in Charleston, proposing that they revive his earlier idea for an opera based on Heyward's novel *Porgy*.

NOTES

1. Joan Peyser, in *The Memory of All That* (New York: Simon and Schuster, 1993), claims that Kaufman and Ryskind did not like George because he was too "pushy." Kaufman's biographers do not bear this out.

2. Lawrence Maslon, "Stars and Swipes," in *Show Music*, Fall 1998, pp. 38–44.

3. *Boston Evening Transcript*, December 22, 1931.

4. Robert Kimball and Alfred Simon, *The Gershwins* (New York: Bonanza Books, 1963), pp. 143–44. Simon became one of the rehearsal pianists. Gershwin, conducting from the pit behind Simon, would correct him from time to time, saying "Not quite so fast," or "that should be an A-flat." Once when friends dropped by after rehearsals George played a "dazzling" set of variations on "Liza."

5. Bennett Cerf, "Trade Winds," *The Saturday Review of Literature*, July 17, 1943, pp. 14–15.

6. Kimball and Simon, *The Gershwins*, p. 151.

7. *New York Times*, August 17, 1932; author identified as "H.T."

8. After George died, Paul Whiteman recorded the *Cuban Overture*, but with a completely new orchestration and with a piano solo added!

9. Steven Gilbert, *The Music of George Gershwin* (New Haven, CT: Yale University Press, 1995), p. 173.

10. The first printing in 1932 contained "splendid" drawings by Constantin Alajalov, that "caught the spirit of the songs," Gershwin wrote in the introduction. The drawings are incredibly racist in their depiction of Afro-Americans. A new printing in 1941 dropped these drawings, as well as the dedication to Kay Swift. That version has on the title page, "Special Piano Arrangements Edited and Revised by Herman Wasserman."

11. Gilbert, *The Music of George Gershwin*, pp. 80–81. The entire *Song-Book* has been recorded as written by several modern pianists.

12. "Our Music Leads Gershwin Asserts," *New York Times*, September 25, 1932.

13. Stanley Green, *Ring Bells! Sing Songs!* (New York: Galahad Books, 1971), p. 62.

14. Gershwin Collection, Library of Congress.

15. Irving L. Kolodin, *Theatre Arts Monthly*, December 1933, p. 967.

16. Stanley Green, *Ring Bells! Sing Songs!*, p. 90.

17. Maslon, "Stars and Swipes," p. 44.

18. Malcolm Goldstein, *George S. Kaufman* (New York: Oxford University Press, 1979), p. 220. The scores of both *Of Thee I Sing* and *Let 'Em Eat Cake* have been recorded in modern versions by the Orchestra of St. Luke's conducted by Michael Tilson Thomas, under the auspices of the Brooklyn Academy of Music. Funding was from Lee Gershwin. Where available the original orchestrations were used. The leading roles were sung by Maureen McGovern, Larry Kert, and Jack Gilford (CBS Records, M2K 42522). Critics were enthusiastic.

19. Henry Cowell, "Overture to the Schillinger System," in *The Schillinger System of Musical Composition*, ed. Lyle Downing and Arnold Shaw (New York: Da Capo, 1978), p. ix.

20. Excerpt in David Ewen, *George Gershwin* (New York: The Ungar Publishing Company, 1970), p. 212. Ewen vigorously rebuts Schillinger's claims.

21. Ibid.

22. *The Schillinger System of Musical Composition*. The claim about Gershwin's lack

of resources is on p. 195, as well as Schillinger's assertion that "Mine" was written at his suggestion.

23. Gilbert, *The Music of Gershwin*, pp. 174–81.

24. Kay Swift's role is somewhat unclear. In the Library of Congress, Gershwin Collection, the entire composition is in her hand; there are discrepancies between it and the published version. It may be that the published version was edited by Albert Sirmay and by Gershwin himself.

25. Joan Peyser, *The Memory of All That*, p. 217. She claims that the sensation reflected a "slow growing tumor on the right temporal lobe of his brain."

26. Some of these broadcasts have been preserved and reissued on various CDs. They provide an excellent record of Gershwin's voice. The recording of *Variations on I Got Rhythm* was broadcast on April 30, 1934, with an explanatory introduction by George.

27. Kimball and Simon, *The Gershwins*, p. 167.

28. Peyser, *The Memory of All That*, pp. 138–39, writes that Gershwin was suffering from "depression, anxiety and personality problems" at this time. Her source is a collection of letters from Julia Van Norman to Gershwin. This lady was obsessively infatuated with Gershwin. He replied only sporadically. Peyser notes, however, that Nancy Bloomer Deussen, who was born in 1931, believes that she is in fact Gershwin's child.

29. Allen Forte, *The American Popular Ballad in the Golden Era* (Princeton, NJ: Princeton University Press, 1995), p. 148.

30. Rosenberg, *Fascinating Rhythm* (New York: Dutton, 1991), p. 238.

31. *The New Grove Dictionary of Music* (1980 edition).

Chapter 10

Porgy and Bess

Was it George Gershwin's destiny to write the first great American opera? He seemed to think so. Even when he was only a young and relatively unknown songwriter, he was groping for a fusion between the dramatic forms of the American stage and the popular jazz rhythms and melodies he was creating for George White's *Scandals*. He spoke of writing a musical version of a play based on the Hebrew folk tale *The Dybbuk*, and even signed a tentative contract in October 1929, but the rights were not free. Later, Gershwin thought he might compose an opera that reflected the urban dynamism of New York City (a foreshadowing of *West Side Story*):

> What I'd like to do would be to write an opera of the melting pot of New York City itself, which is the symbolic and actual blend of the native and immigrant strains. This would allow for many kinds of music, black and white, Eastern and Western, and would call for a style that would achieve, out of this diversity an artistic and aesthetic unity . . . I'd like to catch the rhythms of these interfusing peoples.[1]

It turned out that his initial effort to create an extended musical drama, however, was not about the great melting pot, but about blacks in Harlem, titled *Blue Monday*. It was a relatively short piece, written and produced in the summer of 1922 as a "jazz opera" for that year's version of the *Scandals*. It was crude, but in some respects it anticipated the monumental *Porgy and Bess*.

Gershwin's lyricist at the time, B.G. "Buddy" De Sylva, first had the idea and George White became interested. White and De Sylva were influenced by the success in 1921 of the all-black musical *Shuffle Along*, with a score written by Eubie Blake and Noble Sissle. It had opened in May 1921 after a long road tour and was almost immediately a hit. The Blake-Sissle score featured a song that became quite famous, "I'm Just Wild about Harry," as well as "Love Will Find a Way." During the show's long run, at one point or another the cast included Paul Robeson, Josephine Baker, and the blues singer Adelaide Hall. The show opened the way for other all-black musicals. Suddenly it seemed that all-black musicals might be money makers; *Shuffle Along* ran for over five hundred performances; in New York and on the road it made several million dollars. George White speculated about putting on his own version of a follow-up to *Shuffle Along*.[2] He even hired away two of the stars for his show, tentatively entitled *Shuffle Along of 1923* then changed to *George White's Black Scandals*. White was sued by the *Shuffle Along* company, but prevailed in court. James P. Johnson was hired to write the score for White's show (this may be when he first met Gershwin). White then changed his mind, fearing that the new all-black *Scandals* might compete with his annual *Scandals*. The title for his new show was changed to *Runnin' Wild*. It too was successful, especially James P. Johnson's song "Charleston," which launched the craze for the popular dance. The show opened in October 1923. White may have thought it would appeal to black audiences, but it turned out that the audiences were about three-fourths white. It is very likely that Gershwin saw this show.[3]

It is probable that during this time George White urged De Sylva to develop a black segment for the *Scandals*. When he first heard about it, Gershwin was enthusiastic. White, however, wavered but then revived his interest, which left De Sylva and Gershwin only "five feverish days" to complete their project. Apparently, they had already done some work based on White's initial enthusiasm. Paul Whiteman's orchestra was in the pit for that version of the *Scandals*. Ferde Grofé heard an early version of *Blue Monday* at Buddy De Sylva's apartment. After George died, Grofé wrote: "Even with such a crude performance the work struck me as highly original and as representing a new departure in American music."[4]

The basic plot revolved around a love triangle set in Mike's Tavern, a basement "cafe" near 135th Street and Lennox Avenue in Harlem. Onstage there is a bar and a piano. Upstage center there is a door leading to the street. Before the curtain the leading character, Joe, half-sings: that the ladies and gentlemen should come to Mike's colored saloon to see a colored [Harlem] tragedy enacted in operatic style and like the white man's opera. The theme will be love, hate, passion, and jealousy! The story will be an account of a woman's intuition gone wrong.

For this introduction there is music with a strong blues theme. As the curtain rises, there is Mike the proprietor polishing glasses behind the bar. It is about nine-thirty in the evening. This was followed by a short, bright dance that apparently included White as one of the dancers.

The hero is Joe, a gambler, who is in love with Vi. Her profession is a little vague. The villain is Tom, who entertains at Mike's. At the opening, Sam, who helps out around the tavern, enters. He is berated by Mike for his laziness; the original employed the "N"-word, but later was cleaned up to "good-for-nothin'." Sam sings "Blue Monday Blues," which becomes the main underlying musical theme of the opera.

Sweetpea the piano player enters and plays a few bars. Then Tom enters followed by Vi. She sings the second song of the opera, "Has Anyone Seen Joe?" based on a melody from an earlier Gershwin string quartet, "Lullaby," which was unknown at that time. Bits and pieces of this theme also reappear. Vi and Tom confront each other in a musical dialogue. Tom tries to persuade Vi to forget about Joe and think about him. He tries to kiss her, and they struggle. Vi pulls out a revolver. Tom backs off and Vi then leaves and Sam reprises "Blue Monday Blues."

Joe arrives and confides in Mike that he has won money in a dice game and is going to use it to go south to see his mother. "I haven't seen her now in years, So I sent a telegram that I'll be with her soon. Vi mustn't know that I've gone." Mike asks, "Why can't you tell her you're going?" Joe explains that she is too jealous. She'd never let him go. Joe sings that he wants to see his mother. Joe confides that he awaits a telegram that will confirm his visit. Others arrive followed by Joe and Vi. There is a musical interlude; the music mixes some of the main themes. Vi sings a version of the melody of Joe's spiritual. The jealous suitor, Tom, intimates to Vi that the telegram will be from another woman. The pianist Sweetpea delivers the telegram to Joe, and Vi demands to see it, insisting that it is from a woman. Joe pushes her—"Go on away!" He tears open the envelope and removes the telegram. Vi reaches for her handbag, draws her revolver and shoots Joe. He sinks down and the telegram flutters to floor. Vi picks it up and reads that Joe's mother has been dead three years. Vi begs forgiveness, which Joe grants her (all of this is sung). But it is too late—or almost, because Joe survives just long enough to sing another chorus of the spiritual.

The entire production ran for about twenty minutes. All of the original plot and dialogue have not survived, and this may be a blessing, judging from what has survived. After writing a piano arrangement, Gershwin gave it to Will Vodrey, a black orchestrator for the *Ziegfeld Follies* and the *Scandals*, who wrote out the arrangements for Paul Whiteman's pit orchestra.[5]

It was previewed in New Haven and performed once on Broadway. The production, introduced at the close of the first act of the *Scandals* of 1922, was performed by white singers and actors in black face. George White immediately withdrew it, not so much for its artistic failings, but because it was too depressing for a Broadway musical revue.

It was the first sustained musical effort by Gershwin beyond production numbers for the *Scandals*. He demonstrated that he could integrate 32-bar popular songs with operatic devices. The main themes, including the "Lullaby," were striking melodies, and Gershwin's manipulation of the musical themes and the dramatic action was skillful. "Blue Monday Blues" is more of a genuine blues than Gershwin had written hitherto. He used it to establish the ambience of the tragedy that was to come. He also used Joe's spiritual to bond him to Vi, when she sings the very same melody. In other words, he was striving to adapt operatic forms, which is not too surprising since he was studying classical forms with Kilenyi.

Gershwin was pleased with the chance to write this small opera. It gave him valuable experience in tying together the characters, the action, and the music. Thus, twelve years before *Porgy and Bess*, he had written recitatives and had used musical themes to identify characters and had written underscoring for the dialogue, spoken and sung. In his characteristic ebullience, he was not deterred by the critical attacks. Most often cited, however, is the devastating review by Charles Darnton for the *New York World*: "the most dismal, stupid and incredible black face sketch that has probably ever been perpetrated." Even Gershwin's ever-enthusiastic biographer David Ewen wrote that "The music lacks atmospheric or dramatic interest while the recitatives were stilted and stiffly contrived." Other biographers are quite critical. Edward Jablonski writes that while not "stupid" it is without doubt "dismal, words and music." He brushes off the spiritual as a "mammy song." Rodney Greenberg in his biography follows Jablonski, dismissing the spiritual, which he also calls a "mammy song" for its "sheer mawkishness." Charles Schwartz's biography characterized the production as a "dismal failure." Recent scholarly research has demonstrated that the reviews were in fact mixed, including some highly favorable ones.[6]

This small opera led indirectly to *Rhapsody in Blue*, because it inspired Whiteman's respect for Gershwin.[7] Gershwin's music also foreshadows the *Rhapsody*, especially his piano sketch. Whiteman was also impressed by *Blue Monday* and after the success of the *Rhapsody* in 1924 he hoped to repeat the favorable reception of his Aeolian Hall concert with a similar concert at Carnegie Hall. The new centerpiece would be *Blue Monday* with a new orchestral arrangement by Ferde Grofé and a new title, *135th Street*. Grofé's version, which became standard, drew on the Vodery score but used the *Rhapsody in Blue* instrumentation, with wailing clarinets and wah-wah muted trumpets.

This Whiteman version was performed on December 28, 1925, at Carnegie Hall, but in a concert version without sets. This may have been because the original dialogue and plot could not be accurately reconstructed. When De Sylva was asked about it, he admitted he could not remember the dialogue. This version too was criticized ("an extremely dreary affair"), although a review in the *New York Times* (December 30, 1925) described it as twenty minutes of as vivid grand opera as has yet been provided by an American composer. One critic who witnessed this revival wrote that Gershwin demonstrated the possibilities of jazz as legitimate operatic material when handled with imagination. Olin Downes, who had heard the score rehearsed, wrote in the *New York Times* (January 2, 1926): "In the score itself there is excellent material . . . there are not only some good melodies, but certain genuinely dramatic passages, some use of dissonance that is striking and germane to the stage situation." Another review said that there "were moments when Gershwin almost succeeded in making this absurd business sound like an opera."

A recent modern analysis summed up the role of *Blue Monday* in Gershwin's evolution:

> Compared to *Porgy and Bess* it [*Blue Monday*] pales in many ways. But like all of Gershwin's works (early or late) *Blue Monday* is pivotal in his compositional maturation, the first of several conversely shaky and sure steps in fresh directions. Here is a failed experiment, yes, but bold-like-genius, and without it his later greater contributions would not reflect the scope that they do.[8]

Revivals of *Blue Monday*, however, have not fared well. In 1953 there was a production for the TV series *Omnibus*. One reviewer concluded that while the performance had a certain curiosity value, otherwise it proved most ordinary and pedestrian. Another reviewer (Jack Gould in the *New York Times*) added that Gershwin apparently forgot this work and his judgment should be respected. This, of course, is not the case. Gershwin remembered it and years later could even quote favorable reviews.

Whiteman later claimed that he liked the themes in *Blue Monday* better than the *Rhapsody*, but this sounds like a justification for his failed Carnegie Hall concert. In any case, the idea of a longer, more serious piece of music was not alien to Gershwin when he was approached by Whiteman in the winter of 1923–24 to write the *Rhapsody*.

It was at about this very time, late December 1925, when Gershwin was involved with Whiteman's revival, that he became intrigued with DuBose Heyward's novel *Porgy*. Almost certainly because of his recent exposure with the *Blue Monday* revival, he saw in *Porgy* the basis for an opera. His attachment to this idea began when he was given the book by either Emily Strunsky or Kay Swift during tryouts for *Oh, Kay!* (the summer of 1926). Gershwin was not much of a reader, but once he opened the novel he found that he could not put it down; other sources claim he read himself to sleep, after strenuous days of working on the new show.[9] In any case, he wrote immediately to Heyward proposing to turn it into an opera.

What was it about *Porgy* that attracted Gershwin? Writing *Blue Monday* was surely one reason. He saw in the life of Afro-Americans links to spirituals, to jazz and the blues—which he found compelling. He also felt an affinity for African-American lifestyle, or so he professed. In an interview shortly before the revival of *Blue Monday*, Gershwin said that he would certainly write an opera: "I shall write it for niggers [*sic*]. They are always singing. They have it in their blood. I have no doubt that they will be able to do full justice to a jazz opera." A friend, he said, was looking for a libretto and he did not expect difficulty in finding principals for the solo parts. "There will probably also be a nigger orchestra. I am very hopeful about the success of such a venture."[10]

A decade later, after the opening of *Porgy and Bess*, he made similar remarks: because the story dealt with "Negro life in America," the music could reflect the "drama, the humour, the superstition, the religious fervor, the dancing and the irrepressible high spirits of the race."[11] Although a decade separated *Blue Monday* from *Porgy and Bess*, Gershwin may well have seen some parallels between these stories and even the characters (e.g., Cokey Lou in *Blue Monday* foreshadows Sporting Life in *Porgy*). He also was intrigued because *Porgy* was a "folk tale," and the music could therefore be folk music, not original folk songs, but new ones written by Gershwin himself.

When first approached by Gershwin, Heyward's wife Dorothy was turning his novel into a stage play, even though DuBose did not believe it was possible to extract a play from the novel. Thus, he had to turn down Gershwin's overture, but he indicated an interest. When they spoke after Gershwin's letter, Gershwin was vague and noncommittal. Apparently he was not disappointed, since he was not ready for such a major undertaking. He felt that he was not technically or musically equipped for the mammoth project of a grand opera, and claimed that he had to steep himself in the foundations of concert music. This is exactly what Gershwin did for the decade that separated *Blue Monday* and *Porgy and Bess*. He made enormous strides as a composer in the technical sense. He taught himself to orchestrate and mastered the traditional forms and devices—fugues, canons, counterpoint. Rather pompously he once explained to Vernon Duke that he had been using all of these techniques without realizing it, and doing so correctly but only by pure instinct. By studying, however, he could incorporate them into his music with greater skill and self-confidence.

He did not return to the idea of *Porgy* until March 1932, after the premiere of his *Second Rhapsody*. While still basking in the success of *Of Thee I Sing*, he wrote Heyward again proposing to collaborate in writing an opera. Why he reverted to an opera at this juncture is not clear; perhaps his success in handling the diverse musical requirements of *Of Thee I Sing* made him think that an opera would not be as difficult as others imagined. Or it is possible that he recognized that his contemporaries had written rhapsodies and concertos, but had avoided opera. This time the Heywards were receptive and discussions began. A contract was signed in October 1932.[12]

DuBose Heyward had an impeccable pedigree: one of his ancestors, Thomas Heyward, had signed the Declaration of Independence. The family had been plantation owners, but by 1885 Edwin Heyward was working in a rice mill when his son DuBose was born (DuBose was a family name on his mother's side). His father died, and his mother, Janie, moved the family to Charleston. Janie took an active interest in the study of the Afro-Americans residing in the low country and the outer islands around Charleston. She became an expert in the so-called Gullah culture and dialect and lectured on the subject. (Gullah was a corruption of Angola, the area in West Africa where the slaves transported to South Carolina had lived.) DuBose picked up an interest from his mother's encouragement.

As a young man he was sickly, suffering from a bout of polio. He began to write poetry and short stories, and his work was published occasionally. He met his wife, Dorothy Kuhs, at the MacDowell Colony, a summer camp for artists, and they were married in the summer of 1923. She was from Ohio, and the Southerners of Charleston did not take to her. But she won Harvard's prize for playwriting that guaranteed a Broadway production of her play, *Nancy Ann* (she beat out Thomas Wolfe in the competition). DuBose was still a relatively unknown writer, however, when he decided to give up his part-time insurance business and concentrate on writing a novel about Negro life in Charleston.

In addition to his mother's experience, DuBose had gained some practical insights. At one point he worked for a steamship line on the Charleston waterfront where he observed the Negroes working on the wharves. He was also moved by his observations of the black community in an area called "Cabbage Row," an old tenement that had once been a grand house in colonial times but had degenerated into a slum. It was not too far from Heyward's own home, and he could hear the distant sounds and vicariously absorb the life of Cabbage Row.

Heyward wanted to humanize the experience of the inhabitants through the tale of a character he first called "Porgo." He was modeled on a crippled beggar whose mode of transportation was a cart drawn by a goat. He was called "Goat Cart Sam" and was known to many around Charleston. His name in fact was Sammy Smalls, but he had died or disappeared by the time *Porgy* would have made him famous. He was not known to Heyward, who was intrigued by a newspaper clipping reporting his arrest for brawling.

The novel was published in 1925 to generally favorable reviews. The critics found it a new approach to the subject of southern blacks. The basic story became well-known. The locale is "Catfish Row." The main character is Porgy, a crippled beggar. In the novel Heyward describes him:

> There was something Eastern and mystic about the introspection of his look. He never smiled, and he acknowledged gifts only by a slow lifting of the eyes that held odd shadows in them. He was black with the almost purple blackness of unadulterated Congo blood.[13]

In the stage play and the libretto for the opera the Heywards describe Bess: "Bess is slender, but sinewy; very black, wide nostrils, and large, but well-formed mouth. She flaunts a typical, but debased, Negro beauty."

A modern writer named Kendra Hamilton, who grew up in Charleston, noted that her own grandmother, Anna Hamilton and her grandmother's friend, Mrs. Sarah Dowling were well aware of "Goat Cart Sam." They told her:

> Oh, he was a mean man.... A drunk and whatnot.... And that Bess business—it wasn't no Bess. They just wrote it up as a story and put all this Sporting Life and stuff in it. Of course, there were people *like* that

> . . . he had plenty of girlfriend[s]. He used to beat 'em, beat 'em with his
> little goat whip. Us children been scared of him, that Sam, . . . Oh, Lawd,
> you'd see (Sam) just going along, just a-singing, a body in a cart with
> two wheels.[14]

DuBose and Dorothy set about the task of transforming the play into the libretto of an opera. As they completed scenes they sent them to Gershwin. The opening scene of the opera is a summer evening in Catfish Row; a group is slowly dancing, and in the background Clara sings to her baby the opera's best-known song, "Summertime." A second group begins shooting dice. Porgy enters and joins the game, and then Crown, a brutish stevedore, obviously drunk, enters and takes a place in the game; he is accompanied by Bess. The dope peddler Sporting Life is on hand to supply Crown and Bess with some "happy dust" and liquor. The game degenerates into a fight; Crown kills another player, Robbins, and flees leaving Bess behind. All doors are shut to her, but Porgy gives her refuge, and she remains with him for the next month. Her presence transforms the lonely Porgy ("I Got Plenty o' Nuttin' "). Later, when the inhabitants of Catfish Row embark on a picnic on Kittiwah Island Porgy urges Bess to go along; he is confident of their relationship ("Bess, You Is My Woman Now"); on the island Sporting Life entertains the crowd ("It Ain't Necessarily So"). Crown is hiding on the island and forcibly takes Bess. She eventually escapes and returns, and is again taken in by Porgy, but she is delirious. She confesses to Porgy her vulnerability to Crown's enticements.

During a hurricane, Crown returns to Catfish Row to claim Bess. However, he leaves during the storm to help Clara and Jake, who are caught by the hurricane. When he returns Porgy fights and kills him. The police drag Porgy away, not as the culprit, but as a witness to identify Crown's body, which terrifies Porgy. Bess is alone and Sporting Life tempts her with "happy dust." Bess yields to his temptation ("There's a Boat Leavin' Soon for New York") and leaves Catfish Row with him. Porgy finally returns and learns of Bess's disappearance. He is determined to follow her, even to New York ("beyond the customs house"). He leaves Catfish Row as he and the other inhabitants sing a final spiritual, "I'm on My Way," and the curtain falls.[15]

Two of Gershwin's biographers noted: "It is astonishing today how innovative the treatment of black life in 'Porgy' was."[16] Nevertheless, almost every observer could not help but note the incongruities: a Russian Jew from the Lower East Side and a white southern aristocrat collaborating to write an opera about life in the Negro quarter of Charleston, South Carolina.

It turned out that Heyward and Gershwin were compatible. They were drawn together by a mutual interest in creating an authentic "folk opera." Gershwin had been training for it for years, without really acknowledging it, and Heyward and his wife were dramatists with a flare for the lyric theater. Their collaboration, however, was ragged. They communicated mainly by mail; Heyward would finish a scene and mail it to Gershwin, with suggestions as to where a song might fit. They met only occasionally. Heyward was unfamiliar with Gershwin's style of working, especially Gershwin's ability to contemplate the essence of a new composition while doing something else.

Heyward became frustrated as Gershwin seemed to be diverted into one project or another. First, there was a tour with Leo Reisman's orchestra and then a radio show. Heyward wrote of his disappointment that Gershwin was not concentrating on the opera: "Swell show George, but what the hell is the news about PORGY!!! . . . I am naturally disappointed that you have tied yourself up."[17] But he drafted the first scene of *Porgy* by November 12, 1933, shortly after the opening of Gershwin's *Pardon My English*. His original novel and play had included some traditional folk songs, but Gershwin informed Heyward that he intended to write all of the music, including original spirituals. This meant that sooner or later Gershwin ought to visit Charleston. On his way to Florida in December 1933, Gershwin did stop by to meet with Heyward, and they planned on a longer stay later. Accompanied by his cousin Henry Botkin, Gershwin finally spent several weeks on Folly Island in July 1934. "Lonesomeness" had crept in on him quite a few times and he found that the primitive conditions and the easy access to the beach made it difficult to work. He wrote that he had seen and heard some "grand Negro sermons." To the delight of the local blacks, he joined in a prayer meeting and soon took over the "shouting."

Heyward, however, was never quite satisfied that Gershwin had absorbed enough local atmosphere. Heyward, after all, had spent his life in the area studying the ways of the local Negroes, while Gershwin was merely passing through. Nevertheless, Gershwin's ear for the right sounds was finely tuned, and many critics assumed he had borrowed from local traditions. The only borrowed themes, in fact, were the cries of the street vendors, and Gershwin even rewrote them.

Gershwin explained that he believed the opera had to be entertaining. Accordingly, he urged Heyward not to make the scenes too long. He was a great believer, Gershwin wrote, in not giving people too much of a good thing. His constant advice was to shorten the play—by 40 percent, he suggested. Heyward did in fact cut down the play eliminating some entire scenes.[18] Gershwin's feel for the theater was an important dimension of his success. Professor Richard Crawford wrote that Gershwin profited from the fact that he had spent his career submitting his music to the ruthless judgment of mass audiences; thus he knew how to break through an audience's apathy.[19]

As for his own contribution, Gershwin indicated he had started work in February 1934 (soon after he finished his *Variations on I Got Rhythm*). Later he wrote Heyward that he was "skipping about, writing a bit here and a bit there."[20] He reported to Heyward that he had seen Virgil Thomson's opera *Four Saints in Three Acts*, with a libretto by Gertrude Stein. He dismissed Stein's text as the work of a five-year-old.

In a complete turnaround from his usual work style with Ira, Gershwin was setting Heyward's lyrics to music. His brother was busy collaborating with Harold Arlen on a new musical, *Life Begins at 8:40*. In April 1934, Heyward came to New York and stayed with George. Heyward wrote several of his lyrics during that interlude. When Ira became free in the summer of 1934 he began to help by "polishing" some of Heyward's lyrics, according to DuBose's wife. Although he denied even "polishing" DuBose's lyrics, Ira's contribution has been overshadowed somewhat by the fascination with the Heyward-Gershwin collaboration. It is now evident that Ira contributed much more than mere "polishing." He wrote many of the lyrics entirely by himself and some of them in collaboration with Heyward.[21]

For example, it was George who suggested the need for a lighter song for Porgy. He started experimenting at the piano, and both Ira and DuBose exclaimed "that's it!" Suddenly, a title "popped" into Ira's head—"I Got Plenty o' Nuttin.' " George and DuBose were delighted, and DuBose asked if he could take the music back to Charleston and work on it. His lyric was "awkward," so Ira did indeed "polish" it. But, Ira noted, all the rest of DuBose's lyrics were set to music by George with scarcely a change. For some of Ira's lyrics he borrowed from a line in the Heyward play; for example, "I Loves You Porgy" and "Oh, I Can't Sit Down."

Heyward left behind a graphic description of the Gershwin work method: "the brothers Gershwin, after their extraordinary fashion, would get at the piano, pound, wrangle, swear, burst into weird snatches of song, and eventually emerge with a polished lyric." All of this was taking place at George Gershwin's new fourteen-room penthouse apartment in Manhattan at 132 East 72nd Street.[22] (Ira lived across the street.) At one point George wrote himself a note of "things to be done," such as "write prelude to Act I," which he never did. Dubose Heyward eventually sent the Gershwins a libretto marked up by his wife, which George then annotated.[23]

Heyward alone wrote the words to the most enduring song, "Summertime." He drew on bits and pieces from his play, but nowhere in the play is there the most famous lyrics of "Summertime," "when the livin' is easy." [24] It was the first melody Gershwin wrote when he began the score, and of course he played it for anyone he could capture. His listeners were enthusiastic, and he reassured Heyward: "we have an exciting event ahead of us."[25] Richard Rodgers relates that on Christmas Eve 1934, Gershwin and Kay Swift burst into the Rodgers' apartment like "two irrepressible Magi." Dorothy Rodgers was having a difficult time with her second pregnancy, so George and Dick carried her into the living room to a sofa, and George proceeded to play the score for *Porgy and Bess*— almost a year before its Broadway premiere.

Gershwin mused about the basic concept to follow. He wrote that he would not begin a composition until he had all of the themes in his head. He thought it should be a blend of Wagner and Bizet. He explained that Wagner told a complete musical story with no stage breaks, interruptions for dialogue, or explanations by the performers. Moreover, Wagner created a musical signature (leitmotifs) for both the major actors as well as the action. The audience could identify certain musical passages with key performers and this was an aspect that intrigued Gershwin. He could repeat a basic theme many times, varying it and reworking it in tempo, timbre, or style; he had done this on a small scale in *Blue Monday*, and he did so again in *Porgy*. Thus, Wagner hovered over Gershwin's opera. According to Gershwin's close friend Oscar Levant, Gershwin constantly referred to the score of *Die Meistersinger* as a "guide to the plotting of the choral parts and for general precepts in choral writing." In Gershwin's notes for the final spiritual "I'm on My Way," he wrote, "rhythmic figure a la Wagner."

Gershwin did make use of musical signatures for some of his characters, especially Porgy, in a short, five-note blues theme, and he massaged it musically over and over to an impressive effect. For example, Porgy's theme is introduced first by the orchestra, when he first enters and the crowd greets him; this is meant to convey Porgy's attachment to the broader Catfish Row community. Gershwin also demonstrates musically that Bess has been accepted by the community, when she leaves without Porgy for the fateful picnic on Kittiwah Island.[26] Crown has no melodic theme, but a rhythmic pattern identifies him. Gershwin also described Sporting Life as an outsider from the Catfish community by musically using harmonic dissonance.[27] Sporting Life sings "It Ain't Necessarily So," and Gershwin uses fragments of this melody to suggest Sporting Life whenever he reappears.

In his analysis, the musicologist Professor Joseph P. Swain points to the use of Porgy's theme, once established, to move the action musically. At first the music reflects Porgy's struggle against loneliness, but then returns triumphantly after he kills Crown.[28] Bess, however, has no distinct theme; her music adapts to the men she is with—Porgy, Crown, and Sporting Life. One of the most important climaxes occurs when Porgy sings his aria, "Bess, You Is My Woman Now." It is introduced by a few bars from Porgy's theme, and the bond between Porgy and Bess is established when Bess finally joins in and they sing together.[29] At this point the relationship must be explicated by the music and "Gershwin does not fail."[30]

The music underlying the first fight between Crown and Robbins, a furious agitated passage, is repeated virtually without change in the fight between Porgy and Crown. After Porgy kills him, he shouts out—"Yo' Got Porgy Now!" The curtain rings down, but the orchestra triumphantly plays Porgy's theme ending on a major chord, but then punctuated by a sweeping glissando to a sharp dissonant chord.

At the end of the opera, there is also a Wagnerian touch. When Porgy leaves Catfish Row, Gershwin reverts to Porgy's familiar musical signature. As the curtain falls, the final bars begin with the entire orchestra majestically playing two bars of "Bess, You Is My Woman," followed by a fortissimo statement of Porgy's theme, a crescendo to the final beat. What is musically interesting is that the sequence is in one key (E major) but the final harsh chord is an unresolved E major 7th chord, thereby signalling that the story is not completely or truly over for Porgy—a masterful musical touch by Gershwin.

Despite Wagnerian twists, the ponderous and romantic Wagner was a dubious model for Gershwin's style: the great German built huge walls of sound that engulfed the action, the singers, the stage, and the audience. Bizet, on the other hand, was a better model because he used his musical talents to write "song hits," and he spurred the plot and characters, giving them real melodies to be sung. This too appealed to the popular songwriter in Gershwin. In a later conversation with the music critic Irving Kolodin, Gershwin was enthusiastic about Bizet's use of local color.[31]

At this time Gershwin was friendly with another popular songwriter, Vernon Duke, who was an informal advisor while Gershwin was writing *Porgy and Bess*. His given name was Vladimir Dukelsky; he was a fairly recent Russian immigrant, an aspiring classical composer, a student of the famous Russian master Rheinhold Gliere, and a friend of Sergei Prokofiev. Duke and Gershwin hashed over ideas for the opera. Gershwin was insistent that all of the dialogue be sung, or at least set against a musical background. Duke urged a more traditional, pre-Wagnerian approach, with a collection of arias, ensembles, trios, quartets, and so forth. Gershwin resisted because he feared that he would end up writing another musical comedy, with a series of melodies interspersed throughout Heyward's serious stage play.

When Gershwin and Heyward began collaborating, Heyward also suggested that the dialogue be spoken, in order for the action to move more rapidly, but Gershwin prevailed. What Gershwin wanted was a "grand opera," not a Broadway musical. When the Theatre Guild wanted to bill the production as a "folk opera" he also resisted, but finally conceded. After the opening, he justified his decision:

> Since the opening of *Porgy and Bess* I have been asked frequently why it is called a folk opera. The explanation is a simple one. *Porgy and Bess* is a folk tale. Its people naturally would sing folk music. When I first began work on the music I decided against the use of original folk material because I wanted the music to be all of one piece. Therefore I wrote my own spirituals and folksongs. But they are still folk music—and therefore, being in operatic form, *Porgy and Bess* becomes a folk opera.[32]

It is ironic that in the end his most fervent admirers disliked the recitatives that he insisted on, but worshipped the simple songs, such as "I Got Plenty o' Nuttin'," as he feared. Gershwin contended that "The recitative I have tried to make as close to the Negro inflection in speech as possible, and I believe my songwriting apprenticeship has served invaluably in this respect."[33]

It would be many years before Gershwin's conviction was finally vindicated by revivals of the original version or versions close to it in the 1970s. Even after the opening this debate over the use of recitatives continued and for a time muddied the question of whether *Porgy and Bess* was a genuine opera or a musical. Gershwin's insistence on producing it in a Broadway theater did not help his cause. On Broadway he could expect a series of performances, whereas at the Metropolitan the season might include only a few performances. Moreover, Gershwin's insistence on an all-black cast would have posed a problem for the Metropolitan and using mixed races in the cast was out of the question. Gershwin explained that he did not seek the "usual sponsors" because he wanted to develop "something in American music" that would appeal to the "many" rather than the "cultured few."[34]

According to Oscar Levant, Gershwin's acquaintance with formal music was "scattered," but he had some clear preferences that suggest an aesthetic eclecticism, especially for a Broadway songwriter. He tilted toward modern impressionists (Ravel and Debussy), as well as more radical composers. He was impressed by Alban Berg; he had even acquired the score to Berg's opera *Wozzeck* and traveled to Philadelphia to hear it. He owned recordings of Honegger's *Pacific 231*, Berg's *Lyric Suite*, Stravinsky's *Firebird*, Debussy's *Afternoon of a Faun*, Shostakovich's *First Symphony*, Prokoviev's *Classical Symphony*, Richard Strauss' *Salome*, Wagner's *Tristan and Isolde*, and Ravel's *Daphnis and Chloe*. He had studied the score for Stravinsky's *Les Noces*, as well as the works of Milhaud and Schoenberg.[35]

In the 1920s, Gershwin began to feel that his musical ambitions and creativity were outstripping his technical capacity. Then around 1932 he encountered a new teacher, the Russian émigré Joseph Schillinger. For Gershwin the Schillinger "system" of composition was exciting, according to Vernon Duke who studied with Schillinger later. For Gershwin, "who always took a childish delight in the simplest pleasures and discoveries, now had found a toy that was real fun and would also yield great dividends, and unheard of combinations," wrote Vernon Duke. While Duke acknowledged that Gershwin's *Variations on I Got Rhythm* and his *Cuban Overture* owed a lot to Schillinger, he added that Schillinger was *not* a major contributor to *Porgy and Bess*, even though Gershwin was studying with him. On the other hand, during the tryouts for *Porgy and Bess* in Boston, while listening to the orchestra, Gershwin turned to Duke and commented, "Just listen to those overtones."[36]

Schillinger himself, after George died, claimed that "Porgy and Bess was written entirely under my supervision; it took a year and a half, at the rate of three lessons a week (which at the time consumed four and a half hours)." David Ewen, while quoting Schillinger, added that Gershwin's friends could not recall a single incident or remark to substantiate Schillinger's contention.[37] In a letter to the editor of *Newsweek*, Ira rebutted Schillinger vehemently.

Vernon Duke believes, however, that Schillinger did indeed have a liberating effect on Gershwin: His various tunes were now "clothed in appropriate orchestral garb and shone with a new and dazzling brilliance."[38] Oscar Levant believed that there was "considerable evidence" of [Gershwin's] study with Schillinger in *Porgy*. Careful scholarship by Wayne D. Shirley of the Library of Congress has demonstrated that there are several instances in the original score that reflect Gershwin's adaptation of Schillinger's methods; most of these, however, were in passages that were cut during rehearsals or the Boston tryout.[39] The musicologist Paul Nauert, while suggesting that Schillinger's claims did not "ring true," nevertheless concluded that it was generally agreed that the extended, continuous elements of [Porgy] drew "most heavily on the resources of the Schillinger System."[40]

In any case, by January 1935, roughly a year after he began, Gershwin finished the piano score for two of the three acts and finished most of the orchestration by mid-August 1935. He completed the final passages on September 2, 1935. He began sending completed scenes to his publisher and editor Albert Sirmay in mid-February so that they could be sent to the engraver for final printing. Thus a complete, printed score existed before the show opened. Moreover, rehearsals had begun in July, before the score or orchestration had been finished.[41]

Rouben Mamoulian was recruited as the director, since he had directed the original play. The conductor was Alexander Smallens, and the vocal coach was Alexander Steinert.[42] Gershwin personally recruited two of the star performers: Todd Duncan, who would play Porgy, and Anne Brown, who would take the role of Bess. He was very proud of them and his role in discovering them, but his explanation was disconcerting: "we were able to find these people [Duncan and Brown] because what we wanted from them lies in their race," (*New York Times*, October 20, 1935).

The most inspired casting was John Bubbles for Sporting Life (contrary to legend, the part was not written specifically for Cab Calloway). Bubbles was part of the vaudeville team of Buck and Bubbles; he was totally undisciplined, unreliable, and the source of several embarrassing incidents, but marvelous in the part. Gershwin's explanation of the character of Sporting Life was unusual: Sporting Life, instead of being a sinister dope peddlar, is a "humorous, dancing villain who is likable and believable and at the same time evil."

One rehearsal was recorded in the CBS studios on July 19, 1935, and some of it was broadcast on Gershwin's radio program with George conducting. He played (and sang) a few bars of introduction to "Summertime" which was sung by Abbie Mitchell, the original Clara. This session also included a version of "Bess, You Is My Woman Now," sung by Todd Duncan and Anne Brown, the original Porgy and Bess. Kurt Weill (who had fled from Hitler) attended one rehearsal in the company of Ira Gershwin. Weill was a recent arrival in the United States, but already renowned as the composer of the *Three Penny Opera*. After the rehearsal, he commented: "It's a great country where music like that can be written and played." George Gershwin often rehearsed the orchestra himself. Just before leaving for the out-of-town tryout, Alexander Smallens conducted the entire score at Carnegie Hall for a selected group. Ira Gershwin was in attendance and wrote: "Until then only George knew what it would sound like. I couldn't believe my ears. That wonderful orchestra and full chorus on the stage. I never realized it would be like that. It was one of the great thrills of my life."[43] Ira was particularly struck by George's reservoir of musical inventiveness, resourcefulness, and craftsmanship. Ira cites "Summertime" as an example, but also Bess' song to Crown, "What You Want Wid' Bess?" became a rhythmic aria, which is then superimposed by Crown's theme to become a duet.

Ira was not alone in his admiration. His brother too was quite taken by his own accomplishment. After the first day of rehearsal, Gershwin called the director Rouben Mamoulian late at night, and told him:

> I just had to call you and tell you how I feel. I am so thrilled and delighted over the rehearsal today. Of course, I always knew *Porgy and Bess* was wonderful, but I never thought I'd feel the way I feel now. After listening to that rehearsal today, I think the music is so marvelous, I don't believe I wrote it.[44]

This was typical of Gershwin, Mamoulian observed. He could look at himself in a detached way, as if he were looking at somebody else. Whatever he liked he praised. He happened to like his own music, too, so he praised it without any self-consciousness or false modesty. Alex Steinert, who conducted the choral work, said much the same thing about Gershwin's objectivity. And DuBose Heyward echoed this appraisal: he saw himself realistically and impersonally—a man who "knew what he wanted and where he was going."[45]

The out-of-town tryout in Boston on September 30, 1935, was a sensation: "Gershwin must now be accepted as a serious composer," noted the *Boston Transcript*. The audiences insisted that the authors come onto the stage (George was dressed in white tie), and held them there for a long ovation. Nevertheless, the production was much too long and the Gershwins, Heyward, Smallens, and Kay Swift spent the evening talking through the needed revisions. Mamoulian and Steinart were impressed with Gershwin's willingness to cut his own work, but Kay Swift claimed later that he was deeply wounded by the process. She too was depressed that the original score would never be heard. Todd Duncan agreed that Gershwin was quite hurt by the cuts.

The net result—the score was cut by one-quarter!—an ironic outcome in light of Gershwin's urging Heyward to shorten his scenes. One of the casualties was the opening. It had been Heyward's idea for the curtain to open on a darkened stage; the music would come from a lone piano player, performing a "ragtime" tune, that would merge into the clanging of St. Michael's chimes. Then would come the overture introducing Catfish Row. The piano music composed by Gershwin was later published as "Jaszbo Brown," the title of one of Heyward's poems, and can be heard in recent full recordings of the original score. Gershwin moved it to the opening of the first act, rather than keeping it as a prologue. It is clearly not "ragtime," but closer to a modern blues. It was cut down before the first Broadway version, and then eliminated. Also cut was the "Buzzard

Song" sung by Porgy in Act II, Scene 1. This was an important cut, because the appearance of a buzzard was intended to be a symbol of bad times to come. Gershwin himself, however, proposed to cut it because of the strain on Todd Duncan's voice. He had to sing his major aria, "Bess, You Is My Woman Now" a few minutes after the "Buzzard Song." Other cuts reduced the opera to three hours, about right for Broadway.[46]

These changes and subsequent ones have given rise to some controversy over just what should be considered the "authentic" score. Recent versions that have returned to what Gershwin originally "intended" or "envisioned" are based on the piano vocal score that was given to the publisher for printing before the Boston opening. There were cuts in the Boston production and even after the opening in New York. For example, the version that opened that first night in Boston had already suffered cuts during rehearsals. One score used by the conductor, for example, has three layers of cuts, reflecting the different stages of production. Charles Hamm, after a thorough study of five existing scores, some relatively newly available, pointed out that subsequent claims by producers that they revived the "original" are misleading. Professor Hamm, however, makes an important point: however reluctantly, Gershwin did, in fact, initiate or agree to all the cuts; the version that opened in New York therefore is the version that Gershwin "intended to be played."[47]

The production opened on October 10, 1935, at the Alvin Theater, but it ran for only 124 performances. It closed on January 26, 1936, and then began a short road tour. The Gershwins each lost their investment of about $5,000, as did Heyward.[48] George more than recouped his investment through royalties from the music, which ran over $10,000 in 1935, the year the opera opened. After the road tour ended the "original" version of *Porgy and Bess* was finished.

The reception in New York was divided. Some adored it, some were puzzled, and some hostile. Brooks Atkinson of the *New York Times* thought the operatic form was "cumbersome," and objected that commonplace remarks had to be made into a "chanting monotone." What the theater critic wanted was a musical show with songs that "evoke the emotions of situations and make no further pretensions." Nevertheless, he concluded that Gershwin's music added something vital to the story that had been lacking; as to whether the Gershwin score measured up to the stated intention of writing a "folk opera," Atkinson graciously acknowledged that this was Olin Downes' bailiwick. (This was an odd arrangement, Atkinson reviewed Broadway musicals, but apparently *Porgy* was too "serious," and thus Downes was called in.)

Downes (*New York Times*, October 11, 1935) agreed that the recitatives were "seldom significant," but praised the "flashes of ingenuity . . . and effective use of spirituals." Burns Mantle gave it four stars, his highest award. Lawrence Gilman, an inveterate critic of Gershwin, disliked the "song hits" which he claimed marred the score and were a "blemish upon its musical integrity." John Anderson (*Evening Journal*) found "two-thirds of it mighty dull." Leonard Liebling, however, concluded, "The music is our own soil and our own days."

Porgy and Bess has been engulfed by various controversies. Was it an opera? A musical? Some of both? Was it an authentic portrayal of Negro life? Or stereotypes imagined by white men?

At the time such questions seemed quite important, because the traditional critics insisted on defining how it would be judged, by standards of Puccini or Jerome Kern. In this regard, Gershwin's insistence on the recitatives turned out to be self-defeating. Most of the classical critics did not like them. The music critic, Irving Kolodin, was an exception. He observed the opera in rehearsal for several months and wrote:

> This rhythmic speech has demonstrated its validity and its vitality in numerous operas before, but it has peculiar suitability to the negroes who constitute the characters of *Porgy and Bess*, for it approximates a type of speech they frequently use as a race. Indeed, the declamatory writing in Gershwin's opera is one of the most impressive accomplishments, for its adherence to the characteristics of the persons in the drama, for its excellent sense of word values.[49]

Gershwin's talent for songwriting was also self-defeating. No one could forget the melancholy strains of "Summertime" or the joyous "I Got Plenty o' Nuttin'." Their popularity reinforced the argument that the opera was, in fact, only a thinly disguised musical. Gershwin, however, refused to apologize for the melodies: "I am not ashamed of writing songs," he said. He cited other operatic traditions:

> Without songs it could be neither theater nor entertaining, from my viewpoint. But songs are entirely within the operatic tradition. Many of the most successful operas of the past have had songs. Nearly all of Verdi's operas contain what are known as song hits. *Carmen* is almost a collection of hits.[50]

The composer Virgil Thomson was a major critic. In 1938 he claimed: "Gershwin does not even know what an opera is." With a "libretto that never should have been accepted on a subject that never should have been chosen, a man who should never have attempted it has written a work of considerable power." Thomson's critique was quite racist: The performers should have shown the writers the "folly of trying to get out of Negroes any real enthusiasm for white-man-made art about Negroes." Thomson insisted:

> Mr. Gershwin is here a greater sinner than Mr. Heyward, because his work was executed later. Folklore subjects recounted by an outsider are only valid as long as the folk in question is unable to speak for itself, which is certainly not true of the American Negro in 1935. . . . As for the development, or musical build-up, there simply isn't any. When he gets hold

of a good number he plugs it. The rest of the time he just makes up what music he needs as he goes along.[51]

Edward Jablonski was roundly critical of Thomson, not only because the tone of his criticism was "condescending" but also was "surprisingly uninformed." Jablonski noted that in his review Thomson admitted an unfamiliarity with Gershwin's work and named two pieces that did not even exist (Harlem Night and a second piano concerto). Joan Peyser noted a smarmy anti-Semitism in some of Thomson comments (e.g., a reference to "gefilte fish orchestrations"). Jablonski also noted that Thomson's assessment reflected a consensus of the "intellectual" music establishment of the time as well as the mixed (predominantly negative) opinions of the press.

As expected, the modernist critic Paul Rosenfeld was quite harsh:

Porgy and Bess . . . fortifies one's conviction of Gershwin's shortness of the artists's feeling . . . some of the pieces are very bad and empty . . . the score sustains no mood . . . the individual numbers spurt from a flat level, and ending, leave one largely where they picked one up.[52]

Nevertheless, a consensus emerged that *Porgy and Bess* was indeed a grand opera.[53] One eminent authority, the conductor and writer Lehman Engel, wrote about the debate:

It has always seemed to me that this annoyance with *Porgy* is far more than the product of semantics than of anything Gershwin put into his score. It is as if just calling *Porgy* by the name "Opera" serves to assail the sensibilities of those who believe that such a classification is a slur on the dignity of Wagner, Verdi, and Mozart.[54]

Wayne Shirley, the musicologist of the Library of Congress, sees *Porgy and Bess* as an opera comparable to Wagner's *Die Meistersinger* because there is "not just a chorus of mastersingers. Each one of them has a name, a character and all emerge as real people." *Porgy and Bess* is "the American opera" he asserts, just as *Boris Godunov* is the Russian opera and *Tristan and Isolde* is the German opera, and *Carmen* the French or Spanish opera.[55] A similar observation was made by the musicologist Gerald Mast, who wrote that while *Porgy and Bess* plays on white audience's beliefs about stereotypical blacks, grand opera has always relied on characters who were "more passionate" than the average lot of ordinary citizens.[56]

A recent appraisal (1997) of the opera by professor Geoffrey Block concluded that despite its "pretensions and attendant artistic and political controversies [it has] long since demonstrated a stageworthiness matched only by the memorability of its tunes."[57] An incisive musical analysis by Joseph P. Swain (*The Broadway Musical*) emphasized that the "folk" aspect is amply demonstrated by Gershwin's careful, slow development of the community of Catfish Row as a dramatic character in themselves. This comes to fruition when Porgy and the community merge to sing the final spiritual.[58]

The second area of major criticism came from black writers who attacked the opera's racial stereotypes, as depicted in both the music and the text. Hall Johnson, the music critic for *The Afro-American*, wrote:

> The informing spirit of Negro music is not to be caught and understood merely by listening to the tunes and Mister Gershwin's much-publicized visits to Charleston for local color do not amount even to a matriculation in the preparatory school that he needed for his work. [The audience] . . . admired the Broadway Negro style because it does not know the real and its intelligence is not yet insulted when Negro folk-material is mis-stated in foreign terms.[59]

Duke Ellington was also numbered among the original critics. A recent authority on Ellington claimed that he "despised the opera version." In an interview published in December 1935, Ellington did indeed say that Gershwin had "borrowed from everyone from Liszt to Dickie Wells' kazoo band." He also said that "the first thing that gives it away is that it does not use the Negro musical idiom. It was not the music of Catfish Row or any other kind of Negroes."[60] Some months later, in a press release by his publisher Mills Music, Ellington claimed that he was quoted incorrectly from an interview that he believed not to be for publication. But students of Ellingtoniana believe that while the "frank tone is surprising, the manner of delivery would seem to be Ellington's own." Nevertheless, some years after the original opening, Ellington found that he liked the new production of March 1953, which returned to New York after its overseas tour. He cabled the producer—"Your Porgy and Bess the superbest, singing the gonest, acting the craziest, Gershwin the greatest."[61]

Black criticism seems to have been divided between the outsiders—the critics, writers, and sociologists—and the performers.

The 1953 version that Duke Ellington liked provoked some harsh attacks from black authorities. The sociologist Harold Cruse wrote in the 1950s,

> Porgy and Bess belongs in a museum and no self-respecting African American should want to see it, or be seen in it. . . . It portrays the seamiest side of Negro life . . . presumably the image of black people that white audiences want to see.

He warned that *Porgy and Bess* traveled the same tortured path on which African-American culture too often gets to the public: via whites and third parties who give it their own interpretation. A black journalist, James Hicks, wrote that it was the "most insulting, the most libellous, the most degrading act that could possibly be perpetrated against coloured [*sic*] Americans of modern times."[62] A recent critic wrote that black audiences stayed away in droves, and the depictions of black life in Charleston caused periodic revolts among cast members.

William Warfield, who sang *Porgy* in the 1950s, acknowledged the reservations of some black performers—"believe me, there was a time when a black artist thought very seriously as to whether or not he or she should perform in 'Porgy' or 'Show Boat.' " He said, "I remember when our State Department decided to send the 1952 *Porgy* abroad, there was a lot of criticism from black groups about whether this was the right thing to do. . . . Leontyne Price and I both had to search our hearts before we decided to do the [1952] tour."

Nevertheless, Warfield said *Porgy* was the "true American opera, a real masterpiece. Americans have produced many fine things when it comes to opera. . . . But to me "Porgy" towers over all of them." Gershwin had "captured the black spirit incredibly well," because he spent so much time in Charleston and had so many black people sing their songs and spirituals for him. He absorbed all the street calls and the music being sung in the black churches and transcribed it. That's why it is so authentic."[63] Both Todd Duncan and Anne Brown, who sang Porgy and Bess in the original, dismissed charges of racism. (Anne Brown's father, however, was not pleased with the characterization of African-Americans.) Roberta Alexander, who sang Bess at the Metropolitan, said "*Porgy*'s definitely an opera. Anybody who has ever sung it will tell you that." The baritone James Deas, who sang *Porgy* in the winter of 1998 in concert versions presented by the National Symphony Orchestra in Washington, D.C., and then by the New York Philharmonic, said "These characters are of a certain time and place. And I think Gershwin loved them and wrote music for them of tremendous nobility, strength and depth. If I felt there was a condescension, I wouldn't be singing it."[64]

The poet Maya Angelou, who played Ruby on the tour of 1952, recalled the performance in Milan at the famed La Scala:

> This was something unique: famous white American performers had appeared at La Scala, but never blacks, especially not a huge cast of blacks such as *Porgy* provided. Both audience and company were tense. Every member of the cast was coiled tight like a spring, wound taut for a shattering release. The moment the curtain opened, the singers pulled the elegant first-night audience into the harshness of black Southern life. The love story unfolded with such tenderness that the singers wept visible tears.[65]

As for Gershwin himself, there was a whiff of racism in his rather condescending comments when the opera first opened. He wrote that because *Porgy and Bess* deals with Negro life in America:

It brings to the operatic form elements that have never before appeared in opera, and I have adapted my method to utilize the drama, the humor, the superstition, the religious fervor, the dancing and the irrepressible high spirits of the race. If in doing this I have created a new form, which combines opera with theater, this new form has come quite naturally from the material. [It] has all elements of entertainment for the eye as well as the ear because the Negroes, as a race, have all these qualities inherent in them. They are ideal for my purpose because they express themselves not only by the spoken word but quite naturally by song and dance.[66]

On the other hand, Gershwin also defended the lyrics which created a "fine synchronization of diversified moods." Heyward wrote most of the folk songs, while his brother wrote most of the sophisticated songs. He summed up: all of the lines come naturally from the Negro.[67]

After the opening, and before he left New York for Hollywood, Gershwin wrote a suite of themes from *Porgy and Bess*. Unfortunately, it was largely forgotten, because later in the 1940s Robert Russell Bennett was commissioned to write a similar suite that became the concert hall standard. Gershwin's version has been revived under the title *Catfish Row*. A comparison of the two is instructive: Bennett's is the more colorful, more of an expanded Broadway overture, as one might expect from a professional orchestrator. But Gershwin's is much closer to the essential character of the opera, and his orchestration is quite good.

The original Gershwin version of the opera gradually went into eclipse. New, flashier, modern versions, including a movie took over.

The world was still not ready to accept *Porgy* for what it was—grand opera. *Porgy and Bess* was revived in the 1940s on Broadway, but with spoken dialogue and extensive cuts—it had become a musical play. The revival was produced by Cheryl Crawford, who had been the assistant stage manager for the original play, and was later a driving force in the Group Theater. Much of the "dull, draggy" recitatives were eliminated or changed to spoken dialogue; it was a lot of "artificial padding" she concluded. (She was relatively safe in making these comments since Gershwin had been dead for over three years. DuBose Heyward died on June 16, 1940.) Alexander Smallens, who had conducted the original, re-orchestrated much of the score (unthinkable if Gershwin had lived), and the orchestra was much smaller. Indeed, Ira questioned whether the small orchestra could do justice to the score.[68] Nevertheless, *Newsweek* reported that the consensus was that the cuts and clarifications had produced a considerable improvement over the original. Indeed, it was a hit; it ran on Broadway at the Majestic Theater for 286 performances, toured on the road, and then returned to New York. Richard Rodgers wrote that he felt Gershwin made a mistake because it did not work as an opera, because the recitatives were unfamiliar and difficult for Broadway audiences. When it was revived later as a musical play it was an overwhelming success.[69]

Gilbert Chase wrote that the new version was a "far more unified whole, and one of the most touching creations in the theatre."[70] One of the most prominent and strident of the original critics, the composer Virgil Thomson, decided that he liked the new version. Dorothy Heyward attended a performance and found it surprisingly well-done, except for the set, which she believed looked like how the moderately rich lived in Hollywood: Porgy's room was in pink satin wallpaper and a gilded framed oil painting adorned one wall. She wrote: "the designer has apparently never been to Charleston, but you can safely assure him that negro beggars here do not live in that style."[71] She also objected to the billing which read "George Gershwin's Porgy and Bess."

Over the years different versions of the opera were revived. One toured Europe and eventually ended up in the Soviet Union with Ira Gershwin traveling along. In Vienna, only the principals were black! The chorus and the dancers were all made up to look black! The State Department had feared that in Russia the opera would give the wrong impression of authentic black life in the United States. William Warfield disagreed: "I don't think anybody is going to see the opera and think, "That's the way blacks really live. . . . Today we can put the opera in a perspective that was not possible when it was new. For so much has changed in the last 60 years."

Finally, a low point was reached with a movie produced by Samuel Goldwyn. This version reduced the entire production to little more than a musical comedy, with popular black performers Sidney Poitier, Dorothy Dandridge, Sammy Davis Jr., and Pearl Bailey. Goldwyn, never noted for his sensitivity, was inordinately proud of this bastardized version, though he did not intend it as a burlesque. Andre Previn wrote the orchestrations and was the musical director. Mamoulian had been hired as the director, but Goldwyn fired him and hired Otto Preminger, who dropped the recitatives and replaced them with dialogue. Poitier's singing voice was dubbed, and the singing voice of Bess became the voice of a white girl. The *New York Times* film critic Bosley Crowther was impressed—"a fine film version." He concluded that the "eloquence" of the music expressed the opera's characters' "joys and sorrows." Ira Gershwin, however, finally objected and after the first round of showings in June 1959 the film was withdrawn.[72]

The road back to Gershwin's original score began with a production by Sherwin M. Goldman and the Houston Grand Opera in 1976. At long last, the score as it was first envisioned was heard in all its strength and beauty. Leonore Gershwin came to see it and was amazed, quite pleased and enthusiastic. She convinced Ira to give it his blessing. During the tour of this revival Kay Swift, who assisted in the production, occupied the very same seat in the Colonial Theater in Boston that she had in 1935, sitting along side George Gershwin. When it finally came to New York in September 1976, the critics were overwhelmed. Walter Kerr reflected the new consensus when he wrote that it was "Just plain thrilling . . . we can see now that Gershwin made no bones about the rhythmic flesh he was putting on bones. It's all there in the overture, when, after massive chords . . . the jazz piano takes over boldly." However, the chief music critic of the *New York Times* and scholar of classical pianists Harold Schonberg, found it to be three hours of "aimless meandering," but he undermined his own case by dismissing the *Rhapsody* and *An American in Paris* as "junk music." His review was roundly attacked and dismissed as a "fit of pique."[73]

Musicologists began to reevaluate *Porgy and Bess*. One prominent observer attended a performance in New York. He went expecting "splendid show tunes, loosely strung together," but found, instead, a profound surprise: "I saw an opera." This observer, Lawrence Starr, wrote:

Nothing had prepared me for the way in which the supposedly independent "show tunes" [were] harmonically, motivically, and dramatically integrated into a carefully crafted larger entity, but neither was [I] in any way prepared for my amazed realization; about twenty minutes into the performance, that I had lost all consciousness of the fact that the characters in the opera were black, because I was witnessing a pure and compelling human drama, whose implications were restricted to no single race or ethnic group, and which was built around thoroughly involving, complicated and distinct personalities.[74]

Other students of opera began to reevaluate. Composer-critic Eric Salzman, in his survey *Twentieth Century Music*, wrote that "George Gershwin's *Porgy and Bess* (1935) stands apart; Gershwin called it a 'folk opera,' but it is actually a full-scale grand opera." Musicologist Charles Hamm concurred that *Porgy and Bess* was a fully developed opera. He went further in his survey of American music: "It is the greatest nationalistic opera of the century, not only of America but of the world."[75] Conductor Lorin Maazel led the first uncut recording of the work with the Cleveland Orchestra. He commented that Gershwin's compassion for individuals was like Verdi, and his comprehension of them was reminiscent of Mozart. In Maazel's view, Gershwin's grasp of the folk-spirit was as firm and subtle as Mussorgsky's, and his melodic inventiveness rivaled Bellini. Gilbert Chase considered the Houston version a turning point that "demonstrated beyond a shadow of a doubt that Gershwin's opus was not only really American but also truly operatic."[76]

In the final redemption, the Metropolitan Opera produced its own version in 1985, fifty years after the original. *Porgy and Bess* had at last achieved its official immortality. There was still controversy, both sharp criticism and excessive praise. Lee Gershwin did not like it; she said that the "singers were wrong! Everything was wrong!"[77] On the other hand, the critic Douglas Watt thought that it may have been the most important night in the history of the Metropolitan. One critic wrote that the Metropolitan's huge sets turned Catfish Row from a small, hot, claustrophobic and tense place into an open air spectacle, merely a pedestal for great black voices to display their virtuosity. Peter G. Davis thought that it collapsed under the burden of its own respectability. The

New York Times wrote that it was the "ultimate establishment embrace of a work that continues to stir controversy with both its musical daring and its depiction of black life by three white men."[78]

A much publicized production was staged at Glyndebourne, England in July 1986, conducted by Simon Rattle and directed by Trevor Nunn. Some critics thought it better, musically, than the Metropolitan version. Oddly enough, however, the director thought that Porgy had to be more of a man to attract Bess; so he chose to eliminate Porgy's goat cart and to substitute crutches; the goat cart was "Disneyish," Nunn said. Thus in the final scene Porgy, on his way to New York in pursuit of Bess, throws away his crutches, calls for his "coat" (not his goat) and limps off the stage! If the goat cart was Disneyish, then this innovation would seem to be pure Hollywood.

These two productions should have put to rest the debate over the opera's value. *Porgy and Bess*'s chronicler, Hollis Alpert, summed it all up appropriately: "So at long last, *Porgy* was an opera, and a masterpiece at that." As a theater piece, noted another commentator, it easily meets the criteria for opera once established by Richard Strauss: It has pathos, comedy, and high drama, and each of these elements is expressed through a wide variety of music.

As for the alleged racism, nothing in Gershwin's music condescends to racial stereotypes. Gershwin's music was intended to ennoble Heyward's characters. After all, Heyward's novel ends with Porgy in despair, but the stage play and the opera end with Porgy, supported by Catfish Row, struggling to embark for New York to find Bess: Porgy and the chorus sing, "I'm on My Way" and this musical climax unifies the love and spirit of Catfish Row. The Gershwin version expresses the triumph of the human spirit.

Had he written mediocre music, the entire affair would probably have been long forgotten. But the majesty of his score forced both critics and proponents to focus on the opera for decades. The composer Ned Rorem agreed with Gershwin—"Melody is what makes a composer a composer," he wrote. The vocal solos in *Porgy and Bess* were arias, rather than songs because they were "non-extractable," and the tunes followed where the words led rather than being "stuffed into a thirty-two bar cage."[79]

Why did *Porgy and Bess* finally prevail? Steven E. Gilbert, in his extensive study of Gershwin's music, concluded: "It was Gershwin's crowning achievement: a grand coalescence of inspired melodies and intellectual sophistication. It was the best of Gershwin past and present." The music historian Richard Crawford found that what made *Porgy and Bess* unique among American operas was its universal familiarity: "Almost every American breathes in some of Porgy and Bess: it is part of the American musical vernacular."[80] Joseph Swain makes the same point: "From the vantage point of fifty years of history, it seems that *Porgy and Bess* is one of those rare works, comparable to perhaps the master films of Chaplin, that make the leap from a local popular tradition into world-class art."[81]

Fifty years after *Porgy and Bess*'s first performance, *The New Oxford*

Dictionary of Music wrote: "[It] has not only never been equalled in its genre, it has not even been approached." To be sure, Gershwin would have been especially proud of such an accolade and of the Metropolitan's much-belated production fifty years after his opera's premiere. From the beginning he wanted to create a work that would last.

NOTES

1. Isaac Goldberg (supplemented by Edith Garson), *George Gershwin: A Study in American Music* (New York: Frederick Ungar Publishing, 1958), p. 275.

2. The new attention to black musicals was evident in a song introduced by Gilda Gray in the 1922 *Ziegfeld Follies*, entitled "It's Getting Dark Over Old Broadway": Blacking up was the "latest rage." Quoted in Ann Douglas, *Terrible Honesty* (New York: Farrar, Straus and Giroux, 1995), p. 354.

3. Allen Woll, *Black Musical Theatre: From Coontown to Dreamgirls* (Baton Rouge: Louisiana State University Press, 1989), pp. 82–90.

4. Ferde Grofé, in *George Gershwin*, ed. Merle Armitage (New York: Longmans, Green, 1938), p. 27. This encounter demonstrates that Gershiwn and Grofé were professionally acquainted for some time before George wrote the *Rhapsody*.

5. Why Vodery was chosen for the orchestration rather than Grofé is not known. Probably Grofé was busy writing the arrangements for the entire *Scandals* for Whiteman; it may also be that Gershwin recommended Vodery, and that White knew him from his planning for the show that became *Runnin' Wild*."

6. John Andrew Johnson, "Gershwin's Blue Monday (1922) and the Promise of Success," in *The Gershwin Style*, ed. Wayne Schneider (New York: Oxford University Press, 1999). This is an important scholarly contribution to understanding the opera; it is based on extensive research.

7. John Andrew Johnson, "Gershwin's Blue Monday," in Schneider, *The Gershwin Style*, p. 112. He notes the "kinship" between the *Rhapsody* and *Blue Monday*, with its characteristic Gershwin "jazzy, bluesy rhetoric of the 1920s." He also concludes that *Blue Monday* was a model for *Porgy and Bess*, "informed by ten years of experience and study."

8. Ibid., p. 129.

9. He showed a copy of *Porgy* to Nanette Kuttner, his assistant at the time, and told her that he was going to make an opera out of it. Kuttner, in Armitage, *George Gershwin*, p. 239.

10. "When We Have Jazz Opera: An Interview with Mr. George Gershwin," *Musical Canada*, October 1925, pp. 13–14. Gershwin's use of the "n" word seems to have been an aberration; he usually said Negro or colored, at least in public.

11. George Gershwin, "Rhapsody in Catfish Row," *New York Times*, October 20, 1935.

12. Hollis Alpert, *The Life and Times of Porgy and Bess* (New York: Alfred Knopf, 1990). This is the indispensable chronicle of the opera, from its inception through the production at the Metropolitan Opera.

13. DuBose Heyward, *Porgy* (Mattatuck, NY: Amereon House, n.d.) (originally published by George H. Doran, 1925), pp. 12–13.

14. Kendra Hamilton, "Goat Cart Sam: Dubose Heyward's Icon of Southern Inno-

cence," essay included in "Porgy a Critique," American Studies Program at the University of Virginia, 1996; taken from the Internet: http//xroads.virginia.edu.org.

15. The novel and the stage play, as well as the opera, differ in some significant respects, but the basic story is the same.

16. Robert Kimball and Alfred Simon, *The Gershwins* (New York: Bonanza Books, 1963), p. 175.

17. James M. Hutchisson, *DuBose Heyward: A Charleston Gentleman and the World of Porgy and Bess* (Jackson: University of Mississippi Press, 2000), p. 145.

18. Ibid., p. 148.

19. Richard Crawford, "Gershwin's Reputation: A Note On *Porgy and Bess*," *Musical Quarterly*, April 1979, p. 257.

20. Gershwin's musical sketches and fragments in manuscripts provide no clue to the order in which he wrote. As he once said, he had the music in his mind, but did not necessarily write it down seriatim.

21. Ira wrote the lyrics for some of the most famous songs: "Bess, You Is My Woman Now," "It Ain't Necessarily So," and "There's A Boat Dat's Leavin' Soon for New York." Philip Furia, *Ira Gershwin* (New York: Oxford University Press, 1996), pp. 108–9. Ira's notes and manuscripts in the Library of Congress Collection suggest that he rewrote some of his lyrics extensively, especially "It Ain't Necessarily So" and "I Got Plenty o' Nuttin'." In this collection there is a list of songs by George indicating who would get the credit for the lyrics.

22. Hollis Alpert, *The Life and Times of Porgy and Bess*, p. 82.

23. This annotated copy of the libretto is in the Library of Congress, Gershwin Collection.

24. George (and Ira?) altered slightly one of the famous lines of "Summertime." Heyward had written "Yo' Daddy's rich, chile, and yo' ma's good-lookin'." Ira and George added "Oh," to the beginning of the line and struck out "chile,'" thus eliminating the back to back "ch" sounds. George's handwritten changes are contained in the draft libretto in the Library of Congress, Gershwin Collection. Phillip Furia, *Ira Gershwin*, pp. 108–9, however, gives credit to Ira. In the line "with mammy an' daddy standing by" George reversed the order putting daddy first; a strong "d" helps the musical emphasis which is on the first beat of the measure.

25. When exactly Gershwin wrote the music for "Summertime" is unclear; he said it was the first piece he wrote after he began the score; but his friend Kay Halle claims that he had written several versions that did not satisfy him, until in her apartment late one evening, playing on her baby grand Steinway, he finally finished it.

26. On the draft libretto, at this point of Bess' departure for the picnic, Gershwin wrote "Bess' theme," but the music, written later, does not make this clear.

27. Geoffrey Block, *Enchanted Evenings* (New York: Oxford University Press, 1997), p. 79.

28. Wayne D. Shirley, "Notes on Porgy and Bess," Metropolitan Opera Program, Lincoln Center/Stage Bill, October 1989.

29. The placement of this duet between Porgy and Bess was suggested by Dorothy Heyward in her annotation on the draft libretto.

30. Joseph P. Swain, *The Broadway Musical* (New York: Oxford University Press, 1990), pp. 62–63. He devotes a chapter to *Porgy and Bess*.

31. Irving Kolodin, "Porgy and Bess," *Theatre Arts Monthly*, November 1935.

32. George Gershwin, "Rhapsody in Catfish Row," *New York Times*, October 20, 1935.

33. Gilbert Chase, in *America's Music* (Urbana: University of Illinois Press, 1981), wrote that "history shows that an exclusively aesthetic 'integrity' has never made a successful opera, but many a good tune has" (p. 548).

34. The contract between the Theatre Guild and the Alvin Theater specifies at least a five-week run, but does not mention the requirement for an all-black cast.

35. This list of recordings was donated to the Library of Congress by Ira; George apparently possessed them at the time of his death; the list is not necessarily inclusive; other recordings could have been given away, misplaced, or lost.

36. Vernon Duke, "Gershwin, Schillinger, and Dukelsky," *Musical Quarterly*, January 1947.

37. David Ewen, *George Gershwin: His Journey to Greatness* (New York: The Ungar Publishing Company, 1970), pp. 212–13.

38. Vernon Duke, *Passport to Paris* (Boston: Little Brown, 1955), pp. 312, 319; Vernon Duke, "Gershwin, Schillinger and Dukelsky, Some Reminiscences," *Musical Quarterly*, January 1947, p. 102 ff. There are three notebooks belonging to George that are filled with examples and exercises of his studies with Schillinger; most of the notes are in Schillinger's hand. Library of Congress, Gershwin Collection.

39. Wayne Shirley, "The Rotating of Porgy and Bess," *Musical Quarterly*, Fall 1985; Steven E. Gilbert, *The Music of George Gershwin* (New Haven, CT: Yale University Press, 1995), p. 193. In a musical sketch for the fugue in the fight between Crown and Robbins, Gershiwn wrote the first theme "A" was to be followed by "B" the same theme "backwards, and then "C" the same theme upside down and backwards. This reflects Schillinger's various theories. Library of Congress, Gershwin Collection.

40. Paul Nauert, "Theory and Practice in Porgy and Bess," *Musical Quarterly*, Spring 1994.

41. As a result of the early publication of the score, there are discrepancies between the piano-vocal score, edited by Albert Sirmay for Chappel Music, and the full orchestral score. Wayne D. Shirley, "Reconciliation on Catfish Row," *Quarterly Journal of the Library of Congress*, 38 (Summer 1981).

42. Mamoulian received $500/week, and one percent of the gross over $8,000; Smallens received $200/week during rehearsals and $400/week during the performances; Steinart received $100/week beginning on June 17, 1935.

43. Hollis Alpert, *The Life and Times of Porgy and Bess*, p. 110.

44. Rouben Mamoulian, in Armitage, *George Gershwin*, p. 104.

45. DuBose Heyward, in Armitage, *George Gershwin*, p. 35.

46. Dozens of bars of music were cut; thus, 120 bars of the fugue during the crap game and fight were cut.

47. Charles Hamm, "The Theatre Guild Production of Porgy and Bess," *Journal of the American Musicological Society*, 40 (Fall 1987). This article includes a list of all the cuts in effect for the New York premiere.

48. The individual investors included DuBose Heyward (5%), Ira (5%), Rose Gershwin (10%) (probably paid for by George), Russell Crouse, the Broadway writer and Warren Munsell and Theresa Helburn of the Theatre Guild, each for 5 percent, for a total of 35 percent. The cost was initially estimated at $40,000, but it seems likely that the final expenses were closer to $60,000. George's original investment was listed at

$3,000, but for 1936 his accountant's balance sheet listed his loss on *Porgy and Bess* at $5,917. In addition to his royalty of over $10,000 for 1935 he earned about $6,000 in 1936.

49. Irving Kolodin, *Theatre Arts Monthly*, November 1935, p. 858.

50. *New York Times*, October 20, 1935.

51. Virgil Thomson, *A Virgil Thomson Reader* (Boston: Houghton Mifflin, 1981), pp. 25–27. Thomson's biographer concludes that since *Porgy and Bess* failed, Thomson's critique was in fact an impassioned defense of the opera. Anthony Tommasini, *Virgil Thomson: Composer on the Aisle* (New York: W.W. Norton, 1997), p. 302; Virgil Thomson, *Modern Music*, March–April 1938, p. 183.

52. Paul Rosenfeld, *Discoveries of a Music Critic* (New York: Vienna House, 1972), p. 271.

53. James Standifer, a professor of music at the University of Michigan, produced a PBS television documentary about the opera, which takes note of the criticism by Cruse and Hicks but also cites several favorable comments: for example, Rodney Milnes, author of a review in *Opera*, argued that *Porgy* had to be seen as an opera—both as an inheritor of a long tradition and as an inspiration for much that followed: "Its influence on *Peter Grimes* grows more obvious as time goes by, and there was never any doubt of its influence on *Street Scene*. In the case of both works, the 'folk opera' or 'Broadway opera' labels were the result of managerial nervousness about potential customers being put off."

54. Lehman Engel, *The American Musical Theater* (New York: Collier Books, 1975), p. 141. Engel conducted a recording of the original score in 1951.

55. Wayne Shirley, "Reconciliation on Catfish Row," *Quarterly Journal of the Library of Congress*, 38 (1980–81).

56. Gerald Mast, *Can't Help Singin'* (Woodstock, NY: Overlook Press, 1987), p. 83. He notes that after *Porgy* the verse disappeared from most Broadway songs; and these songs following *Show Boat*'s example became more of a "highly particularized expression of just that character just then just there."

57. Geoffrey Block, *Enchanted Evenings*, p. 84.

58. Joseph P. Swain, *The Broadway Musical*, p. 71.

59. Quoted in Allen L. Woll, *Black Musical Theatre*, pp. 172–73; Hall Johnson's original article appeared in *Theatre Arts Monthly*, January 1936. Johnson was a musician, director of his own choir, and the brother of J. Rosamond Johnson, *Porgy and Bess*' assistant musical coach.

60. There was more than a touch of jealousy in the criticisms by Ellington and Thomson, as explained in Terry Teachout, "Gershwin at 100," *Commentary*, September 1998, and "(Over)praising Duke Ellington," *Commentary*, September 1996.

61. Mark Tucker, *The Ellington Reader* (New York: Oxford University Press, 1993), p. 114. Ellington's turnaround is suspect. It is difficult to see how the 1953 version was more "Negro" than the 1935 original, which Ellington had attacked: that is, that the music did not reflect Catfish Row or any other kind of Negro. More likely Ellington was reluctant to criticize such major stars as Leontyne Price and William Warfield.

62. Quoted in James Standifer, "The Complicated Life of Porgy and Bess," notes for "Porgy and Bess: An American Voice," PBS Television.

63. Interview with William Warfield by John Ardoin, PBS, Great Performances, "Porgy and Bess: An American Voice," 1999.

64. Roberta Alexander quoted in Paul Thomason, *Opera News*, August 1998. James

Deas quoted in Cori Ellison, "Porgy and Bess and Music's Racial Politics," *New York Times*, December 13, 1998.

65. Quoted in James Standifer, "Porgy and Bess: An American Voice," PBS, February 1999.

66. George Gershwin, *New York Times*, October 20, 1935.

67. Ibid.

68. Ira had a good point. In recordings of excerpts from the 1942 version, the orchestra sounds thin, while the voices, Todd Duncan and Anne Brown, sound strong.

69. Richard Rodgers, Foreword to Robert Kimball and Alfred Simon, *The Gershwins*, p. xiii.

70. Chase, *America's Music*, p. 429.

71. Letter, December 20, 1941, to Warren Munsell; Library of Congress, Gershwin Collection, Theatre Guild folders.

72. There were occasional offers for the rights to a movie version; one of the first in 1942 was for $100,000 from Metro that was brusquely dismissed by Ira. Warner Brothers in 1944 paid $20,000 for the film rights to a segment of the opera, "Summertime," and "I Got Plenty o' Nuttin' " to be included in the film biography of George Gershwin, *Rhapsody in Blue*. The Goldwyn version was revived for a Gershwin Centennial Festival: "Porgy and Bess—The film," *ISAM Newsletter*, Fall 1998; this article includes brief reviews by James Standifer, Professor of Music at the University of Michigan and Margo Jefferson, cultural critic for the *New York Times*.

73. The Houston Opera production was recorded and released by RCA, Red Seal in a three-disc set, RCD3-2109. The cover is labeled "George Gershwin's Porgy and Bess."

74. Lawrence Starr, "Toward A Reevaluation of Gershwin's *Porgy and Bess*," *American Music* (Summer 1984).

75. Charles Hamm, *Music in the New World* (New York: W.W. Norton, 1983), p. 450.

76. Ibid.; Chase, *America's Music*, p. 548.

77. Allan Jalon, *Los Angeles Times*, February 11, 1987.

78. The Metropolitan Opera produced *Porgy and Bess* again in September 1989. The *New York Times* reviewer, Donal Henahan, wrote (September 29, 1989) that the work "continues to look and sound as overblown as ever." This writer attended a performance a few days later and could not disagree more.

79. Ned Rorem, "Living with Gershwin," included in *Settling the Score: Essays on Music* (San Diego, CA: Harcourt Brace Jovanovich, 1988), pp. 8–9; the music critic Terry Teachout, reviewing the future of American opera, wrote in *Commentary*, March 2000 that, "To date American opera has produced one masterpiece, George Gershwin's *Porgy and Bess* (1935)."

80. Richard Crawford, "Gershwin's Reputation: A Note on *Porgy and Bess*," *Musical Quarterly*, April 1979.

81. Swain, *The Broadway Musical*, p. 71.

Chapter 11

Hollywood

George Gershwin was a New Yorker. His music seemed to reflect the city's hustle and bustle. He often said that the roots of his music were in the famed melting pot of the great metropolis. He said that he wrote for "young girls sitting on fire escapes on hot summer nights in New York and dreaming of love."[1] It is ironic, therefore, that the final year of his life was spent in Hollywood, where he died in 1937.

Like Gershwin most of the major songwriters of the 1920s were also New Yorkers (with the notable exception of Cole Porter). Songwriters made their fame and fortune within those few square blocks called Tin Pan Alley or in their shows that played along Broadway. Yet, many of them chose to migrate to Hollywood in the 1930s. Vincent Youmans was an early arrival. Rodgers and Hart were there for several years. Kern spent most of his time there after 1934, finally settling there permanently. Oscar Hammerstein, Yip Harburg, and Harold Arlen were in and out of Hollywood. Cole Porter shuttled back and forth. Irving Berlin came periodically, but he resisted the temptation to abandon New York. He said he felt "slow" in Hollywood. Nevertheless, of all the transplanted easterners his movie music was the most successful.

By 1933, Hollywood was recovering from its earlier disenchantment with musicals that had followed the first burst of enthusiasm for *The Jazz Singer*. Warner Brothers took the lead in a new round of musicals. It produced a minor classic entitled *42nd Street*, with music and words by Harry Warren and Al Dubin (they even appeared briefly in the film—as songwriters). It included an early Busby Berkeley dance number built around Ruby Keeler (formerly Mrs. Al Jolson) and staged to the music of the title song. The score featured "Shuffle Off to Buffalo" as well as the title song. It was the ultimate backstager, featuring one of show business' great lines by Warner Baxter, playing the director, to the understudy, Ruby Keeler, who on short notice is about to go on for the ailing leading lady: "You've got to come back a star." Of course she does. (It was remade as a stage musical in 1980, with many Warren-Dubin songs added and produced by David Merrick to great acclaim. It had a very long run.)

The movie was hailed as the prelude to a possible cycle of musicals, and indeed others soon followed. Busby Berkeley's elaborate staging and imaginative use of the camera made "movement" in films all the rage. Next came *Gold Diggers of 1933*, also with a score by Warren and Dubin, featuring the "Shadow Waltz," and "The Gold Diggers Song," ("We're in the money"). It too was successful. The third piece in this trio was *Footlight Parade*, starring James Cagney and Joan Blondell, and again with Dick Powell and Ruby Keeler. Its principal songs were the easily forgotten "Honeymoon Hotel" and "Shanghai Lil," but it had an extravagant waterfall number staged by Berkeley.

The contrast between Hollywood's musical revival and the depressed state of affairs along Broadway was increasingly obvious. The lure of Hollywood was nearly irresistible. A composer could make far more money for a minimal effort in Hollywood; a few songs for a movie written over two or three months could yield more than even a very successful Broadway show that might take months to organize and run for less than a year. For example, in 1933 Vincent Youmans received $8,000 for four songs. Kern had a contract for $5,000 a week for four weeks. Both Kern and Irving Berlin even negotiated a percentage of the profits.

As interest in musicals began to revive, the studio executives once again turned to the greatest names from Broadway. The major studios were interested in having "hit" songs, but the musical knowledge of the producers and many of the directors was too limited to understand the creative process. The studios could not expect to monopolize the songwriters with established reputations, so the studios put together rudimentary staffs, with resident songwriters, musical arrangers, and conductors.

One of the most successful in these categories—indeed, the most successful songwriter—was Harry Warren. He and his lyricist Al Dubin both came to Hollywood by way of Broadway and Tin Pan Alley. Warren had written several hits in the mid-1920s ("Nagasaki" and "Rose of the Rio Grande"), and he was also associated with the fledgling movie industry in and around New York (Vitagraph Pictures). For a time he alternated between Hollywood and New York. He wrote "Cheerful Little Earful" with Ira Gershwin, but eventually he moved to the West Coast and remained there the rest of his life, earning seven academy award nominations and four Oscars. Warren had some of the same qualities as Berlin: he could write in almost any vernacular.

As the movie musicals began once again to blossom, especially at the box office, the quality became erratic. In effect the arbiters of popular music were the Hollywood producers. When Darryl Zanuck asked to preview Kern's songs, Kern indignantly declined, saying that he did not give samples. Nonetheless, even the established composers had to bend to the system; they lost control over whether and how their songs would be used. The final film might have only snatches of a song. "You're Devastating," one of Kern's fine songs from *Roberta*, was relegated to background music in the film version. New songs were demanded but then discarded. Only "Night and Day" remained of Cole Porter's *The Gay Divorce*. The hit of the film was "The Continental," written not by Porter, but by Con Conrad who won an Academy Award for it.

Judgments about music seemed particularly quixotic. For example, "Over the Rainbow" was cut from *The Wizard of Oz* three times. Richard Rodgers composed "Lover" and played it for Darryl Zanuck, who asked "could he make it better?" The studios bought some of the music publishing houses and thereby acquired the rights to individual songs as well as to Broadway productions. Thus, the major songwriters were more and more vulnerable to the whims of commercialism. Harry Warren frequently complained of the "illiterates" in the front office of the studios he worked in for fifty years. While watching a recording of one of his numbers he told the director that the lyrics were wrong; the director dismissed the problem: "what's the difference, who'll know?"

When Rodgers and Hart finally left Hollywood, Rodgers felt obligated to say goodbye to Irving Thalberg, who had hired them. He was ushered into the inner sanctum, where Thalberg, Hollywood's "Last Tycoon" and young genius, was conducting a staff meeting. Thalberg's "glassy stare" made it obvious to Rodgers that Thalberg had not the faintest idea who Rodgers was. Years later in his autobiography, Rodgers would write: "to Thalberg we were all faceless, anonymous cogs."[2]

Despite the mindless intervention of the studio chiefs, the overall musical direction in Hollywood was gradually assumed by competent musicians retained as full-time staff by the studio, including orchestrators and composers for the background music. This latter category was almost unknown on Broadway; in a film, music would be woven into and out of the action and this required planning, orchestrating the score, rehearsing the orchestra, and finally recording the sound track. All of this was painstaking, and gradually became more and more important not only to musicals but to straight dramas. Thus, composers such as Alfred Newman, Max Steiner, and Erich Korngold became as important to the studios as the best-known songwriters. This inevitably made for friction with the newcomers from Broadway.

Nevertheless, the Broadway expatriates produced a magnificent collection of songs, much of it for the dance team of Fred Astaire and Ginger Rogers. The more modern camera techniques created a new freedom. As a result of the influence of Busby Berkeley, the emphasis in musicals was shifting to dancing. Irving Berlin was hired to write for an Astaire-Rogers picture. Despite some unpleasant early experiences with film musicals, Berlin was able to adapt to the medium, and over many years he produced some of his best work for the movies. Indeed, for Astaire and Rogers Berlin wrote some of his most inspired songs about dancing: "Cheek to Cheek," "Change Partners," and "Let's Face the Music and Dance." Even Jerome Kern, who had trouble accommodating to the new swing dancing, wrote "I Won't Dance" carried over from a failed musical, as well as "Waltz in Swing Time" and "Never Gonna' Dance." He wrote "Bojangles in Harlem," Astaire's only performance in black face. Oddly enough, the Gershwins, who had made their reputation with rhythm numbers, turned to the more romantic ballads for Astaire and Rogers, although they did contribute "Shall We Dance."

On Broadway it was no surprise to an audience when the hero or heroine of a musical broke into song, often followed by a dance routine. It was expected. Even if discomforted by the incoherence of the music and the plot, the audience could still savor the ambience of a live show: the stunning costumes, the brilliant sets, the excitement of a new hit show, including the sound of the live pit orchestra. There was no way black-and-white films could capture this aura. In the early years of talking pictures, Broadway shows were eagerly adopted, but the results were disappointing. Even stars such as Marilyn Miller could not re-create on film her radiant presence in *Sally*. Sometimes a few songs were grafted onto a thin melodrama. This meant long scenes of dialogue and action with most of the music then crowded together. Hollywood, still conditioned by the silent movies, simply could not adjust to the sound of music; one reason was that the music was recorded and often the sound track was a disaster. Moreover, in a film the segue into a song was simply too awkward. This was the unfortunate experience of the Gershwins when they wrote for Fox's *Delicious*. The same was also true of Rodgers and Hart's first film, *The Hot Heiress*.

With the advent of Busby Berkeley and his extravagant dance sequences, a new breed of actor and performer was required. The emphasis on dance, however, created a challenge. Writing for the "swing" dances of the 1930s was far different from Broadway. On the stage the dances were dictated by the space and time allotted to any number; it was usual for the melody to be replayed for several choruses while the dances were spun out. But in the movies, where the action could be more dramatic and sweeping, the music and dancing had to be tailored to the new techniques. Fred Astaire was dismayed, when he first reported for work, to find a proliferation of cameras, a huge set, and an "audience" of various technicians.

As a consequence, Astaire and his choreographer Hermes Pan developed a new work routine. He would rehearse his numbers in private, away from everybody including the director, often using only a rhythm tape as the music or his own pianist. Mark Sandrich, the director of the Astaire-Rogers epics was thus often in the dark, as were the composers.

In the beginning Astaire and Rogers were not a team, even though they both gravitated to Radio-Keith-Orpheum (RKO). Rogers had been making nonmusical movies since *Girl Crazy* and had settled in Hollywood. Her big break was a role in *42nd Street*, playing "Anytime Annie," and she sang "Shuffle Off to Buffalo." She wanted to be a dramatic actress, but in the era of Jean Harlow, she was cast as a hard-boiled blonde. By the time she joined Astaire in their new partnership she had made twenty pictures.

Astaire pursued a rocky road to Hollywood. There is an infamous, probably apocryphal anecdote of a studio scout report about Astaire: "Can't Act. Can't Sing. Balding. Can dance a little." The Gershwins, of course, knew Astaire from their experience in *Lady Be Good!* and *Funny Face*. After a successful performance in Schwartz and Deitz's revue *The Band Wagon*, Astaire was on his own; Adele had married Charles Lord Cavendish and had retired. Without Adele, Fred starred in Cole Porter's *The Gay Divorce* (November 1932). One reviewer noted that Fred stopped every few minutes to look offstage, as if expecting and hoping his sister would appear. Another wrote, "Two Astaires are better than one." On the other hand, Fred's solo dancing was praised.

RKO had bought the rights to the show and put Astaire under contract in July 1933. At first David Selznick was enthusiastic, but after a screen test Selznick sidetracked him to a new film called *Flying Down to Rio*, with music by Vincent Youmans. Astaire's contract allowed him to travel to London for the British version of *The Gay Divorce* in the fall of 1933, but in between he reported for *Flying Down to Rio*. Before that he learned that he was "loaned" to MGM for a small role in *Dancing Lady*, starring Clark Gable and Joan Crawford. Many thought this was the equivalent of being buried alive.

In any case, his role in *Flying Down to Rio* was downgraded. Delores Del Rio would be the star playing opposite Gene Raymond. Astaire was paired with Ginger Rogers, the inspiration of young aggressive producer named Pandro S. Berman, who had taken over the faltering RKO and was breathing some new life into it. For this he needed topflight music and he offered to pay for it, even though Berman could not really afford it because the studio was nearly bankrupt. RKO had been formed in the late 1920s by Joseph P. Kennedy (the future president's father). Kennedy had set it up as a holding company of the old Keith-Albee vaudeville chain, the United Booking Office, and RCA—hence the title Radio-Keith-Orpheum, or RKO. Kennedy also owned Pathe Pictures, which he sold to his new company, RKO at a handsome profit for himself. This prompted cries of manipulation, and some congressmen urged an investigation of the movie industry. Kennedy was denounced as the "chief racketeer" in this swindle. By the time Berman took over in an effort to salvage RKO, Kennedy was gone. RKO had nothing left—nothing but Fred Astaire and Ginger Rogers!

The two were not eager to become a permanent team, even though they were friends and had known each other in New York, where they had enjoyed a brief flirtation when Astaire coached Rogers for a dance number in Gershwin's *Girl Crazy*. In *Flying Down to Rio* the score was delightful: Fred danced with Delores Del Rio to "Orchids in the Moonlight" and only danced with Ginger to a lavish production of the "Carioca." While in London Astaire assumed that his role in films was over; he thought that *Flying Down to Rio* was a "turkey," but was surprised to learn that the film was successful and his role was praised: "The main point of *Flying Down to Rio* is the screen promise of Fred Astaire," wrote *Variety*. As more or less promised to Astaire, next came *The Gay Divorcee*, the new title, because a "Gay Divorce" was an unacceptable idea for the new, more conservative Hollywood. Astaire protested being linked to Ginger Rogers: "I did not go into pictures to be teamed with anyone," he wrote to his agent Leland Hayward.[3] Cooler heads prevailed and once again Astaire and Rogers danced the "Continental," but their big number was "Night and Day." Fred sang a chorus and then persuaded Ginger to dance—their first real duet in the movies. And then they were joined together in the film version of Jerome Kern's *Roberta*. These were not starring roles, however.

While *Roberta* was in production, Berman decided to start a major effort, a new musical in which they would be the real stars, with a score by America's best-known songwriter. Irving Berlin was signed in November 1934 for this new musical, which became *Top Hat*, the first of three pivotal movies that clinched the careers of Astaire and Rogers and turned them into a legend. For *Top Hat* Berlin wrote "Top Hat, White Tie and Tails." It became one of Astaire's most popular numbers. Berlin was a treasure for his performers; he found the right lines for what they were doing. Others, including Kern and Gershwin, wrote fine songs, perhaps musically more interesting than Berlin, but not more appropriate. Berlin also wrote the masterful "Cheek to Cheek." These two songs—"Top Hat" and "Cheek to Cheek"—were the strongest songs of the movie. Arlene Croce, the dance critic who studied and wrote an analysis of all of the Astaire-Rogers films, believes that the singing of "Cheek to Cheek" was the "high point" of this most famous of all Astaire-Rogers numbers.[4] That score also included "Isn't It a Lovely Day" and "No Strings."

Astaire then bargained for his own share of the profits in the next picture, *Follow the Fleet*. In this new film Astaire was in a sailor's uniform, no white tie and tails. Berlin's score was again excellent: "I'm Putting All My Eggs in One Basket," "Let's Face the Music and Dance," "Let Yourself Go," "Get Thee Behind Me Satan," and "We Saw the Sea." The two movies together were an incredible burst of Berlin's creativity, probably the high point of his career, at least until *Annie Get Your Gun* ten years later.

An Astaire-Rogers picture was ideal for any songwriter, including the Gershwins. Irving Berlin wired them that there was "No set up in Hollywood that compares with doing an Astaire picture." The reason that songwriters liked Astaire so much were obvious in his performances. He sang a song as written without embellishments. He enunciated the lyrics clearly and displayed a feel for the meaning of the story told by the lyrics, and he had a fine sense of the rhythm. Jerome Kern felt that Astaire could do no wrong.

The next Rogers and Astaire vehicle was *Swing Time*, with music by Kern. Despite an excellent score, the film had not fared as well at the box office as its predecessors. George saw *Swing Time* after he arrived in California and liked it. Somewhat pompously he wrote: "Although I don't think Kern has written any outstanding hits, I think he did a very creditable job with the music and some of it is really delightful. Of course, he never was really ideal for Astaire, and I take that into consideration."[5] He was right about the incompatibility of Astaire and Kern. Fred Astaire complained to the lyricist Dorothy Fields that Kern could not write a rhythm song he could dance to.

No shrinking violet, Berman set his sights on the Gershwins for the next Astaire-Rogers show. First, however, there were several months of haggling, before they signed their contract. The Gershwins had received $100,000 for their previous Hollywood deal in 1930 with Fox studios and expected much the same. But times had changed. Gershwin was "no longer perceived as the indefatigable winner he had been." When the studio balked Gershwin's agent wired him, "They are afraid you will only do high brow songs." Gershwin indignantly replied "rumors about highbrow music ridiculous. Am out to write hits." In New York, Gershwin was being lauded for having demonstrated that Tin Pan Alley could produce a serious composer (*Porgy and Bess*), while in Hollywood this was considered a liability. Of course, true to his word, Gershwin did indeed write several hits. After the film was completed, he commented that the studio realized "Gershwin can be a low brow."[6]

The new Gershwin film would be the seventh Astaire-Rogers combination. RKO was running into problems, however. Whereas *Top Hat* had earned a profit of over $1 million, *Swing Time* had not done as well at the box office (profits of $830,000). Thus, RKO offered the Gershwins $60,000 for twenty weeks and pro rata thereafter. The Gershwins countered with an offer of $75,000 but suggested that they could write the score in sixteen weeks for $60,000. Finally, the deal was closed: $55,000 for sixteen weeks and an option for a second picture at $70,000, to be executed forty-five days after completion of the first picture. Six months after the starting date of the second picture the Gershwins would then be free to engage in other deals. An interesting stipulation inserted by the Gershwins no doubt, was that no other songs would be interpolated, and the score was to be published by the Gershwins' new company, Dawn Music.[7]

In August 1936 the two brothers embarked on a TWA flight for Glendale. The last time any New York audience heard Gershwin in a live performance was at the Gershwin night at Lewisohn Stadium. The crowd was smaller than usual; there were empty seats and "that is news," wrote a reviewer. Gershwin complained but was reassured that it was one of New York's hottest nights on record.

Nevertheless, he left town on a plaintive note. According to his mother, when George left he told her not to worry because in a couple of months he would be back in New York. Nevertheless, a change may well have been welcomed in the wake of the disappointments over *Porgy and Bess*. George's hopes for a London production of his opera had evaporated. Moreover, Broadway was drying up as the Great Depression deepened. Hollywood offered a chance to make some money. This was Ira's rationale. He pointed out that they were still living on the royalties from *Of Thee I Sing*. (This was stretching things.) George never paid much attention to his financial status. Despite the Depression, in 1935, for example, he created trusts for his mother and Ira of $15,000 each. When he arrived in Hollywood he opened a bank account with a deposit of $7,500, a healthy sum for 1936, which he quickly built up to over $35,000.[8]

Before leaving for California Gershwin exclaimed to his cousin Henry Botkin, that this year he wanted to get married. It was an odd remark, since the decision to go to the West Coast as a movie songwriter entailed an important personal break with Kay Swift. They agreed they would not see each other while he was away, and would use the time to reconsider their relationship. What lay behind this decision was never revealed by Gershwin. Perhaps he resisted the pressure to solidify their relationship, since Kay Swift had been divorced and was free to marry. Gershwin obviously was not yet prepared for this step. Despite their agreement to set aside their relationship temporarily, Gershwin's letters suggest a growing anxiety over this decision.

One other event complicated Gershwin's last year. While he was in Beverly Hills his longtime and very close friend and musical mentor Bill Daly died (December 1936). For the first time in many years he was without his two closest friends and musical colleagues—Kay Swift and Bill Daly. It is a testimony to the maturity of his talent that his creativity did not suffer. Indeed, the completely new melodies (i.e., not trunk songs) he wrote for his last three films were outstanding—"vintage Gershwin."[9]

The Gershwins—George, Ira, and Lee—moved into a house on Roxbury Drive after a "fierce struggle" to find a suitable home to rent. They finally settled in and George loved it, he wrote. It was a posh neighborhood that included the homes of movie stars. In New York, George had a separate apartment on 72nd Street, and Ira and his wife lived in their own apartment across the street. Now they were back within the same house. Joan Peyser comments that this was a "self-destructive act," explained by Gershwin's fear of being alone. George was occasionally critical of Lee, but some (Oscar Levant) think he was unjust, because she ran their household with "great skill." Nevertheless, while some remembered her "generously," others spoke of her "cruelty."[10]

Both of the Gershwin brothers were proud of their large, Spanish-style stucco house that had both a swimming pool and a tennis court, to the envy of "our less fortunate Hollywood friends." George was an avid tennis player and their court was actively used. One of his tennis partners was Arnold Schoenberg! At first George seemed happy. The script for the Astaire-Rogers movie was not yet finished so they had time on their hands. George spent a weekend at Lake Arrowhead, where he had a "grand time." The Gershwins gave a large party for "Moss Hart's teeth" (i.e., caps with porcelain). Seventy-five people were expected. He instructed his secretary in New York to send out fifteen of his favorite paintings, as well as his own paints.

They adopted a social circle of Jerome Kern, Sam Behrman the playwright, Moss Hart, Yip Harburg, Harold Arlen, Harpo Marx, and of course Oscar Levant. George wrote that Hollywood was "getting some brains." He was delighted to find a point of view that was "progressive." The producers were buying "new talent."[11] In another letter he concluded, "Hollywood has taken on quite a new color since our last visit six years ago." There were many more people in the business in Hollywood who talked the language of "smart showmen" and therefore it was "much more agreeable working out here." He noted their many friends from the East: "All the writingmen and tunesmiths get together in a way that is practically impossible in the East." He saw a great deal of Irving Berlin and Jerome Kern at poker parties and dinners. All in all the feeling was very "gemutlich."[12]

Once he settled in Hollywood, George resumed his romantic activities, including flirtations with movie stars, especially Simone Simon; of course, he played down these slight attachments—"a movie star is a movie star." He even went dancing with Ginger Rogers, which in itself was a testimony to his self-confidence. But there was a much more serious attachment to Paulette Goddard.

This affair turned out to be quite intimate and intense. How serious it was is still something of a mystery. Goddard's biographer describes her relationship with Gershwin as a "sweet, romantic scene between a married woman and dying genius."[13] She was uncommonly beautiful and charming. "Mmm. She's nice. Me likee," he wrote to Mabel Schirmer after he was seated next to her at a dinner party in March. Gershwin fell in love, his friends claimed. Edward Jablonski describes it, however, as a "fruitless infatuation and a brief fling." To be sure it was fruitless in the end, but most sources describe it as more than a "fling." Paulette Goddard said that George fell in love with her because she was "unattainable—absolutely unattainable was what excited him." The author Anita Loos, a close friend of Goddard's, recalled that Gershwin "came to life in her presence as nobody had ever seen him before."[14] That he fell in love is plausible but Loos' claim about coming to "life" as never before is surely an exaggeration.

In any case, Gershwin contemplated taking his furnishings out of storage and setting up house in Hollywood. He even began to speculate on marriage, though Goddard was married to Charlie Chaplin (whether, in fact, they were married was uncertain, though they both allowed that rumor to spread without denials). Chaplin apparently tolerated her infidelity, but Gershwin's friends warned him that she would not break off with Chaplin. When the affair finally ended is not clear. Chaplin's biographer claims that she broke it off in May, while other versions claim that Gershwin ended the affair when he learned that she was having a liaison with another man. By mid-May Gershwin played down the affair in letters to his sister and mother. In answer to his mother's inquiry about Goddard, George wrote that he saw her "less frequently." A week or so later, he wrote his sister that he took the "young lady out a couple of times," but doubted that it would go much further.[15]

Goddard is not a reliable witness. She claimed that George lived with his family—"his mother was alive then." While his mother visited him in Hollywood, she lived in New York. Goddard claimed that the last Sunday she was with him he was screaming in pain. Goddard ordered his valet to pack his bag and to take him to Cedars of Lebanon, where doctors located a tumor the "size of an orange," and then he died. This is wildly fanciful. In another version she even called Chaplin for advice, who recommended "Doctor Reynolds," who put him in the hospital, according to Anita Loos (in Loos' version the tumor was the "size of a fist"). Goddard also told friends that his family blamed her for

George's condition, because she had rejected him. She claimed she tried to visit him several times but was refused. George was not even informed of her visits (there may be some truth to this).

Before the Goddard affair, George seemed pleased with his new surroundings, and said California had a lot to offer. He informed one of his friends back East that he was writing in a pair of shorts—"everything out here goes along pretty serenely." The work thus far was not difficult, and he and Ira were taking it easy. Yet there was a note of homesickness. Gershwin wrote that he fully intended to return to New York after his last picture. George Kaufman and Moss Hart wanted the Gershwins for a new musical in November. In one letter (October 1936) he noted that there was going to be a "good deal of musical activity starting in NYC soon, so don't fail to keep me informed." He remarked that he didn't get to see many papers "out here," and he had to know the news. He wrote that he naturally missed New York and would "probably miss it more as time goes by."[16]

As for his music, Gershwin was becoming somewhat defensive about his new position as a Hollywood songwriter. In one interview he said that he would leave the incidental music to the "hacks." He was obviously irritated by the studio's handling of his music. Contrary to his dismissal of the incidental music, he wrote a great deal of such music for *Shall We Dance*—a waltz and a ballet. He wrote a delightful musical interlude for Fred and Ginger. They were both walking their dogs along the deck of an ocean liner, as Fred tried to catch Ginger's attention. For this Gershwin did not leave the music to the "hacks," but composed an engaging original piece, usually called "Promenade." He wrote out a two-piano version, along with notations for the orchestration. Moreover, he was quite friendly with the so-called "hacks," who included the orchestrator Edward Powell, a student of Schillinger's, as well as his friend from Broadway Alfred Newman, who had conducted two versions of the *Scandals*.

Nevertheless, he was wounded by the haphazard approach to his music and took refuge in pretending indifference. In New York he was lionized, but he complained that in Hollywood sometimes he was regarded as little more than hired help. At parties he was expected to play as part of the entertainment. At the other extreme, he was ignored, sometimes not asked to play, or at social outings there was no piano or music.

By late October the Gershwins were finishing their score for *Shall We Dance*. "So far every body is happy," George commented. The show was a romantic comedy in which Fred portrays a sham Russian ballet dancer who pursues Ginger, a Broadway star. Although the Gershwin brothers had not written for a musical since 1933, their work for their first picture did not suffer. Gershwin was indeed writing in a different style. Deena Rosenberg points out that his songs for Astaire in the 1930s differ from those written for Astaire in the 1920s; the world was "darker," and Ira's lyrics urged people to dance and sing as an antidote to their troubles. She also wrote:

George's music is different, too. It is, on the whole, less given to the repetition of melodic fragments against shifting harmonies that was characteristic of George's twenties style. . . . The mature Gershwin song has an unself-conscious, almost conversational flow, and what Dick Hyman calls "built-in swing."[17]

In his analysis Steven Gilbert writes along the same lines: "Gershwin's last songs are indeed different, in other ways than phrasing and structure. Carefully written accompaniments, contrapuntal bias, the thoughtful selection of key, a flirtation with quartal harmony, and the influence of Gershwin's study with Joseph Schillinger marked the last songs in special ways.[18] Another musicologist finds that Gershwin's music for "Slap That Bass," and "A Foggy Day" show a new "artistic maturity" in handling blue notes, integrating them into a "wide-ranging but remarkably consistent individual style."[19]

Shortly after arriving in Hollywood, Gershwin had indeed written to his secretary Zena Hannenfeldt asking for the "rhythm and scale books from Schillinger and instruction how to use them." What might have been appropriate for *Porgy and Bess* was not suitable for Hollywood, and Gilbert notes that the published version of his songs for the movies were simplified compared to Gershwin's manuscripts.[20]

At the time, however, a *Variety* review of their movie music commented that the "lyrics were more interesting than melodies," which were not fashioned for "popular acceptance." Ira said that he was proud of *Shall We Dance*. It was a smart score, with lots of hits; all the songs were smart, a little too sophisticated—"maybe that was a mistake, to put so many smart songs in one picture."

In any case, Gershwin's occasional brooding did not seem to affect his movie music. The score for *Shall We Dance* was on the whole a happy one (probably reflecting Ira's mood more than George's).[21] There were some outstanding melodies, especially "They Can't Take That Away from Me" (which appeared all too briefly in the film). Gershwin thought this song had "distinct potentialities of going places." He complained that the studio had not taken advantage of his songs, and had thrown one or two away without any kind of "plug." More could have been done with the songs, he believed, especially "I've Got Beginner's Luck." It was sung by Astaire, but cut off when dogs in the shipboard kennel start howling.

The singing left something to be desired, he said; he complained that the story did not allow for any singer other than Fred and Ginger, and "the amount one can stand of those two is quite limited." This rather acid comment was uncharacteristic. Nevertheless, he vowed that in his next picture, he was going to make sure that he would have a "much better break" on the vocal side.[22]

George Gershwin was right, of course, about the treatment of his music. The presentation of the musical program was erratic. The best numbers were presented back-to-back. "Let's Call the Whole Thing Off," after two choruses of singing, became a fine Astaire-Rogers dance number on roller skates. Then in the very next scene came the romantic ballad "They Can't Take that Away from Me," sung by Astaire, but only the verse and one chorus and then a fade-out. One song, "Wake Up Brother and Dance," was scrapped altogether. The finale, "Shall We Dance," was written at the request of the producers. It is marred by a weird ballet featuring Harriet Hoctor's acrobatics.

With this movie Gershwin entered the swing era of big bands. In the early 1930s there was an important change as jazz gave way to swing, as played by the bands led by superior musicians from the earlier Jazz Age: Benny Goodman, the Dorsey brothers, Harry James, Woody Herman, and the black musicians Duke Ellington, Count Basie, and Jimmie Lunceford. These bands were appreciative of superior music by Gershwin, Kern, or Porter.

As the swing style caught on with the general public, new dancing followed and the bands reached larger and larger numbers of young people; they toured throughout the country playing popular dance halls, they made recordings and appeared on "live" radio shows. Some of the bands or band leaders even began to appear in movies. The orchestrations for *Shall We Dance*, especially for the dances, are clearly in a swing time mode, and they sound quite different from the Broadway fare. Early in the movie Fred Astaire says to his manager, "jazz went out with flappers." Gershwin seems to have made the transition without much difficulty. "Slap That Bass" for Fred Astaire was clearly a swing dance. Indeed, even the ballads are in the swing vernacular. "They All Laughed" was a particularly witty lyric by Ira. The worksheet that has survived includes some clever unused lines, rhyming crepes suzette with the safety of Gillette.

Shall We Dance was favorably received. Richard Rodgers, in Hollywood at that time, commented to his wife that the picture was "generally admired," but the "damn fools all hate George's score . . . they're swell tunes anyway." Forty years later, Alec Wilder, in his opus on popular songs, agreed with Rodgers. The last songs of Gershwin struck him as generally excellent. Despite the complexities of *Porgy and Bess*, Gershwin's final songs were in fact simpler—and in many ways better. Gerald Mast concurs: of the twenty songs written for the Gershwins' last three films, "a dozen are among their most memorable gems."[23] As *Shall We Dance* was finished the studio took up the option on their contract for another Astaire movie.

During the winter holidays Frances and Rose were visitors. Both found George in good health and good spirits. He even commented to a reporter that he would probably stay in Hollywood to work on his more serious compositions; no doubt this was said to promote the release of *Shall We Dance*. He did write, after his family's visit, that they had "cheered him up." Before that there were many nights where he wished for the "warmth of New York." After their visit he lost that "rather painful feeling." He told his mother that he enjoyed hiking in the woods and was speculating about his future. He told her that he expected to have enough money to go to Europe and then settle down in New York for some serious work. He felt he was only beginning. He told his sister much the same thing, that he had not "scratched the surface" of serious music; he would stay in Hollywood for a time to make enough money to go back East to work on symphonies, chamber music, and operas.[24] This same message was conveyed to his cousin Henry Botkin, who recalled that George said his sole purpose had been to make money, that he was dissatisfied with Hollywood and the people there; he was "wasting his time."[25]

The gloomier moments persisted. In a letter to Mabel Schirmer he wrote, "There's nothing like the phony glamor of Hollywood to bring out the need for one's real friends." Indeed, his correspondence with Mabel Schirmer "puts all the Hollywood year, almost from its inception, into a steadily darkening spectrum."[26] Thus, he wrote her: "Perhaps, dear Mabel, this is our year. A year that will see both of us finding that elusive something that seems to bring happiness to the lucky; the pendulum swings back, so I've heard, and it's about due to swing back to a more satisfying state."[27]

Despite a great deal of talk about new compositions, Gershwin did not write a note of any new work (other than the movie songs). Why? A plausible explanation for his inactivity as a composer seems to be that at first he enjoyed the new experience, including a fascination with the techniques of moviemaking. There is no doubt, however, that after some time he became more and more frustrated with Hollywood and the treatment of his music. His hopes of producing a revival of *Porgy and Bess* for the West Coast had fallen through. Even the climate was enervating. Scott Fitzgerald said that the climate "wears you down." Finally, George's illness began to manifest itself by the spring of 1937.

Was Gershwin gun-shy because of the mixed reaction to *Porgy and Bess*? Perhaps, but he did explore some post-movie possibilities. The last entry in his Hollywood tune book contains an entry marked "suite," with additional "comments," followed by a list: "working class, idle rich, intolerance, children, fear, nature," but no music. It is likely that this was a sketch for a ballet. He seemed to oscillate between writing a symphony, a string quartet, and an opera. He urged DuBose Heyward to give some thought to a new play for an opera. He also met the playwright Lynn Riggs to talk about an opera. This is one of those footnotes to musical history: Gershwin and Riggs never collaborated, but it would be a Riggs play that would become Rodgers and Hammerstein's *Oklahoma!* As usual Gershwin was still toying with further study. In Hollywood he renewed his acquaintance with Arnold Schoenberg, and the great composer became a frequent guest at the Gershwins' tennis court. Also in Los Angeles he met the composer Ernst Toch, another refugee from Hitler.

Gershwin wrote to ask Schillinger for advice; should he study with Schoenberg or Toch? Schillinger answered: both; Schoenberg for four-part fugues, and Toch for a symphony. Writing a string quartet, however, seemed to intrigue Gershwin most at this stage. He mentioned it to Schoenberg, who came to like and admire Gershwin and wrote a moving eulogy after George died. No music for that quartet was ever found, however.

After *Shall We Dance* both Astaire and Rogers wanted to end their partnership. Astaire did not want to keep repeating the same plot, and Rogers wanted to turn to serious roles. Astaire thought that without Rogers he could do more solo work. The studio was disappointed with the financial return of *Shall We Dance* (a decline to about $400,000 gross profit) and therefore agreed that a change in the Rogers-Astaire formula might be advised (RKO was wrong; the next film lost money). That picture was *A Damsel in Distress*, with Astaire; but Ginger Rogers was replaced by a fine actress named Joan Fontaine, who unfortunately could not sing or dance. Her part was that of a young British girl, which was probably why she was selected. The script was based on an older P.G. Wodehouse story about an American in London who falls in love with a young lady who resides in a nearby castle. Wodehouse was enlisted to work on the script, after what he described as a "frightful" version "all about crooks" by an "ex-drugstore clerk" was thrown out. He commented to Guy Bolton that picture-writing "made one feel as if one were working with one's hands tied."[28]

The Gershwins thought that the casting would allow them to use more of their songs. One observer noted, "the musical tone of the film is bright and brittle, assertive, witty and imaginative; deeply felt but never mawkish or sentimental—just the way Gershwin would have wanted it."[29] Nevertheless, the Gershwins were perhaps too optimistic. For example, "Nice Work if You Can Get It" was quite unusual with its intriguing dissonant harmonies, and was the exception to the rule that he was writing simpler melodies. It was a trunk song from an earlier period. Gershwin composed at the piano, though he admitted it was bad practice (so did most popular songwriters). Often he wrote an original version in intricate keys that sounded richer and fuller on the piano, but he made a note that the published version should be in a simpler key. Gershwin's original manuscript of "Nice Work" is in the key of D-flat, but it was published in the key of C and sung in that key and in B-flat in the film.

In the movie, however, a small group sang "Nice Work" and butchered this brilliant creation; it was repeated but as the background music for a long Astaire drum solo and dance. "Things Are Looking Up" is in many ways a typical Gershwin song—romantic but not slow or dragged out. It evolves into a dance by Astaire as Fontaine merely watches. She does manage a few dance steps, but not exactly gracefully. The scene works well, however, partly because of the music and partly because of Astaire's clever moves to conceal his partner's lack of dancing. No studio juggling could get around the major song of the picture, "A Foggy Day in London Towne" (the original title). It is given a full treatment—"one of the most visually arresting moments in [Astaire's] career."[30] It was also one of Alec Wilder's favorite Gershwin songs. An interesting aside is that George wrote it originally in the key of E, a unusual key (the same as the slow theme in *Rhapsody in Blue*), but he wrote on the manuscript "in F," a far more conventional key for publication.

The film opened with "I Can't Be Bothered Now," a lively melody that served as the background for a dazzling Astaire solo dance. Later in the film there was a long, humorous dance routine, with Astaire and George Burns and Gracie Allen, to a new song, "Stiff Upper Lip." If the film had not been so far along

George Gershwin might have written a special number, but Robert Russell Bennett orchestrated Gershwin's song into a five-minute dance, the highlight of the show. Hermes Pan received an Academy Award for his direction of the sequence.[31] According to John Mueller, *Damsel in Distress* "is one of the most unrelievedly delightful films Astaire ever made." Moreover, Mueller considers the Gershwin score "probably the best ever written for an Astaire film—and therefore for any movie musical."[32]

It is something of a creative miracle that this score was ever born. For by then George Gershwin was beginning to suffer from headaches; the first overt sign came in early February 1937, but perhaps he suffered even earlier. Some of Gershwin's friends and casual acquaintances claimed he was experiencing headaches well before he went to Hollywood.[33] If so, while in New York he did not complain about his condition to any of his immediate family or close friends.

There was a noticeable sign of trouble when he had a mental lapse while he was playing in early February in the Hollywood Bowl. Oscar Levant noted this and teased him about it, and drew a surprisingly angry reply. All accounts of the illness that eventually killed him date back to this incident. It turned out to be a manifestation of a fatal physical disorder, but his friends tended to ascribe his headaches to a psychological aversion to Hollywood. Harold Arlen recalled that during his last year Gershwin was very often unhappy and uneasy. "Lots of other people were writing well—Rodgers, Porter, others [e.g., Porter's *Red, Hot and Blue* and Rodgers' *Babes in Arms*] and, of course, George liked to be kingpin. I knew something was wrong with him . . . and I thought it was Hollywooditis."[34] This was the common conclusion of others, that he was depressed by Hollywood.

It was not too surprising that his family and friends failed to recognize his real physical problems. By the spring of 1937 Gershwin felt increasingly alone and frustrated. Several years after his death, Ira said that he was not so much a part of the songs as he would be in New York, where he was always consulted as to how numbers should be done. But in Hollywood, when the contract ended the writers were through. Then everything was left to the studio to do whatever they wanted.

One by one his old friends from New York—Harburg, Arlen, Rodgers, and Hart began to peel off, returning to New York. Kern suffered a heart attack in March 1937. Gershwin seemed to be more and more determined to go back to New York. His music was played, but usually only if Gershwin performed at the concerts. Particularly frustrating were the difficulties in mounting a version of *Porgy and Bess* on the West Coast.

Obviously, at the time of the February incident Gershwin knew what Levant did not, that there was a real problem. The headaches persisted and more frequently there were also dizzy spells. The headaches came in the morning and often awakened him, so that he was doubly tired. "He felt abandoned, friendless, and once told Paul [Mueller] that despite everything he had, he really had no friend in the world." He reassured his mother, however, that everyone was "feeling well," and despite a "hectic period" this would be his last picture. He wrote Frances that he had gone through a "tough time." His condition worsened. In a letter he wrote in May he said he was "dragging himself to work."[35]

After finishing *A Damsel in Distress*, the Gershwins switched studios, and began to work on a film for the boorish Sam Goldwyn. In May he told his friend and colleague Albert Sirmay, who was visiting Hollywood, that the only thing that held him was his contract and the money he needed to make, so he could get out of Hollywood and return to New York, in order to concentrate on the composition of more artistic works.

The Gershwins' new picture for Goldwyn was *Goldwyn Follies*, a "super, stupendous" production, as Gershwin sarcastically described it. It proved to be an exceedingly frustrating experience. On one occasion Sam Goldwyn requested that Gershwin preview his songs, a sort of audition; he commented that he hoped Gershwin could write "hits like Irving Berlin" (who was in fact a personal friend of Goldwyn's). This infuriated Gershwin, who was already ill. But Alfred Newman, a friend of Gershwin's and the musical director for the movie, who was present, remembered that Goldwyn was quite enthusiastic. Some time earlier Gershwin had written "Love Walked In," which he referred to as a "Brahms" song, mainly because of its very plain, church-like harmony. It too was based on a trunk song written in his tune book in September 1931, six years before the *Goldwyn Follies*. Ira thought it was too much of a "pop" song, and argued against it. He even summoned help from Yip Harburg to adjudicate the argument. Eventually he gave in, but disliked his own lyric. In his commentary Alec Wilder found it "very restrained, lucid, direct, warm and without pretense . . . it is surely close to a concert song."[36]

The other major song for Goldwyn was "Our Love Is Here to Stay" (sometimes the title drops "Our") It was an original, written specifically for the movie. It turned out to be Gershwin's very last song. An undated manuscript of this song in Gershwin's hand exists, showing the main theme of the first nine bars that differs somewhat from the final version. Michael Feinstein, who worked for Ira Gershwin as a musical secretary many years later, commented that this song illustrated Gershwin's meticulous musicality: the first three pick-up notes leading into the chorus would normally be without harmony; but Gershwin harmonized each note thus greatly enhancing the main melody itself. A valid point, except that the manuscript in Gershwin's hand contains no harmony at all, only a melody line. This fragment is not dated in his tune book, so it may have been written sometime earlier. It is possible that Gershwin wrote more than this fragment, because Oscar Levant heard the entire song, but the few bars in the tune book are all that survived in George's hand.

After Gershwin's death Ira felt obligated to complete the melody for the picture and to add a verse. He turned to Vernon Duke who finished the melody and wrote a verse—and took credit. Oscar Levant had heard the melody several times and he helped Duke to complete it without claiming any credit. Years later Ira Gershwin recalled that it was he who wrote not only the lyrics but music for the verse and dictated it to Duke. The movie was released well after Gershwin died, but "Love Walked In" made it to the Hit Parade for fourteen weeks and was ranked number one for four straight weeks.

There are various versions of Gershwin's final weeks and days. They more or less agree on the details of what happened, but there is controversy over his treatment, or lack thereof. After George died, his friend George Pallay wrote a long letter to Irene Gallagher, Max Dreyfus's secretary. He gave a number of details of the last days and particularly the operation. He claimed to have been selected by the family to serve as intermediary with the physicians. Most biographers have drawn on this letter in varying degree.[37] Edward Jablonski's version is probably the most accurate and complete, but he seems determined to shield Ira and Lee from any blame.

After his mistake in the February concert, Gershwin had a medical exam and was given a clean bill of health, so to speak. Some accounts (Charles Schwartz) claim that he called Zilboorg, who suggested that his problem was physical, thus absolving himself of any blame for failing to recognize Gershwin's malady earlier. Zilboorg recommended a therapist, Dr. Eugene Simmel. Edward Jablonski does not mention the consultation with Zilboorg. Since Schwartz was favorably disposed toward Zilboorg, he specifically included Zilboorg's claim that Gershwin's problem was physical. For years Zilboorg's wife went out of her way to denounce accusations that her husband failed to recognize Gershwin's real problem. She did so when she met Michael Feinstein, who was baffled, since he had not heard the old charges of neglect against her husband.[38]

Gershwin "quickly forgot the entire matter in the press of daily living," Schwartz concluded. David Ewen writes, however, that Gershwin continued to suffer brief blackouts; for example, in April there was an incident of dizziness while sitting in a barber's chair (the source is Pallay's letter). By June he began to experience more severe headaches and dizziness. According to Ewen, "on one or two occasions he was found sitting in his bedroom with the shades drawn, bent over; his 'eyes glazed'; with each passing day he grew increasingly jumpy, irritable and restless."[39]

Edward Jablonski, who has thoroughly investigated these last months, does not confirm this particular incident, but writes that in the latter days of May 1937, Gershwin became "unnaturally moody, lost his temper at times, became critical of things, people and events."[40] His headaches were so bad that both Ira and Lee urged him to have a physical exam. On June 9, a "battery" of physicians (Jablonski's term) examined Gershwin at home and found nothing. The lead examining physician was Dr. Gabriel Segall, recommended by Gershwin's psychiatrist, Dr. Simmel. Segall's reports stated that Gershwin had been suffering headaches over a three-month period (beginning in early March) but the headaches disappeared after eating; there also were dizzy spells at least once a day. His physical examination failed to reveal any "abnormalities," was the conclusion.[41] The day after this exam George wrote his mother that he had not been feeling particularly well, and had been examined by Segall, who told him there was nothing of a serious nature, but would investigate further.

There was an interval of almost two weeks between these exams and the decision to enter the hospital for more examinations. Sam Behrman saw him around this time, and they went for a drive. George was behind the wheel, but there was something odd about him; he was subdued, shadowed, according to Behrman.[42] Over the next few days his condition must have deteriorated. Thus, in mid-June Oscar Levant visited and found him upstairs in his bedroom crouched on the floor beside his bed shielding his eyes. Gershwin had lunch on June 22 with his agent Arthur Lyons and Paulette Goddard (Ewen lists the participants as George Pallay and Constance Collier, as well as Goddard). Gershwin's behavior was so uncharacteristic—detached, distracted, uninterested—that his companions concluded there was something seriously wrong. They finally persuaded him to undergo a complete medical exam—X-rays, blood tests, and so on—which took place at Ceders of Lebanon Hospital between June 23 and June 26.[43]

Gershwin himself must have recognized the seriousness of his problem, otherwise he probably would not have submitted to these exams. But nothing seemed to be physically wrong. One neurologist, Dr. Eugene Ziskind, however, suspected a problem with his brain. This was before the era of CT-Scans, and Gershwin vehemently rejected a spinal tap that might have revealed a tumor. (Modern medical practice holds that a spinal tap under certain conditions could be fatal.) His medical record concluded: "most likely hysteria."[44]

The failure to turn up any physical disabilities encouraged his friends in their belief that he was suffering from a psychological reaction to the humiliations and frustrations of Hollywood. This, in turn, encouraged him to seek psychiatric help from Dr. Simmel, who began to suspect that Gershwin's problem was organic (at least that is what he later claimed). After George's death, P.G. Wodehouse, who was in Hollywood, wrote his wife that what was "gruesome" was that everyone had treated his illness so lightly. When he encountered Lee Gershwin at a party, she explained that George couldn't come but his illness was "simply something psychological." Shortly before George died, Mrs. Edward G. Robinson invited Wodehouse to a party for Gershwin, scheduled for July 14; when Wodehouse commented that he thought George was ill, she "smiled in a sort of indulgent, knowing way and said 'Oh, *he's* all right. He'll be there,'—again suggesting that he was doing a sort of prima donna act."[45]

In some accounts, after his physical exam he began to sleep better and mentioned headaches less frequently; there were "moments of cheerfulness and clear thinking, planning for his comfort and work," according to George Pallay.[46] About this time a news item in Walter Winchell's column reported that Gershwin was ill, which produced a flurry of inquiries. Ira reassured his mother as well as his sister, who was traveling abroad. George's secretary, Carol Stevens, reported to Rose on June 30 that "Mr. George is feeling much better, and expects to be completely well in a few days." George sent a telegram to Julia Van

Norman on June 30, remarking that he had left the hospital, feeling somewhat better, and expected to be better in a week or so.[47] However, a private male nurse named Paul Levy was engaged, and then signs of a physical lack of coordination reappeared.

When he collapsed outside the Brown Derby restaurant, one of his party said to disregard him because he only wanted attention. Jablonski reports this incident without naming names, but Peyser identifies Lee as the culprit. This is a startling incident: George Gershwin collapsing on the pavement, without being taken to a hospital? Later, when George had trouble using his silverware and knocked over his drinking glass, Lee ordered him from the table. As he climbed the stairs, Ira saw the look on his face, and later commented that he would never forget it. That Ira would tolerate such mean-spirited treatment of his brother is amazing—if true.

But there were also irrational episodes—all originating from accounts by Oscar Levant and Vernon Duke, who were not present—but unerringly repeated by his biographers. Indeed, Joan Peyser raises serious questions about Ira and Lee's inaction in the final weeks as George's symptoms worsened in such an alarming way. "One would have expected them to seek out a great neurosurgeon. . . . But they did not act. On the contrary, the last weeks saw virtually no action at all."[48]

In 1998, Joan Peyser went further and blamed George's psychoanalyst Gregory Zilboorg. She wrote: "Zilboorg's most heinous crime was providing Leonore Gershwin, Ira's wife, with the rationale for the neglect of her brother-in-law's symptoms that friends and associates had found alarming." Jablonski dismisses Peyser's implication that Lee Gershwin was responsible for the neglect of George's symptoms as "pure nonsense."[49] He insists that at no point did Lee Gershwin stand in the way of George's medical exams; nor was Zilboorg consulted. Dr. Ernst Simmel, his analyst in California, also concluded that his problem was organic, not psychosomatic, in Jablonski's account. This version is accurate to a point, but it serves to exonerate Ira and Lee, Jablonski's patrons. Still, Ira's passivity in this final phase is indeed puzzling, although he never wanted to look for trouble. There is no doubt that Simmel was called in before George's examination at Cedars of Lebanon; almost certainly on Zilboorg's recommendation. So, Joan Peyser has a point.

In any case, friends who saw George were shocked. He was listless to the point of refusing to play the piano. One evening before dinner, Lillian Hellman noticed that he made mistakes while playing casually during conversations. When Hellman approached him he had stopped and was looking at his hands, and momentarily did not recognize her. On another evening he had dinner with Irving Berlin and his daughter Mary Ellin. Gershwin played and listened while Berlin's daughter played a little. Later Berlin pointed out to his daughter that she may have been one of the last people to hear George Gershwin play. After dinner Lee and Ira found him sitting on the car's running board, his head in his hands, groaning. "He's doing it again," Lee complained. Behrman, Oscar Levant, and the screen writer Sonya Lieven visited George on Saturday evening, July 3: "It was not the George we all knew." He was very pale, and the light had gone from his eyes. He even refused to play the piano. After they left, the three of them concluded that he was seriously ill.[50]

Following his psychiatrist's advice, Gershwin moved out of Ira's house on July 4, to stay by himself with his valet and a male nurse. Yip Harburg was leaving for New York and offered his house. Why moving out of the Roxbury house was advisable is a mystery. Dr. Simmel is quoted as saying that he wanted to shield him from Hollywood's parlor psychiatrists—further confirmation that Simmel did not yet fully understand Gershwin's true illness. Nevertheless, the move certainly depressed him. His valet Paul Mueller claimed (in 1990) that this was Leonore's idea, according to Peyser: Mueller said, "they couldn't wait to get rid of him."[51] This seems unfair to Ira. Sam Berhman, however, was appalled. He later claimed to be outraged at the complacency over the diagnosis and the trust in the psychiatrist. Berhman insisted on another medical test, but had to leave for New York. When Harburg, Harold Arlen, and his wife stopped in to say goodbye, Gershwin pathetically said that all his friends were leaving him. "His life had taken on a nightmare quality in this strange, desolate house: the parties over, the piano silent, the laughter gone," wrote Jablonski and Stewart.[52]

Visitors were discouraged, but Ira came by to see him on Thursday, July 8. On the following day, July 9, Ira came by but was told George was asleep. Three doctors, Ziskind, Segall, and Simmel, were present earlier for two hours, according to their bills. That evening he fell down, lapsed into a coma, and was rushed to Cedars of Lebanon Hospital around midnight of July 10.[53] Various tests were conducted, and in the afternoon a spinal tap confirmed the existence of a tumor. An immediate operation was ordered. There was a frantic search to locate the eminent neurosurgeon Dr. Walter Dandy, in the Washington area, but by the time he was found and ready to fly to California it was too late to wait any longer. He conferred with the doctors and agreed with the need to proceed immediately. Another eminent surgeon, Dr. Howard Naffziger, was brought to the hospital from Lake Tahoe at about 9:30 in the evening as a consultant.[54] A bulletin was released around 9:00 P.M. describing George's condition as "critical"; news stories described him as near death.

A five-hour operation began shortly after midnight on July 11. The surgeons located a cyst. This news cheered up his friends and family, since a cyst could be removed. Ira was reassured, but then the physicians discovered beneath the cyst an extremely malignant tumor, embedded deep in the brain. Lee Gershwin was told the truth by their friend George Pallay, who acted as a liaison between the doctors, the family, and a large group of friends that had collected on the floor below. They all left and returned home in the early morning at 6:15. George was taken back to his room at 7:00 A.M. and soon took a turn for the worse. A telephone call informed Lee that George Gershwin had died at 10:35 A.M. He was all alone.

Could he have been saved by earlier action? In her biography of Gershwin, Joan Peyser quotes a noted neurosurgeon who studied Gershwin's case history and concluded that he probably had been suffering some of the symptoms for three years (this would be about the time he began his therapy and started on *Porgy and Bess*). His condition thus could have been treated.[55] Jablonski disputes this implication. In his biography he wrote: "From the beginning Gershwin never had a chance. (Even today glioblastoma is difficult to treat.) An earlier diagnosis would have made little difference in the final outcome . . . [even] Had it been possible to remove the tumor, or the bulk of it, it would have recurred."[56] Charles Schwartz shares this same judgment. Yet the question remains how the tumor grew so rapidly between the first overt symptoms in February and the last few weeks of his life. Jablonski quotes a letter from the noted neurosurgeon Walter E. Dandy, to the effect that nothing more could have been done.[57] George might have recovered for a "little while" but the tumor would have recurred very quickly. "For a man brilliant as he . . . a recurring tumor would have been terrible; it would have been a slow death."

NOTES

1. Edward Jablonski and Lawrence Stewart, *The Gershwin Years* (New York: Doubleday & Company, 1958), p. 331. The text includes a reproduction of Martin Lewis' etching *The Glow of the City* that reflects Gershwin's sentiments.

2. William G. Hyland, *Richard Rodgers* (New Haven, CT: Yale University Press, 1998), pp. 98–99.

3. Bill Adler, *Fred Astaire* (New York: Carroll and Graf, 1987), p. 106.

4. Arlene Croce, *The Fred Astaire and Ginger Rogers Book* (New York: E.P. Dutton, 1972); also see Gerald Mast, *Can't Help Singin'* (Woodstock, NY: Overlook Press, 1987).

5. Robert Kimball and Alfred Simon, *The Gershwins*, p. 205.

6. Joan Peyser, *The Memory of All That* (New York: Simon and Schuster, 1993), p. 259.

7. In the 1920s the Gershwins formed their own publishing company, New World Music, as well as Gershwin Publishing, but leased the distribution rights to Harms and Chappell. Gershwin Publishing lost money, in part because it paid advances to George.

8. George's pay from RKO was $2,338/week; when he went to work for Goldwyn this increased to $2,505/week.

9. Kimball and Simon, *The Gershwins*, p. 200.

10. Peyser, *The Memory of All That*, p. 271; Jablonski and Stewart, *The Gershwin Years* (1996 ed.), pp. 309–10. Lawrence Stewart worked as an assistant to Ira, and is quite sympathetic toward Lee.

11. Library of Congress, Gershwin Collection, Letter to Julia Van Norman.

12. Jablonski and Stewart, *The Gershwin Years*, p. 248.

13. Julie G. Gilbert, *Opposite Attraction: The Lives of Erich Maria Remarqué and Paulette Goddard* (New York: Pantheon Books, 1995).

14. Anita Loos, *Fate Keeps on Happening: The Adventures of Lorelei Lee and Other Writings*, ed. Ray Pierre Corsini (New York: Dodd, Mead, 1984).

15. Library of Congress, Gershwin Collection, Correspondence Folders.

16. Ibid., p. 287.

17. Deena Rosenberg, *Fascinating Rhythm* (New York: Dutton, 1991), p. 326.

18. Steven E. Gilbert, *The Music of Gershwin* (New Haven, CT: Yale University Press, 1995), p. 208.

19. Larry Starr, "Ives, Gershwin, and Copland: Reflections on the Strange History of American Art Music," *American Music*, Summer 1994.

20. Gershwin's original melodies, as written by him for his tune books, or in final copyist version, are generally fuller in the right hand than the published versions, which were probably edited for simplicity by "Doc" Sirmay. Gershwin, however, carefully reviewed the edited versions, and occasionally corrected mistakes, and even made small changes in the harmony.

21. Gilbert, *The Music of Gershwin*, p. 211. He believes that the score of this movie "ranks with the best of the Gershwin stage musicals."

22. Library of Congress, Gershwin Collection, Correspondence Folders.

23. Gerald Mast, *Can't Help Singin'*, p. 85.

24. Kimball and Simon, *The Gershwins*, p. 214.

25. Rose, Henry Botkin, and Albert Sirmay each gave affidavits quoting Gershwin, at the time his will was probated; apparently they were testifying to the effect that his sojourn in Hollywood was temporary in order to persuade the New York courts that he was not a resident of California and subject to state taxes. Sworn statements in Library of Congress, Gershwin Collection.

26. Jablonski and Stewart, *The Gershwin Years*, p. 287.

27. Kimball and Simon, *The Gershwins*, p. 205.

28. P.G. Wodehouse, *Yours, Plum*, ed. F.L. Donaldson (New York: James Heineman, 1990), pp. 131–32.

29. John Mueller, *Astaire Dancing* (New York: Alfred Knopf, 1985), p. 128.

30. Ibid., p. 136.

31. The entire dance sequence was recorded from the original score: *Gershwin Overtures*, EMI CDC-747977 2.

32. Mueller, *Astaire Dancing*, p. 127.

33. Peyser, *The Memory of All That*, p. 262. She claims that Gershwin's failures as a composer created an "unremitting stress that could contribute to a breakdown of his immune system."

34. Kimball and Simon, *The Gershwins*, p. 203.

35. Jablonski and Stewart, *The Gershwin Years*, p. 289.

36. There is a Gershwin melody, written apparently for a show with Ed Wynn in 1919, that is remarkably similar to "Love Walked In."

37. George Pallay builds up his own role as a confidant, and goes out of his way to excuse the physicians and psychiatrists for failing to detect any symptoms until the very final days. Text in the Library of Congress, Gershwin Collection, Miscellaneous Correspondence. A somewhat different version was written by Vernon Duke, who claims he heard it from Lee Gershwin. Duke, *Passport to Paris* (Boston: Little, Brown, 1955), pp. 351–52.

38. In Vernon Duke's version, Simmel conferred with Zilboorg; supposedly Simmel saw Gershwin every day. Duke, *Passport to Paris*, p. 351. Simmel's bills date back to June 19, that is, before Gershwin entered Cedars of Lebanon for his check-up.

39. David Ewen, *Gershwin: His Journey to Greatness* (New York: The Ungar Publishing Company, 1970), p. 279.

40. Jablonski, *Gershwin*, p. 318, quoting George Pallay's letter; Pallay wrote, "Four weeks ago, he seemed unhappy and a bit moody. He was critical of things, people and events."

41. According to Pallay a "big neurologist" (Segall?) examined Gershwin's head for possible symptoms and declared there was "no indication of any symptoms of brain disease." Charles Schwartz, *Gershwin* (Indianapolis: Bobbs-Merrill, 1973), also reports a neurological exam on June 20 that proved negative. Other sources do not confirm this exam; Jablonski, *Gershwin*, pp. 318–19.

42. S.N. Behrman, *People in a Diary* (Boston: Little, Brown, 1972), p. 251.

43. Jablonski, *Gershwin*, p. 318; Ewen, *Gershwin: His Journey to Greatness*, p. 279; Peyser, *The Memory of All That*, p. 292, gives the date as June 20.

44. Jablonski, *Gershwin*, p. 319; Peyser, *The Memory of All That*, p. 292. The source is, again, George Pallay's letter. Peyser adds that this summary also included Gershwin's statement that he had suffered from insomnia four months before, "when he was in love" (a possible reference to Goddard).

45. Wodehouse, *Yours, Plum*, p. 66.

46. Pallay letter; Jablonski and Stewart, *The Gershwin Years*, p. 290.

47. Gershwin Collection, Library of Congress, Correspondence Folders.

48. Peyser, *The Memory of All That*, p. 297.

49. Joan Peyser, *New York Times*, October 4, 1998; Edward Jablonski, *New York Times*, October 25, 1998.

50. Behrman, *People in a Diary*, pp. 253–54.

51. Peyser, *The Memory of All That*, p. 293. All sources claim that Goldwyn brusquely took George off the payroll, complaining that he was tired because he was out carousing with Paulette Goddard until late hours; but George's bank account shows that he continued to receive his weekly salary until the week he died.

52. Jablonski and Stewart, *The Gershwin Years*, p. 292. Vernon Duke claims that George was in the new house for two weeks [*sic*], and that on July 9, Ira and Lee stopped by to consult the physicians: "Lee remembers seeing six doctors testing George's reflexes as she entered the bedroom." *Passport to Paris*, p. 351.

53. Drs. Ziskind, Segall, and Simmel all indicated in their billing that they were present on July 10 for 4–5 hours.

54. These eminent doctors' services were by no means free. Dandy charged $1,000 for his telephone consultation; Dr. Naffziger charged $2,500 for his consultations at the operation. The actual operation was performed by Doctor Carl Rand, whose fee was $12,500. All the bills were paid out of George's estate or by Ira.

55. Peyser, *The Memory of All That*, p. 296.

56. Jablonski, *Gershwin*, p. 324.

57. Ibid.

Chapter 12

Personality

Several years after George died, Ira complained that he wished some of those who thought they knew his brother would not write stories about him. George was never brassy and never hard to get along with. He was shy, reserved, a sweet guy. His real friends, of which there were many, knew him that way too. His sister Frankie said much the same thing—a closed-in person, very sweet and protective. Ira made his comments in 1946, when anecdotes had accumulated about George's oversized ego and insensitivity. So it is no surprise that Ira wished to safeguard his brother's image of a sweet guy.[1]

Shy, reserved, sweet, protective—these were the characteristics that emerged in the portrait first etched by Isaac Goldberg in his biography (published in 1931). Given George (and Ira's) participation in helping Goldberg, it was almost an autobiography. It is this Goldberg version that subsequent biographers have had to wrestle with.

Sixty years later another biographer (Joan Peyser) was far more skeptical. She suggested two different images: On the one hand there was the picture of a vigorous young man, at one with post–World War I New York, a "self-involved cocky Manhattanite who monopolized the piano at parties from Fifth Avenue to Long Island's grand estates." On the other hand, Ms. Peyser added, there was a vastly different image: Gershwin's version of himself was that of a melancholy, thoughtful man quite different from the popular view. One might think that his music would provide the vital clues. The musicologist Wayne Schneider commented that while Gershwin was probably the most famous American composer, he was also one of America's least known and appreciated composers. Professor Charles Hamm makes roughly the same points: that there has been an absence of disciplined theoretical, analytical, or historical discourse on Gershwin and his music. Much of what we think we know about him and his music is based on popular journalists' literature, much of it highly problematic in theory and method. Thus, as Ira feared, George's portrait has become blurred. But this was probably inevitable.

Who, then, was the real George Gershwin?

It depends in part on when such a question might be posed: when he was a young man, or when he had become the mature artist of the 1930s?

When he was a young man breaking into professional music he seemed quite happy, ambitious, of course, and also enormously self-confident. Irving Caesar, the lyricist of "Swanee," knew Gershwin before his rise to fame and thus provides an early glimpse of the young man. He found Gershwin "very sweet and very soft and quite sensitive." Gershwin had "great faith and confidence in his music," but "there was nothing modest about him. I don't mean that he was overbearing, but he had self-confidence, and rightly so."[2]

Over a decade later observers would offer a different assessment. Rouben Mamoulian knew Gershwin when he directed *Porgy and Bess* in 1935. He found Gershwin complex: between the "simple gaiety" of a child and the clear serenity of the old, "there was much in him that was neither as simple nor as clear, nor perhaps, as happy."[3]

Gershwin was an attractive man. He was slightly above medium height (5 feet, nine and a half inches), of an athletic build; Kay Swift said that being slim, long legged, and fast moving, he looked taller than his actual height. He was dark-complexioned, with dark eyes to match. He had a heavy beard, and later was going alarmingly bald. His smile over a slightly protruding jaw was "almost cryptic; it is not an affirmation but a question." Indeed, this countenance gave him a "particular, unobtrusive charm," wrote Isaac Goldberg: "Gershwin's rugged ruddy masculinity and general dynamism undoubtedly enhanced his appearance."[4] His private secretary in the 1920s, Nanette Kuttner, was impressed by her first encounter: "here was no art pose, but a blatant earthiness . . . he was alive, lusty."[5] George's friend, the songwriter Harold Arlen, described George's "questioning look—which to me meant humility. His greatness lay not only in his dynamic talent, drive and sureness, but that questioning look."[6]

A rather refined description was provided by a surprising source, the English writer Osbert Sitwell, who knew Gershwin only casually but admired his music:

> He possessed a fine racial appearance; nobody could mistake him for anyone but a Jew . . . his personality was plain in his whole air, he was modest in bearing, and I never noticed a trace of the arrogance with which he has been credited.[7]

Gershwin's good friend, playwright S.N. Behrman, wrote that "popular composers are a race apart, like dancers and kings." Gershwin was indeed a man of many parts. Songwriter and composer, of course, but he was also an accomplished athlete—golf, tennis, skiing, boxing, and horse riding, as he called it. He was an excellent dancer, too, supple and graceful, as testified to by no less than Fred Astaire. He had a small gym in his last apartment including a punching bag. He was a fan of the prize fights and often attended matches in New York. Once he offered a lady friend the choice of attending the fights or a performance of *Porgy and Bess*; she perversely chose the fights, which proved her last outing with Gershwin. Athletics were an antidote for his loneliness, but also an outlet for his innate competitiveness, not to say aggressiveness.

A biographer (Charles Schwartz) noted that the quick almost automatic reflex that he demonstrated again and again in his improvisations at the piano also were evident in the sports he played. Tennis seems to have been his favorite when he lived in Hollywood. He played regularly on the court at their rented home in Beverly Hills. One observer of a match between Arnold Schoenberg and Gershwin noted that Gershwin was relentless and hard-driving, but played to the audience, where he found admiration and praise a stimulant. Schoenberg was a much older man and a more calculating strategist, as befitted the inventor of the twelve-tone system, and in the end he prevailed.[8]

As an avid golfer, Gershwin shot in the low nineties, occasionally breaking into the eighties. His friend Emil Mosbacher claimed that George was more nervous in a golf match than on an opening night on Broadway. He could drive about two hundred yards, but had a slice that cut down his distance. His strongest game was pitching and putting. This part of the game requires strong concentration and steady nerves, and Gershwin, once he set himself a task, was single-minded almost to the point of obsession. Even in sports Gershwin competed with himself. When he played golf with friends he conceded strokes, but if he won, he would insist on another match conceding even more strokes. Having proved his dominance, he was generous.

Despite his penchant for sports, for much of his life Gershwin was not in the best of health. He frequently complained of trouble with his stomach. What exactly he suffered from is unclear, but it involved occasional nausea, dizziness, and vomiting. He tried occasional dietary fads (yeast and sour cream) but without much success. It could have been psychosomatic, and some friends thought he sought psychiatric help in order to do something about his stomach. Gershwin himself referred to his malady as "composer's stomach," because it flared up during periods of intense concentration. His condition seemed to intensify more when he turned to his larger compositions. It started in 1922, when he was writing *Blue Monday*; he was then twenty-four. When writing *Porgy and Bess* in 1934 his stomach trouble seemed to worsen; it continued for the rest of his life.

For most of his life he lived with his parents and his brothers and sister. Most accounts suggest that it was a reasonably congenial arrangement. Ira also lived at home, even after he married. After George and Ira enjoyed some commercial success the family moved to a larger duplex on 110th Street on the West Side, and then to a five-floor apartment complex at 33 Riverside Drive. George occupied a top floor study and apartment. His future secretary described her first impression:

You rang the front door bell, a terrier yelped, a maid neither prompt nor neat answered, or his mother or his sister Frances. And you were shown to a small elevator. On the way left of the entrance hall you saw a mirrored room, its formal design routed by a ping pong table; George's touch. Mounting past numerous bedrooms, past a parlor with two pianos, you reached the top. This was his.[9]

In the front of his apartment was a livingroom, with a fireplace and a grand piano, and a balcony. In the back was a bedroom, flanked by a small study. Above his desk was a picture of Prince George signed "From George to George." He finally moved to his own penthouse on East 72nd Street, and Ira and Lee occupied a penthouse directly across the street.

He seems to have been comfortable at home—probably because he was free to do what he pleased. Oscar Levant found the Gershwin family quite undemonstrative. It is also probable that he did not want to be alone, as his sister speculated. Friends who visited him commented on the near-chaotic surroundings, all sorts of people coming and going, but Gershwin liked it.

Isaac Goldberg attributed George's contentment with his family life to traditional strong Jewish bonds, but there was little evidence of religion in the Gershwin family. Only Ira was bar mitzvahed. George had little to say about religion, his own or in general. He occasionally referred to his Russian roots, but seldom to his Jewish roots. During one Passover, his friend Kitty Carlisle attended a seder with him; it was performed in Hebrew by Oscar Levant, with George chiming in, but in mad jazz rhythms. Some critics have strained to detect a strong Jewish influence in Gershwin's music, but Ira scoffed at this idea. Goldberg believed that George must have heard snatches of Yiddish folk songs. This may be true, but Gershwin portrayed his own music as quintessential American, and never ascribed his music to a Jewish influence.

Both parents carried over strong Russian and Yiddish accents. Both brothers must have understood some Yiddish. Their parents often played cards with Boris Thomashevsky, the founder of the Yiddish theater on Second Avenue. George's piano playing supposedly interfered with their card games. Ira and George "hung out" with young Milton and Harry. Michael Tilson Thomas, the conductor of the San Francisco Orchestra and the grandson of Boris Thomashevsky, believes that George was influenced by Jewish music; however, when George was offered a chance to collaborate on a Jewish musical, the other composer, Sholom Secunda, a Juilliard graduate, refused to join with an amateur.[10] Joseph Rumshinsky, the conductor of the Yiddish theater musicals, claims to have remembered George from his early days.

Their mother insisted that the boys learn proper English and was determined that her children would be assimilated. George had no trace of an accent, and George and Ira were assimilated to the degree that was possible in the years after World War I. The 1920s, however, was an era of growing anti-Semitism. Show business offered some sanctuary from rabid anti-Semitism, but it is likely that George was subjected to anti-Semitic incidents. He never referred to them nor did Ira.

George and Ira belonged to a social circle that revolved around young middle-class New York Jews whom George met through his work as a Remick's song plugger. Herman Paley was a song plugger there, and his brother Lou wrote some lyrics with George. They introduced him to the Strunsky family, especially Emily, who married Lou Paley. Ira married Emily's sister Leonore. The Strunskys were a prosperous real estate family. This circle included the Strunskys' cousin Mabel Pleshette, who married Bob Schirmer. She became George's life-long close friend and confidant.

George Gershwin, however, was never the young Jew in Manhattan struggling to break free of the ghetto. He was not ashamed of his roots, but he did not glorify them. There is no doubt, however, that he was ambitious and sought recognition, but not because he was determined to overcome his Jewishness. True, his near obsession with playing the piano at social gatherings brought him a measure of acclaim and recognition—and ridicule. It became almost a joke; Cole Porter wrote a humorous lyric about a party in which Gershwin did *not* play.

Fortunately, his ambition was buttressed by a willingness to take a chance, at least in music. Writing the mini-opera *Blue Monday* was a gamble for a popular songwriter, and it failed, embarrassingly so; but composing *Rhapsody in Blue* was an even more dangerous gamble. After all, it could easily have failed as well. As a young man he could afford to gamble, because he was unusually self-confident and talented. Kay Swift commented that he knew how good he was. He would have been a "jackass" not to.

George was increasingly dependent on Ira, whom a friend described as George's "guardian angel." It was obvious to everyone that Ira venerated George. Yet even after Ira began writing some lyrics and George had been writing for the *Scandals* for three years, they did not collaborate, except for an occasional song. Even then Ira chose a pseudonym (Arthur Francis), lest he be accused of trading on his brother's name. That they should collaborate on their first show, *Lady Be Good!* was not George's idea, but the proposal of the producer Alex Aarons.

In any case, as a result of that show George and Ira became even closer both professionally and personally. They worked at night, usually at George's initiative, but Ira was also a night person. After returning from a social outing he would summon Ira, if he felt like writing. He composed at the piano. Ira would listen over and over to George's new melody. Finally, Ira would find a phrase, usually for a title, somewhere near the final notes of the refrain. Often they would argue, but on the whole their work went smoothly. Their aunt Kate Wolpin, however, claimed that there was in fact a friendly rivalry brought on by George's compulsive competitiveness.[11]

Ira was reclusive, but George obviously enjoyed socializing. As he became well-known he moved up the social ladder. Jules Glaenzer, a vice president of

Cartier's, sponsored him in New York society as he did Richard Rodgers. Whereas Rodgers and his wife Dorothy were both from upper-middle-class families, and moved easily into the realm of higher society (as did the wealthy Cole Porter), Gershwin was neither suave nor polished. His initial entree into New York society was as a piano player, a virtual entertainer, but gradually he became a guest on his own at soirees and weekends—not with the Whitneys or Vanderbilts, but only a step below.

Oscar Levant believed that social outings were a diversion from work and a satisfaction of his need for companionship. Whether playing the piano at parties, attending the fights, or taking in a show with a lady friend, he sought an escape from his fear of loneliness. His sister thought he would seek out companionship rather than spend an evening by himself. His cousin Henry Botkin, the painter, agreed that George was insecure in so many ways that it was really unbelievable. Botkin related that George would often invite him over for dinner, because otherwise he would be all alone. Botkin commented later that one kept wondering why George was in that particular condition.

If loneliness was something he feared, it might be thought that he would have had many really close friends, but that was not so even though he was quite gregarious. Of course he knew most of his songwriting colleagues and was friendly with them, especially Irving Berlin, Jerome Kern, and Richard Rodgers, but they were not close confidants. He was generous with his colleagues, and loaned some of them money. He encouraged Harold Arlen early in Arlen's career and Vernon Duke was virtually a Gershwin protégé. He was quite considerate of Kurt Weill when Weill first arrived in America. When George was occupied elsewhere he did not seem to mind that Ira wrote lyrics with others, like Vernon Duke and Vincent Youmans. For his part, as Oscar Levant noted, George had a "curious partiality" for successful well-to-do people of the "stock broker type, with whom he could play golf and go on week-ends." Emil Mosbacher was one such friend.[12]

In his socializing, he was not hampered by his lack of education. For most young Jews before World War I, education was the route out of the ghetto. Gershwin, however, was not well-educated, especially when compared to Ira, who attended the prestigious Townsend Harris High School and then City College. George graduated from grammar school, but was then directed by his parents to the High School of Commerce, the equivalent of a vocational school. He was supposed to learn the rudiments of accounting. He was "disillusioned," according to Goldberg, an odd way of putting it, since he could not have had any illusions; he was simply following his parents' direction.

Gershwin was no intellectual, not because he was ignorant or insensitive, but because he was too preoccupied with his other activities to be contemplative. He knew none of the major literary figures of his generation. He read very little; he owned no library to speak of. Reading *Porgy* was an exception, and the book was a gift. His environment was largely formed by show business. He had a quick mind, however, and was attuned to the nuances and subtleties of the written word. His articles for newspapers and magazines were literate and insightful (writing about music of course). He was an avid letter writer, and Ira proudly pointed out that George's letters were grammatically correct with no spelling errors. In some of his letters, especially after he moved to Hollywood, he was quite articulate in revealing many of his inner thoughts and concerns.

Occasionally, he was exposed to an intellectual atmosphere. The Saturday evenings he spent with Herman and Lou Paley and the Strunskys were lively discussions of almost every topic—art, music, and politics. His cousin, the painter Henry Botkin, known to the Gershwins as Harry, was an intellectual and Henry's brother B.A. Botkin, known as Ben, was an outstanding sociologist.

Gershwin, however, was absorbed in his music. So it is not surprising that musicians would see him in a special light. They remarked on the similarity between Gershwin's personality and his music. Serge Kousevitsky wrote: "To speak of George Gershwin the composer, is to approach the real, the essential part of his being." Harold Arlen also commented on the link between Gershwin's music and his personality: "I believe that anyone who knows George's work, knows George. The humor, the satire, the playfulness of most of his melodic phrases were the natural expression of the man."[13] This was also Kay Swift's view: "he was exactly like his music in person. It is a curious thing—I think most of us fail to hide in our work; it was especially true of George, he was exactly like his work." Ira concurred but employed a different set of comparisons—"vibrant, dynamic, honest and charming."[14]

Which music was like him? The boisterous *Rhapsody in Blue*, written when he was twenty-five, would fit Arlen's description of humor and playfulness. But what of his last song, the plaintive "[Our] Love Is Here to Stay," written just before he died when he was thirty-eight? Here, surely, was a different man—more introspective, occasionally gloomy, worried and uncertain of his future. Alex Steinert, his vocal coach for *Porgy and Bess*, quoted a rather pitiful remark by Gershwin around this time: "I am thirty-eight and famous, and rich, but profoundly unhappy. Why?"[15]

As for outlets other than music, unlike his brother George was not involved in politics. Immigrant families were wedded to reading the Jewish Daily *Forward*, a socialist newspaper. Given this background Ira and his friends in New York and Hollywood were generally on the far left. Joan Peyser claims that George was shunned by some of these friends because he was so nonpolitical, or too conservative. He was listed in 1924 among the show business personalities supporting Al Smith. Moreover, George could not have written the music for *Strike Up the Band*, *Of Thee I Sing*, and *Let 'Em Eat Cake* without absorbing some political lore from George Kaufman and Morrie Ryskind. In 1936, when the Gershwins moved to Hollywood, some of their friends were highly political—Edward G. Robinson and Lillian Hellman, for example. Gershwin was as concerned as everyone with Hitler. In a letter he noted "depressing moments too, when talk of Hitler and his gang creep into conversation. For some reason or other the feeling out here is even more acute than in the East." This in itself

Typical Kike

is puzzling, since two of his friends, the composers Arnold Schoenberg and Kurt Weill then on the West Coast, were refugees from Hitler's oppression. On one occasion he became quite upset when the conversation turned to Hitler's evil ways, but he did not join any of the anti-fascist front groups in Hollywood. It is an interesting aside that the lyricists, who worked with words and ideas— Oscar Hammerstein, Yip Harburg, and Ira—were immersed in politics, but the music writers, Gershwin, Kern, Porter, and Youmans, were not (Irving Berlin was an exception). When George returned from his vacation in Mexico in 1935, after visiting Diego Rivera who was a Trotskyite by then, George said in a newspaper interview, "I'm going to interest myself in politics. I talked a great deal with Diego Rivera, and with his radical friends, who discussed at length their doctrines and their intentions." He went on to say, "I'm going to try to develop my brains more in music . . . to match my emotional development." Nothing came of it, however. After George died, Issac Goldberg commented that after this trip to Mexico Gershwin became more conscious of economic and sociological problems. It is difficult, however, to imagine George Gershwin as the champion of Trotskyism or communist orthodoxy.[16]

Among his hobbies were photography and painting—both as a collector and painter himself. His photography had an almost professional quality. He was urged to take up photography by his psychoanalyst, Gregory Zilboorg; presumably it was a form of therapy. But many of his photos were dark and forbidding, with heavy shadows and accents. For some reason he tried to create rather grim settings. A photo of his friends Emily Strunsky and Mabel Schirmer is composed of two ghostly white faces against a stark black background. It is also an interesting comment that he included himself in his own photos: for example, a rather eerie time exposure of himself and Irving Berlin, a similar time exposure of himself, Lou Paley, and Edward G. Robinson, of Kay Swift's daughter Andrea, and finally a time exposure of himself. There is nothing happy about these posed photographs.

He took up painting at his cousin's urging around 1929. Ira had been painting for some time, and his Aunt Kate believed that George started painting to compete with Ira, who finally quit. According to Merle Armitage, a friend, art critic, and collector, Gershwin took to painting with the same "gusto" that he gave to his music.[17] He had the good fortune to enjoy the influence and help of his cousin, the artist Henry Botkin, who said that painting came "remarkably naturally to Gershwin." Gershwin himself said to Rosamond Walling, who was an aspiring painter and questioned his turn toward painting: "Of course I can paint! If you have talent you can do anything. I have a lot of talent."

His style was influenced by his favorite artist, Georges Rouault. He was fascinated by what Armitage described as Rouault's "heavy use of color, his sense of form and his bold treatments." He was enthralled by the "life and spirit" that animated Rouault's work. According to Botkin, Rouault's "power and depth" was evident in Gershwin's portraits.[18]

He painted portraits of his grandfather (1933), his mother (1936), Ira (1932),

Emily Paley (1933). He did a humorous self-portrait showing himself in the act of painting but dressed in white tie, tails, and a top hat. (Ira trumped him by painting a self-portrait of himself painting a portrait in his underwear.) Among his surviving works there is a still life entitled "Orchid," a portrait of a Negro child, which he hung in his apartment, and his last oil portraits of Jerome Kern and Arnold Schoenberg, copied from photographs. He also painted a self-portrait in a checkered sweater, which has become rather well-known, and is on display at the Gershwin exhibit in the Library of Congress.[19]

It was perhaps inevitable that his paintings would be compared with his music. Merle Armitage, for example, is persuaded that his painting was like his music—not modern in the sense of Picasso or Braque, but in a solid middle ground (a curious description of his music). His mastery grew with each picture, Armitage believed: "He was in love with color and his palette in paint closely resembled the color of his music. Juxtaposition of greens, blues, sanguines, chromes, and grays, fascinated him (again, this seems odd, since the color associated with his music was blue). He did enjoy using a variety of colors and positioning them in unusual patterns (in other words, like "Fascinating Rhythm").[20] His mentor, Henry Botkin, said that as his painting progressed he displayed how the "specific moods of his musical compositions" had given "a vital form and emotional strength to his paintings," and "the intense, dynamic impulses of his music became the dominating force in his paintings." This makes little sense; he did not begin painting until he had already composed the *Rhapsody*, the *Concerto in F*, and *An American in Paris*. His painting did not in the least resemble his *Variations on I Got Rhythm*, or the *Cuban Overture*; perhaps one might draw a comparison with the *Second Rhapsody*. That composition might qualify in Botkin's description of intense and dynamic impulses.[21]

After he died some of his work was exhibited at a gallery in New York. One critic wrote that while he was not yet great as a painter, that was merely because he had not yet had the time—but he was "distinctly on the way to that goal."

Botkin guessed that he bought about 200 paintings for Gershwin. Armitage believed that Gershwin's collection of paintings was quite revealing. He had acquired a Picasso oil, "The Absinthe Drinker," which he left to his mother. He also acquired a Utrillo, some Modiglianis, as well as works by his friend David Siquerios, and many others that amounted to a quite valuable collection. Shortly before he died he urged Armitage to acquire a Kokoschka on his trip to Europe. Kokoschka had painted a portrait of Arnold Schoenberg. Comparing his with Gershwin's shows that Gershwin was still quite conventional. Among the moderns, he appreciated Paul Kleé; after studying a Kleé watercolor with a magnifying glass, he stopped abruptly and exclaimed, that his music would not stand up under that kind of scrutiny.

There is a striking sculpted head of Gershwin created by the artist Isamu Noguchi in 1929. Noguchi described his work: "An exterior of self-assurance verging on conceit does not hide the thoughtfulness of a rich and sensitive nature." Gershwin's turn toward painting, however, astonished Noguchi. He wondered whether it reflected Gershwin's doubts over the adequacy of music as a form of "complete expression," or was it merely a diversion? After Gershwin's death Noguchi decided that Gershwin was perhaps "fleeing from the exorbitant expectations which are heaped upon genius in the 'public eye'; painting was his solace."[22]

Noguchi's speculation that Gershwin was fleeing from exorbitant expectations does not coincide with Goldberg's. This was a man who wore "his unprecedented celebrity as lightly as if it were a cane . . . moving easily, confidently," according to Goldberg. "No affectations. No embarrassing habits that cling to one from earlier, more humble days, and surroundings. *Simplicity*, and even, at moments, an *engaging naivete*. Above all, no desire to make an effect" (emphasis added). Goldberg continued: "His modesty is not a mask for swollen self-esteem."[23] Not surprisingly, David Ewen, in his early writing about Gershwin, concurred: "it was not innocence but wisdom that brought Gershwin that unassuming *simplicity* which was so often interpreted as *naivete*." A more cynical source, Alexander Woollcott, who knew Gershwin from the 1920s, nevertheless supported Goldberg and Ewen's analysis: "Master Gershwin was profoundly interested in himself, but unlike most of us, he had no habit of pretense. He was beyond, and, to my notion, above, posing."[24]

Kay Swift commented along the same lines:

> *He did not take himself seriously as a person, not a bit*. He wasn't pompous. I think he took his music seriously and I think he thought of it as something he had to do and looked at it almost reverently because it was that good.[25] (emphasis added)

Yet, there persist stories of his cockiness. They are derived mainly from anecdotes, many from Oscar Levant, meant to be humorous. Indeed, some of the more humorous ones are repeated in every biography. This is the line taken by Charles Schwartz: "It is clear that he was not the 'simple,' 'unaffected,' and 'modest' man Goldberg described. Nor would one expect him to be."[26]

Pushy, cocky, conceited—all characteristics that seem at variance with the widespread view among his friends that he was naive. The songwriter Arthur Schwartz ("Dancing in the Dark"), an admitted admirer, wrote: "He had such charm and naivete about his own work and himself that there was no feeling on the part of any of us composers or any of his friends who were constantly with him that his egocentricity was objectionable." David Ewen agreed that Gershwin's egocentricity was never objectionable. Even Charles Schwartz concedes that Gershwin's behavior was "frequently tinged with an artlessness and naivete that was appealing in so talented a person."[27]

Mitch Miller, later famous as a conductor of popular music, encountered Gershwin in 1934 when Gershwin toured with Leo Reisman's orchestra: "Gershwin was always sweet. He never raised his voice. He did not have a commanding personality. He was the consummate craftsman. Gershwin had a poker face. It was impossible to judge his reactions. He never looked exultant or distressed."[28]

Edward Jablonski and Lawrence Stewart claim that "Of all creative geniuses George Gershwin was one of the least personally sensitive; instead he was so youthfully brash, so confident in his work, that he seems never to have succumbed to doubts or imagined insults."[29] A musician who knew Gershwin rather well was Alexander Steinert, the vocal coach for *Porgy and Bess*. He wrote that Gershwin completely believed in what he was doing. "He knew he had something to say, and he said it."[30]

One aspect of Gershwin's life that commands a near universal consensus was his infatuation with women. There is a long list of ladies he squired around New York and Hollywood. He also had many nonromantic women friends, especially Emily Strunsky and her cousin Mabel Schirmer. His letters suggest he felt comfortable confiding in them. Mabel Schirmer's niece maintains that the relationship with her aunt was nonromantic, but not because of Gershwin's lack of trying. It was Schirmer who believed that if they had an affair it would ruin their friendship, and apparently Gershwin acquiesced.

Goldberg addressed the subject of Gershwin and the ladies, but gently. While gentleman may prefer blondes, Goldberg wrote, George preferred "more sober leanings . . . toward the intellectual type of femininity. Not the blue-stocking but the woman of sympathetic intelligence—the woman who, perhaps like his mother, can handle situations with delicacy yet with firmness." (To associate his mother with "delicacy" is a considerable stretch).[31] Artist and caricaturist Al Hirschfeld saw George at parties in the late 1920s and 1930s—but never saw him go steady in any sense of that word: "George was so in love with work that he seemed asexual to me. Like [Frank] Crowninshield and [Alexander] Woollcott. Neither was homosexual or interested in women; their passions were all tied up in their work."[32] The possibility of Gershwin's latent homosexuality is raised in the biographies of Schwartz, Kendall, and Greenberg, but all three dismiss the idea.

Frances Gershwin said, "George was always looking for a woman to marry. He talked about marriage a lot. Even as far back when we were living on 110th Street, he would say how he wanted a beautiful home with beautiful dishes and beautiful glasses. He wanted everything to be beautiful. But when you don't have nurturing parents you don't know how to give love."[33] Rosamond Walling, a young lady he romanced in 1928–30 and supposedly proposed to, commented that "he never made me feel needed. He didn't need me." This was a common observation from most of the women he knew.[34]

There are some potentially jarring aspects of Gershwin's relations with women. Consider the strange case of Julia Thomas Van Norman. She had started their friendship by writing him an admiring letter. They became pen pals and then close friends. Joan Peyser believes he may have fathered a daughter by her. Moreover, Peyser claims that Gershwin fathered a son by a chorus girl, Marilyn Manners (stage name). This young man, named Alan, later publicly laid claim to his parentage, many years after George died. His claim was strenuously rejected by the Gershwins. David Ewen ignores this affair; Charles Schwartz notes the claim, without pronouncing on its validity. But Joan Peyser goes into it at some length.[35]

His habit of frequenting brothels, of course, was never mentioned until the biography by Charles Schwartz appeared. Schwartz related an incident in Paris in which Jules Glaenzer and Buddy De Sylva secretly observed Gershwin performing sex with a prostitute in a brothel; his performance they found surprisingly perfunctory; but to their surprise, he bragged about his prowess.[36] Jablonski takes note of this alleged incident but casts doubt on the source (by the time Glaenzer related it to Schwartz, Glaenzer was a very old man). Peyser believes that Gershwin wanted always to project the image of a great lover; this incident suggested to Peyser that perhaps his potency, so pleasurable to him at the age of nine [according to Goldberg], had started to decline about the same time he began to suffer his stomach pains (speculation refuted by the testimony of Goddard and Swift).

Gershwin apparently held totally unrealistic standards for women that no one could match. He craved and searched for an ideal; but women who approached his ideal were safely married (e.g., Kay Swift and Paulette Goddard). Gershwin supposedly believed that "failure in marriage is not be to debited to the institution so much as to the competence of the partners."[37] Edward Jablonski concludes: "Gershwin loved and needed the companionship, but marriage seemed to him a rather drastic step—and he idealized it."[38] Alan Kendall, in his biography, agreed. He wrote that as Gershwin moved into more sophisticated society, he met many women who threw themselves at him "yet he never seemed to take advantage of their offers, nor to find the right sort of partner with whom he felt able to settle down. . . . This is often a problem of Jewish men whose mothers have filled the traditional matriarchal role. They find it extremely difficult to form a relationship with a woman, no matter how much they may wish to do so."[39]

His idealization of marriage probably explains his relationship with Kay Swift. She was the one woman whom he loved and could have married before he left for Hollywood. All his biographers accept the genuineness of an intimate Swift-Gershwin romance. Jablonski wrote that she brought to the relationship her "native wit, practical intelligence, worldly sophistication, sensitivity, as well as musically retentive mind, a keen ear, and background of [musical] study." David Ewen wrote that Gershwin came as close to being "completely in love with her as he did with any woman, and he remained devoted to her longer than to any."[40] Jablonski more or less agreed.

Decades later she confided in Michael Feinstein (Ira's musical secretary) that George was "the best lover she ever had."[41] Swift was divorced in 1934, probably in hopes of marrying George. George's mother was cool, if not opposed, because Kay was not Jewish and was divorced. Swift's oldest daughter also opposed her mother's relationship. Swift later acknowledged this. Gershwin tried to win over her children, but he was clumsy with children and his efforts did not work. Ira claimed George's relationship with Kay was hampered by his reluctance to take on the responsibility for her children. It seems also likely that he was put off by their rejection. Near the end of his life he confessed to his valet that he had made a "terrible mistake" in leaving Kay Swift. When interviewed for a 1987 television program she commented that during George's stay in Hollywood they were both "miserable." She told her granddaughter, Katharine Weber, that had George lived she imagined that indeed they would have been married, "but probably also would have been divorced."[42]

This entire relationship is somewhat disturbing, and does not speak well for Gershwin. Both of them seemed to have had a callous disregard for the effects of their long public affair on Kay Swift's marriage or on her children. Moreover, once her marriage was dissolved, Gershwin avoided any commitment to marriage. Jimmy Warburg said that when he confronted Gershwin and told him to go ahead and marry Kay "the composer fled in panic from his office." This statement comes from Jimmy Warburg's third wife, and is probably imaginary. There is no other evidence of such a Gershwin-Warburg confrontation.[43]

His involvement with Swift led him to became interested in finding the "real" Gershwin. She recommended that he see a therapist. Accordingly he enlisted as a patient of her psychoanalyst, Gregory Zilboorg, a Russian émigré who had fled the Bolshevik Revolution. He remained an "old-fashioned" socialist, according to Lillian Hellman, who was one of his patients. S.N. Behrman disliked him and considered him "boorish," but admitted that everyone was in therapy. Frances Gershwin said that George went to Zilboorg because he wanted to "improve himself." He felt "inadequate" because of his lack of education.[44] Oscar Levant lumped George's psychoanalysis with his turn toward Schillinger for musical instruction. In both cases, Levant saw a reflection of George's curiosity about himself, to find out about himself "scientifically, rather than emotionally." According to Levant his sessions proved him to be "enthusiastically unneurotic."

David Ewen apparently consulted Zilboorg when he wrote his biography of Gershwin. He wrote that Gershwin sought Zilboorg after failing to find any relief from what he called his "composer's stomach." Zilboorg (not surprisingly) told Ewen that he had diagnosed a neurosis, without specifying its manifestation or its cause.[45] Ewen concluded that Zilboorg helped Gershwin by making him somewhat less self-centered and inhibited. Charles Schwartz insisted that in Zilboorg Gershwin found someone who was exceptional on many levels, aside from his "outstanding" credentials as a psychiatrist and analyst. According to Schwartz, during the year or so that Gershwin was Zilboorg's patient, their relationship was an exceptionally good one: besides Gershwin's respect for Zilboorg's professional skills, there were many areas of common interest because of the psychiatrist's broad background in art and related fields: "Gershwin came to lean quite heavily on Zilboorg for psychological support."[46] Although he stopped seeing Zilboorg after their unpleasant Mexican outing, they remained friendly, according to Schwartz, who noted, however, that Gershwin complained to friends that he was not getting much out of his analysis. It cost him $3,280 for 1935.

Schwartz's conclusions are unconvincing. He was obviously badly biased by the testimony of Zilboorg's wife, whom he sought out. She insisted that Zilboorg had never divulged any of Gershwin's analysis and had behaved ethically throughout. This is simply not true. According to Kay Swift, Zilboorg discussed Gershwin's analysis with her! Indeed, Zilboorg seems to have discussed all of his patients' analyses with everyone. Moreover, Zilboorg had sexual relations with Kay Swift, according to Kay Swift's granddaughter.[47]

For Gershwin the Zilboorg episode is truly bizarre. Zilboorg was recommended to Kay Swift by her sister-in-law Bettina Warburg, a trained psychoanalyst. At one point Zilboorg was treating both Kay and Jimmy Warburg, as well as Kay's lover, George Gershwin, and Jimmy and Kay's cousin, Eddie Warburg (who continued for many years), and, briefly, one of Kay's daughters. In Mexico, Zilboorg had separate sessions with Eddie, George, and a third friend, then gathered them together to reveal and discuss their analyses! Zilboorg is described by Kay Swift's granddaughter as "a notorious psychoanalyst who was eventually forced out of practice for his unorthodox and manipulative methods, was part Renaissance man and part Svengali."[48] He threatened Kay Swift with publicly exposing the content of hers and George's analyses if they married. His behavior finally led to charges against him for unethical behavior and a censure by his professional colleagues.

Perhaps there was a legitimate need for analysis. George's letters do reveal a restlessness and loneliness. Joan Peyser sees a darker, self-destructive motive; in selecting Zilboorg Gershwin added to the malevolent circle around him— Leonore, Levant, and Schillinger.[49] Kay Swift later admitted to Edward Jablonski that her recommendation to Gershwin was a "mistake." One can only wonder how much harm his treatment did to Gershwin. In his biography Alan Kendall comments that analysis can be "very destructive" for some, and perhaps Gershwin "saw the implicit danger to his talents," and withdrew. "Or his instinct for self-preservation asserted itself in time."[50]

To sum up: The image of the sweet, unassuming, indeed modest man, simple, naive, as pictured by his partisans is not wrong, but it is incomplete. It applies mainly to the younger man. After he suffered setbacks on Broadway (*Pardon My English*) and encountered diminished enthusiasm in the concert hall (the *Second Rhapsody*), followed by the relative failure of *Porgy and Bess*, Gershwin seems to have become gloomier, taking a more melancholy view of life and of his own situation. It was at this point that he stopped his therapy, decided to defer marriage with Kay Swift, and made arrangements to leave for Hollywood. As it turned out he regretted his decision to break with Kay Swift and was frustrated and disenchanted with Hollywood. He died determined to return to the safety of New York.

There was always a darker shadow, for he was fundamentally far more complex than his public persona. Rouben Mamoulian commented that "George did not live easily. He was a complicated, nervous product of our age. There was in him an intricate and restless combination of intellectual and emotional forces. Conflicting impulses clashed within him and played havoc."[51]

Kitty Carlisle (who later married Moss Hart) also suggested a picture of Gershwin in the mid-1930s that was different from the popular image:

> People felt very protective about him. Why I don't know. He was successful. He was good looking, women adored him, he had money. He had everything, but yet there was something vulnerable, childlike. He needed approval. Yes, maybe that's it. And you felt it.[52]

Perhaps Kay Swift caught the essence of Gershwin better than his critics and analysts: beneath his confident, bluff exterior, there was buried a "sad Russian."

NOTES

1. Edward Jablonski, ed., *Gershwin Remembered* (Portland, OR: Amadeus Press, 1992), pp. 51, 87.

2. Robert Kimball and Alfred Simon, *The Gershwins* (New York: Bonanza Books, 1963), pp. 67–68.

3. Rouben Mamoulian quoted in *George Gershwin*, ed. Merle Armitage (New York: Longmans, Green, 1938), p. 56.

4. Isaac Goldberg (supplemented by Edith Garson), *George Gershwin: A Study in American Music* (New York: Frederick Ungar Publishing, 1958), p. 9.

5. Nanette Kuttner in Armitage, *George Gershwin*, p. 237.

6. Harold Arlen quoted in Jablonski, *Gershwin Remembered*, p. 76.

7. Osbert Sitwell quoted in Jablonski, *Gershwin Remembered*, p. 59.

8. Albert Heinik Sendrey, "Tennis Game," in Armitage, *George Gershwin*, pp. 102–12.

9. Nanette Kuttner in Armitage, *George Gershwin*, p. 238.

10. John Ardoin, "An Interview with Michael Tilson Thomas." from the Internet series Great Performers: Carnegie Hall, Meet the Artists (www.pbs.org/wnet).

11. Joan Peyser, *The Memory of All That* (New York: Simon and Schuster, 1993), p. 156.

12. Oscar Levant, *A Smattering of Ignorance* (New York: Doubleday, 1940), p. 171.

13. Arlen quoted in Jablonski, *Gershwin Remembered*, p. 75.

14. Kimball and Simon, *The Gershwins*, p. 66.

15. Ibid., p. 155.

16. *New York Times*, December 17, 1935; Edward Jablonski and Lawrence D. Stewart, *The Gershwin Years* (New York: Doubleday & Company, 1958), p. 244.

17. Merle Armitage, *George Gershwin, Man and Legend* (New York: Duell, Sloan and Pierce, 1958), p. 63.

18. Henry Botkin, "Painter and Collector," in Armitage, *George Gershwin*, p. 139.

19. Color reproductions of some of his paintings are included in Kimball and Simon, *The Gershwins*, beginning on p. 154.

20. Armitage's article in *George Gershwin*, the collection he edited, p. 14.

21. Botkin in Armitage, *George Gershwin*, p. 139.

22. Noguchi, quoted in Armitage, *George Gershwin*, p. 210.

23. Goldberg, *George Gershwin*, p. 10.

24. Alexander Woollcott excerpt from "George the Ingenuous," *Cosmopolitan*, November 1933, quoted in Jablonski, *Gershwin Remembered*, p. 44.

25. Kay Swift, quoted in Jablonski, *Gershwin Remembered*, p. 82.

26. Charles Schwartz, *Gershwin: His Life and Music* (New York: Da Capo, 1979), p. 110.

27. Arthur Schwartz, quoted in Jablonski, *Gershwin Remembered*, pp. 80–81.

28. Quoted in Peyser, *The Memory of All That*, p. 216.

29. Jablonski and Stewart, *The Gershwin Years*, p. 226.

30. Alexander Steinart, "Porgy and Bess and Gershwin," in Armitage, *George Gershwin*, p. 45.

31. Goldberg, *George Gershwin*, p. 19.

32. Peyser, *The Memory of All That*, quoting Al Hirschfeld, p. 90.

33. Peyser, *The Memory of All That*, p. 157.

34. Rosamond Walling remarks in Kimball and Simon, *The Gershwins*, p. 138; Kitty Carlisle Hart notes that Gershwin's "proposals" were part of his style, just as were the special waltzes he kept on his piano composed for each new girl friend. She too believed that George did not behave as if he really needed the recipients of his proposals. *Kitty* (New York: St. Martin's Press, 1988), p. 69.

35. Peyser, *The Memory of All That*, p. 157.

36. Schwartz, *George Gershwin*, pp. 51–52.

37. Goldberg, *George Gershwin*, p. 20.

38. Jablonski, *Gershwin*, p. 298.

39. Alan Kendall, *George Gershwin* (New York: Universe Books, 1987), p. 35.

40. Ewen, *George Gershwin: His Journey to Greatness*, 2nd enlarged ed. (New York: The Ungar Publishing Company, 1970), p. 144.

41. Michael Feinstein, *Nice Work if You Can Get It* (New York: Hyperion, 1995), p. 65.

42. Katharine Weber, "The Memory of All That," in *A Few Thousand Words about Love*, ed. Mickey Pearlman (New York: St. Martin's Press, 1998), p. 24. Kay Swift remarried twice, and continued writing music. She died in January 1993.

43. Ron Chernow, *The Warburgs* (New York: Vintage Books, 1994), p. 333.

44. Peyser, *The Memory of All That*, p. 218.

45. One of Zilboorg's patients claimed that Zilboorg said that Gershwin's only "romance was with his enema bag." This disgusting statement, if true, is evidence that Zilboorg discussed his analysis with others.

46. Schwartz, *George Gershwin*, p. 273.

47. Peyser, *The Memory of All That*, pp. 216–30, 263.

48. Zilboorg was both brilliant and malevolent. On the one hand, he published extensively under such esoteric titles as "Mind, Medicine and Man" (1943); "The Medical Man and the Witch in the Renaissance" (1935). On the other hand, his outrageous ethics led to his downfall.

49. Peyser, *The Memory of All That*, p. 217.

50. Kendall, *George Gershwin*, pp. 136–37.

51. Mamoulian quoted in Jablonski, *Gershwin Remembered*, p. 71.

52. Kitty Carlisle Hart quoted in Kimball and Simon, *The Gershwins*, p. 168.

Chapter 13

Keeping the Flame

When George Gershwin died the news of his death was featured on the front page of the July 12 *New York Times*: GEORGE GERSHWIN, COMPOSER, IS DEAD, and the subhead read "Master of Jazz Succumbs." He was described as a "composer of his generation, and a child of the twenties." Eulogies would stress two themes: that Gershwin was a "bridge" between the world of jazz and the concert hall, and that he was the voice of America.

His memorial services were huge gatherings of notables. In New York, the honorary pallbearers included W.C. Handy, Paul Whiteman, Ferde Grofé, Max Dreyfus, George M. Cohan, and former mayor Jimmy Walker. In attendance were Mayor Fiorello La Guardia and Governor Herbert Lehman. In California the honorary committee included Jerome Kern, Rodgers and Hart, Arnold Schoenberg, Ernst Toch, Irving Berlin, and Fred Astaire. At that memorial service Oscar Hammerstein II read a eulogy that began:

> Our friend wrote music
> and in that mould he created
> Gaiety and sweetness and beauty.[1]

In New York, several thousand people gathered for the service at Temple Emman-u-El on Fifth Avenue. The eulogy was delivered by Rabbi Samuel Wise, who described Gershwin as the "singer of songs of the American soul." The *New York Times'* memorial editorial (July 13) asserted, "As a composer he bridged the gap between the cultured and uncultured music lovers of the nation as no one had done before him." In doing so, Gershwin became a "figure of great and even lasting importance in our national music."

In his eulogy titled "Hail and Farewell" for the *New York Times* (July 18), Olin Downes went further: "George Gershwin had a unique position in American music." Downes explained that Gershwin proved that significant creation was possible in the terms of [the] popular national idiom [jazz]." Gershwin was the "connecting link" between the "serious" and "popular" composers of America. His accomplishments reflected his natural talents as well as the conditions of his times—the growth of urban life at the expense of the agricultural environment of early America, as well as the "Babylonic epoch when every body was so gay and everything so flush and amusing." Musically speaking Gershwin talked "the language that his countrymen and generation knew." It was Gershwin who took his generation to an appreciation of "good" music. Even Downes, however, could not resist the chance to take a mild crack: "Doubtless the author of the 'Rhapsody in Blue' was overrated," but he went on to write that the composer of the *Rhapsody* had a "strong and lasting influence for the good of American composers."

Mammoth memorial concerts soon followed. On August 9, 1937, at Lewisohn Stadium a record audience of over 20,000 turned out. It was the largest in the history of that stadium (only a year earlier Gershwin had made his final appearance to a disappointing crowd). This time the program was staggering. A medley from *Of Thee I Sing*; the *Concerto in F*, played by Harry Kaufman with the New York Philharmonic conducted by Alexander Smallens. There was a selection from *Porgy and Bess* sung by original cast members Anne Brown, Todd Duncan, and Ruby Elzy. After intermission came a medley from *Strike Up the Band*, and then *An American in Paris*, followed by Ethel Merman singing "The Man I Love" and "They Can't Take That Away from Me," and ending with her great triumph from *Girl Crazy*, "I Got Rhythm." Finally came *Rhapsody in Blue*, "a fitting conclusion to an altogether fitting tribute," according to the review in the *New York Times* (August 10, 1937). That review concluded that "the evening was one of unremitting pleasure," but ended with a poignant commentary on the occasion: "one left the stadium thinking how little this harassed world could afford to lose a voice of such captivating esprit, such natural wit, such abundant potentiality."

Even Lawrence Gilman relented and softened his criticism. In notes for the concert program he wrote that Gershwin's achievement was "remarkable." He had developed a new kind of music of "unforgettable gusto, skill and fascination." *Variety* concluded that the concert was a real triumph, and it proved "the amazing versatility of the boy from Brooklyn, who once thought it was sissified to play the piano." In Hollywood there was a memorial concert on September 9. Oscar Levant played the *Concerto in F*, and Jose Iturbi played the *Rhapsody*.

His music flourished. His last movie, *The Goldwyn Follies*, was finally released the following spring. The movie got poor reviews, but not the music. The major song, "Love Walked In," made it to the radio Hit Parade where it became the number-one song.

Ironically it was Hollywood, which Gershwin had come to dislike, that perpetuated his music, at least for a time. Arthur Freed, the songwriter-turned-musical-czar at MGM, produced two movies that simply borrowed the title of

Gershwin shows. First came *Strike Up the Band* with Judy Garland and Mickey Rooney. The story had nothing to do with the original Broadway show and only the title song was used. *Lady Be Good!* became a musical comedy starring Robert Young and Ann Sothern playing two feuding songwriters. Again, it had nothing to do with the Broadway original, but used more Gershwin, including "Fascinating Rhythm," and "So Am I." The hit of that movie was an interpolated song by Kern and Hammerstein, "The Last Time I Saw Paris," sung by Dinah Shore, which won the Academy Award. *Broadway Rhythm* featured Lena Horne singing "Somebody Loves Me." The *Ziegfeld Follies* revived the humorous "Babbitt and the Bromide," deadpanned by Fred Astaire and Gene Kelly. Soon thereafter Freed returned to Mickey and Judy for a version of *Girl Crazy*; the plot loosely resembled the old Broadway show and most of the Gershwin music was revived, including two elaborate production numbers by Busby Berkeley: "Fascinating Rhythm" and "I Got Rhythm" in a lengthy grand finale sung by Judy Garland, accompanied by a huge chorus and an expanded orchestra led by Tommy Dorsey.[2]

Hollywood was not quite finished with George Gershwin. Next came his biography on film, appropriately titled *Rhapsody in Blue*. The script went through several versions, including one by Ira and an early one by Clifford Odets, who saw the film as an opportunity to tell the story of American Jews. Ira Gershwin was not taken with this idea, and settled for a more mundane story written by his friend Sonya Levien, who knew the Gershwins from their stay in Hollywood in 1930. It was adapted by Howard Koch and Elliot Paul. John Garfield was a candidate for the lead, but George was finally portrayed by Robert Alda. George's girlfriends were invented: Julie Adams (played by Joan Leslie), a singer who introduced some of his songs, and Christine Gilbert (portrayed by Alexis Smith), a sophisticated, expatriate artist who encouraged his serious side. Both women abandoned him, realizing that he was completely dedicated to his music. Also fictionalized was his old music teacher "Professor Frank" who died in bed listening to Whiteman's *Rhapsody in Blue* concert. Oscar Levant played himself.

The film included many Gershwin songs: Al Jolson sang "Swanee," and there were cameo appearances by Paul Whiteman and George White, as well as scenes from *Blue Monday*. Levant was puzzled by the attention to *Blue Monday*. The producers explained that they wanted to show a Gershwin failure to emphasize his later successes. The film made fun of Morris Gershwin, who judged the value of George's compositions by their length, which he measured with his pocket watch.

The movie was released in 1945 in black and white to moderately good reviews. Later, one Gershwin biographer found it an inaccurate and highly romantic conception. On the other hand, the film continued the emphasis on Gershwin's Americanness. The character portraying the mythical Professor Frank advises him to become an American voice. Max Dreyfus, played by Charles Coburn, comments that George writes "of America, for Americans," and the sophisticated "Christine Gilbert" says that George is "America personified." The movie was filmed and released during World War II, and Warner Brothers obviously wanted to give it a patriotic emphasis.[3]

Ira was devastated by his brother's death. He never fully recovered. For a time he went into virtual seclusion. He wrote some songs with Jerome Kern, but not until 1940 did he really emerge when he agreed to write the lyrics for a new Broadway show by Moss Hart and Kurt Weill, *Lady in the Dark*. In effect, his main occupation became the self-appointed keeper of the flame. George left no will, so his mother inherited his estate. His assets were valued at $341,089; the residual value of George's compositions valued at $50,125. The New York tax court, not noted for its musical acumen, assessed *Rhapsody in Blue* at $20,000, *An American in Paris* at $5,000, and the *Concerto in F* at $1,750. His cash and insurance came to $228,811 offset by debts of $38,810.

George's collection of songs, books, unpublished manuscripts, and various sketches were kept by Ira, who began to organize an archive. His home took on the air of a shrine (though not accessible to outsiders), according to Michael Feinstein who was Ira's assistant for several years. Ira kept a careful watch over his brother's legacy, using his influence to block new productions or radical revisions he did not like. Ira was quite sedentary when Feinstein worked for him before he died in 1984. When recalling his association with his brother, the stories always seemed to revitalize him. Yet he felt guilty that he had survived and George had not, and his feelings of guilt apparently increased as he grew older. Once he privately told Feinstein he believed he saw the apparition of George sitting in his bedroom and smiling.

With the help of Kay Swift, who knew George's music better than anyone, Ira constructed some songs with new lyrics based on unused melodies. One of them was used as a theme song for the New York World's Fair. Ira and Kay Swift used some others for the score of a new movie, *The Shocking Miss Pilgrim*, set in the 1870s and starring Betty Grable and Dick Haymes. This experiment with resurrected Gershwin songs was not very successful. There were some clever new songs—"Aren't You Kind of Glad We Did," an unusually saucy lyric for Ira. "Back Bay Polka" was a cute take-off on self-righteous Bostonian primness. Only one song made any impact: that was the love song, "For You, For Me, For Evermore."

It is puzzling why Ira resorted to this particular project. Probably his determination to keep the memory of his brother alive influenced his judgment. Even more disconcerting was a second movie, *Kiss Me Stupid*, also with posthumous Gershwin songs. Apparently Ira did it as a favor for the producer Billy Wilder. It too was unsuccessful. Ira wrote Kay Swift, "Too bad about 'Kiss Me Stupid.' The songs never had a chance." Ira himself, however, compiled a book of some of his lyrics with introductory comments on each entry, published in 1959 as *Lyrics on Several Occasions*. It is an invaluable guide to how he and his brother worked together to develop many of their more famous songs, as well as some lesser-known ones.

A much more successful movie project soon followed. Arthur Freed asked Ira if he would sell the title of *An American in Paris* for a movie he was contemplating for Gene Kelly. Ira agreed if the film used Gershwin music. Freed eagerly accepted. The successful lyricist of *Brigadoon*, Alan Jay Lerner, was engaged to write the screen play, and Kelly choreographed a new dance routine for the ballet of *An American in Paris*, which was reorchestrated under Ira's supervision. More than ten older songs were also used, and Ira wrote some new lyrics. Inevitably, Oscar Levant was recruited for a part; he eventually played the *Concerto in F* in an amusing montage in which he was the soloist, the conductor, and a member of the audience. The movie was a major hit. It revived the beautiful "Love Is Here to Stay," for Gene Kelly and Leslie Caron. Also outstanding was a production number for George Guetary singing "I'll Build a Stairway to Paradise." Lerner received an Academy Award as did the picture itself.

It was ironic that Gershwin's music was being featured more in Hollywood than on Broadway. Eventually, however, writers went to work to create his biography. First came a collection of reminiscences, anecdotes, and commentary by a wide variety of Gershwin's friends, colleagues, and critics. A book was arranged and edited by Gershwin's newfound friend in California, Merle Armitage. He was an impresario who had promoted the first all-Gershwin concert in February 1937 in Hollywood (it was at this concert that Gershwin first faltered, a symptom of his fatal illness). Armitage was an authority on art, and he and George had formed a close bond. The Armitage collection of memories published in 1938 was entitled simply *George Gershwin*. The articles included Gershwin's Broadway colleagues—Berlin, Arlen, Kern, Grofé, Whiteman, and two reprints of articles by Gershwin. Perhaps the most significant was a brief essay from Arnold Schoenberg. The composer was a friend of Gershwin's in Hollywood. While writing a tribute, Schoenberg took a few cuts at the critics:

Many musicians do not consider George Gershwin a serious composer. But they should understand that, serious or not, he is a composer—that is, a man who lives in music, expresses everything, serious or not, sound or superficial, by means of music, because it is his native language. . . . It seems to me beyond doubt that Gershwin was an innovator. What he has done with rhythm, harmony and melody is not merely style. It is fundamentally different from the mannerism of many a serious composer.[4]

The composer George Anthiel contributed a tribute to the Armitage collection. He too was disdainful of Gershwin's critics for their ill manners and ignorance, which had not changed since George's death.[5]

A full-scale biography of Gershwin was an obvious target. The first outing was a children's biography by David Ewen. Even in that category it was pathetic, laced with completely imaginary conversations and dialogue. Ewen was indefatigable, however, and he was soon into a major biography. He had known

George and Ira reasonably well, and received some encouragement and assistance from Ira. Titled *A Journey to Greatness: The Life and Music of George Gershwin*, it was an informative and sympathetic treatment. Written in 1956, the introductory chapter noted that Gershwin's music was heard "more often and in more places than it was two decades ago." As befitting the title, Gershwin's life was portrayed as a journey: "One of the most impressive and singularly significant facts about Gershwin is the way he progressed toward a single goal from his boyhood on. He sought from the very first to achieve artistic validity as a composer through popular music." The music critic Irving Kolodin found Ewen's book too limited: "What is lacking, however, is a sense of the man seen whole as well as admiringly." More important, Kolodin revived the old controversy about Gershwin and jazz.

> Perhaps what is fundamentally disturbing about Ewen's view of Gershwin, at this point, is the repeated references to him as a "composer of jazz," one who made jazz respectable, who—in Walter Damrosch's too pithy phrase—"took jazz out of the kitchen." It is painful to repeat it again, but the notion of Gershwin as composer of jazz is essentially false. . . . It was Gershwin's function to occupy a middle ground, between formal and informal music rather than "classical and popular."[6]

Ira Gershwin, commenting in private in a letter about Ewen's biography, found him "no great stylist, but the most comprehensive thus far."

For some years it stood as the "definitive" work alongside Isaac Goldberg's older biography. Ewen, however, failed to acknowledge Goldberg's pathbreaking work, from which he borrowed large amounts of information.

Shortly after Ewen's publication, two other authorities collaborated on a new biography of both George and Ira, entitled *The Gershwin Years* (1958). It included much that was new, especially in several revised editions. The authors were Edward Jablonski, a writer and Gershwin enthusiast, and Lawrence D. Stewart, who had worked with Ira as an assistant. Their book was heavily illustrated and used extensive photographs, many by Gershwin himself; it also used reproductions of original letters and pages from his music manuscripts. One reviewer noted that while too loose to be a full-scale biography, it was a "thoroughly delightful book that gives a fascinating and comprehensive picture of the era suggested by its title." The authors too were highly sympathetic and acknowledged their great debt to Ira. It was disdainful of Ewen's earlier biography, which was dismissed as "not serious," but came to largely the same conclusion as Ewen: "The enduring significance of this man is felt in the blood and felt along the heart when his music is played."[7]

One of the authors, Edward Jablonski, was on his way to becoming the definitive authority on Gershwin. On his own, without any collaborators, he wrote a "concise" biography of George Gershwin, published in 1962, with an introduction by Harold Arlen.

These biographical tributes to Gershwin were interrupted by a critical, icon-oclastic and revisionist biography by Charles Schwartz, entitled *Gershwin: His Life and Times* (1973). It included an introduction—"An Appreciation"—by Leonard Bernstein, who lauded Gershwin, but not without noting his deficiencies: "What's important is not what's wrong with the *Rhapsody*, but what's right with it." Schwartz's purpose, he wrote, was to bring into better focus Gershwin's life and music. Bernstein stressed that despite all that had been written about him, "there are many aspects of his life and work that are practically unknown." As Virgil Thomson noted in the blurb for the book jacket, Schwartz "tells all."

Schwartz did indeed probe into some dark corners, such as Gershwin's sex life, his psychotherapy, and his overbearing ego. Schwartz's service was in forcing other biographers to deal with facets of Gershwin heretofore covered over. Subsequent writers found it necessary either to acknowledge or refute Schwartz's interpretations. Schwartz's appendix analyzing Gershwin's music strains to place Gershwin in a Jewish tradition of musical composition. Ira complained that its distortions concerning the strained relations between him and his mother were "willful."

Two new authors did not bother with Schwartz. Robert Kimball was (and is) a noted analyst, editor, and archivist of lyrics and his co-author Alfred Simon had worked as a rehearsal pianist for Gershwin. They produced a beautifully illustrated coffee-table book, *The Gershwins* (1973), with an introduction by Richard Rodgers. It is a valuable collection with reminiscences by many colleagues, as well Rodgers' own appreciation and a very thorough introduction by the music critic John S. Wilson. One of the volume's most appealing features was a center folio of color photographs of George Gershwin's paintings, including his "Self Portrait in Checkered Sweater," a line drawing of his studio in Folly Beach, where he gathered material for *Porgy and Bess*, a grim portrait of his mother, paintings of Lee Gershwin, Emily Strunsky, his grandfather, and a self-portrait in Opera Hat (not included in the color folio are his striking portraits of Arnold Schoenberg or Jerome Kern, among his last work).

The upshot was that a great deal of information about George Gershwin was forthcoming. It was left to Edward Jablonski again to tie it all together in a "definitive" biography, *Gershwin: A Biography*, published by Simon and Schuster in late 1987. Over four hundred pages were stuffed with almost everything anyone could want to know about George Gershwin (Jablonski's bibliography omits Schwartz's book).[8] In addition to being overwhelmingly sympathetic, its weakness is the sparse analysis of Gershwin's music. In his blurb for the book jacket Michael Feinstein, the popular entertainer who had been Ira Gershwin's musical secretary, wrote: "The only book on Gershwin to own." Well, not quite.

By far the most critical and unsympathetic biography was written by Joan Peyser. For several years (1977–1984) she was the editor of *The Musical Quarterly*. She was the biographer of Leonard Bernstein and the composer/conductor Pierre Boulez. She turned to Gershwin because she found that much that had

been written about him was channelled in one direction by the influence of
Leonore Gershwin, who turned a "complex man into a two-dimensional figure."
Peyser was determined to unearth new information about Gershwin and she
succeeded, but only in part. In particular, she located a young man who claimed
to be George Gershwin's illegitimate son, but whose claim was vehemently
denied by the Gershwin family. She also located George's mother's family (Kate
Wolpin); she conducted interviews with several women acquaintances of Gershwin who kept letters and diaries.

Much of her book, however, is burdened with "rancid gossip" and "psycho-
babble" according to the *Kirkus Review* (March 15, 1993). Although other reviews were quite critical, her book nevertheless turned a corner.[9] Subsequent
writings about Gershwin had to take into account her claims. Two books about
Gershwin, Rodney Greenberg's *George Gershwin* (1978) and Alan Kendall's
George Gershwin (1987), adopted her conclusions about the illegitimate Alan
Gershwin. Gershwin loyalists, like Jablonski, of course sharply dissented.[10]

What finally came into focus was indeed a complex man, with human frailties
and failings. What did not come into focus was the wellspring of his creativity.
None of his biographers could go beyond the early conclusions that he was
natural genius, an "irrepressible melodist." Deena Rosenberg's biography *Fascinating Rhythm* (1991), provided a detailed musical analysis covering most of
the major songs; her book, written with Ira's help, was reviewed as a "pleasure,
intriguing and insightful, casting new light on the Gershwin genius." In the
reissue as a paperback, she emphasized Gershwin's close ties to the urban life
of New York.

The illustrious critic Henry Pleasants took note of the fact that the biographies
up to that time (1974) contributed to an understanding of the personal phenomenon, but all were more "intimately concerned with the personality than the
music." On the seventy-fifth anniversary of Gershwin's birth, Pleasants made
an interesting comparison with Beethoven. Just as no earlier composer had been
as German as Beethoven, no other composer was "as utterly American as Gershwin."[11]

The various revelations about his life and times did not affect the appreciation
of his music. At first, however, there were few revivals of his musicals, mainly
because they were too badly dated for modern audiences, and several of the
originals had succeeded mainly because of the stars (the Astaires and Gertrude
Lawrence). Finally, Broadway caught on: If not the old books, then why not
use the music in a new setting? Two shows resulted. *My One and Only* starring
Tommy Tune and Twiggy used the music from *Funny Face*. The new book was
by Peter Stone and Timothy S. Mayer, the musical "concept" was by Wally
Harper, with orchestrations by Michael Gibson.

Michael Feinstein was Ira's musical representative as the show took shape.
Feinstein objected to the distortion of the original score; for example, he was
disturbed by the orchestration of " 'S Wonderful," which featured a ragtime
counterpoint to the melody. On this and several other conflicts with the pro-

ducers and the stars, Ira capitulated, and Lee Gershwin became indignant over Feinstein's effort to preserve the authenticity of the score. The new score did feature several Gershwin songs that were seldom heard—"I Can't Be Bothered Now," from *Damsel in Distress* and "Blah, Blah, Blah," from the movie *Delicious*. Later in the production there was a show-stopping dance by Tommy Tune and Honi Coles to "Sweet and Low Down," from *Tip Toes*. Near the end came a rousing version of "Kickin' the Clouds Away."

After considerable turmoil—a rewritten book, new orchestrations, and considerable doctoring by many including Mike Nichols—the show finally opened at the St. James theater in May 1983 to good reviews—"a happy spin down memory lane," according to Frank Rich's review in the *New York Times*. It was billed as "The New GERSHWIN Musical." The producers claimed that Ira made significant contributions, but Feinstein commented that this was "bull." Nevertheless, when Feinstein played for Ira a recorded version of the entire show's opening night in Boston, Ira was quite moved by the enthusiastic reception, which made him "extremely happy." The show played for over seven hundred performances—far longer than any Gershwin show.

There were several re-creations of older shows that used the original book and orchestrations or careful reconstructions. But *Lady Be Good!*, for example, failed to arouse much enthusiasm, not because of the music, but because the plots were simply too outdated. Not so with a substantially altered Broadway remake of *Girl Crazy* entitled *Crazy for You*. With stunning new choreography by Susan Stroman and loaded with Gershwin's music it was highly successful (February 1992). It too was billed as "The new GERSHWIN Musical Comedy." There were twenty-three musical numbers, including the quite rare "The Real American Folk Song is a Rag," and two virtually unknown songs, "Tonight's the Night" and "What Causes That?" The book was by Ken Ludwig, who commented that the original book for *Girl Crazy* was "terrible," and had to be thrown out completely. The stars were Harry Groener and Jodi Benson. The critic Frank Rich wrote (*New York Times*, February 20, 1992) that the exact moment when Broadway finally rose up to grab the musical back from the British, was when *Crazy for You* "uncorked the American musical classic blend of music, laughter, dancing, sentiment and showmanship, with a freshness and confidence rarely seen during the 'Cats' decade."

Some of the music for these songs came from a treasure trove of musical manuscripts discovered at a Warner Brothers' warehouse in Secaucus, New Jersey. This cache included songs by Kern and Berlin as well as Gershwin and others. Ira was still alive and amazed at the discoveries; he was able to explain some of the rare items. It was this collection that included songs from *Primrose*, the British show that never reached America; among the manuscripts were orchestrations by George Gershwin, which were proof that even by the time of the *Rhapsody* he had learned to orchestrate.

Perhaps the most impressive musical tribute to Gershwin came from an unusual source, the jazz singer Ella Fitzgerald. With musical arrangements by

Nelson Riddle, she recorded over fifty songs on three compact discs under the title "The George and Ira Gershwin Song Book" (1959). It included mainly the vintage Gershwin hits, but also some unusual songs—"Just Another Rhumba," written for a the movie *Shall We Dance* but not used, and two posthumous songs—"For You, For Me, For Evermore" and "Aren't You Kind of Glad We Did?" from the movie *The Shocking Miss Pilgrim*. Ira liked the recordings including the new swing arrangements by Nelson Riddle. He admired Ella Fitzgerald's clear diction, and did not object to the innovative arrangements backing her up. He even contributed some revised lyrics. Gershwin afficionados were not as impressed. Charles Hamm, for example, thought that Riddle's "neoromantic, 1950s ethic [style]" robbed the songs of "all vitality and rhythmic life." (It is difficult to imagine that Ella Fitzgerald could rob any song of rhythm.)

Finally, due to the largess of Lee Gershwin, new recordings were made of early Gershwin shows based mainly on the original orchestrations, libretto, and lyrics restored under the supervision of Tommy Krasker—*Lady Be Good!*, *Strike Up the Band* (two versions), *Oh, Kay!*, *Girl Crazy*, and even *Pardon My English*. *Of Thee I Sing* and *Let 'Em Eat Cake* had been recorded earlier, and separate recordings were made of *Tip Toes* and *Tell Me More*. So almost the entire Gershwin output for Broadway was available once again in nearly original versions, sung by first-rate casts and played by fine orchestras (omitted thus far is *Funny Face*).[12] The Smithsonian Museum, however, reconstructed *Funny Face* for a long-playing record using some of the contemporary recordings of 1927–29 by Fred and Adele Astaire, but including some non-Gershwin songs from the British production.

Then came the a marvelous triumph, a new recording in 1986 of the entire program of the Paul Whiteman Aeolian Hall concert of 1924.[13] In addition to being an authentic version of the *Rhapsody*, it had the virtue of re-creating the context of the entire concert, which opened with a re-creation of the Original Dixieland Jazz Band's "Livery Stable Blues." The recording did not, however, follow the original program meticulously; a few songs were substituted, but not Gershwin's.[14]

Finally came the centenary of George's birth. One enterprising student of Gershwin's music, Professor Edward Berlin, discovered 531 compact discs of Gershwin's music listed on the Internet.[15] There were endless concerts all around the country. Carnegie Hall opened its season with an all-Gershwin concert conducted by Michael Tilson Thomas. The reviewer for *New York* Magazine, Peter G. Davis, wrote:

> Is *Rhapsody in Blue* jazz or concert music? Are his show tunes fit material for slumming opera singers? Does anyone still care? Symphony orchestras across the land are celebrating Gershwin's centenary with entire programs devoted to his music. *Porgy* is now firmly ensconced in the world's opera houses, and even his Broadway musicals are recorded on CDs with the

same scholarly care bestowed on fourteenth-century motets. Yes, in 1998 Gershwin is right up there with Bach, Beethoven and Brahms.[16]

An invaluable contribution was the electronically regenerated recordings of Gershwin's original piano rolls. The project was organized and supervised by Artis Wodehouse. Here for the first time were Gershwin's technique and creative interpretations from as early as 1916, even though the recordings were reproduced by modern electronic techniques. There have been two volumes (1992–93) including more than a dozen songs, not all by Gershwin. In addition, a similar transcription of his piano rolls was issued, which included some of his songs and many of the songs by other songwriters.[17]

Public reminders of Gershwin took place from time to time. In 1963 there was a tribute to George at Lincoln Center that featured his paintings and photographs. Ira and Lee came from Hollywood. Harold Arlen, Burton Lane, and "Yip" Harburg turned out. In 1968, the Museum of the City of New York staged a major exhibition of paintings, music, his Steinway and Rosewood desk, and various memorabilia, entitled "GERSHWIN: George the Music/Ira the Words." Ira attended, worried that he might have to make a speech. Characteristically, Ira proposed calling the exhibit: "PRINCIPALLY GEORGE (and incidentally Ira)." This was rejected, of course; one of the organizers, his musical secretary Lawrence D. Stewart, commented, "the networking of genius cannot so casually be rated or separated." Mayor Lindsay proclaimed the week as "Gershwin week." Another event occurred in September 1968 on the anniversary of George's birthday. ASCAP presented a plaque at the home in Brooklyn where George was born in 1898. At the ceremonies the glee club of the George Gershwin Junior High sang his songs.

In February 1970 a new ballet, *Who Cares*, choreographed by George Balanchine, was danced by the New York City Ballet. Balanchine took the *Song-Book* as a text and included seventeen songs, orchestrated by Hershey Kay. The music for "Clap Yo' Hands" came from an original Gershwin piano recording. A pas de deux was danced to "The Man I Love." It was an ironic celebration. It was for Balanchine that Gershwin was supposed to score a ballet for the movie *The Goldwyn Follies*, but he died without even starting it. *Who Cares* was a classical ballet in two parts and highly successful. Balanchine graciously attributed the success to the audience's familiarity with the words and music. The Clive Barnes review for the *New York Times* (February 6, 1970), however, was incredibly snide and tone-deaf: Balanchine was attempting to "rehabilitate" music that had become "either the raw melodic material for jazz, or music that has degenerated into Musak noises of elevators and airplanes."

Occasionally, there was an appreciation of Gershwin's music from an unexpected quarter. In 1979, Woody Allen chose Gershwin's works as background music for a film. Titled *Manhattan*, it was Allen's usual highly humorous romp, and the music, performed by either an orchestra or a jazz group, seemed to fit the story perfectly. Gershwin was after all the quintessential Manhattanite. The original soundtrack was recorded by the New York Philharmonic conducted by Zubin Mehta.

Gradually, a scholarly appreciation of Gershwin began to take shape. First came Alec Wilder's major survey of popular songwriters up to the 1950s. Published in 1972, *American Popular Song* was quite forthright in recording Wilder's likes and dislikes. He admitted that he was guilty of heresy in that his enthusiasm for Gershwin often "guttered out" when he closely examined some of Gershwin's sacrosanct melodies. He decided, for example, that Gershwin was not in the same league as Rodgers or Kern as pure melodists. On the other hand, he expected to find that Gershwin's melodies would be heavily dependent on "opulent harmonies," but in fact he found that while Gershwin's harmonic sense was superb, his melodies did have a life of their own. It is best that Wilder speak for himself on some of Gershwin's individual songs:

> *Swanee*—"cheerful and aggressive, but without any distinction."
>
> *I'll Build a Stairway to Paradise*—"stiffly contrived and synthetic."
>
> *Somebody Loves Me*—"[not] a great song; straightforward, little concerned with syncopation, and spare."
>
> *Lady Be Good!*—"monotonous and almost pedestrian."
>
> *That Certain Feeling*—"neat as a pin."
>
> *Someone to Watch Over Me*—"harmonically ingenious."
>
> *Maybe*—"totally satisfying."
>
> *Funny Face*—"as a melody it does little, goes no particular place and makes no particular point."
>
> *Embraceable You*—"a marvelous illustration of simplicity and economy."
>
> *How Long Has This Been Going On?*—"back to [Gershwin's] repeated note device and here it works very well. The main strain harmonically is very fine. . . . The release is very good and is an intrinsic part of the song."

Overall, Wilder pointed out that Gershwin was an aggressive composer, compared to, say, Kern, whom he found to be passive by contrast. This aggressiveness broke through in Gershwin's use of repeated notes. For example, in one of Gershwin's very last songs—"They Can't Take That Away from Me"—Gershwin handles the repeated notes "perfectly," Wilder wrote. While "A Foggy Day" also uses repeated notes, in this case, according to Wilder, "it is a most tender and moving song, a far from aggressive song . . . has a heart break quality, not one note of which I would change." Wilder's evaluation was quite high, but he acknowledged a general reservation: for him, no other writer provoked such disparate reactions as Gershwin, because there seemed to be a "vaguely transparent theater curtain between him and what he sought musically."[18]

Jablonski and Stewart are critical of Wilder for "blinding himself to published scholarship" and making free with facts and occasionally drawing conclusions which established evidence refutes. "This is a casual and not unpleasing book; but it is to be read more for the expressions of Wilder's tastes than for historically accurate accounts of material."[19]

Deena Rosenberg's biography closed the gap in earlier biographies with her extensive musical analysis of his songs. Like Wilder she was quite high on Gershwin as both a melodist and harmonist, but her analysis emphasizes Ira's lyrics, as an example of his "creative mastery over colloquial English," set to "a series of lush, provocative harmonies and a slow but swinging rhythm." She notes that while "Yip" Harburg said that George's music had an infectious sense of play, so too did Ira's whimsical rhymes and devices such as repeating a line but altering its meaning.

One writer noted that while there was a sort of Gershwin renaissance, there was the lingering feeling that Gershwin was closer to becoming a Sousa or Lehar than a "real" composer. For example, while there were seventy-two performances of *An American in Paris* during the 1984-85 season, not one performance by the six largest orchestras was for an adult subscription concert. Gershwin was in danger of being relegated to the pops concerts and youth festivals.[20] An exception was a major program by the Brooklyn Academy of Music of Gershwin's works, conducted by Michael Tilson Thomas; this led to the full-scale recordings of "Of Thee I Sing" and "Let 'Em Eat Cake."

More recently, two new analyses have appeared. Professor Allen Forte of Yale University analyzed the romantic ballads written in the period 1924 through 1950, relying on a method of analysis developed by Herbert Schenker. He included one chapter on Gershwin. Professor Forte analyzes in detail six of Gershwin's better-known ballads, beginning with "Somebody Loves Me," through "Nice Work if You Can Get It." Forte is impressed with Gershwin's innovative abilities. Citing "How Long Has This Been Going On?", he writes that:

> the song is far from common place in many of its features, not least of which is the way it begins. . . . Based upon its harmonic groupings and two note motives, [is a] the very Gershwin-like melody of the chorus. . . . It is difficult to imagine a melodic confirmation more unlike that of the model ballad of the time, most clearly exemplified in many of those composed by Jerome Kern.[21]

Steven E. Gilbert, using roughly the same methodology as Forte, devoted his entire book to Gershwin: *The Music of Gershwin* (1995). Gilbert notes that a "just appraisal" of Gershwin has been difficult because American music has been split between "high" and "low" culture. As an immigrant's son having first made his reputation as a Broadway songwriter, Gershwin had difficulty finding a niche in the world of "serious" music. In Gilbert's view, therefore, Gershwin's songs had yet to be studied seriously; hence his book. Perhaps Gilbert's view is summed up in the opening line of his second chapter—"nobody dislikes a Gershwin tune."[22]

In short, Gershwin's Broadway songs, which had been taken for granted and in many cases forgotten along with the shows that encased them, have undergone a positive reevaluation. Gershwin's major songs have not faded, of course, but under the scrutiny of technical analysis they gain in stature.[23]

This same process of reexamination was applied to *Porgy and Bess*. It too was the subject of new analytical work, the result of which has been to enhance its stature as well. Hollis Alpert wrote an exhaustive history of the opera, not only the original, but its subsequent productions through the performances at the Metropolitan. His survey included the various foreign productions, including the unprecedented production in Leningrad and Moscow for Soviet audiences. In an amusing aside, Alpert notes a production in Berlin in which the picnickers on Kittiwah Island were wearing Reeboks; in this same production a man dressed as Abraham Lincoln was sitting in the box at stage left and behind him were two mannequins dressed in a Union and Confederate uniform![24]

Professor Joseph Swain, in his musical analysis of the opera, concludes: "its appeal to sophisticated opera audiences and popular musicians alike has only increased by leaps and bounds.[25] Another musicologist, Professor Geoffrey Block, in his *Enchanted Evenings*, provides an overview of the opera's evolution, but adds a succinct musical analysis. In Block's view Gershwin excelled at using his melodies and musical themes to elaborate the central theme of Porgy's loneliness.[26] Finally, the movie version of *Porgy*, which had been withdrawn, was screened for a rare occasion in November 1998 at a special Gershwin Centennial Festival sponsored by the Institute for Studies of American Music. Three new reviews of the film were published, and were more favorable than some of the original criticisms.[27]

A sort of Gershwin renaissance was further stimulated by a new volume edited by Wayne Schneider, *The Gershwin Style*. It included singular essays by a number of scholars. Perhaps most interesting was an essay by Charles Hamm ("Towards A New Reading of Gershwin"), who urged that it was high time for another look at Gershwin's life and music. He suggested that Gershwin had been the victim of the intellectual penchant for pigeonholing composers according to European categories. Since Gershwin did not fit easily, he was banished by a generation of "modernists." Hamm also suggested that Gershwin was misunderstood, or at least not well understood intellectually. He was more politically aware than usually given credit for, and Hamm called for a reconsideration of Gershwin's ideology. His premature death shifted control over his music to his family, and according to Hamm, many performances violated the "letter and spirit" of his music.[28] To hell with his damn Kike politics.

It is impossible to write about George Gershwin without citing the novelist John O'Hara's famous quote from an article for *Newsweek* (July 15, 1940). He wrote: "George died on July 11, 1937, but I don't have to believe that if I don't want to."

A fine tribute. But rarely quoted was O'Hara's additional thought: "I am a little sorry now that I did not like George, that I was not his friend."

NOTES

1. Full text reprinted in Robert Kimball and Alfred Simon, *The Gershwins* (New York: Bonanza Books, 1963), p. 230.

2. Hugh Fordin, *MGM's Greatest Musicals* (New York: Da Capo, 1996), pp. 84–89.

3. Charlotte Greenspan, "Rhapsody in Blue: A Study in Hollywood Hagiography," in *The Gershwin Style*, ed. Wayne Schneider (New York: Oxford University Press, 1999), pp. 145–59.

4. Arnold Schoenberg in *George Gershwin*, ed. Merle Armitage (New York: Longmans, Green, 1938), pp. 97–98.

5. Ibid., p. 115.

6. Irving Kolodin, *Saturday Review of Literature*, January 15, 1956.

7. Edward Jablonski and Lawrence Stewart, *The Gershwin Years* (New York: Doubleday & Company, 1958), p. 281. Subsequent editions contain significantly more material.

8. Jablonski's book was thoughtfully and favorably reviewed by William H. Youngren (*Commentary*, December 1987). The writer dismissed Ewen's biography as "fanciful and riddled with errors," and criticized Schwartz's book as "compulsively mean-spirited."

9. Recent reviews of the biographies by Peyser, Schwartz, and Rosenberg are included in passing in Brad Leithauser's review of Philip Furia's biography of Ira; *New York Review of Books*, October 17, 1996.

10. Jablonski and Stewart, *The Gershwin Years* (1996 ed.), commented unfavorably on both Schwartz and Peyser, pp. 379–80. The main text is a reprint of their 1973 edition, but the discography and bibliography are updated to 1996.

11. Henry Pleasants, "Gershwin Season," *Stereo Review*, January 1974.

12. One insightful review of this particular output notes that many of the familiar tunes sound "strangely unlike the classic songs we know." Not a shortcoming of the performances or recordings, but a demonstration of how "dramatically aesthetic standards have changed." Edward A. Berlin, "Gershwin on Disc," *Institute for Studies in American Music Newsletter*, Fall 1998. Restored versions of *Tip Toes* and *Tell Me More* were performed in concert versions, and recorded in 2001 (New World Music, 2 CDs, 80598–2).

13. "Paul Whiteman's Historic Aeolian Hall Concert of 1924," with piano soloist Ivan Davis, reconstructed and conducted by Maurice Peress. Music Masters, MMD 60113T.

14. Francis Davis, *Outcats* (New York: Oxford University Press, 1990), p. 187. Edward A. Berlin, "Gershwin on Disc," comments that Maurice Peress' treatment stands out for the style of playing he gets from prominent instruments: "Containing many interesting details, the recording merits consideration."

15. Edward Berlin, "Gershwin on Disc," *Institute for Studies in American Music Newsletter*, Fall 1998. Professor Berlin offers a well-informed review of the major CDs.

16. Peter G. Davis, "Of Thee We Sing," *New York*, October 12, 1998.

17. *Kickin' the Clouds Away: Gershwin at the Piano*, Klavier Music Productions, K 77031.

18. Alec Wilder, *American Popular Song* (New York: Oxford University Press, 1972), pp. 121–61.

19. Jablonski and Stewart, *The Gershwin Years*, p. 394.

20. Kenneth LaFave, "Gershwin, Hollywood and the Unanswered Question," *Keynote*, August 1986.

21. Allen Forte, *The American Popular Ballad of the Golden Era* (Princeton, NJ: Princeton University Press, 1995), p. 157.

22. Steven E. Gilbert, *The Music of Gershwin* (New Haven, CT: Yale University Press, 1995), p. 8.

23. There is no need to enumerate the hundreds of performances of Gershwin songs by jazz artists. "I Got Rhythm" has been a particular favorite. It is discussed by Professor Richard Crawford, *The American Musical Landscape* (Berkeley: University of California Press, 1993), ch. 7, p. 213.

24. Hollis Alpert, *The Life and Times of Porgy and Bess* (New York: Alfred Knopf, 1996).

25. Joseph P. Swain, *The Broadway Musical* (New York: Oxford University Press, 1990), p. 71.

26. Geoffrey Block, *Enchanted Evenings* (New York: Oxford University Press, 1997), pp. 60–84.

27. *Institute for Studies in American Music Newsletter*, Fall 1998; reviews by George Cunningham, Professor of Africana Studies and American Studies, Brooklyn College; Foster Hirsch, Professor of Film Studies, Brooklyn College; James Standifer, Professor of Music, University of Michigan; and Margo Jefferson, cultural critic for the *New York Times*.

28. Charles Hamm, "Towards a New Reading of Gershwin," pp. 3–17, in *The Gershwin Style*, ed. Wayne Schneider. The book was reviewed by Stephen Banfield of the University of Minnesota; while he generally approved, he found it a "mixed bag." In a similar vein as Hamm, Carol Oja (*Musical Quarterly*, Winter 1994) surveys the critical treatment of Gershwin by the "modernists" in the 1920s; she covers the same ground in her book, *Making Music Modern* (New York: Oxford University Press, 2000).

Michael Feinstein is a boring hack. No talent!
Ira's bitchy wife can go to hell.

Chapter 14

American Music

Where does George Gershwin stand in the pantheon of American music? It is not an easy question. Long after Gershwin died, one scholar summed him up: "We Americans . . . have yet to make up our minds about Gershwin."[1] When he was alive he was America's most famous composer and sixty years after he died, he still remains the best known. During his lifetime the critics were favorably disposed toward him for both his Broadway and concert works. Despite complaints about defects in his craftsmanship, it was recognized that he spoke in the musical language of his countrymen and his generation: "he brought a distinctive subtlety to the jazz style of the inter-war American musical theatre."[2] Or, as another source declared, he "originated a novel type of symphonic jazz."[3]

From the beginning of his concert career in 1924, however, there was a sustained and determined effort by a dedicated faction of critics and intellectuals to banish him from the sanctuary of serious American music and relegate him to the fringes of "low-brow" music. Gershwin made critics "uneasy," because they could not classify his music according to traditional European standards. He was regarded as an interloper. His concert work too often evoked the sounds of Tin Pan Alley, and his compositions were therefore dismissed. The popularity of performances of his work by prominent orchestras contributed to doubts about the "worthiness" of his compositions as serious music. "We see Gershwin as a great natural talent, to be sure, but technically suspect, and working in a commerical realm quite separate from the neighborhood in which true art is created."[4] His greatest achievement, *Porgy and Bess*, was ignored for decades or attacked as a musically inadequate opera corrupted by racist stereotypes.

Gradually, however, the tide turned. Scholars began to appreciate that Gershwin's work reflected a genuine Americanism: "his melodic talent and a genius for rhythmic invention" made him a "genuinely important American composer."[5]

Had he lived to absorb such praise, the operative words for him would have been "American composer." He often said that his music represented the thoughts and aspirations of the American people. "My people are Americans. My time is today," he wrote in 1927. Even some of his most severe critics, while disdaining jazz, the blues, and ragtime, never denied that when these elements were brought together by Gershwin the results were truly American music. In the *New York Times* (July 18, 1937), Olin Downes wrote after Gershwin died that "It was only in Gershwin's generation that Americans took with ardor to good music. He came on the scene about the right time, to make the link between the 'serious' and the 'popular' composers of America."

This Americanism was an important characteristic. Before World War I, music written by American composers was not widely recognized as reflective of American culture. One of the most prominent American composers, Edward MacDowell, was a product of training in Europe, especially Germany. When he finally returned to the United States he rejected that idea of a national music— "purely national music has no place in art." Later, however, he did adopt some American Indian themes in his compositions. But nothing in his works signified a distinguishing Americanism.

On the other hand, Charles Ives was a truly national American composer, perhaps the most outstanding; his music had an "unmistakable nationalistic character—yet his music went virtually unnoticed and had no impact on either the musical life of the country or on other composers."[6] He stopped writing music around 1920, and his music was rarely programmed by the major orchestras. Ives' famous *Concord Sonata* was written in 1919, but not performed until 1939! Ives had nothing to do with jazz, though he liked to listen to ragtime. His music was American to the extent that it reflected his concepts of life in New England; he borrowed often from traditional and folk songs and patriotic airs. Since there were few recordings, he temporarily faded into obscurity.[7]

European influences were also evident in the pedagogy in leading universities and conservatories. As H.L. Mencken quipped, "There are two kinds of music, German music and bad music." A musical career meant studying in Europe. Before World War I, Americans "flocked" to Germany, as Virgil Thomson put it. The first full-time professor of music appointed at Harvard, John Knowles Paine, studied in Germany for three years. Horatio W. Parker, who taught Ives at Yale, also studied for three years in Germany. But German music, for political reasons, became unpopular during World War I. By the 1920s a generation of fledgling American composers born in the 1880s and 1890s was maturing. For them the "new things" were coming from Paris. Debussy and Ravel were the rage. Many Americans travelled to Paris to study with Nadia Boulanger. This new generation, however, was determined to express a fundamental Americanism in their music. Americanism, however, could not be easily defined. It lacked a national focal point. Was it folk music? Or spirituals? Or jazz and the blues? Should these sources be grafted on European forms, or used to create something distinctly new?[8]

The times were ripe for a fusion of popular American music and European forms—or what came to be called "symphonic jazz." It was, after all, the Jazz Age. George Gershwin was on hand to break new ground with *Rhapsody in Blue* in 1924. His background made him an ideal candidate to make "a lady out of jazz," as the commentators kept writing.

Others, of course, were moving in the same direction, striving to emphasize their Americanness. Aaron Copland, still in Europe, was absorbing jazz in small Parisian and Viennese cafes, and proposing to incorporate it in his compositions as a student of Nadia Boulanger in Paris. The French composer Darius Milhaud had drawn on jazz for his ballet music *La creation du monde*. Gershwin's critics were fond of pointing out that Milhaud's composition was written before *Rhapsody in Blue*. That composition was irrelevant to Gershwin; it was never heard in the United States before 1933. It owes as much to Stravinsky as it does to jazz.[9]

Gershwin, then, was truly a pioneer, unwitting perhaps. Yet it was Gershwin who "demystified" classical music and made it accessible to people who had not listened to such music.[10] He greatly benefitted from the advent of two forms of early mass media, the radio and the phonograph. He even adopted, and was adopted by two great American institutions, the weekly radio program and, of course, the movies.

Why was Gershwin criticized so sharply? Some of the criticism reflected a cultural antipathy to his "low-brow" music but some "betrayed anti-Semitic and nativist sentiment."[11]

> Less secure in their cultural position than their European colleagues, Paris-trained American composers such as Copland and Virgil Thomson may have felt threatened when Gershwin's concert works were taken seriously by critics while theirs were treated as monstrosities.[12]

By the 1930s the modernist composers and critics had prevailed, and were effective in fixing Gershwin's image.[13] "They relegated Gershwin to a lesser realm, even though his works often shared programs with theirs."[14] They resented Gershwin's easy access to the major orchestras to perform his work; they resented his "low-brow" successes on Broadway and his pretensions to "high-brow" status; and they resented his commercial success. The composer Roy Harris (another student of Boulanger) said that the "harassing problem" for a composer was how to become economically and socially recognized as a worth-contributing citizen. This statement explains some of the resentment; Gershwin had obviously achieved the economic and social recognition that Harris and his colleagues sought.

Gershwin's comments suggest that he was stung by criticism. For example, he dismissed his former teacher Rubin Goldmark. While noting Goldmark's first "feeble" steps toward an American music, he dismissed Goldmark's *Negro Rhapsody* as far removed from the American spirit as Goldmark himself. (Goldmark was a pupil of Dvorak). He described Copland as a "very talented young man," but lumping him in with Bloch and Leo Ornstein, he asked why such consummate musicians failed in their attempts at American music. Gershwin's answer was easy, he said: "they were trained by Europeans; they were rigidly raised in European musical traditions." Fortunately, he added, neither Irving Berlin nor I were taught by European masters." Therefore, they could both "plunge wholeheartedly into this new culture that is America."[15]

Over the decades Gershwin's reputation fluctuated. A sustained undertone of criticism continued: *The Oxford Dictionary of Music* (1985) in its article on Gershwin concluded that "His larger-scale works, melodically remarkable as might be expected, suffer from his haphazard mus[ical] education and lack of grounding in counterpoint, theory, etc." *The New Grove Dictionary of Music and Musicians* (1980 edition) went further:

> Gershwin has only limited experience in developing musical material . . .
> his serious works are structurally defective. The orchestral and piano
> pieces are filled with repetitive rather than developed melodies, motifs,
> sequences and ostinatos, and often sections are separated by abrupt pauses,
> but the melodic materials are usually so attractive that they compensate
> for any shortcomings.[16]

Some well-known histories of American music dismissed Gershwin with a few sentences. A respected textbook, *Music in the United States* by H. Wiley Hitchcock, downgraded *Porgy and Bess* for its reliance on some "memorable songs"; it was a "more pretentious but hardly more artistically successful contribution [compared to his Broadway shows]. This passage was slightly softened in a subsequent edition: "hardly more artistically successful" was changed to a "*perhaps not more* artistically successful contribution." On the other hand, in both editions, the authors cited a quotation from Professor Richard Crawford to the effect that *Porgy and Bess* was "full of moments that show Gershwin at his most convincing." Finally, in this same textbook, Gershwin's *Three Preludes* were relegated to a class of "unpretentious but charming trifles, among the very best "household music of the 1920s."[17] Trifles!!

On the other hand, Professor Charles Hamm, in his survey of American music was more generous. While citing the criticism of Lawrence Gilman and other critics for harping on Gershwin's deficiencies in compositional skill, Hamm concluded that Gershwin's "episodic, fragmented, mosaiclike formal designs," growing out of Tin Pan Alley, helped to give him that which no "serious" composer of the 1920s could achieve—"a sense of being *truly American in character*"[18] (emphasis added). Some other histories are also more generous:

> Gershwin clearly achieved that which no other American composer before
> him had achieved despite his casual musical education, namely: the cre-
> ation of substantive music that found a world wide audience in his lifetime

and has remained a major part of the repertoire ever since. After Gershwin, American classical music became focused as it had never been focused before. And the world began to sit up and listen.[19]

Each new generation of writers seemed to discover Gershwin for the first time. The criticism of Gershwin for his lack of technique began to fade. The historian of America music, John Tasker Howard (*Our American Music*), wrote that while in the first edition of his book in 1931 he had placed Gershwin in the category of popular music and jazz, in his new edition in 1946 he had changed his mind: "It is time to change the emphasis on Gershwin's twofold output, and to present him in the gallery of serious composers." Gershwin "evolved an idiom of his own that is unmistakably American."[20]

Gilbert Chase, in his impressive survey, described *Porgy and Bess* as "the most individual American opera that has been successfully produced, and it may very well be a pioneer in establishing a native school of American opera."[21] Martin Gottfried attended a version of *Blue Monday* in 1975. He wrote, "hearing prime Gershwin that you've never heard before is an exhilarating experience, the best kind of treat" (*New York Post*, November 29). The British critic Kenneth Tynan, after listening to a program of Gershwin's songs performed by Steve Lawrence and Edie Gorme, wrote in his diary (April 5, 1976): "the greatest composers of the twentieth century are Berlin, Rodgers, Porter, Kern and Gershwin, *et. al*? . . . Even with middling American talents [like Lawrence and Gorme] one feels such a glow, such a pressure of *bonhomie*, such an unforced, unservile wish to please, that one is disarmed and conquered."[22] Later, in 1988, after the discovery of the treasures of the Secaucus warehouse, *New York Times* critic Stephen Holden commented that "the Gershwins' brash romantic pop songs exude a street-wise vigor that still stands as the prototype of the collision of cultures in New York City's melting pot."[23] Critics still took account of his failings of technique, but warned against driving such points into the ground, emphasizing instead that Gershwin's "big" works succeeded because of the "sheer vitality, the originality and high quality of the musical ideas."[24] In January 1999, there was a program of four concertos: Gershwin's *Second Rhapsody*, Ravel's *Concerto for the Left Hand*, and concertos by Gershwin's friends Oscar Levant and Vernon Duke. The critic Anthony Tomasini wrote, in his review of this performance for the *New York Times*, that Gershwin exercised a lasting influence on many of the traditionally trained composers of his time and also demonstrated to his Broadway colleagues that they too had something of value to say in concert music. Finally, Arthur Jacobs, an English critic and editor of *Opera Magazine*, wrote a good summary in his *A Short History of Western Music*:

Back in the 1930s, when composers such as Copland and Harris were reaching out to draw the vernacular idiom into the established forms and modes of serious music, one man successfully crossed the frontier in the other direction, raising the vernacular idiom itself to the dignity of a true and fully conscious art. He was George Gershwin.[25]

Copland paid no attention to Gershwin and the *Rhapsody* in an article entitled "1926: America's Young Men of Promise." Yet in 1932, reviewing concerts he heard at Oxford, he wrote of *An American in Paris*, in the journal *Modern Music*: "It was an interesting phenomenon to witness how well, in spite of various technical difficulties, it withstood being transplanted into an alien milieu (i.e., Oxford). It will be a long time before (Europeans) see him in proper perspective, as the best composer of light music that America has yet had."[26]

Of course, this was damning with faint praise, consigning Gershwin to "light music." Moreover, Copland still omitted Gershwin when he reiterated his choices of the best composers of the new generation in 1936 in a follow-up article in *Modern Music* (the mouth organ of the modernists). When the original article was reissued in 1963 Copland defended himself by claiming that at the time Gershwin had only two concert pieces to his credit, and was regarded in "everybody's book" as a composer of popular songs.

It is ironic that Copland and Gershwin should emerge as competitors if not antagonists. Under other circumstances they might even have become colleagues. They shared a common background. They were born a year apart in Brooklyn. Both were Jewish sons of Russian immigrants (Lithuanian in Copland's case). Both grew up in the environs of New York. Gershwin moved from Brooklyn to various locations in Manhattan, but Copland remained in Brooklyn. Both studied with Rubin Goldmark, though at different times. Copland was a serious student, but Gershwin quit after a few lessons. It is an interesting speculation how they might have fared if their paths had not diverged. As Gershwin went to work for George White's *Scandals*, Copland went to Europe to study with the legendary Nadia Boulanger. After three years he returned to the United States to find that Gershwin was semi-famous for *Rhapsody in Blue*.

They were often compared in the 1920s, because both were associated with jazz as a source of their music. When he was in Mexico in the early 1930s, Copland wrote that at last he had found a country where he was as "famous as Gershwin." Thus Copland's jazz-based *Piano Concerto* was praised while Gershwin's concerto was dismissed as a "hash derivative." While Edmund Wilson found Copland had a gift similar to Stravinsky's, he found Gershwin "mechanical and unsatisfactory." Even Gershwin's sometime teacher Henry Cowell entered the fray, praising Copland for writing classical music based on jazz, but denouncing Gershwin for failing to create "anything worthy in this idiom."[27] Copland never really joined this fight; it was not his nature. And he did not need to: by the 1940s Gershwin was dead and musicologists had embraced Copland as the true leader of the new modern American music.

They did meet in the 1930s. Copland mentioned an evening at the Gershwins during which George encouraged Oscar Levant to play his *Sonatina* for Copland. Levant subsequently became an admirer and defender of Copland. Gershwin and Copland also met later in Hollywood where, on one occasion, they were face-to-face at a party. With the opportunity for conversation, they found they had nothing to say to each other. It is difficult to imagine a taciturn Gershwin. A coolness may be explained by Copland's association with Paul Rosenfeld and Virgil Thomson, Gershwin's most vicious critics.

Nevertheless, they both shared a common goal—to express an Americanness in their music. Gershwin found his spirit of America in urban life, in the blues and jazz motifs. Copland began along these same lines, but he gravitated toward using folk music. He said he wanted to write music that related to America but also sounded American. He explained in his Charles Eliot Norton Lectures (1951–52) that:

> Our concern was not with the quotable hymn or spiritual: we wanted to find a music that would speak of universal things in a vernacular of American speech rhythms. We wanted to write music on a level that left popular music far behind—music with a largeness of utterance wholly representative of the country that Whitman envisaged.[28]

Gershwin probably would not have agreed. He did not want to leave popular music "far behind." While he too was striving for "American speech rhythms," his focal point was not universal, nor "wholly representative of the country," but rather of life in New York in the 1920s—at least until the 1930s when he created *Porgy and Bess*. He might even have agreed with Virgil Thomson's flippant statement that the way to write American music was to be an American and then "write any kind of music you want."

Gradually Gershwin and Copland drifted in different directions. One critic noted that Copland's common denominator was the sense of something expansive. He caught the emptiness of the city and the quiet of the endless flatland, as if they were the same thing.[29] This set him apart from Gershwin, who knew nothing of the endless flatland or the quiet city. He knew the glittering Great White Way of Broadway. He knew the blues that Bessie Smith sang about, which seemed foreign to Copland. Indeed, Copland dismissed jazz because it represented two emotions: the blues and a wild, grotesque abandon. Such statements suggest that Copland was obviously unaware of the sensuous Billie Holiday or the lyrical Bix Beiderbecke.

On the other hand, Professor Howard Pollack, the biographer of Copland, also suggests some similarities between Copland and Gershwin:

> Their music features formal and stylistic similarities, including rhythmic, melodic, and harmonic traits derived from ragtime, jazz, city blues, and various folk styles . . . their work engages similar themes: the restlessness, excitement, and loneliness of contemporary urban life; the absurdities of American affectations and pretenses; and the resilience of the human spirit.

Such themes characterize a wide range of their compositions, including their major works for the stage, *Porgy and Bess* and *The Tender Land*.[30]

Shortly after Gershwin died, the modernist composer, musicologist, and critic Frederick Jacobi wrote an appraisal in *Modern Music*. While noting Gershwin's popular appeal of "making people fall in love with his music," Jacobi concentrated on Gershwin's failings. His "larger and more pretentious" works lacked "precisely the qualities which were otherwise so much his own: style, shape and that indefinable thing called authenticity." Jacobi cited the *Three Preludes* as proof that Gershwin's ideas were essentially "short of breath." He lacked the ability to "draw them out, to make them unfold from within themselves." He had much the same criticism of a lack of development in the *Concerto in F*. Rather foolishly, however, Jacobi predicted that *An American in Paris* would become more popular than the *Rhapsody*, and, in a triumph of myopia, he prophesied that *Porgy and Bess* would be "the first to go."[31]

If Aaron Copland stands at one end of the spectrum of American music, at the other end is Duke Ellington.

The claims made for Copland as America's greatest composer are contested by Ellington's partisans. They insist that he, not Gershwin, or Copland for that matter, was the quintessential American composer. Their reasoning is that the only authentic American music is jazz; that the roots of jazz are black music played by blacks; that Ellington was the foremost black composer, writing in the jazz idiom, and hence he was the foremost American composer. "In Ellington we hear the story of the Negro, maybe the most American of Americans."[32] The black writer and critic Albert Murray wrote, in *Stompin' the Blues*, "I don't think anybody has achieved a higher aesthetic synthesis of the American experience than Duke Ellington expressed in his music." He also proclaimed that Ellington's works "represent far and away the most definitive musical stylizing of life in the United States."[33] Or, as an Ellington biographer put it, "Ellington's music summarized the American experience."[34] Even Aaron Copland wrote in 1938: "[T]he master of them all is still Duke Ellington . . . by which I mean, he comes nearer to knowing how to make a piece hang together than the others."

While Gershwin and Copland shared an ethnic and cultural heritage, no one could have been further from that cultural milieu than Edward Kennedy Ellington. Nevertheless, there are superficial parallels. Ellington and Gershwin were born about the same time (September 1898 for Gershwin and April 1899 for Ellington). They started to study music as young piano students about the same time. Both were tempted by other professions—Ellington as a painter, Gershwin as an athlete. Both started their musical careers on the low rungs on the ladder: Gershwin as a song plugger and Ellington as a pianist in small clubs. Both were impressed and influenced by the Harlem stride pianists.

Both were superb melodists. Both were "miniaturists," that is, they wrote short songs. Gershwin wrote the bulk of his music for the theater or the movies, while Ellington wrote instrumentals exclusively for his own orchestra. Both prided themselves on being self-taught. Both taught themselves the art of orchestration. Both were helped by friends and colleagues: Gershwin by Bill Daly and Ellington by Billy Strayhorn—a songwriter, orchestrator, and confidant, who wrote Ellington's most famous jazz song "Take the 'A' Train." Both wanted to break the bonds of 32-bar songs; Gershwin did so with *Rhapsody in Blue*; Ellington did so many years later with his orchestral suites, especially *Black, Brown and Beige*.

They both composed at the piano and transcribed their songs and other compositions for orchestra. Both were influenced by ragtime, more than most scholars admit. Ellington wrote some early rags, as did Gershwin; neither persisted in this idiom for long. Gershwin was meticulous in writing down his songs in a piano version, but Ellington was more haphazard; since his orchestra was always at hand, he could write down a few lines and then ask his gifted sidemen to improvise various parts, until a complete arrangement emerged.[35]

Both were attracted to the blues. Gershwin appropriated blue notes so consistently that he is thought of as a blues composer. An early example is "Somebody Loves Me"; but the recording by Paul Whiteman in the year it was written unfortunately makes it clear that the blue inflections were easily subsumed by the popular style of the period. Even the *Rhapsody*, replete with blue notes, gives way to a more European mode in the slow passage. On the other hand, there are distinctly blue refrains in *Blue Monday*, in the *Concerto in F*, and in *An American in Paris*.

Ellington became wedded to the blues in the traditional twelve-bar or eight-bar form, in major and minor. "Ellington was the greatest manipulator of blues form and blues feeling," wrote Stanley Crouch.[36] He gravitated toward the blues, first under the influence of James P. Johnson, and then under the influence of his sidemen, especially trumpet player Bubber Miley. It was Miley who wrote several of the Ellington orchestra's early instrumentals ("East St. Louis Toodle-Ooo"). Miley played a growl trumpet style with a mute and a plunger, devices that he had picked up from the famous King Oliver. The trombone player, Sam Nanton, played a similar style, and Johnny Hodges on the alto saxophone was an extraordinary blues master, as was the clarinetist Barney Bigard. Thus, Ellington could "manipulate the blues style, and inject its shape and sound into the orchestral body of his music."[37]

Their paths crossed occasionally. Ellington finally settled in New York about the time Gershwin wrote *Rhapsody in Blue*. He played at the Hollywood Inn with a small band. The club was described by a band member as the "Black Hole of Calcutta." The bandstand was so small that Ellington had to play the piano from the dance floor. Occasionally, there was a fire, but the owner always warned the band members to take their instruments home the night of the fire. According to Ellington's longtime drummer Sonny Greer, Paul Whiteman and his sidemen frequented the place after hours; Gershwin probably did so as well.

Ellington and his orchestra played on stage in Ziegfeld's 1929 musical *Show Girl*; their big number was Gershwin's "Liza," sung and danced by Ruby Keeler.

In the 1930s, Gershwin often came to the Cotton Club, and it was said that Whiteman and Gershwin gave Ellington music the title of "jungle music." Although Ellington had no special relationship with Gershwin, Oscar Levant said that Gershwin greatly admired Ellington's "Creole Love Song."

There is no real basis for comparing Ellington and Gershwin as songwriters. Ellington's songs have a distinctly different quality, in part because they were written for and performed by his orchestra, not as songs but as instrumentals. Thus, they have a sound all their own. No one would mistake Ellington's "Mood Indigo" or "Sophisticated Lady" for a Gershwin song. Ellington, however, was not averse to success in Gershwin's bailiwick—Tin Pan Alley: "From a purely commercial standpoint, Ellington and Gershwin were equally welcome in Tin Pan Alley, but their ideas were poles apart. . . . That the two were of different races and from different backgrounds is not relevant; both men were supremely gifted writers of good tunes."[38]

After Ellington died (1974), the jazz scholar and composer Gunther Schuller placed Ellington "in the pantheon of musical greats, the Beethovens, the Monteverdis, the Schoenbergs, the prime movers, the inspired innovators. . . . [Thus], Ellington has been generally considered to be the most important composer in the history of jazz."[39] A radically different aspect was offered by the critic Terry Teachout in his comparison of Gershwin to Ellington:

> Unlike Ellington, Gershwin realized early on that he would never master the larger forms on his own. Not only did he study composition, he also familiarized himself with a wide range of classical music, up to and including the works of such modernists as Arnold Schoenberg and Alban Berg. This course of study made it possible for Gershwin to produce a series of "classical" compositions of increasing structural complexity . . . Ellington, by contrast, gave no indication of even recognizing that his limitations were limitations. At no time did he seek formal training, and to the end of his life his musical culture remained severely restricted.[40]

This is devastating and probably goes too far. It follows from Teachout's conclusion that both Albert Murray and Stanley Crouch's claims for Ellington "may be to some extent the product of a racial myth," which explains Murray's insistence that Ellington was more authentically "American" than Ives or Copland, or his implication that this alleged authenticity somehow made Ellington a better composer.[41]

On the other hand, while commentaries about Ellington by black writers reflect a bitter resentment, often at the expense of other composers, including Gershwin, they have a point. Whereas Copland and Gershwin are identified as "American composers" in the *New Oxford Dictionary of Music*, Ellington is described only as a "black jazz musician." Ellington's longer, more serious compositions deserve better than that.

The unbridled enthusiasm of Ellington's partisans has recently been tempered somewhat by a greater appreciation for Gershwin. Thus the critic Stanley Crouch on the occasion of Gershwin's Centenary praised his work and brushed aside criticism that he was racist.[42]

As musicians Copland and Ellington can be compared to Gershwin but neither was anything like his person. The one man who was probably closest to a replica of Gershwin was Leonard Bernstein, albeit a generation later (born in 1918). He admired Gershwin and came to be a skilled performer of his works. Bernstein and his boyhood friend Sid Ramin (later an outstanding Broadway orchestrator) were enchanted by *Rhapsody in Blue*. They played a two-piano arrangement incessantly. In July 1937, during Parents Weekend at Camp Onata, Bernstein, a camp counselor, heard that Gershwin had died. He asked for quiet and played *Prelude No 2*. There was no applause when it was over, only a heavy silence in the hall; "As I walked off I felt I *was* Gershwin," he said.[43] When relating this incident to his biographer, Joan Peyser, also Gershwin's biographer, Bernstein broke out in a fit of coughing, an emotional reaction he claimed to recalling Gershwin's death.

Bernstein, however, admired Gershwin more for his commercial success and popularity than for his music. Bernstein wrote his senior thesis at Harvard (March 1939) on "The Absorption of Race Elements into American Music," a lively account of how "two of his favorites, Gershwin and Copland," had responded creatively to Jazz and Latin American influences. At Harvard, however, Bernstein rejected Gershwin as a potential role model and instead chose Copland. Joan Peyser believes that this choice reflected Bernstein's awareness that Copland could do much more for his career than the long-dead Gershwin.[44]

Bernstein and Gershwin nevertheless invite comparison, though separated by a full generation. Both were Jewish; both were sons of Russian immigrants. Both were "crossover" artists. Bernstein wrote very successful Broadway shows, but he returned to "serious" composing and especially conducting. Gershwin crossed in the opposite direction; after *Rhapsody in Blue* he returned to Broadway for *Lady Be Good!* Both were skilled pianists. Both used "jazz" as ingredients of their more serious compositions. Both were rejected by authentic jazzmen.

While both were very ambitious and sought public acclaim, in the end Bernstein was far more successful as a national figure because of his television performances. Bernstein also gained notoriety as a radical, left-wing political activist.

Bernstein's musical education was miles beyond Gershwin's. He graduated from Harvard, where he was a student of Walter Piston. He attended the Curtis Institute in Philadelphia where he studied conducting with Fritz Reiner, and became a protégé of Serge Koussevitzky and Aaron Copland at Tanglewood. He wound up as the renowned conductor of the New York Philharmonic.

Gershwin's ghost, however, seemed to hover over Bernstein. The composer William Bolcom wrote, "The only American composer comparable to Gershwin is Leonard Bernstein." Bernstein, continued Bolcom, was addicted to "grand statements," but in contrast there is a "sunniness" in Gershwin's songs and concert literature.[45] A critic commented on his *Wonderful Town*: "There hasn't been any one around like Bernstein since George Gershwin for jauntiness, tricky and intriguing modulations and graceful swoops with simple and pleasant melody." Irving Caesar, when he met Bernstein in 1941 at a social occasion where Bernstein played, commented that he reminded Caesar of Gershwin. In 1945 when Bernstein conducted a performance of *Rhapsody in Blue*, from the piano, Paul Bowles commented that he was the incarnation of Gershwin. In 1948 he conducted at a concert for Israeli soldiers in embattled Jerusalem; he chose the *Rhapsody* for his program.

As Professor John Warthen Struble concluded in his history of American classical music: "[Bernstein] was by far the most dynamic public *personality* in American classical music of the 1950s through the 1970s . . . and came closer than any of his colleagues to duplicating Gershwin's extraordinary achievement."[46]

Yet Bernstein also delivered a vicious attack on Gershwin, clothed in high praise. "You can't just put four tunes together, God given though they may be and call them a composition." David Schiff describes this so-called interview as "the most lethal anti-Gershwin brief filed by the Copland forces." The article, a self-interview, was entitled "A Nice Gershwin Tune."[47] Bernstein said, "I don't think there has been such an inspired melodist on this earth since Tchaikovsky . . . but if you want to speak of a 'composer,' that's another matter."[48]

Bernstein softened his criticism in 1973, when he wrote an "Appreciation" for Charles Schwartz's highly critical biography of Gershwin. For that book, Bernstein wrote that Gershwin was a victim of "higher criticisms" that did not permit Gershwin's name to enter the category of significant composers:

> This is sad, because Gershwin was certainly one of the true authentic geniuses American music has produced. Time and history may even show him to be the truest and most authentic of his time and place. . . . Gershwin's tragedy was not that he failed to cross the tracks, but rather that he did, and once there in his new habitat, was deprived of the chance to plunge his roots firmly into the new soil.[49]

It may well be that Gershwin intended to "plunge his roots into the new soil" when he finished with Hollywood. This is the burden of the remarks he made shortly before he died. But, at the same time, he was dickering for a new Broadway show. Maybe Broadway would indeed have been his direction. In Hollywood he wrote no new classical pieces, but did write a collection of quite enchanting songs.

There is no need to gild the reputation of Gershwin as a popular composer and songwriter. His work in both fields has easily stood the test of several generations. Professor Richard Crawford has concluded that while Gershwin's music "ensures him a place in American music history," it is not the one anticipated by his partisans. Indeed, his achievement in bridging the popular and classical world seems less important—his legacy is the "sheer musical satisfaction" his compositions provide his listeners.[50]

Gershwin, Copland, Ellington—each in his own way contributed to the creation of a body of genuine American music. None could claim that title exclusively. The country is too large, too ethnically diverse, and the sources of music too varied for a distinctive American music to emerge from the career of a few men, no matter how talented the practitioners. What stands out about George Gershwin is that he was a pathfinder in 1924 and 1925, when Bernstein was a young boy, Ellington was an unknown piano player in nightclubs, and Copland was just emerging to make his mark.[51]

His life was cut tragically short, giving rise to speculation of what he might have accomplished: "there can be little doubt that had he lived longer he would have progressed to considerable symphonic achievement."[52] Maybe. Yet even before he died he created his own monument: no other songwriter, jazz musician, or American composer has written anything approaching *Porgy and Bess*.

His friend and colleague Irving Berlin put it best: "We were all pretty good songwriters, but Gershwin was something else. He was a composer."

Music should be listened to - not analyzed !

NOTES

1. David Schiff, "Misunderstanding Gershwin," *Atlantic Monthly*, October 1998.

2. *The New Oxford Companion to Classical Music*, ed. Denis Arnold (New York: Oxford University Press, 1983), article signed by Paul Griffiths, p. 578.

3. *Britannica Book of Music*, ed. Benjamin Hadley (Garden City, NY: Doubleday/ Britannica Books, 1980), p. 315.

4. Richard Crawford, "Gershwin's Reputation: A Note on *Porgy and Bess*," *Musical Quarterly*, April 1979.

5. Nicolas Slonimsky, in *Baker's Dictionary of Music*, ed. Richard Kassel (New York: Schirmer Books, 1997), p. 348.

6. Charles Hamm, *Music in the New World* (New York: W.W. Norton, 1983), p. 414 on MacDowell; p. 303 on Ives.

7. A performance of the *Concord Sonata* in 1939 by John Kirkpatrick was enthusiastically reviewed by Gershwin's *bête noire*, Lawrence Gilman; he is credited with bringing national prominence to Ives' work. J. Peter Burkholder, *Charles Ives: The Ideas Behind His Music* (New Haven, CT: Yale University Press, 1985), p. 3.

8. Hamm, *Music in the New World*, p. 424.

9. Carol Oja, "Gershwin and the American Modernists," *Musical Quarterly*, 78/4 (1994), pp. 658–59. Professor Oja points out that Milhaud's work was "obscure" in New York in the 1920s. Milhaud visited the United States in 1922 and was impressed by the "primitive qualities" of the American Negroes' music; by their "tremendous rhythms and expressive melodies." *Musical Canada*, April 1925, pp. 40–41.

10. Ibid., p. 16.

11. Terry Teachout, "Gershwin at 100," *Commentary*, September 1998.

12. David Schiff, "Misunderstanding Gershwin," *Atlantic Monthly*, October 1998, p. 104.

13. Carol J. Oja, *Making Music Modern* (New York: Oxford University Press, 2000), pp. 303–10.

14. Schiff, "Misunderstanding Gershwin," p. 104.

15. George Gershwin, "Fifty Years of American Music," *The Hebrew American*, November 1929.

16. *The New Grove Dictionary of Music and Musicians* (London: Macmillan, 1980), p. 303. The latest edition (New York: Grove, 2001) has a much more extensive article, including an analytical section, a list of his shows and songs, and a bibliography. The text is by Richard Crawford.

17. H. Wiley Hitchcock, *Music in the United States* (Englewood, NJ: Prentice Hall, 1988; 4th ed., written with Kyle Gann, 2000), pp. 206–7. The fourth edition still refers to the *Three Preludes* as "charming trifles," but adds "*and perfectly honed* trifles." This edition refers to the *Rhapsody*'s success for its "unique melange of stylistic sources." Another textbook, Bryan R. Simms, *Music of the Twentieth Century: Style and Structure* (New York: Schirmer Books, 1996) includes one brief reference to Gershwin, p. 420.

18. Hamm, *Music in the New World*, p. 424.

19. John Warthen Struble, *The History of American Classical Music* (New York: Facts on File, 1995), p. 122.

20. John Tasker Howard, *Our American Music*, 3rd ed. (New York: Thomas Crowell, 1946), p. 247; (4th ed., 1965), p. 424.

21. Gilbert Chase, *American Music*, 3rd ed. (Chicago: University of Illinois Press, 1987), p. 428. Chase also writes that the Houston Opera Company's production demonstrated "beyond a shadow of a doubt that Gershwin's opus was not only really American but also truly operatic," p. 548.

22. Kenneth Tynan, *Diaries of Kenneth Tynan*, ed. John Lahr (New York: Bloomsbury, 2001), p. 313.

23. Stephen Holden, *New York Times*, January 17, 1988. The author heard about 70 songs from the Secaucus collection.

24. Alan Rich, "By George," *New York Magazine*, September 10, 1973.

25. Arthur Jacobs, *A Short History of Western Music* (New York: Drake Publishers, 1973), p. 313.

26. Aaron Copland, "Contemporaries at Oxford," *Modern Music*, November–December 1931, p. 20.

27. Carol Oja, *Making Music Modern*, pp. 352–356.

28. Quoted in Hitchcock, *Music in the United States*, p. 191.

29. Samuel Lippman, quoted in Pollack, *Aaron Copland*, p. 529.

30. Howard Pollack, "Copland and Gershwin," essay prepared for the American Musical Society Convention in Toronto, 2000.

31. Frederick Jacobi, "The Future of Gershwin," *Modern Music*, November–December 1937, pp. 3–7.

32. Stanley Crouch, *Always in Pursuit* (New York: Pantheon Books, 1998), p. 45.

33. Albert Murray, *The Blue Devils of Nada* (New York: Vintage Books, 1996), p. 83.

34. John Edward Hasse, *Beyond Category: The Life and Genius of Duke Ellington* (New York: Simon and Schuster, 1993), p. 404.

35. Richard Crawford, the chapter entitled "Duke Ellington and His Orchestra," in his *The American Musical Landscape*, (Berkeley: University of California Press, 1993), pp. 186–87.

36. Stanley Crouch, *Always in Pursuit*, p. 44.

37. Ken Rattenbury, *Duke Ellington: Jazz Composer* (New Haven, CT: Yale University Press, 1990), p. 50.

38. Ibid., p. 89.

39. Cited in Terry Teachout, "Overpraising the Duke," *Commentary*, September 1996.

40. Ibid.

41. Ibid.

42. Stanley Crouch, *New York Times*, August 30, 1998.

43. Joan Peyser, *Bernstein: A Biography* (New York: Billboard Books), pp. 45–46.

44. Peyser, *Bernstein*, p. 51.

45. William Bolcom, *New York Times*, August 30, 1998.

46. Struble, *The History of American Classical Music*, pp. 234–35.

47. Originally in *The Atlantic Monthly* 1955, reprinted in Leonard Bernstein, *The Joy of Music* (New York: Simon and Schuster, 1959), p. 57.

48. Bernstein's thesis about Gershwin's "tunes" was skillfully refuted by Larry Starr, "Musings on 'Nice Gershwin Tunes,' Form and Harmony in the Concert Music of Gershwin," in Schneider, *The Gershwin Style*.

49. Leonard Bernstein, "An Appreciation," in Charles Schwartz, *Gershwin: His Life and Music* (New York: Da Capo, 1979), no page number.

50. *The New Grove Dictionary of Music and Musicians* (2001), p. 753; the text of this entry is by Richard Crawford; the text for the entry in *The New Grove Dictionary of American Music* (New York: Norton, 1986), also written by Crawford, is slightly different.

51. Charles Hamm, "Toward a New Reading of Gershwin," in Schneider, *The Gershwin Style*, p. 17. Professor Hamm writes that while Gershwin was in no sense an innovator in his popular songs, his "classical" pieces became popular: "There were no important precedents for them and sociohistorical analysis enables us to see them as important 'modeling' and 'prophetic' works, much more than his popular songs. This merely confirms Gershwin's own judgment on these matters."

52. *The Oxford Dictionary of Music*, 2nd ed., ed. Michael Kennedy (New York: Oxford University Press, 1994), p. 337.

Selected Bibliography

There is no lack of information about George Gershwin's life and music. Thanks largely to the efforts of his brother Ira and Ira's wife, Leonore, a private archive was created after George's death. Gradually this material was donated to the Library of Congress, where a Gershwin collection was created and still exists in the Music Division. There is also a permanent exhibit ("Here To Stay"), open to the public, in the Jefferson Building of the Library. On display are several original manuscripts, George's self-portrait, and his piano, among other items.

The Gershwin collection is a national treasure. It includes orchestrations, piano-vocal scores, musical sketchbooks, and lyric sheets, much of it in the handwriting of both Gershwins. For example, in the collection is George Gershwin's handwritten score for *Porgy and Bess*. There are also dozens of scrapbooks, extensive correspondence, and photographs of George, Ira, their family, and friends. As the curator of the collection, Raymond A. White, has commented, "a unique acquaintance and an immediacy are gained through seeing original documents" (Library of Congress, "Information Bulletin," September 1998).

In the era of television there have been several shows devoted to Gershwin (e.g., "Gershwin Remembered" in the *Omnibus* series), and performances of *Porgy and Bess*. Of course, there are dozens and dozens of recordings of George's music. Under the sponsorship of Leonore Gershwin, almost all of George and Ira's major Broadway shows have been re-created and recorded by modern casts and orchestras, based to the extent possible on the original manuscripts. George's close friends and colleagues have recorded their interviews with Tony Thomas: *George Gershwin Remembered*, taken from a Canadian Broadcast radio documentary in 1961 (Facet # 8100).

Not surprisingly, there are several biographies. By one count there are about twelve in print or accessible. These are included in the list that follows. Special mention should be made, however, of Norbert Carnovale's *George Gershwin: A Bio-Bibliography* (Greenwood Press, 2000). It is a truly amazing compilation of a bibliography about his life and works, both orchestral and Broadway, a filmography, a discography, and much more. Also indispensable is Walter Rimler, *A Gershwin Companion* (Ann Arbor, MI: Popular Culture, 1991).

In the bibliography that follows, some other works are singled out for special comments.

GERSHWIN

Armitage, Merle, ed. *George Gershwin*. New York: Longmans, Green, 1938. A memorial collection of remembrances by musicians, friends, and others; published a year after George's death, it also includes some excerpts from articles by George Gershwin. A new edition was reprinted by Da Capo in 1995, with a new introduction by Edward Jablonski.

Behrman, S.N. *People in a Diary*. Boston: Little, Brown, 1972.

Bernstein, Leonard. *Findings*. New York: Simon and Schuster, 1982.

Bernstein, Leonard. *The Joy of Music*. New York: Simon and Schuster, 1959.

Carnovale, Norbert. *George Gershwin: A Bio-Bibliography*. Westport, CT: Greenwood Press, 2000. As noted, this is a truly invaluable compilation.

Crawford, R. "Rethinking the Rhapsody." *Institute for the Study of American Music (ISAM) Newsletter*, 28/1 (1998).

Crawford, Richard. *The American Musical Landscape*. Berkeley: University of California Press, 1993.

Crawford, Richard. *America's Musical Life*. New York: W.W. Norton, 2001.

Croce, Arlene. *The Fred Astaire and Ginger Rogers Book*. New York: E.P. Dutton, 1972.

Crouch, Stanley. *Always in Pursuit*. New York: Pantheon Books, 1998.

Davis, Francis. *Outcats*. New York: Oxford University Press, 1990.

Ewen, David. *George Gershwin: His Journey to Greatness*, 2nd enlarged ed. New York: The Ungar Publishing Company, 1970. The first edition was published in 1958. The author claimed that Ira Gershwin was a helpful source.

Feinstein, Michael. *Nice Work if You Can Get It*. New York: Hyperion, 1995. The author was for several years the assistant to Ira Gershwin.

Furia, Philip. *Ira Gershwin*. New York: Oxford University Press, 1996.

Gershwin, George. *George Gershwin's Song-Book*. New York: Simon and Schuster, 1932.

Gershwin, Ira. *Lyrics on Several Occasions*. New York: Knopf, 1959. A selection of lyrics (not all Gershwin songs) with commentary by Ira on how they were written or used. An especially important source.

Gilbert, Steven E. *The Music of Gershwin*. New Haven, CT: Yale University Press, 1995.

Goldberg, Isaac, supplemented by Edith Garson. *George Gershwin: A Study in American Music*. New York: Frederick Ungar Publishing, 1958; originally published New York: Simon and Schuster, 1931. This is a basic source; both George and Ira helped the author, who planned to update his work, but died a year after George. The original ended before *Porgy and Bess*; the update by Edith Garson takes the narrative through George's death.

Green, Stanley. *Ring Bells! Sing Songs!* New York: Galahad Books, 1971.

Greenberg, Rodney. *George Gershwin*. London: Phaidon Press, 1998. The author is British; part of a series, "Twentieth Century Composers."

Hamm, Charles. *Music in the New World*. New York: W.W. Norton, 1983.

Hutchisson, James M. *DuBose Heyward*. Jackson: University Press of Mississippi, 2000.

Jablonski, Edward. *George Gershwin*. New York: G.P. Putnam, 1962. A short book, part of a series, "Lives to Remember."

Jablonski, Edward. *Gershwin: A Biography*. New York: Doubleday, 1987. Considered by many to be the definitive account. A subsequent edition contains an updated discography.

Jablonski, Edward, ed. *Gershwin Remembered*. Portland, OR: Amadeus Press, 1992. Selected excerpts from writings by many friends, critics, and commentators, as well as George and Ira.

Jablonski, Edward and Lawrence D. Stewart. *The Gershwin Years*. New York: Doubleday & Company, 1958. There have been several subsequent editions. The third edition was published by Da Capo in 1996; each new edition has incorporated significant changes, especially in the final chapters and the bibliography. Stewart was an assistant to Ira Gershwin.

Jacobs, Arthur. *A Short History of Western Music*. New York: Drake Publishers, 1973.

Kashner, Sam and Nancy Schoenberger. *A Talent for Genius: The Life and Times of Oscar Levant*. New York: Villard Books, 1994.

Kendall, Alan. *George Gershwin*. New York: Universe Books, 1987. The author is British; first published in Great Britain.

Kimball, Robert, ed. *The Complete Lyrics of Ira Gershwin*. New York: Knopf, 1993. Incorporates many of Ira's commentaries; an indispensable resource.

Kimball, Robert and Alfred Simon. *The Gershwins*. New York: Bonanza Books, 1963. In the style of a coffee-table book, but loaded with information, including numerous valuable comments from friends and acquaintances. Simon was a rehearsal pianist for Gershwin shows; includes a preface by Richard Rodgers.

Kresh, Paul. *An American Rhapsody*. New York: E.P. Dutton, 1988.

Lawrence, A.H. *Ellington*. New York: Routledge, 2001.

Levant, Oscar. *The Memoirs of an Amnesiac*. New York: G.P. Putnam, 1965.

Levant, Oscar. *A Smattering of Ignorance*. New York: Doubleday, 1940.

Mast, Gerald. *Can't Help Singin': The American Musical on Stage and Screen*. Woodstock, NY: Overlook Press, 1987.

Mellers, Wilfrid. *Music in a New Found Land*. New York: Oxford University Press, 1987.

Mordden, Ethan. *Make Believe: The Broadway Musicals of the 1920s*. New York: Oxford University Press, 1997.

Oja, Carol J. "Gershwin and American Modernists of the 1920s." *Musical Quarterly*, 78/4 (1994).

Oja, Carol J. *Making Music Modern*. New York: Oxford University Press, 2000. An important new analysis of the modernists' campaign against Gershwin.

Nauert, P. "Theory and Practice in Porgy and Bess: The Gershwin-Schillinger Connection." *Musical Quarterly*, 78 (1994).

Peyser, Joan. *The Memory of All That*. New York: Simon and Schuster, 1993. The most iconoclastic of all biographies, but containing considerable new information.

Rattenbury, Ken. *Duke Ellington: Jazz Composer*. New Haven, CT: Yale University Press, 1990.

Rosenberg, Deena. *Fascinating Rhythm: The Collaboration of George and Ira Gershwin*. New York: Dutton, 1991. The author, the daughter-in-law of "Yip" Harburg, enjoyed the cooperation of Ira Gershwin; it includes extensive musical analysis.

Rosenstiel, Leonie. *Nadia Boulanger: A Life in Music*. New York: W.W. Norton, 1998.

Schneider, Wayne, ed. *The Gershwin Style*. New York: Oxford University Press, 1999.

Schuller, Gunther. *Early Jazz*. New York: Oxford University Press, 1968.

Schuller, Gunther. *The Swing Era*. New York: Oxford University Press, 1989.

Schwartz, Charles. *Gershwin: His Life and Music*. Indianapolis: Bobbs-Merrill, 1973; reprint, New York: Da Capo, 1979. The Da Capo edition has been used in this book. It is a highly critical and skeptical treatment, revealing new information and interpretations.

Shirley, Wayne D. "Reconciliation on Catfish Row." *Quarterly Journal of the Library of Congress*, 38 (1980–81).

Shirley, Wayne D. "Scoring the Concerto in F." *American Music*, 3 (1985).

Starr, Larry. "Toward a Reevaluation of Gershwin's Porgy and Bess," *American Music*, 2/2 (1984).

Struble, John W. *The History of American Classical Music*. New York: Facts on File, 1995.

Sudhalter, Richard M. *Lost Chords, White Musicians and Their Contributions to Jazz, 1915–1945*. New York: Oxford University Press, 1999.

Suriano, Gregory R., ed. *Gershwin in His Time: A Biographical Scrapbook, 1919–1937*. New York: Gramercy Books, 1998. A collection from memoirs, reviews, and articles by George and Ira.

Swain, Joseph P. *The Broadway Musical; A Critical and Musical Survey*. New York: Oxford University Press, 1990.

Thomson, Virgil. *A Virgil Thomson Reader*. Boston: Houghton Mifflin, 1981.

Tucker, Mark, ed. *The Duke Ellington Reader*. New York: Oxford University Press, 1993.

Weber, Katharine. "The Memory of All That." In *A Few Thousand Words about Love*, ed. Mickey Pearlman. New York: St. Martin's Press, 1998. This is an essay by Kay Swift's granddaughter, commenting on the relationship between Kay Swift and George Gershwin. Insightful and unique.

Weber, Nicholas Fox. *Patron Saints*. New York: Knopf, 1992; reprint, New Haven, CT: Yale University Press, 1995.

Wilder, Alec. *American Popular Song: The Great Innovators 1900–1950*, ed. James T. Maher. New York: Oxford University Press, 1972.

Wilk, Max. *They're Playing Our Song*. New York: Zoetrope, 1986.

Woods, Ean. *George Gershwin*. London: Sanctuary Publishing, 1996.

Wyatt, R. "The Seven Jazz Preludes of George Gershwin." *American Music*, 7 (1989): 68–85.

GENERAL

Atkinson, Brooks. *Broadway*. New York: Macmillan, 1970.

Bergreen, Laurence. *As Thousands Cheer: The Life Of Irving Berlin*. New York: Viking Penguin, 1990.

Bordman, Gerald. *The American Musical Revue, from the Passing Show to Sugar Babies*. New York: Oxford University Press, 1985.

Bordman, Gerald. *American Musical Theatre: A Chronicle*. New York: Oxford University Press, 1986.

Bordman, Gerald. *Days to Be Happy, Years to Be Sad: The Life and Music of Vincent Youmans*. New York: Oxford University Press, 1982.

Bordman, Gerald. *Jerome Kern: His Life and Music*. New York: Oxford University Press, 1980.

Bowers, Dwight Blocker. *American Musical Theater, Shows, Song and Stars*. Washington, DC: Smithsonian Press, 1989. A companion to the Smithsonian recordings of the same title.

De Long, Thomas A. *Pops: Paul Whiteman, King of Jazz*. New York: New Century Publishers, 1983.

Engel, Lehman. *The American Musical Theater*, rev. ed. New York: Collier Books, 1975.

Ewen, David. *The Life and Death of Tin Pan Alley*. New York: Funk and Wagnalls, 1964.

Fordin, Hugh. *Getting to Know Him*. New York: Random House/Ungar, 1977; reprint, New York: Da Capo, 1995. An outstanding biography of Oscar Hammerstein.

Fordin, Hugh. *The World of Entertainment*. New York: Doubleday, 1975.

Furia, Phillip. *The Poets of Tin Pan Alley*. New York: Oxford University Press, 1990.

Green, Stanley. *Encyclopedia of the Musical Theatre*. New York: Da Capo, 1976.

Hamm, Charles. *Yesterdays: Popular Songs in America*. New York: W.W. Norton, 1979.

Hyland, William G. *The Song Is Ended*. New York: Oxford University Press, 1995.

Jasen, David A. *Tin Pan Alley*. New York: Donald I. Fine, 1988.

Kanter, Arnold. *The Jews on Tin Pan Alley*. New York: Ktav Publishers, 1982.

McCabe, John. *George M. Cohan: The Man Who Owned Broadway*. New York: Da Capo, 1973.

Merman, Ethel, with George Eells. *Merman, An Autobiography*. New York: Simon and Schuster, 1978.

Mordden, Ethan. *Broadway Babies*. New York: Oxford University Press, 1983.

Mordden, Ethan. *The Hollywood Musical*. New York: St. Martin's Press, 1981.

Rodgers, Richard. *Musical Stages*. New York: Random House, 1975.

Shaw, Arnold. *The Jazz Age: Popular Music in the 1920s*. New York: Oxford University Press, 1987.

Smith, Cecil. *Musical Comedy in America*. New York: Theater Books, 1950.

Traubner, Richard. *Operetta*. New York: Oxford University Press, 1983.

Waters, Edward N. *Victor Herbert: A Life in Music*. New York: Macmillan, 1955.

Whitcomb, Ian. *Irving Berlin and Ragtime America*. New York: Limelight, 1988.

Wodehouse, P.G. and Guy Bolton. *Bring on the Girls*. New York: Limelight, 1984.

Index

About the Author

WILLIAM G. HYLAND served a long career with the United States government—at the White House, the State Department, and the NSC—and for ten years was the editor of *Foreign Affairs Quarterly.* He is the author of many works on international politics, as well as *The Song Is Ended: Songwriters and American Music, 1900–1950* and *Richard Rodgers.*